*Greater China:*
*The Next Superpower?*

# Studies on Contemporary China

The Contemporary China Institute at the School of Oriental and African Studies (University of London) has, since its establishment in 1968, been an international centre for research and publications on twentieth-century China. *Studies on Contemporary China*, which is sponsored by the Institute, seeks to maintain and extend that tradition by making available the best work of scholars and China specialists throughout the world. It embraces a wide variety of subjects relating to Nationalist and Communist China, including social, political, and economic change, intellectual and cultural developments, foreign relations, and national security.

Volumes in the Series:

Art and Ideology in Revolutionary China, *David Holm*
Demographic Transition in China, *Peng Xizhe*
Economic Trends in Chinese Agriculture, *Y. Y. Kueh and R. F. Ash*
In Praise of Maoist Economic Planning, *Chris Bramall*
Chinese Foreign Policy: Theory and Practice, *edited by Thomas W. Robinson and David Shambaugh*
Economic Reform and State-Owned Enterprises in China 1979–1987, *Donald A. Hay, Derek J. Morris, Guy Liu, and Shujie Yao*
Rural China in Transition, *Samuel P. S. Ho*
Agricultural Instability in China 1931–1990, *Y. Y. Kueh*
Deng Xiaoping: Portrait of a Chinese Statesman, *edited by David Shambaugh*

# Greater China:
# The Next Superpower?

*Edited by*
DAVID SHAMBAUGH

OXFORD UNIVERSITY PRESS
1995

Oxford University Press, Walton Street, Oxford OX2 6DP
Oxford New York
Athens Auckland Bangkok Bombay
Calcutta Cape Town Dar es Salaam Delhi
Florence Hong Kong Istanbul Karachi
Kuala Lumpur Madras Madrid Melbourne
Mexico City Nairobi Paris Singapore
Taipei Tokyo Toronto
and associated companies in
Berlin Ibadan

Oxford is a trade mark of Oxford University Press

Published in the United States
by Oxford University Press Inc., New York

British Library Cataloguing in Publication Data
Data available

Library of Congress Cataloging in Publication Data
Data available
ISBN 0–19–828934–0

1 3 5 7 9 10 8 6 4 2

Printed in Great Britain
on acid-free paper by
Biddles Ltd.,
Guildford & King's Lynn

# Contents

Go With Your Feelings: Hong Kong and Taiwan Popular Culture

*Thomas B. Gold*

*Wang Gungwu*

# List of Contributors

DAVID SHAMBAUGH is Senior Lecturer in Chinese Politics at the School of Oriental and African Studies, University of London, and Editor of *The China Quarterly*. He specializes in Chinese domestic politics, military affairs, foreign relations, and the international politics and security of Asia. His publications include *The Making of a Premier* (1984), *Beautiful Imperialist* (1991), *American Studies of Contemporary China* (1993), *Chinese Foreign Policy: Theory and Practice* (1994), and *Deng Xiaoping: Portrait of a Chinese Statesman* (1995).

ROBERT F. ASH is Senior Lecturer in Economics with reference to China and Head of the Contemporary China Institute at the School of Oriental and African Studies, University of London. He has published widely on various aspects of the Chinese economy, including *Land Tenure in Pre-Revolutionary China* (1976) and *Economic Trends in Chinese Agriculture* (1993).

HUGH D. R. BAKER is Professor of Chinese at the School of Oriental and African Studies, University of London, and author of *A Chinese Lineage Village* (1968).

RICHARD LOUIS EDMONDS is Senior Lecturer in Geography at the School of Oriental and African Studies, University of London. He has published widely on various aspects of geography in China and Macau, including *Patterns of China's Lost Harmony* (1994).

THOMAS B. GOLD is Associate Professor of Sociology and former Director of the Centre of Chinese Studies at the University of California–Berkeley. He has published widely on various aspects of society in China and Taiwan. He is author of *State and Society in the Taiwan Miracle* (1986), and is presently writing a book on China's urban private sector.

HARRY HARDING is Professor of Political Science and Dean of the Elliott School of Public and International Affairs at the George Washington University. A specialist in Chinese domestic politics and foreign relations, he has published *Organizing China* (1981), *China's Foreign Relations in the 1980s* (1984), *China's Second Revolution* (1987), and *A Fragile Relationship* (1993).

BRIAN HOOK is Senior Lecturer in Chinese Studies at the University of Leeds, and the former editor of *The China Quarterly*. A specialist on Hong Kong affairs, he is editor of the *Cambridge Encyclopedia of China*.

CHRISTOPHER HOWE is Professor of Economics with reference to Asia at the School of Oriental and African Studies, University of London. A specialist on various aspects of the Chinese, Japanese, and Asian-Pacific economies, he is author of *Employment and Economic Growth in Urban China, 1949–1957* (1971), *Wage Patterns and Wage Policy in Modern China, 1919–1972* (1973), *Shanghai: Revolution and Development in an Asian Metropolis* (1981), *The Foundations of the Chinese Planned Economy* (1989), and *The Origins of Japanese Trade Competitiveness* (1994).

Y. Y. KUEH is Professor of Economics and Dean of the Faculty of Social Sciences at Lingnan College, Hong Kong. He has published extensively on various aspects of the Chinese economy, including *Economic Trends in Chinese Agriculture* (1993) and *Agricultural Instability in China* (1995).

SHAO-CHUAN LENG is Compton Professor of Government emeritus at the University of Virginia. He has published numerous studies on politics and law in the People's Republic of China and the Republic of China on Taiwan, including *Chiang Ching-kuo's Leadership in the Development of the Republic of China on Taiwan* (1992) and *Reform and Development in Deng's China* (1994).

CHENG-YI LIN is Associate Research Fellow of the Institute of European and American Studies at the Academia Sinica in Taiwan. He has written on American policy towards China and Taiwan.

CHONG-PIN LIN is a Resident Scholar at the American Enterprise Institute in Washington, DC. An expert on Chinese military and security affairs, he has also written on domestic Chinese politics and foreign policy. He is the author of *China's Nuclear Weapons Strategy* (1988).

QI LUO is Research Assistant at the Contemporary China Institute, School of Oriental and African Studies, University of London. He has written about Chinese industrial policy and foreign trade and investment in southern China.

WANG GUNGWU is Vice Chancellor of the University of Hong Kong. His many writings include *The Structure and Power in North China During the Five Dynasties* (1963), *China and the World Since 1949* (1977), *Community and Nation* (1981), *China and the Overseas Chinese* (1991) and *The Chineseness of China* (1993).

MICHAEL YAHUDA is Reader in International Relations at the London School of Economics and Political Science, University of London. An authority on China's foreign relations and the international politics of the Asia-Pacific, his books include *China's Role in World Affairs* (1978) and *Towards the End of Isolationism: China's Foreign Policy After Mao* (1983).

# Introduction: The Emergence of "Greater China"

## David Shambaugh

The post-Cold War world is witnessing the reconfiguration of international relations with the emergence of new actors and relationships on the world stage. These new actors and patterns of relations are reshaping the familiarities of the post-war era. As the new millennium approaches, one has the sense that the world is in transition from one epoch to another. Among the new realities of our era is the emergence of "Greater China."

As the contributions which follow illustrate, Greater China is a complex and multifaceted phenomenon which exists even if the term to describe it is not entirely apt. Greater China comprises various actors, dimensions and processes. Together they pose a potential challenge to the regional and international order. Some already speak of Greater China as the world's next superpower. If the political obstacles can be overcome and China reunified under a single sovereign authority, it is likely that superpower status will become a reality. Even if *de jure* unification does not come to pass and Taiwan remains outside the fold, the *de facto* strength and influence which comprise Greater China will only increase with time. The formal obstacles to *unification* are indeed formidable, but the informal processes of *integration* gather pace with each passing day.

It is not unimaginable or unrealistic to assume that early in the 21st century the combined Gross Domestic Product (GDP) of Greater China will surpass those of the European Community and United States; it will be the world's leading trader and in possession of the world's largest foreign exchange reserves; it will be a source of state-of-the-art high technology and scientific and medical advances; it will be the world's largest consumer; it will garrison the world's largest military establishment; and may become a member of the Group of Nine nations (including Russia). By some estimates, Greater China will also overtake Japan as the dominant regional power, with Shanghai and Hong Kong the financial nexus of East Asian economic dynamism.

With such prospects a distinct possibility,[1] it is a propitious time to examine the phenomenon of Greater China, in its various dimensions, so as to provide some analytical clarity to a complex and increasingly diverse subject. This volume is not definitive, but it does go some way towards

---

1. This scenario depends very much on the assumption that China itself holds together as a national economic and political unit. Increased regionalism, devolution of power and decline of central authority in China are not insignificant trends that may lead to the fragmentation of the Chinese nation-state in the post-Deng era. This is, of course, only one of several possible alternative futures facing China. See Robert Scalapino, "China in the Late Leninist Era," *The China Quarterly* (Dec. 1993), pp. 949–71; David Shambaugh, "Losing control: the erosion of state authority in China," *Current History* (September 1993), pp. 253–59; and Harry Harding, "China at the crossroads: conservatism, reform or decay?" *Adelphi Paper* 275 (London: International Institute for Strategic Studies, 1993), pp. 36–48.

setting out the parameters (and hence the concept) of Greater China, its constituent parts, and its efficacy and limits. The articles which follow both assess the individual components and discrete dimensions of Greater China, and endeavour to explore their linkages and implications. They also adopt an interdisciplinary approach as the multifaceted nature of the Greater China phenomenon warrants.

## The Dimensions of Greater China

Conceptualizing the phenomenon of Greater China is a difficult task. Indeed, at the conference which led to this volume considerable time was devoted to assessing the validity of the concept and term "Greater China," even if it was generally recognized that the phenomenon of growing interactions and interdependencies within the constituent parts of China existed. The conferees did not accept as given that because the term "Greater China" had gained currency it was necessarily accurate or appropriate. At one point they came to the brink of dismissing the utility of the term altogether, as it was thought too vague, too pejorative and implied expansionism. For many Asians, "Greater China" conjures up images of Japan's wartime "Greater East Asian Co-Prosperity Sphere." Consensus eventually emerged, however, that if "greater" was equated with "larger" it was an adequate term to describe the activities in, and interactions between, mainland China, Hong Kong, Macao, Taiwan and the offshore islands, and Chinese overseas.

In his introductory essay, Harry Harding explores the concept of "Greater China": its origins, usages, variations, difficulties and realities. Harding's contribution does much to gain conceptual control over the vagaries of the phenomenon and, in so doing, delineates its various facets. Harding distinguishes between the economic, cultural and political aspects of Greater China (one might add the military/strategic and foreign policy dimensions as well). While pointing out that in each of the three realms there exists increasing interaction and convergence among the geographic constituent parts, he also notes that each has its own "centre" and there consequently exist limits to mutual influence. As is noted by subsequent contributors, Greater China is largely an *informal* phenomenon, lacking institutionalization. Harding aptly points out that in addition to the generally recognized *integrative* aspects of the Greater China phenomenon, there also exist *disintegrative* factors that inhibit convergence. He also notes the many reservations felt – largely within Chinese and Asian communities – about both the term and concept of Greater China, and he places it in historical perspective, as a reminder that Greater China is neither a new term nor new concept. Harding also introduces some balance into recent discussions, which have tended towards the alarmist by those who emphasize the potential aggregate economic and military might of Greater China. Finally, he stresses that Greater China is a series of *processes* with an indeterminate end. While to date analysts have mostly emphasized the integrative aspects, Harding cautions that integration is not an inexorable trend that will lead over time to national unification. Intra-Greater China interactions also create a variety of social, cultural, economic and political fissures – which could as easily accelerate *dis*integrative processes as vice versa.

If one looks at Greater China from an economic or cultural perspective, the relevance of nation-states and political entities is minimized. People, ideas, investments and goods are transcending political and territorial boundaries largely irrespective of the governments under which they live. Yet, as Michael Yahuda's contribution makes clear, a duality of state and non-state interactions exist. It is the interaction between the two, and indeed the influence that the latter exerts on the former, that characterize Greater China and is the subject of Yahuda's article. Yahuda observes that the informal dimension of relationships within Greater China comes quite naturally to Chinese more accustomed to *guanxi*-based ties than institutionalized, legal forms of sovereign interaction. He explores principally the relationships among Hong Kong, Taiwan and the People's Republic of China, and what the frictions between them mean for the emergence of Greater China. The interrelationships between these three governments (plus, in the case of Hong Kong, Great Britain) remain contentious amidst considerable flux. The delicate process of the retrocession of Hong Kong to PRC sovereignty in 1997 and the "flexible diplomacy" of the Republic of China on Taiwan pose significant challenges to the government in Beijing, and these are analysed. Like Harding, Yahuda concludes that there exists a disjunction between the economic and political aspects of Greater China. The former creates pressures for integration while the latter augur for separate national identities. Yahuda concludes that the evolution of politics in Beijing, Hong Kong and Taipei will be the ultimate determinant for the realization of Greater China.

More than anything else the concept of Greater China has arisen to account for the rapidly growing economic ties between Taiwan, Hong Kong and mainland China. If taken together, these three entities' combined economic prowess presently account for the world's third largest GNP, largest foreign exchange reserves and third largest foreign trade turnover.

The economic nexus of the three is, of course, Hong Kong. Performing its traditional entrepôt role, approximately 70 per cent of commercial investment in China today either originates in or flows through the territory. Hong Kong itself is the largest source of foreign direct investment in the PRC, although a growing percentage are "reinvestments" by PRC subsidiary corporations in Hong Kong (the PRC may have as much as $20 billion invested in the colony, though no one knows for sure and it is very difficult to calculate). Hong Kong's cumulative investment in China stood at nearly $25 billion in 1990, and by some estimates may reach twice that amount by the end of 1993. The integration of the Hong Kong and southern Chinese economies over the past decade is truly extraordinary. Today Hong Kong manufacturers employ more workers in south China than in Hong Kong itself. Approximately two-thirds of Hong Kong manufacturing is now located in the Pearl River Delta.

Since 1988–89 much new investment in China has come from Taiwanese investors, who by the end of 1992 had invested a cumulative total of approximately $10 billion on the mainland ($5.5 billion in 1992 alone). Until the end of 1987 Taiwan's cumulative investment on the mainland totalled only $100 million, but after 1988 the Taiwan government relaxed the travel ban and gave the go-ahead for business to accelerate trade and investment with the mainland. Trade consequently mushroomed, with the balance heavily in Taiwan's favour. Hong Kong accounts for approximately 40 per cent of the mainland's foreign trade (although most is re-exported to other destinations), and it serves as the principal trans-shipment point for indirect trade with Taiwan (although much trading and illegal smuggling takes place directly across the Strait). Estimates vary concerning the total value of two-way indirect trade between Taiwan and the PRC, but Taiwan's Board of Foreign Trade projects $10.4 billion for 1993, up from $7.41 billion in 1992. The growing importance of the mainland market for Taiwan traders cannot be understated; at current levels of growth mainland China will replace Japan as Taiwan's third largest export market within the next two or three years. Taiwan's investments in Hong Kong are also rising markedly, and vice versa.

In brief, the law of comparative advantage has stimulated rapidly rising levels of trade and investment between Taiwan, Hong Kong and southern China. This is the subject of the article by Robert Ash and Y. Y. Kueh. Ash and Kueh detail the commercial interactions between these three entities and show how economic integration is taking place.

In their contribution Luo Qi and Christopher Howe argue that economic integration is in fact a region-wide phenomenon throughout the Asia-Pacific. Luo and Howe examine trade and investment patterns within East Asia and place Taiwan's mainland investments in this broader perspective. Their case study of Taiwanese investment in the Xiamen Special Economic Zone is a detailed examination of the evolution of Taiwan's commercial approach to the mainland and its impact. They note that a variety of factors stimulated Taiwanese businessmen to look across the Strait for new markets, among them an appreciating New Taiwan Dollar; rising production costs on Taiwan and the appeal of low wages and relatively cheap land on the mainland; and the opportunity to take advantage of higher PRC export quotas. Luo and Howe conclude that while the experience has not been without its problems, overall, Taiwanese capital has transformed Xiamen and Fujian and has helped create "confidence-building measures" for politicians on both sides of the Taiwan Strait, thus contributing to the growing *rapprochement*.

While the expanding (and often illegal) movement of capital and goods across the Taiwan Strait increases integration within Greater China, a political gulf still exists. But even in this respect, as Chong-Pin Lin demonstrates, the gap has narrowed considerably in recent years. The impetus for this has predominantly come from the authorities in Taipei, although Beijing has reciprocated in kind while still attempting to frustrate Taiwan's bid for international recognition. Lin details the process of growing accommodation between the two governments that not long ago were frozen in armed confrontation. He carefully traces both the governmental and non-governmental interactions, as well as the governmental decision-making process on each side. Substantial political and military tensions still exist and the two sides remain a long way from reunification, but Lin's analysis demonstrates the "thickening" of ties and the establishment of a *modus vivendi* across the Strait since 1988–89. The ROC–PRC *rapprochement* is another case in international relations proving how non-governmental inter-actions can build bridges and initiate détente between hostile governments. As ROC President Lee Teng-hui responded when asked in 1990 about the enduring lessons of the Cold War, "Willy Brandt's policy of *Oestpolitik* proved farsighted and correct."[2]

Parallel and contributing to the growing ties between Taiwan and main-land China has been a dramatic liberalization of domestic politics on Taiwan. Less than a decade ago Taiwan remained dominated by a single ruling party that was intolerant of opposition, ruled through coercion, and clung to the dual fictions that Taiwan was a democracy and that the "Republic of China" was the legitimate government of all China. Times have changed. Today Taiwan's polity is one of the liveliest and most democratic in Asia; the strengthening of the Legislative Yuan and formation of the Democratic Progressive Party, Taiwan New Party and variety of lesser parties have diluted the Kuomintang's predominant power; the termination of martial law and abolition of the "period of national mobilization for the suppression of the Communist rebellion" have curbed the once pervasive strength of the security services; and the government has abandoned its claim to represent and rule all of China. In their contribution Shao-chuan Leng and Cheng-yi Lin describe and document this dramatic transition and the parameters of political change on Taiwan in recent years. Leng and Lin offer a careful examination of the process of political pluralization and maturation on the island. It has by no means been a smooth transition, with the ruling Kuomintang's grip on power growing more tenuous each year. Leng and Lin detail the ups and downs of the process and examine the implications for the future.

Political change in Hong Kong has not been as dramatic as on Taiwan, but, as Brian Hook shows in his article, perhaps just as significant. In both cases, the rise of a middle class and growth of civil society spurred demands for improved and more institutionalized forms of political participation. Yet in Hong Kong the pressure was not that of a hegemonic ruling party but the joint constraint of a governing colonial administrative apparatus, on the one hand, and the penetration of the colony by PRC operatives on the other. As Hook reveals, these processes had been at work for some years, but the double "shock" of the 1989 killings in Beijing and the 1992 proposals by Governor Chris Patten for accelerating democratization prior to the colony's 1997 retrocession to China jointly served to alter fundamentally the dis-course and substance of Hong Kong politics. Hook examines the impact of these events on local politics in Hong Kong, as well as the evolving struggle between Beijing and London over the interpretation and implementation of the Joint Declaration leading up to and beyond 1997.

Political change is usually reflective of more fundamental social change. In his contribution, Hugh D. R. Baker examines the changing lifestyles of the

---

2. Interview in Taipei, 13 November 1990.

Hong Kong citizenry and finds a number of distinctive trends. Perhaps most profound is the all-encompassing urbanization of Hong Kong. Rural life in the New Territories has virtually vanished, with the entire population becoming – in one way or another – tied into the urban commercial economy. Concomitantly, Baker notes the increased wealth in the colony, which in turn has facilitated the growth of a true middle class. Along with rapid economic development and rising incomes (and prices) have come demands for improved social services and a change in leisure pursuits. Baker concludes that Hong Kong remains a society that lives for the moment, but also that it faces 1997 with increased trepidation. This is why emigration figures have trebled in the last decade, now averaging approximately 60,000 per annum.

An often forgotten component of Greater China is Macao. A small enclave in the Pearl River Estuary, Macao is dwarfed in all respects (except gambling) by neighbouring Hong Kong. Nevertheless, it still makes its economic contributions to Greater China. Richard Louis Edmonds details these and other aspects of the territory still administered by Portugal but due to revert to China in 1999. One has the impression that Macao is homogeneous and relatively placid, but Edmonds provides examples of considerable diversity and unrest. He also elucidates Macao's growing economic integration with Zhuhai and the Guangdong economy more generally. Edmonds concludes that 1999 may prove a rude shock for Macao's population. Without improved specialization of production, he observes, economic dominance of Macao by Hong Kong and Guangdong will be unavoidable.

When one thinks of the impact of "outer China" (Hong Kong, Taiwan) on "inner China" (the PRC), politics and economics come to mind. But what about culture? Anyone who walks the streets of mainland Chinese cities, or even the dusty roads of interior rural villages, cannot help but be struck by the pervasiveness of what might be called a Greater Chinese popular culture. As Thomas B. Gold's contribution reveals, this has its origins among the under-40 generation in Hong Kong and Taiwan. Karaoke bars, MTV, KTV, discos, pornography, rock and rap singers and film stars from Hong Kong and Taiwan have all penetrated the consciousness of mainland China's youth. For this generation it is not Deng Xiaoping who rules China, but Taiwan's popular singer Deng Lijun (Teresa Teng). Gold shows how information technology and the movement of people in and out of China have contributed to the replacement of the Party by the party. What Gold calls *Gang-Tai* (Hong Kong–Taiwan) popular culture has become a vital component linking Greater China together.

One of the more controversial aspects of the Greater China phenomenon is the Chinese overseas, who reside outside continental China or Taiwan. Does one include the diaspora of South-east Asia, the ethnic Chinese communities in Europe and North America, or even the state of Singapore as members of Greater China? Wang Gungwu brings his considerable perspective and many years of analysing the Chinese overseas (a term he deliberately prefers to "overseas Chinese" or *huaqiao*) to his discussion of this aspect of Greater China. In so doing, Wang also posits considerable reservations about the concept and term "Greater China."

As China and the world progress towards the 21st century, the Greater China phenomenon will loom larger. Whether or not "Greater China" is the most appropriate term, there is little doubt that the entities, processes and phenomena which comprise it will increasingly be felt in regional and global terms.

# The Concept of "Greater China": Themes, Variations and Reservations*

## Harry Harding

The world is suddenly talking about the emergence of "Greater China." The term has appeared in the headlines of major newspapers and magazines, has been the topic of conferences sponsored by prominent think-tanks, and is now the theme of a special issue of the world's leading journal of Chinese affairs. It thus joins other phrases – "the new world order," "the end of history," "the Pacific Century" and the "clash of civilizations" – as part of the trendiest vocabulary used in discussions of contemporary global affairs.

As is so often the case with the phrase of the moment, however, the precise meaning of "Greater China" (usually rendered as *dazhonghua* in Chinese) is not entirely clear. In essence, it refers to the rapidly increasing interaction among Chinese societies around the world as the political and administrative barriers to their intercourse fall. But different analysts use the term in different ways. Some refer primarily to the commercial ties among ethnic Chinese, whereas others are more interested in cultural interactions, and still others in the prospects for political reunification. Some observers focus exclusively on Hong Kong, Macao, Taiwan and mainland China, others incorporate Singapore, and still others include the overseas Chinese living in South-east Asia, America and Europe. To some writers, "Greater China" is simply a way of summarizing the new linkages among the far-flung international Chinese community; to others, it is a prescription of the institutions that should govern those ties.

Even more important, "Greater China" is a controversial concept. To some observers, the formation of a Greater China is an inexorable and irreversible process – the resurrection of a wide range of natural economic and cultural relationships that were long restricted by artificial political obstacles. In contrast, other analysts stress the remaining barriers to economic interaction, cultural exchange and political integration among Chinese societies, and insist that the creation of Greater China will be a turbulent and ultimately unsuccessful undertaking. Moreover, where some see the emergence of Greater China as an attractive possibility both economically and culturally, others regard it as all too reminiscent of past attempts to create empires by military force, and argue that both China and the rest of the world would be better off without it.

This article is an attempt to explore the various meanings of the term "Greater China," as well as to capture some of the controversy surrounding it. It makes three basic arguments. First, the term "Greater China"

*This is a revised version of a paper presented at the conference on "Greater China," convened by *The China Quarterly* in Hong Kong on 4–5 January 1993. I am grateful to the participants in the conference for their valuable criticisms and suggestions. I also wish to express my appreciation to Scott Kennedy, my research assistant at the Brookings Institution, for his invaluable help in assembling material.

subsumes three relatively distinct themes: economic integration, cultural interaction and political reunification within the international Chinese community. Each of these variants of Greater China has different boundaries, has different capitals or centres of activity, and takes different institutional forms. Secondly, within each of these three themes, there are many variations. Some authors simply use different terms – whether in Chinese or in English – to express pretty much the same ideas. In other cases, however, different terms reflect significantly different meanings. These variations, in turn, often reflect different assessments of the boundaries of Greater China, and different evaluations of the feasibility of institutionalizing it. Finally, Greater China is a problematic idea. Some analysts question its feasibility, given the disintegrative forces that continue to separate the various elements of the global Chinese community. Others question its desirability, either for China or for the rest of the world. It is important to understand the reservations surrounding the idea of Greater China, as well as its rationale.

## The Origins of "Greater China"

In the English language, the word "greater" is often used to suggest a coherent economic and demographic region that spans administrative borders. The term "Greater London," for example, refers to the city and its suburbs, even though those suburbs may lie outside the jurisdiction of the municipal government. Similarly, the term "Greater New York Metropolitan Area" refers to the economic system that takes New York City as its hub, but includes parts of at least three states. In these contexts, the entity is regarded as the product of largely natural economic and social forces, which render political boundaries obsolete or irrelevant.

In a political or strategic setting, however, the term "greater" often has a much more pejorative connotation. Here, it refers to a state's expansion of its political boundaries to include territories formerly outside its control. Although occasionally justified in terms of uniting an ethnic group divided by political frontiers, this is not usually a natural process, but may actually occur by force. The most common examples are the "Greater Germany" (*Grossdeutschland*) that Hitler intended to unite all the "Germanic peoples" of Europe as the core of an even larger German Empire, and the Greater East Asia Co-Prosperity Sphere, designed by Japan to include most of East Asia. Other imperial powers have occasionally employed the term in this way as well: the phrase "Greater Britain" was used briefly in the 1860s to refer to what was later called the British Empire.[1]

Although the specific term "Greater China" is a fairly recent one, it has quite a long pedigree. The concept can be traced to the traditional distinction, made first by Chinese and then adopted by Western geogra-

---

1. Stephen Uhalley, Jr., " 'Greater China': what's in a name?" paper presented to the Regional Seminar on "Greater China," sponsored by the Center for Chinese Studies, University of California at Berkeley, February 1993, p. 2.

phers, between "China Proper" (*Zhongguo benbu*) and what was variously called "Outer China" or the "Chinese dependencies" (*shudi* or *fanshu*). "China Proper" referred to those areas that were directly controlled by the central administrative bureaucracy. For most of the Qing Dynasty, it consisted of the 18 provinces primarily populated by Han Chinese. In contrast, "Outer China" or the "dependencies" referred to other areas, primarily peopled by ethnic minorities, that were under the suzerainty of the Chinese state and whose subordination was ensured by force if necessary. During the Qing, these included Manchuria, Mongolia, Chinese Turkestan and Tibet.[2]

Together, China Proper and Outer China were normally called the "Chinese Empire," but references to the combination of the two regions as "Greater China" date at least to the 1930s. In 1934, George Cressey used the term when calculating the geographic area of the country. Six years later, Owen Lattimore used it to describe the combination of "China within the Great Wall" (that is, China Proper) and its six "frontier zones" (which he described as "Manchukuo," outer Mongolia, Inner Mongolia, Chinese Turkestan, Tibet proper, and the "Tibet–Chinese frontier provinces of Ch'inghai [Qinghai] and Hsik'ang [Xikang]").[3]

In the 1940s, the term "Greater China" also appeared on a number of United States government maps, with, depending on the map, two different connotations: political and topographic. In some cases, it was used to imply that the Republic of China claimed territories that had once been part of the Chinese Empire, but that the Nationalist government did not presently control. A map published in 1944, for example, included outer Mongolia, Manchuria, Tibet and Xinjiang as part of "Greater China," even though not all of these territories were controlled by the Chinese government of the time.[4] In other cases, the phrase referred to geographic features that were customarily associated with China, but that spilled across international boundaries into other jurisdictions. Thus, one map of the mountain ranges of "Greater China" showed the Himalayas, the Tianshan mountains and the Shikote Akin range, even though they lay either partly or entirely outside the boundaries claimed by the Republic of China.[5]

2. On the distinction between "China Proper" and the rest of the Chinese Empire, see William Darby, *Darby's Universal Gazetteer* (Philadelphia: Bennett and Walton, 1827), p. 154; J. Calvin Smith, *Harper's Statistical Gazetteer of the World* (New York: Harper and Brothers, 1855), p. 402; and *Lippincott's Gazetteer* (Philadelphia: J. B. Lippincott, 1883), p. 464. The term "Outer China" is used, together with "China Proper," in *China Proper*, Geographical Handbook Series, No. 530 (Washington, D.C.: U.S. Department of the Navy, Naval Intelligence Division, July 1944). On the related terms "outer territories" and "dependencies," see Edwin John Dingle (ed.), *The New Atlas and Commercial Gazetteer of China*, 2nd ed. (Shanghai: The North-China Daily News and Herald, 1918?).
3. George Babcock Cressey, *China's Geographic Foundations: A Survey of the Land and Its People* (New York: McGraw-Hill, 1934), p. 53; and Owen Lattimore, *Inner Asian Frontiers of China* (New York: American Geographic Society, 1940).
4. U.S. Office of Strategic Services, "Greater China," 1944. See Uhalley, "What's in a name?"
5. U.S. Department of the Interior, Bureau of Mines, Foreign Minerals Division, "Sketch map of the principal mountain ranges in Greater China," Map No. 170, June 1947.

The more recent usage of the concept of Greater China first emerged in Chinese-language sources in the late 1970s, largely to discuss the expansion of economic ties between Hong Kong and mainland China that was resulting from the post-Mao reforms, and to highlight the prospects that a similar growth might occur in the commercial relations between Taiwan and the mainland. Perhaps the first such reference can be found in the June 1979 issue of a Taiwanese journal, *Changqiao* (*Long Bridge*), which advocated the creation of a "Chinese Common Market" that would link Taiwan, Hong Kong, Macao, Singapore and the Chinese mainland.[6] In Hong Kong, one of the first to use a similar concept was the futurologist Huang Zhilian who, in 1980, devised the terms *Zhongguoren gongtongti* (Chinese community) and *Zhongguoren jingji jituan* (Chinese economic grouping) to refer to economic co-operation among Hong Kong, Taiwan and the mainland.[7]

In English, the first contemporary use of the term "Greater China" appeared about five years later, in the mid to late 1980s. At first, a few writers employed it to refer to the possibility of a politically reunified China, as when *The Economist* mentioned that Taiwan might eventually join a "greater China confederation."[8] But it was more frequently used to describe the expansion of commercial ties among the three main Chinese economies. *Business Week*, in an article entitled "Asia's new fire-breather," referred to "Greater China" as the prospective result of the "three-way economic integration" of Hong Kong, Taiwan and the mainland, and as a more "comfortable" and "apolitical" path to reunification than any formal political settlement.[9] Around two years later, the *Los Angeles Times* described Greater China as a "superpower on a drawing board," the result of the economic integration and possible political reunification of Hong Kong, Taiwan, Macao and the mainland.[10]

In the early 1990s, the concept of Greater China is becoming steadily more commonplace. Chinese writers continue to devise variations on the concept of an integrated Chinese marketplace, and to a lesser degree to propose formulas for the political reunification of their country. At least two major international conferences, attended primarily by Chinese, have been held specifically to discuss the concept of an integrated Chinese economy, and many others have touched on the idea as part of a different agenda.[11] Several major American research institutions and foreign affairs organizations have popularized the term through their publications and

6. Cited in *Far Eastern Economic Review*, 20 July 1979, p. 24.

7. Huang Zhilian, *Meiguo 203 nian: Dui "meiguo tixi" de lishixue yu weilaixue de fenxi* (*America at 203 Years: An Analysis of the Historiography and Futurology of the American System*) (Hong Kong: Zhongliu, 1980), pp. 915–929.

8. "Too rich to stay a lonely beacon," *The Economist*, 28 March 1987, p. 21. See also *The Financial Times*, 9 December 1985, Section III, p. VII.

9. "Asia's new fire-breather," *Business Week*, 10 October 1988, pp. 54–55.

10. " 'Greater China': superpower on a drawing board," *Los Angeles Times*, 12 June 1990, Section H, p. 1.

11. The first conference was held in Hong Kong in January 1992; the second in Stanford in June 1993. See Uhalley, "What's in a name?" pp. 13–14.

conferences.[12] Multinational corporations use the concept to describe their marketing or investment strategies in Asia, and several mutual funds have appropriated the term as well.[13] "Greater China" is rapidly becoming part of the standard lexicon of international affairs, whose meanings and implications deserve careful scrutiny.

## A Transnational Chinese Economy

The most common theme in contemporary discussions of Greater China is the integration of the world's various Chinese economies, surmounting the political boundaries that once divided and isolated them. This first aspect of Greater China is reflected in the enormous increase in the trade between Hong Kong and mainland China over the last 15 years, and the more recent but equally rapid growth of trade between Taiwan and mainland China since the mid-1980s. Hong Kong's trade with mainland China, most of it entrepôt transactions, grew from $5.7 billion in 1980 to more than $80 billion in 1992. During the same period, Taiwan's trade with the mainland increased from around $300 million to $7.4 billion. And, according to Taiwan's accounts, its trade with Hong Kong, including some of its entrepôt trade, rose from $2 billion in 1980 to $17 billion in 1992. For each of the three Chinese economies, trade with the other two has become an important part of its global economic relations.

Investment has also been rising. It has been estimated that Taiwan has now invested a cumulative total of $6.7 billion in mainland China and another $2 billion in Hong Kong, that mainland China has invested a total of $20 billion in Hong Kong (although none yet in Taiwan), and that Hong Kong has invested $10 billion in mainland China and a further $1.2 billion in Taiwan. If these figures are accurate, they suggest that cross-investment within these three parts of Greater China is in the order of nearly $40 billion. The investment provided by overseas Chinese entrepreneurs in South-east Asia and North America would increase the total still further.[14]

12. See, for example, Andrew Brick, "The emergence of Greater China: the diaspora ascendent," Heritage Lectures, No. 411 (Washington, D.C.: The Heritage Foundation, 9 September 1992); David Lampton *et al.*, *The Emergence of "Greater China": Implications for the United States*, Policy Series, No. 5 (New York: National Committee on U.S.–China Relations, October 1992); Pamela Baldinger, "The birth of Greater China," *China Business Review*, May–June 1992, pp. 13–17; and Harry Harding, "The U.S. and Greater China," *China Business Review*, May–June 1992, pp. 18–22. The articles in *China Business Review* were drawn from a conference on "American Economic Relations with Greater China," jointly organized in February 1992 by the U.S.–China Business Council and the American Enterprise Institute.

13. One of the first firms to announce a "Greater China" marketing strategy – regarding Hong Kong, Taiwan and mainland China as a single consumer market – was the Swiss watchmaker Rado. See *Bangkok Post*, 25 December 1989. Coca-Cola has also adopted a similar strategy; see *South China Morning Post*, 29 October 1991. Of several closed-end mutual funds making investments in Hong Kong, Taiwan and mainland China, the one managed by Invesco Mim is called the "Greater China Opportunities Fund," while the one managed by Baring International is called the "Greater China Fund."

14. For further details on the level of economic interactions among the principal Chinese economies, see the article by Robert Ash and Y. Y. Kueh in this issue.

The emergence of this transnational Chinese economy is most often portrayed as the result of the economic complementarities that presently exist among Hong Kong, Taiwan and the mainland. Mainland China has an interest in gaining access to capital, technology and know-how from Hong Kong and Taiwan, and especially to gain their co-operation in penetrating markets in third countries. Conversely, manufacturers in Hong Kong and Taiwan have an interest in finding alternative bases of production, as higher wages, stronger currencies and environmental re-strictions make it increasingly expensive to produce goods at home. In addition, Hong Kong and Taiwan – like other economies – are keen to exploit the large and rapidly growing markets on the Chinese main-land, especially at a time of recession and perceived protectionism in the United States, Europe and Japan.

The realization of these economic complementarities, in turn, is facili-tated by the cultural ties among these Chinese societies. It is frequently asserted that a common culture, a common language, family ties and ancestral roots all make it somewhat easier for Chinese to do business with one another than to engage in commercial relations with foreigners. In addition, prosperous Chinese entrepreneurs outside mainland China may be more willing to absorb losses in their dealings in the People's Republic out of a belief that they are assisting in the economic develop-ment and modernization of their motherland.

Another crucial factor has been the more accommodating posture taken by the governments concerned. Both Beijing and Taipei adopted policies in the 1950s that were extremely inhospitable to the maintenance of normal commercial relations among the three principal Chinese econom-ies. The People's Republic chose a strategy of autarkic socialist development which assigned a minimal role to foreign trade and which virtually barred foreign investment, except for a brief period in which a limited amount of Soviet investment was tolerated. Because of its hostile political relationship with the mainland, Taipei banned virtually all economic contacts across the Taiwan Strait. From this perspective, mainland China's decision to welcome and promote foreign trade and investment in the post-Mao era has been one critical stimulant for the creation of this transnational Chinese economy. Another has been the willingness of the Taiwan government to remove some of the barriers to commercial relations with its rival on the mainland.

So far, this analysis makes the emergence of a transnational Chinese economy appear to be a prime example of the "natural economic territo-ries" – the economic systems spanning political boundaries – that can develop when governments allow them.[15] And, to a large degree, the growing commercial interactions among Hong Kong, Taiwan and the Chinese mainland do represent the construction – or, in many cases,

15. The term "natural economic territories" has been popularized by the American politi-cal scientist Robert Scalapino. See his *The Last Leninists: The Uncertain Future of Asia's Communist States* (Washington, D.C.: Center for Strategic and International Studies, 1992), p. 20.

the resurrection – of normal economic ties that had been interrupted by 30 years of central planning in the People's Republic and by 35 years of hostility between Beijing and Taipei. Hong Kong is resuming its original role as the entrepôt for southern China, whereas Taiwan is developing a natural position as a growth centre for Fujian and much of the Chinese coast.

It is becoming increasingly evident, however, that more than natural economic forces are at work. The governments of the principal Chinese societies are not simply removing past obstructions and adopting a neutral posture towards economic relationships. Instead, they remain deeply involved in promoting and guiding the commercial ties among their economies. What is more, they are doing so for strikingly different motives. From Beijing's perspective, economic interaction is viewed as a way of facilitating the eventual political reunification of China. The mainland Chinese government has therefore adopted a series of policies to stimulate commercial relations with Hong Kong and Taiwan, most notably the creation of special economic zones directly opposite them, for political as well as for purely commercial reasons. Hong Kong, in turn, regards economic ties with the mainland as a way of cushioning its return to Chinese sovereignty in 1997, in that they will give Beijing a large and direct stake in preserving the territory's political viability and economic prosperity throughout the transition. On Taiwan, in contrast, economic interaction with the mainland is seen in the short term as a lever for extracting political concessions from Beijing, especially with regard to renouncing the use of force against the island and allowing Taiwan a larger voice in international affairs, and possibly a way of promoting democratization as well. Over the longer term, many on Taiwan regard economic integration as a more feasible and more tolerable form of national unity than formal political reunification.

The emergence of this new transnational Chinese economy has evoked a multitude of analytical concepts and prescriptive formulas. A search of both Chinese and English language materials has thus far identified no fewer than 41 variations on this particular theme, ranging (in alphabetical order) from the "Asian Chinese Common Market" through the "Chinese Economic Community" and the "Greater China Economic Sphere" to the "South-east China Free Trade Area." These formulas differ along two principal dimensions: the scope of the territory regarded as being included, and the degree of formal integration being proposed.

Until quite recently, the varying definitions of the geographical extent of the Greater Chinese economy could be portrayed as five concentric circles, all centring on Hong Kong. These included: Greater Hong Kong (Hong Kong, Macao and Guangdong)[16]; Greater South China (Hong Kong, Macao, Taiwan and the south-eastern coast of the People's Repub-

---

16. Eugene Linn, "Hong Kong/Guangdong link: whither the South China NIC?" *Amcham*, Vol. 22, No. 10 (1990), pp. 12–15; Woo Kwong-ching, "The challenge of 'Hong Kong plus'," 2nd ed. (Hong Kong: The Wharf (Holdings) Ltd., November 1991); and Zhang Jiangming, "Nuli cuijin yue-gang-ao-tai jingji hezuo zuoshang xin taijie" ("Work to enable economic co-operation among Guangdong, Hong Kong, Macao and Taiwan to reach a new

lic, extending north perhaps as far as Shanghai)[17]; Greater *Nanyang* (Hong Kong, Macao, South China, Taiwan, Singapore and overseas Chinese entrepreneurs in the rest of South-east Asia)[18]; All China (Hong Kong, Macao, Taiwan and the entire People's Republic)[19]; and Greater China (Hong Kong, Macao, Taiwan, the People's Republic, Singapore and overseas Chinese throughout the world).[20] The emergence of these variations reflects, to some degree, the changing realities of commercial interaction within the transnational Chinese economy. At the beginning, the economic ties between Hong Kong and Guangdong dominated the process: Hong Kong accounted for the bulk of China's foreign investment and foreign trade, and the largest share of Hong Kong's trade and investment relations were, in turn, with Guangdong. As a result, discussions of "Greater China" understandably focused on the inner concentric circles that lay closest to Hong Kong.

By the end of the 1980s, however, Taiwan had become a major trading partner and source of investment for mainland China, and investment

---

*footnote continued*

level"), *Gang'ao jingji* (*The Economies of Hong Kong and Macao*), No. 8 (1990), pp. 7–9, citing a proposal by a Hong Kong entrepreneur for a "Pearl River Delta Economic Alliance."

17. Xiu Chunping, "Haixia liangan jingmao fazhan de dongyin, zhang'ai ji gaiyou de quxiang" ("The impetus and obstacles to the development of economic relations across the Taiwan Strait and the trend it should take"), *Taiwan yanjiu* (*Taiwan Research*), No. 1 (March 1991), pp. 45–50; Ting Wai, "The regional and international implications of the South China Economic Zone," *Issues and Studies*, Vol. 28, No. 12 (1992), pp. 46–72; Jin Hongxun, "Zhongguo jingji de yitihua yu 'haixia liangan jingjiquan' shexiang" ("The integration of China's economy and the idea of a 'Cross Strait Economic Circle'," *Taiwan yanjiu* (*Taiwan Research*), No. 3 (June 1991), pp. 44–51; Zhou Bajun, "Cong 'Zhongguoren gongtongti' dao 'hua dongnan ziyou maoyiqu' " ("From a 'Chinese Commonwealth' to a 'South-east China Free Trade Area'," *Jingji daobao* (*Economic Reporter*), 6 November 1989, pp. 3–5; William Yang, "Taiwan: a Chinese economic community is emerging," *Business Taiwan*, 4 May 1992; Sally Stewart *et al.*, "The latest Asian newly industrialized economy emerges: the South China economic community," *Columbia Journal of World Business*, Vol. 27, No. 2 (1992), pp. 30–37; and Zhong Yuanfan, "Jianli yu fazhan huanan jingjiqu" ("Construct and develop a South China economic zone"), *Gang'ao jingji* (*The Economies of Hong Kong and Macao*), No. 4 (1993), pp. 3–6.

18. Li Huiwu, " 'Yatai shiji' yu 'fan nanzhongguo jingjiquan' de xingcheng" ("The 'Asia-Pacific Century' and the formation of a 'Pan-South China Economic Circle' "), *Gang'ao jingji* (*The Economies of Hong Kong and Macao*), No. 10 (1991), pp. 21–23.

19. Zhou Zhihuan, " 'Zhongguo jingjiquan' chutan" ("An initial exploration of the 'Chinese Economic Circle' "), in Li Jiaquan and Guo Xiangzhi (eds.), *Huigu yu zhanwang – Lun haixia liangan guanxi* (*Review and Prospect – On Cross-Strait Relations*) (Beijing: Current Affairs Publishing House, 1989), pp. 294–304; Fang Sheng, "Guanyu 'Zhongguo jingjiquan' de sikao" ("Reflections on a Chinese Economic Circle"), in *ibid.* pp. 305–316; An-chia Wu, "The political implications of the 'Coordination of Chinese economic systems'," *Issues and Studies*, Vol. 28, No. 4 (1992), pp. 1–9; Charng Kao, "A 'Greater China Economic Sphere': reality and prospects," *Issues and Studies*, Vol. 28, No. 11 (1992), pp. 49–64; and Huang Wentao, " 'Zhongguo jingji guanxiqun' de fazhan yu 'Zhongguo jingjiquan' de kunzhi" ("The development of the 'China Economic Relations Grouping' and the obstacles to a 'China Economic Sphere',") *Taiwan yanjiu* (*Taiwan Research*), No. 1 (March 1991), pp. 23–31.

20. *Changqiao*, June 1979, cited in *Far Eastern Economic Review*, 20 July 1979, p. 24; Cheng Chu-yuan, "Dazhonghua gongtong shichang de gouxiang" ("The idea of a Greater Chinese common market"), *Zhongguo shibao* (*China Times*), 9 June 1988, p. 2; David Carnes, "Taiwan: Chinese prosperity sphere begins to take shape," *Business Taiwan*, 16 March 1992; and Brick, "Emergence of Greater China."

from both Hong Kong and Taiwan had spread from Guangdong up the coast and into the interior. Even more recently, overseas Chinese entrepreneurs in South-east Asia have shown a more visible interest in conducting trade and investment with the People's Republic. In an empirical sense, therefore, the boundaries of the transnational Chinese economy have steadily expanded in all directions. As this occurred, analysis began to incorporate the outermost of the concentric circles, whose boundaries lay farther from Hong Kong.[21]

But the analysis of the transnational Chinese economy is a prescriptive exercise, as well as a descriptive one. One clear division among those who address the concept has fallen between those who wish to include Singapore and overseas Chinese in Greater China and those who do not. The former often believe that expanding the geographic area of the transnational Chinese economy will make it more dynamic, more efficient and ultimately more powerful. Conversely, the latter often hold that explicitly including overseas Chinese is highly risky, in that it will raise fears in South-east Asia that China has hegemonic ambitions in the region and will produce suspicions that overseas Chinese are expected to be more loyal to their motherland than to their place of residence.

The second dimension along which analyses of the transnational Chinese economy vary involves the degree of formal economic integration that is being envisaged. In fact, most discussions are extremely vague on this point, referring ambiguously to an economic "circle," "sphere" or "zone" linking the various economies, without providing much detail on the institutional or legal structures involved. To the extent that these issues are addressed, however, there has been a growing tendency to favour informal patterns of economic activity over formal institutional arrangements. In other words, just as the geographical scope of the transnational Chinese economy has been expanding, the prescriptions for its organizational structure have become steadily less ambitious.

Of course, some of the earliest discussions of the transnational Chinese economy did imply a rather high degree of formal economic integration. Drawing on the theoretical literature on economic integration, as well as experience in Europe and elsewhere, some analysts proposed the creation of a "free trade area" (*ziyou maoyiqu*) linking the various Chinese economies, implying the elimination of tariff barriers to goods passing among them. Others advocated the formation of a "common market" (*gongtong shichang*), which would involve the establishment of a common set of tariffs for all goods entering the region from abroad. And a few, drawing a parallel with the European Economic Community, recommended the organization of a Chinese Economic Community (*jingji gongtongti*), which would entail not only free trade within the area and common tariffs with non-members, but also the unrestricted mobility of

21. Some analysts predict that the boundaries of the transnational Chinese economy will continuously expand over time. See, for example, Fu Dongcheng, "Xianggang, taiwan, dalu jingji tonghe de qianjing" ("The prospects for economic unification among Hong Kong, Taiwan and the mainland"), *Zhongguo shibao zhoukan* (*China Times Weekly*), 5–11 January 1992, pp. 15–22.

the factors of production (especially capital and labour), the co-ordination of monetary and fiscal policies, and the creation of common social welfare mechanisms.[22]

Over time, however, analyses have become considerably more modest institutionally.[23] Instead of envisaging a high level of economic integration, governed by formal intergovernmental institutions, many observers now advocate a more informal process of "consultation" or "co-ordination," in which governments will attempt to facilitate commercial relations rather than trying to negotiate formal trading blocs or common markets.[24] This trend appears to be occurring for several reasons. First, there is a greater awareness of the barriers that would exist even to the creation of a free trade area, let alone a fully-fledged economic community. Hong Kong's status as a free port makes it impossible to envisage its inclusion in a Chinese free trade area, unless the rest of Greater China were also willing to eliminate tariffs on imported goods.[25] The gaps between the standards of living, economic institutions and legal systems on the Chinese mainland and those in Hong Kong and Taiwan also make extensive economic integration highly problematic.[26] Moreover, Taiwan and mainland China do not yet have official political relations, direct air

22. These distinctions are drawn in Zhou Bajun, "Cong 'Zhongguoren gongtongti' dao 'hua dongnan ziyou maoyiqu' " ("From a 'Chinese Commonwealth' to a 'South-east China Free Trade Area' "). See also Cheng Chu-yuan, "Dazhonghua gongtong shichang de gouxiang" ("The idea of a Greater Chinese common market"); Gao Xijun [Charng Kao], "Zhongguoren ruhe miandui jingji bilei? Jianli 'yazhou huaren gongtong shichang' de tantao" ("How should Chinese confront economic blocs? On the construction of an 'Asian Chinese Common Market' "), *Yuanjian* (*Distant View*), 15 October 1988, pp. 101–105; and Yu Yuanzhou, "Lun jianli 'Zhonghua jingji gongtongti' " ("On constructing a 'Chinese Economic Community' "), *Gang'ao jingji* (*The Economies of Hong Kong and Macao*), No. 2 (1993), pp. 14–16.

23. This is evident in the work of Cheng Chu-yuan, one of the leading analysts of a transnational Chinese economy. Compare his recent "Da Zhonghua jingjiquan de xingcheng yu qianjing" ("The formation and prospects of the Greater China Economic Circle"), *Zhongguo shibao zhoukan* (*China Times Weekly*), 6–12 June 1993, pp. 34–37, with his earlier "Dazhonghua gongtong shichang de gouxiang" ("The concept of a Greater Chinese Common Market").

24. See, for example, Li Shuiwang and Liu Yingxian, "Canjia 'Zhonghua jingji xiezuo xitong' yantaohui youguan" ("Concerns after participating in a symposium on a 'system for co-ordinating the Chinese economies' "), *Taisheng* (*Voice of Taiwan*), April 1992, pp. 17–19; and Liu Yingxian and Luo Xiangxi, "Cong liangan jingmao guanxi fazhan kan 'Zhonghua jingji xiezuo xitong' de jianlai ji kunnan" ("Viewing the construction and difficulties of a 'system for co-ordinating the Chinese economies' from the development of cross-Strait economic and trade relations"), *Taiwan yanjiu* (*Taiwan Research*), No. 2 (1992), pp. 36–44.

25. This point was first made by Yun-wing Sung, in "Non-institutional economic integration via cultural affinity: the case of mainland China, Taiwan, and Hong Kong" (Shatin: Hong Kong Institute of Asia-Pacific Studies, Chinese University of Hong Kong, 1992).

26. See, for example, Xu Donghai, " 'Dazhongguo jingji gongtongti' shexiang yu pinggu" ("The idea and critique of the 'Greater China Economic Community' "), *Gongdang wenti yanjiu* (*Research on Communist Party Issues*), Vol. 16, No. 1 (January 1990), pp. 73–78; Yen Tzung-ta, "Taiwan investment in mainland China and its impact on Taiwan's industries," *Issues and Studies*, Vol. 27, No. 5 (May 1991), pp. 10–42; Gao Chang, "Haixia liangan jingji zhenghe kexingxing fenxi" ("An analysis of the feasibility of cross-Strait economic integration"), *Taiwan jingji yanjiu yuekan* (*Taiwan Economic Research Monthly*), Vol. 14, No. 6 (June 1991), pp. 67–74; and An-chia Wu, "Political implications."

or sea links, or a trade or investment agreement. This makes discussion of a high level of economic integration seem most premature.

Questions of feasibility aside, analysts both in China and abroad have also expressed reservations about the desirability of forming a highly institutionalized transnational Chinese economy. In Taiwan, and to a more limited degree even in Hong Kong, there is the fear that economic integration with the mainland would lead to a "hollowing out" of local industry.[27] This would be particularly true, according to one analysis, if Taiwanese and Hong Kong entrepreneurs shifted their entire production processes and research and development effort to the mainland, not just the simpler assembly operations.[28] Paradoxically, some mainland economists have expressed parallel concerns: that the complete removal of barriers to trade and investment relations with Hong Kong and Taiwan would confront mainland manufacturers with unbeatable competition, and thus would exacerbate the problems of bankruptcy and unemployment in the state sector in the People's Republic.[29] In each society, in other words, analysts are viewing the process of full economic integration with some apprehension, worrying that their own economy will gain the least benefit and suffer the greatest dislocation.

The creation of a formal Chinese economic community would also raise the same issues as the organization of any international economic bloc: the fear of those outside that they will be disadvantaged, and even the apprehension of those inside that their other economic linkages will be attenuated. Thus, several analysts in China have warned that talk of an institutionalized transnational Chinese economy could alienate other countries in Asia, especially members of ASEAN, who would be excluded from it. Similarly, observers in the United States have speculated that the economic integration of Hong Kong, Taiwan and mainland China would divert more trade and investment from third countries than it would generate. Some analysts in Japan are apprehensive that the formation of a Chinese economic community would produce an "export machine" with which the rest of the developing world could not compete, and whose output the developed nations could not absorb. Conversely, observers in Taiwan (and, interestingly, in mainland China as well) have

---

27. Huang Ruiqi, "Liangan jingmao jiaoliu dui guonei chanye fazhan zhi yingxiang" ("The effect of cross-Strait economic and trade interchange on the development of domestic industry"), *Taiwan jingji yanjiu yuekan*, Vol. 14, No. 6 (June 1991), pp. 43–46. For a similar concern about Hong Kong, expressed by the chairman of a Hong Kong Chinese industrialists' association, see Liang Qinrong, " 'Qian dian hou chang' moshi yu Xiang Gang jingji fazhan luxiang," ("The 'store in front, factory in back' model and the path for Hong Kong's economic development"), *Jingji daobao* (*Economic Reporter*), No. 2 (1993), pp. 49–50. For a more sanguine view, written by a mainland scholar, see Zhang Guanhua, "Taiwan 'chanye kongdonghua' wenti zhi tantao" ("An inquiry into the 'industrial hollowing-out' of Taiwan"), *Taiwan yanjiu* (*Taiwan Research*), No. 4 (1992), pp. 33, 34–39.

28. Liu Ruitu, "Poxi guonei shengchang waiyi dalu" ("An analysis of the movement of domestic industry to the mainland"), *Taiwan jingji yanjiu yuekan* (*Taiwan Economic Research Monthly*), Vol. 14, No. 6 (June 1991), pp. 32–37.

29. Pei Wuwei, "Dui 'Zhongguo jingjiquan' de jingji fenxi" ("An economic analysis of the 'Chinese Economic Circle' "), *Yatai jingji – Zhongguo de duiwai kaifang* (*Asia-Pacific Economies – China's Opening to the Outside World*), No. 2 (1993), pp. 54–59.

cautioned that the creation of a transnational Chinese economy might somehow cut off or attenuate their existing economic relations with Japan, the United States and the rest of the world.

Increasingly, therefore, discussions of the transnational Chinese economy are featuring the significantly different concept of a network of overlapping and interlocking economic territories, some large and some small, rather than a single unified economic bloc. According to one early version, presented by the Hong Kong scholar Huang Zhilian, these economic territories might include Greater South China centring on Hong Kong and Taiwan, a Yangzi Circle focused on Shanghai, a Bohai Circle linking Tianjin and Dalian to South Korea, and a South-west China Circle connecting Sichuan and Yunnan to South-east Asia.[30] To this list others would add the Tumen River region, linking north-east China, Russia, Japan and the two Koreas; and a North-west Circle, connecting western China to Russia and the bordering Central Asian republics.

This conception differs from earlier discussions of "Greater China" in several ways. First, it is more multi-nodal, in that these emerging economic circles and networks are no longer seen as centring exclusively on Hong Kong, as earlier versions tended to be. It is still acknowledged, of course, that Hong Kong will continue to provide much of the capital investment for the entire Asia-Pacific region, and to serve as an entrepôt for much of its trade. But a number of other key cities are also depicted as centres of economic growth, with Taipei, Shanghai, Tianjin, Dalian and Chongqing occupying a much more prominent place than they did in earlier versions. Whatever its economic logic, this approach has more political appeal than a concept that assigns the central part solely to Hong Kong.

Secondly, unlike the earlier versions of "Greater China," most of these smaller economic circles are not solely Chinese. Although some (such as Huang Zhilian's Greater South China) still link territories exclusively or largely settled by Chinese, and others (such as the South-west China Economic Circle) involve connections with overseas Chinese entrepreneurs, there are those (such as the Bohai Circle and the North-west Circle) which foresee interaction with economies where ethnic Chinese do not play a dominant role. Thus, Japan, Russia, India and North America are centrally involved, whereas they were virtually excluded from the first portraits of Greater China.

And thirdly, the discussion of these transnational economic circles envisages a relatively low degree of formal institutionalization. Although governments will be involved in breaking down the administrative barriers to trade and investment, and in building the physical infrastructure that can promote commercial transactions, there is as yet little talk of

30. Huang Zhilian, " 'Xi Taipingyang diqu chanye xiezuo xitong' chubu gouxiang" ("Initial conception of a 'western Pacific regional industrial co-ordination system' ") *Jingji daobao* (*Economic Reporter*), 18 July 1988, pp. 14–15. See also his *Xianggang zouxiang ershiyi shiji: "Huaxia tixi" yu "taipingyang shidai" de tansuo* (*Hong Kong Moves Toward the 21st Century: An Exploration of the "Cathaysian System" and the "Pacific Era"*) (Hong Kong: Chinese Press Publishing, 1989).

forming these regions into formal free trade areas or common customs territories. Instead, there is more emphasis on building infrastructure, exchanging information and harmonizing regulatory policies.

In short, the new vision of the transnational Chinese economy involves a set of smaller economic circles, integrally connected to larger economic regions, such as the emerging Asia-Pacific economic community, rather than focused primarily on internal interaction. It also emphasizes relatively spontaneous commercial activity, rather than the negotiation of formal trading arrangements. To its advocates, it therefore promises the best of both worlds: the benefits of new commercial opportunities that cross international borders, without the economic or cultural exclusivity – or the political ambition – associated with earlier conceptions of a "Greater China."

## A Global Chinese culture

The second core concept subsumed under the heading of "Greater China" involves the increasing cultural interaction of people of Chinese descent, again across international boundaries. Like economic integration, this trend can be captured in a few simple statistics. People from Taiwan now visit mainland China around one million times every year. The volume of visits between Hong Kong and the People's Republic is several times higher. The flow of mail across the Taiwan Strait has now reached 24 million pieces per year, and telephone calls from the mainland to Taiwan amount to 40,000 per day. The popular culture of Hong Kong and Taiwan has a growing audience on the mainland, and exchanges of artists, performers and writers between Taiwan and the mainland are steadily increasing.

The growth of these kinds of exchanges represents the reintegration of the transnational Chinese society that had been created by the centuries-old diaspora from the heartland of China to other parts of the world. The flow of Chinese overseas began in the Ming Dynasty with the resettlement of Chinese merchants to South-east Asian trading ports. It continued with the emigration of thousands of Ming sympathizers to Taiwan in the 17th century; with the flow of emigrant labour around the world in the 19th and early 20th centuries; with the flow of political refugees from Communism to Hong Kong, Taiwan, South-east Asia and North America in the mid-20th century; and with the continuing stream of students and scholars to the West over the last hundred years.

The political division of China in 1949 profoundly disrupted the normal contacts within this global Chinese society, just as it prevented the exercise of normal commercial contacts. The People's Republic generally viewed overseas Chinese as being contaminated with bourgeois values; the Nationalist government on Taiwan cut off all cultural and humanitarian exchange with the mainland. Although both Taiwan and the mainland maintained ties with Hong Kong and with groups of sympathetic Chinese abroad, the level of interaction within the international Chinese community was far lower than it would normally have been.

With the fall of these political barriers, cultural exchange could rapidly resume, reflecting the natural desire for interaction among those enjoying a common culture. Families divided since 1949 longed for reunion. Overseas Chinese wanted the opportunity to visit their native places, historical sites or scenic spots on the mainland. Artists and performers wished to exchange their work; intellectuals and scientists were eager to share their views on topics of common concern. Ordinary Chinese wanted to enjoy the stimulation of films, songs and literature produced in their own language but in a different social setting. Moreover, the global revolution in transport and communication has greatly facilitated the resurrection of these kinds of cultural exchange. Jet travel has made it easier and less expensive for Chinese around the world to visit one another. Telephones and fax machines have promoted regular communication among friends and families. Audio tapes, video cassettes and satellite broadcasting have all encouraged the exchange of popular culture.

To this degree, the recreation of a global Chinese culture has been a natural process: the product of a common ancestry, facilitated by modern communications. But, as with commercial ties, many of the governments involved have not been neutral or disinterested observers. The leaders of mainland China have viewed cultural and humanitarian exchanges, like economic relations, as a way of promoting the reunification of the country. The rediscovery of a common cultural identity, they believe, will produce a desire for political reintegration. The Nationalist government has favoured cultural ties across the Taiwan Strait for a related but slightly different reason: not so much to create a demand for reunification as to forestall the demand for independence. Moreover, many in Taipei believe that cross-Strait contacts, by graphically revealing the differences in living conditions between the two sides, will bolster the legitimacy of the Kuomintang while undermining that of the Communists.

Thus far, the reintegration of the global Chinese community has been the least extensively discussed of the three core versions of Greater China.[31] It is here, more than in economics or politics, that both description and prescription are lagging well behind reality. Nevertheless, a number of distinct variations on the common theme of renewed cultural contact are already evident in the few writings on the subject.

Perhaps the dominant tendency in the analysis is an emphasis on high culture. Most writings on the subject focus on the growing interaction among Chinese intellectuals around the world, which they portray as the continuation and renewal of a 150-year search for a modern Chinese culture. Tu Wei-ming, perhaps the most articulate advocate of this view, has portrayed the process as one by which Chinese intellectuals can overcome their "sense of impotence, frustration, and humiliation" and

31. There has, however, been at least one multilateral conference on the subject. The meeting, called "Prospects for Cultural China: Concept and Reality," was co-sponsored by the Chinese University of Hong Kong, the Taibei Hong Kong–Macao Association, and the *China Times*, and was held in Hong Kong in March 1993. See *Zhongguo shibao* (*China Times*), 21 March 1993, p. 22.

find identity "not only as Chinese but as thinking and reflective Chinese in an increasingly alienating and dehumanizing world."[32]

Tu's vision of what he calls a global "Cultural China" raises several profound and interrelated questions. First, who should be included in it? Not surprisingly, Tu includes all those of Chinese descent, whether living in predominantly Chinese societies (such as Taiwan, Hong Kong, Singapore and the mainland), or as minorities in Chinese communities overseas. More controversially, he also includes those non-Chinese with a personal or professional interest in China: "individuals, such as scholars, teachers, journalists, industrialists, traders, entrepreneurs and writers, who try to understand China intellectually and bring their conceptions of China to their own linguistic communities." Tu thus defines the membership of a global Chinese culture culturally, rather than ethnically: it consists of all of those, from whatever ethnic background, who participate in the "international discourse of cultural China" and who thereby join in the creation of a modern Chinese identity.[33]

The second crucial question raised by Tu's concept concerns the capital of his Cultural China. Traditionally, the Chinese state has sought to ensure that the cultural and political capitals of the nation were one and the same, so as to ensure that the prevailing intellectual climate would conform with political orthodoxy. Thus, the leaders of the People's Republic today would presumably wish to see Beijing, and possibly Shanghai, serve as the centres for modern elite Chinese culture. Conversely, political dissidents, dissatisfied with the status quo, wish there to be several centres of cultural life that remain autonomous of the political capital. For them, the intellectual capitals should not be restricted to Beijing or Shanghai but should also include Taipei, Hong Kong and Singapore, and, equally important, the overseas dissident communities in Cambridge, Princeton and Paris. Tu Wei-ming inclines toward the second position. The subtitle of his article – "The periphery as the center" – implies his major theme: that the "periphery will come to set the ... cultural agenda for the center."[34] Or, as he puts it elsewhere, "a significantly weakened center may turn out to be a blessing in disguise for the emergence of a truly functioning Chinese civilization-state."[35]

And this, in turn, leads to the third and ultimately most critical question: the content of the modern Chinese identity that will be produced by the "international discourse of Cultural China." In essence, different centres are associated with different themes, particularly in the crucial area of political culture. Many intellectuals, let alone political leaders, in Beijing, Shanghai and Singapore are advocating a modernized version of traditional Chinese political culture, drawing heavily on Confucian concepts of politics to create a political system that is technocratic, hierarchical and orderly. In contrast to this neo-authoritarian vision, the

32. Tu Wei-ming, "Cultural China: the periphery as center," *Daedalus*, Vol. 120, No. 2 (1991), p. 2.
33. *Ibid.* pp. 12–13.
34. *Ibid.* p. 12.
35. *Ibid.* p. 15.

prevailing view among Chinese intellectuals in Hong Kong, Taipei and overseas is for a much more democratic version of modern Chinese culture, with the organizational and ideological pluralism associated with liberal democracies in the West. The outcome of this debate will not only have a profound effect on the structure of the various Chinese polities, but also, as will be noted later, have significant implications for the political evolution of the rest of the world.

Alongside this there is also a phenomenon that is much more populist in character: a transnational popular Chinese culture, shaped not by modern literati but by commercial artists, musicians and writers. Although this is rapidly becoming a reality, it has not yet become a prominent part of discussions of a global Chinese culture. Still, harbingers of this concept are apparent in the view of a group of Taiwan and Hong Kong television executives that direct satellite broadcasting of Chinese-language programming will soon create a "Chinese television global village,"[36] and in the opinion of at least one mainland Chinese scholar that there is emerging a Chinese "civilizational community" (*shengming gongtongti*) characterized by a "pan-Chinese culture" (*fan Zhonghuaxing wenhua*).

This populist version of a global Chinese culture raises the same issues of participants, capitals and content that have been generated by the more elitist variants. One such question concerns the role of ethnic minorities in forging Chinese popular culture. Chinese officials have long insisted that the Manchus, Tibetans, Mongols and Hui are not only citizens in the Chinese state, but have been assimilated into a common Chinese culture.[37] Increasingly, however, many Chinese writers and artists take the opposite position: that national minorities not only absorb Chinese culture, but also provide values, meanings and artistic vocabularies that can enrich it.[38] Relatedly, one can imagine controversy over the degree to which overseas Chinese are regarded as consumers of Chinese popular culture, or as creators of it. As a result, there will be intense rivalry to serve as the geographic centres of popular Chinese culture. At first, it seemed clear that Hong Kong and Taiwan would play such a role, at least in music and film. Their products were more professionally produced, more technically sophisticated and unconstrained by the orthodox styles and subjects of the cultural bureaucracy on mainland China. More recently, however, the cultural centres of mainland China have made a strong resurgence. This is not only because of the easing of the political restrictions imposed after the Tiananmen crisis of 1989, but also because many believe that problems and trends in mainland society can only be reflected by their own artists and writers. Thus, Guangzhou, Shanghai and Beijing (in music), and Beijing and Xi'an (in film) are challenging the near-

36. *Zhongguo shibao zhoukan* (*China Times Weekly*), 26 April–2 May 1992, pp. 40–53.
37. David Yen-ho Wu, "The construction of Chinese and Non-Chinese identities," *Daedalus*, Vol. 120, No. 2 (1991), p. 162.
38. See, for example, Leo Ou-fan Lee, "On the margins of the Chinese discourse: some personal thoughts on the cultural meaning of the periphery," *Daedalus*, Vol. 120, No. 2 (1991), pp. 207–224.

monopoly in successful popular culture once held by Taipei and Hong Kong.

The content of popular Chinese culture is also a matter of dispute. Most observers agree that that produced outside the mainland is primarily individualistic, materialistic or even hedonistic in character. It is highly likely that the official overseers of culture in Beijing will therefore seek to encourage, as a counterweight, a more orthodox popular culture that embodies collective values, patriotism and asceticism. It is conceivable that the battle between these two versions of Chinese popular culture could be as intense as the struggle among Chinese elites between the proponents of democracy and the advocates of neo-authoritarianism.

And yet, sceptics argue that the emergence of global Chinese culture must overcome two set of daunting obstacles. First, political barriers still play a restrictive role in cultural matters, just as they do in economics. Although Communist leaders are much less intolerant of unorthodox popular culture than they were in the Maoist era, there are still periodic complaints against "spiritual pollution" from abroad, and there are informal limits on the number and type of films and television programmes from Hong Kong and Taiwan that can be exhibited on the mainland.[39] If anything, the barriers on Taiwan are even higher: there are restrictions on the content of mainland publications that can be sold on Taiwan, bans on the public exhibition of mainland films and television programmes, and even regulations concerning the amount of time that mainland performers can appear on the screen in co-produced movies. Political mistrust continues to hamper intellectual exchanges in the social sciences and contemporary humanities. Some worry that these barriers will not only impede cultural interaction, but also ensure that cultural products intended for a transnational audience (such as broadcast on the Chinese-language channel of Star Television) remain bland and non-controversial.

Other analysts have suggested that the main obstacle to the creation of a global Chinese culture will not be the barriers imposed by central governments, but rather the competing attraction of local sub-cultures. And, indeed, the democratization of political life on Taiwan and the decay of political controls on the mainland are producing a noticeable resurgence of local identity. In Taiwan, in Guangdong, in Shanghai and in other parts of mainland China, there is a renewed interest in local history, folk religion and culture, and a rise in the use of local dialect. By extension, there is presumably less interest in national history, in high national culture and in the use of *guoyu* or *putonghua*.

In reply it can be said that these trends are not unprecedented, nor do they negate the possibility of the emergence of a global Chinese culture, at both the elite and popular levels. As Myron Cohen has written, "that differentiation and integration may occur concurrently, especially in complex societies, should hardly come as a surprise.... The generation or

39. As one informant put it, historical dramas are encouraged, whereas programmes showing daily social life in Taiwan and Hong Kong are not.

preservation of [local] differences was the flip side of the creation of [national] uniformities in late traditional Chinese culture." There was always a tension between the national orthodox culture (which the state sought to promulgate, but never expected commoners to master fully) and local sub-cultures (some aspects of which were tolerated by the state, while others were suppressed).[40] Thus one should not regard the question of cultural identity as a zero-sum situation, in which one form of identity can exist only at the expense of another. The creation of a global Chinese culture, in other words, can exist at precisely the same time as the renaissance of local sub-cultures.

A similar debate concerns the likelihood that large numbers of Chinese overseas will become part of a global Chinese culture. Some argue that, compared to the past, more overseas Chinese are seeing themselves as permanent emigrants, rather than temporary sojourners, and are abandoning their Chinese citizenship in favour of foreign nationality. Generation by generation, they will therefore assimilate into their adoptive cultures, intermarry with people of different backgrounds, lose their knowledge of Chinese language and culture, and even abandon much interest in China. Outside East Asia, their ethnicity may prevent their full absorption into their new societies. Even so, they may define that ethnicity in other ways than Chinese, in the way that many younger Americans of Chinese descent see themselves as Asian-Americans, rather than specifically as Chinese-Americans.

In response, defenders of the concept of a global Chinese culture again argue that cultural identity is not an either-or affair. Wang Gungwu, the leading scholar of overseas Chinese, has insisted that working and studying abroad does not necessarily eradicate a sense of Chineseness, but rather helps to define it and even to strengthen it.[41] He emphasizes the ongoing significance of ethnicity, noting that "most [overseas Chinese] live in countries where denial [of their Chineseness] would be useless."[42] He also predicts that the globalization of the world economy and the improvements in communication and transport technology will make it both convenient and imperative for overseas Chinese to maintain at least a partial identity as members of a global Chinese culture.

## A Reunified Chinese State

The final theme associated with the term "Greater China" is the reunification of the Chinese state after a period of division. Of the three core concepts under discussion here, this is the one with the deepest roots in Chinese history. In traditional times, the boundaries of the Chinese empire were never static. The size of the empire shrank when the vitality of the central government declined: peripheral territories, parts of Outer

40. Myron L. Cohen, "Being Chinese: the peripheralization of traditional identity," *Daedalus*, Vol 120, No. 2 (1991), pp. 113–134, at p. 121.
41. Wang Gungwu, "Among non-Chinese," *Daedalus*, Vol. 120, No. 2 (1991), p. 136.
42. *Ibid.* p. 154.

China, became autonomous or fully independent. In periods of severe decay, China Proper might itself be divided, falling victim to foreign invasion, or disintegrating into a number of rival Chinese states. But the subsequent phase in the dynastic cycle was that, in time, the empire would reconstitute itself. A strong political force would reunify the provinces of China Proper, re-establishing a powerful central government. It would then use a combination of economic blandishments and military force to reassert China's suzerainty over Outer China. The boundaries of the resulting empire might not be precisely the same as before, but the process was similar, and became an important part of Chinese political culture. As John Fairbank wrote of the situation in 1949, "the history of past dynastic foundings predisposed the Chinese people to expect and welcome the return of central power."[43]

The last years of the Qing Dynasty provide an excellent example of the process of territorial disintegration during a period of political decay. As the empire weakened, it was stripped of land. Some of these lost territories were part of China Proper, beginning with the Portuguese occupation of Macao in 1557, and continuing with the other colonies, concessions and leased areas (such as Hong Kong, Guangzhouwan, Qingdao and Dalian) seized by the Western powers along the Chinese coast in the 19th century. But foreign powers also seized more peripheral regions: Russia took eastern Siberia; Japan seized the Ryukyus, Taiwan and Korea; France colonized Indo-China. With the collapse of the Qing, the process of disintegration went even further: Outer Mongolia, Tibet and Turkestan all became independent of China, at least *de facto*, in 1911–12; and Manchuria, as Manchukuo, became a separate state under Japanese influence in 1932.

Although the defeat of Japan in the Second World War returned Taiwan and Manchuria to China, the Chinese civil war produced further division of the country, when the Communists seized control of mainland China and the Nationalists retreated to Taiwan. Thus by 1949, what had been a single empire under the Qing had been divided into five separate entities: the People's Republic of China, the Republic of China on Taiwan, the Mongolian People's Republic, Hong Kong and Macao.

Since then, both the Nationalist and Communist governments have been committed to the reunification of China. But what should be the boundaries of a reunified Chinese state? In the 1950s, a few high school textbooks published on Taiwan carried maps suggesting that Nationalist China would seize all of Siberia and much of Soviet Central Asia after the defeat of the Soviet Union and Communist China in a world war, but there is no evidence that the Kuomintang ever took such grandiose plans very seriously.[44] Instead, the Nationalist government has taken the consistent position that China should include all of China Proper, plus Taiwan,

43. John K. Fairbank, "The Reunification of China," in Roderick MacFarquhar and John K. Fairbank (eds.), *The Cambridge History of China*, Vol. 14 (Cambridge: Cambridge University Press, 1987), p. 22.
44. See Uhalley, "What's in a name?"

the South China Sea, Tibet, Xinjiang and Manchuria. Until recently, Mongolia has also been a part of the Kuomintang's conception of Greater China, but in the past few years Taipei has shown a growing willingness to acknowledge Mongolia to be a separate, independent nation.

The perspective of the Chinese Communist Party (CCP) is even more pertinent to an analysis of the prospects of a reunified China. In fact, over time the CCP has taken quite different views of its territorial claims. One issue has concerned Taiwan. At its Second Congress in 1922, the Party called for the unification of China, but did not mention Taiwan as part of the territory to be included within its borders.[45] In an interview with Edgar Snow in 1936, Mao Zedong made the same point more explicitly. Likening Taiwan to Korea, Mao said that both territories should become independent states following the defeat of Japan, rather than being reattached to China.[46] However, the CCP's policy toward the island soon changed. Once the Nationalists had relocated to Taiwan, the CCP called for the reunification of Taiwan with the rest of China – a position it has held consistently ever since.

The CCP's views on the status of outer Mongolia have also varied over the years. Before 1949, CCP documents portrayed Mongolia, Tibet and Xinjiang as having the same status: as minority areas not part of China Proper, which would formally be given the right of secession and independence, but which would "automatically" (in Mao's word) become part of a federal Chinese state after the Communists' seizure of power.[47] After 1949, however, presumably under pressure from the Soviet Union, Beijing recognized the independence of the Mongolian People's Republic. And yet Mao and other senior Chinese leaders have periodically hinted that they still considered outer Mongolia to be part of China, as do some younger people in mainland China today.

The last boundary question concerns the fate of other territories, historically subject to Chinese suzerainty, that fell under the control of foreign powers during and after the 18th century. Chinese maps published in the early 1950s depicted these territories in extensive detail, suggesting that the Communist government still held some claim to them. Moreover, at the beginning of the Sino-Soviet dispute, Beijing denounced the treaties with Tsarist Russia that had demarcated the two countries' border, and implied that it still laid some claim to large portions of Siberia. Since the early 1970s, however, the CCP has consistently pledged to accept most existing international borders, with some limited modifications. Its sole remaining claims are to Hong Kong, Macao and the islands in the South China Sea.

Boundaries aside, how should a reunified China be governed? Al-

---

45. "Manifesto of the Second National Congress of the CCP" (July 1922), in Conrad Brandt *et al.* (eds.), *A Documentary History of Chinese Communism* (New York: Atheneum, 1966), pp. 63–65.

46. Edgar Snow, *Red Star Over China* (New York: Grove Press, 1961), p. 96.

47. "Manifesto of the Second National Congress"; "Constitution of the Soviet Republic" (November 1931), in Brandt, *A Documentary History*, p. 223; and Snow, *Red Star Over China*, p. 96n.

though most discussions of a transnational Chinese economy and of a global Chinese culture are of fairly recent vintage, formulas for reunifying China under a single government have a much longer history. These formulas – Communist and Nationalist – can be grouped into four broad categories: "one country, one system"; "one country, two systems"; "one country, two governments"; and "one country, many governments."[48]

Until quite recently, both the CCP and the Kuomintang proposed that the reunification of China be accomplished under a single government, and with a common socio-economic system. Not surprisingly, each party believed that the government that it controlled should serve as China's central political authority; equally predictably, each party advocated that all of Chinese society be organized according to its own ideological model. Thus, for most of the period from 1949 to 1979, the CCP called for the "liberation" of Taiwan, the creation of a socialist economic system on the island and the formation of a provincial government on Taiwan that would be subordinate to the central government in Beijing. In parallel fashion, the Kuomintang's formula for reunification involved the democratization of the mainland's political system, the reform of the mainland economy according to market principles, and then the reabsorption of the mainland provinces under the Nationalist Constitution of 1946. The CCP, in short, envisaged the unification of China under the principles of Marxism-Leninism, the Kuomintang under the *sanmin zhuyi*.

In the early 1980s, however, the CCP significantly modified its formula for reunification, changing from a policy of "one country, one system" to one of "one country, two systems." It announced that, after reunification, Hong Kong, Macao and Taiwan would become special administrative regions of the People's Republic. As such, they would be able to preserve their own social and economic systems, maintain a more democratic form of government than in the rest of China, and enjoy a high degree of autonomy in their internal affairs. In addition, Taiwan was offered the right to maintain its own armed forces. Nevertheless, under this formula all these entities were seen as local jurisdictions under the sovereignty of the central Chinese government.

In response to this Communist initiative, scholars and policy analysts on Taiwan developed a significantly different formula: not "one country, two systems," but "one country, two governments."[49] Under this approach, Taiwan would not only maintain its own economic, social and political system, but would enjoy equal status with the mainland in international affairs. Third countries could have diplomatic relations with both Taiwan and the mainland, and both Chinese governments would be represented in the United Nations and other international agencies. The

48. For another classification and summary of the competing formulas for reunification, see Wen-hui Tsai, "Convergence and divergence between mainland China and Taiwan: the future of unification," *Issues and Studies*, Vol. 27, No. 12 (December 1991), pp. 1–28.

49. This formula is also summarized as "one country, two regions" or "one country, two entities."

principle of "one Chinese nation" would be maintained, but in practice that nation would be divided into co-equal political systems.[50]

To some of its proponents, this formula applies only to a transitional period, during which the remaining gaps between the conditions on Taiwan and those on the mainland make full reunification impossible. As one leading analyst on Taiwan has put it, the concept of "one country, two governments" "does not preclude reunification ..., [but] only provides the room for simultaneous recognition of both political systems within the divided states in the transitional period before the eventual reunification."[51] To others, however, this formula may represent not an interim solution, but a final one. Many analysts on Taiwan believe that the island's culture, economic system, political institutions and standard of living are now significantly different from those on the mainland, and that the gap between them may never be closed. No formula for reunification under a single central government, in their perspective, could guarantee sufficient autonomy for Taiwan to be acceptable to the Taiwanese people. Thus, they believe that, whatever lip service must be given to the concept of "one China," the reality can only be two distinct societies under two separate governments.

Recently, a fourth set of formulas has begun to emerge on both sides of the Taiwan Strait, adopting a federalist approach to China's reunification. Under many of these formulas, the present People's Republic of China would devolve much of its existing political authority to its provinces, while creating a federal national government to facilitate reunification with Taiwan and Hong Kong. Such an approach can therefore be summarized as "one country, many governments." Although federalism has deep roots in the history of contemporary China,[52] its revival in recent years has been most closely associated with the mainland scholar Yan Jiaqi, the former director of the Institute of Political Science of the Chinese Academy of Social Sciences, now living in exile abroad. Yan has proposed the creation of a federal government to govern the present territory of the People's Republic, and then an even looser

50. Some mainland officials and policy analysts appear willing to explore this proposal. See, for example, the report by Tang Shubei of the mainland's Association for Relations Across the Taiwan Strait that the two sides might "commonly share international status" (*gongtong fenxiang guoji diwei*), in *Zhongguo shibao*, 20 June 1993, pp. 72–75. The most recent official statement of Beijing's policy toward Taiwan, however, shows no such flexibility. See "The Taiwan question and the reunification of China," a white paper issued by the Taiwan Affairs Office and the Information Office of the State Council, relayed by Xinhua News Agency, 31 August 1993, in *Foreign Broadcast Information Service Daily Report: China*, 1 September 1993, pp. 43–51.

51. Yung Wei, " 'Multi-system nations' revisited: interaction between academic conceptualization and political reality," paper presented to the 15th World Congress of the International Political Science Association, Buenos Aires, July 1991.

52. See, for example, Jean Chesneaux, "The federalist movement in China, 1920–23," in Jack Gray (ed.), *Modern China's Search for a Political Form* (Oxford: Oxford University Press, 1969), pp. 96–137; and Prasenjit Duara, "Provincial narratives of the nation: centralism and federalism in Republican China," in Harumi Befu (ed.), *Cultural Nationalism in East Asia*, Research Papers and Policy Studies No. 39 (Berkeley: Institute of East Asian Studies, University of California, 1993), pp. 9–35.

confederal structure to incorporate Taiwan, Macao and Hong Kong.[53] As Yan points out, there was a time when the CCP itself endorsed a federal system for China. The Party's Second National Congress in 1922 formally proposed the creation of a "Chinese Federal Republic," and Mao's interview with Edgar Snow made a favourable reference to the concept. And yet, once the Communist Party gained control over the mainland in 1949, it promptly renounced its federalist heritage. Indeed, even though the Communist Party modelled many aspects of its new governing structure after Soviet practice, it specifically rejected the idea of copying the nominally federal structure of the Soviet Union.

Today, Chinese scholars and officials normally reject federalism as incompatible with the official formula of "one country, two systems."[54] Recently, however, there have been signs that the concept may be receiving a more favourable hearing. Deng Xiaoping himself has reportedly said that, if it is more acceptable to Taiwan, federalism may be the most effective strategy for the reunification of China.[55] And interviews with Chinese scholars in the summer of 1993 have suggested much greater openness to the concept than in the past.

And yet, many still have qualms about the desirability of a single reunified China, even under a federal formula. The most obvious reservations are held by people in the territories that might be incorporated in such an entity. Although the fate of both Hong Kong and Macao has now been determined by international negotiations, a majority of people in Hong Kong, and probably a sizeable portion of the population of Macao as well, would have preferred to remain separate from the People's Republic. Around 10 or 15 per cent of the people of Taiwan are in favour of a formal declaration of independence from the mainland, and a much larger number support the indefinite continuation of the status quo. And certainly the overwhelming majority of those in outer Mongolia wish to remain outside a reunified Chinese state.

Many of China's neighbours, too, are apprehensive about the strategic consequences of Chinese reunification. It has already become commonplace in discussions of regional and global matters to aggregate the resources available to the three major Chinese societies to estimate the power of a reunified China. Together, we are told, the foreign exchange

53. Yan Jiaqi, *Lianbang Zhongguo gouxiang* (*The Concept of a Federal China*) (Hong Kong: Ming Bao, 1992). For more on federalism, see Jiang Jingkuan, "Zhongguo tongyi zui lixiang de tujing" ("The most ideal path for Chinese reunification: implement a federal republican system"), *Zhongbao yuekan* (*Central Monthly*), April 1984, pp. 8–10; and Chen Guozhen, "Minzu zijue zhi shi hai shi shenlou?" ("Is ethnic national self-determination a mirage?"), *Zhongguo shibao zhoukan* (*China Times Weekly*), 2–8 September 1989, pp. 13–15.

54. See, for example, Zhongguo tongxunshe (China News Agency), 26 February 1992, in *Foreign Broadcast Information Service Daily Report: China*, 2 March 1992, pp. 37–38.

55. Deng reportedly said that Beijing should give "careful consideration" to the "possibility of post-reunification constitutional changes," including the formation of a "so-called 'federation' or 'confederation.' " *Jing bao*, No. 184 (5 November 1992), pp. 63–64, in *Foreign Broadcast Information Service Daily Report: China*, 6 November 1992, p. 55. Yang Shangkun is reported to have made a similar remark. See *China Post*, 5 May 1993, in *Foreign Broadcast Information Service Daily Report: China*, 12 May 1993, pp. 66–67.

holdings of Taiwan and the mainland dwarf those of any other country; the global trade volumes of Hong Kong, Taiwan and the People's Republic rival those of Japan; and the armies of Taiwan and the mainland would be the largest military force in Asia. Today, such calculations are not that meaningful, since they assume that these resources would be at the disposal of a single political will that does not exist. Were China to be reunified under a powerful central government, however, such an aggregation of resources would indeed have occurred, producing an international actor far more powerful than mainland China is today.

Finally, some mainland Chinese – albeit a minority – also question the desirability of a politically reunified China. They not only admit the social, economic and political disparities between mainland China and Taiwan, but also acknowledge that the differences between the two are not likely to be eliminated in the foreseeable future. In addition, some interpret their country's history as showing that the Chinese nation is more likely to be culturally vibrant and humanely governed if it has several competing centres of political power, not just one.[56]

*Conclusion*

There has been a plethora of terms to describe the system of interactions among mainland China, Hong Kong, Taiwan and people of Chinese descent around the world. The South China Economic Circle, the Greater China Free Trade Area, the Chinese Economic Community, the China Productivity Triangle, the Chinese Economic Circle, the Chinese Federation, the Chinese Commonwealth, the South China NIC, the Chinese Prosperity Sphere, Cultural China, the Cross-Strait Economic Circle and the Chinese Civilizational Community are but a fraction of the terms that have been used by analysts and observers of the subject. Of these terms, however, it is "Greater China" that is becoming, at least in English, the most commonly employed.

Many people object to the use of the term "Greater China." Although it was originally intended in an benign economic sense, as an simile to Greater London or Greater Tokyo, in some quarters it evokes much more aggressive analogies, such as the Greater East Asia Co-Prosperity Sphere or Greater Germany. But despite these objections, the term is likely to survive. Not only does it have a simplicity and familiarity that its rivals lack, but its very vagueness is one of its greatest virtues. In contrast to more specific terms, the phrase "Greater China" does not imply any definite geographic boundaries, is not limited to any specific set of interactions, and does not refer to any definite structures or institutions. It accurately captures both the broad scope and the uncertain outcomes of the phenomenon in question.

It has been suggested that "Greater China" in fact subsumes three

56. See, for example, Ge Jianxiong, *Putianzhixia: Tongyi fenlie yu Zhongguo zhengzhi* (*All Under Heaven: Unity, Division, and Chinese Politics*) (Jilin: Jilin Educational Press, 1989).

distinct, although related, concepts. Economically, Greater China involves the expanding commercial interactions among mainland China, Taiwan and Hong Kong. Culturally, it refers to the restoration of personal, scientific, intellectual and artistic contacts among people of Chinese descent around the world. Politically, it refers to the possibility of the re-establishment of a single Chinese state, reuniting a political entity that was disintegrated by more than a century of foreign pressure and civil war. To a degree, the three themes are interrelated: a common cultural identity provides a catalyst for economic ties, and economic interdependence may lay the foundation for political unification. In theory, therefore, the three aspects of Greater China could merge into a single integrated entity.

At present, however, they are not perfectly correlated. Each of the three faces of Greater China has different boundaries and different centres. Economic Greater China, at this point at least, is largely limited to the coastal regions of mainland China, together with Hong Kong, Macao and Taiwan. Hong Kong is clearly its capital, although Taipei and Shanghai are both rising in importance. Cultural Greater China includes all those of Chinese descent, wherever in the world, who choose to become engaged in what Tu Wei-ming terms the "discourse" on what it means to be Chinese. It has several centres of influence: Hong Kong and Taipei are the most important for popular culture; whereas elite cultural activities are centred in places as diverse as Beijing, Singapore, Princeton and Paris. Political Greater China, if it fully emerges, would include mainland China, Hong Kong, Macao and Taiwan. Its centre would be Beijing, although the degree of central power wielded in the capital remains to be seen.

Moreover, there appears in all three Chinese societies to be a growing acknowledgement of the barriers to the creation of Greater China, especially one with a highly institutionalized form. There are indeed powerful integrative forces in play: a natural economic complementarity among the three economies, the common cultural and ethnic background among the world's Chinese communities, the family ties linking various segments of the Chinese diaspora, and the age-old sense that a powerful China should be a unified China. But against these are working significant disintegrative factors, including differences in level of economic development, in political and economic system and in cultural identity. Moreover, some fear the consequences of closer integration: the dislocations of economic life, the erosion of cultural identity and the loss of political autonomy.

Thus, there is no unanimity among Chinese about the desirability of a Greater China. Instead, different groups of Chinese approach these three sets of concepts with distinctly different degrees of enthusiasm. In mainland China, there is interest in extensive cultural and economic interaction among the People's Republic, Taiwan and Hong Kong, but largely as a way of securing political reunification. On Taiwan, there is also an interest in promoting cultural and economic ties with the mainland, but these are widely regarded as an alternative to political reunification, rather than as a means of achieving it. In Hong Kong, the greatest interest is in the development of economic and cultural ties with South China, largely as a method for cushioning the transfer of political sovereignty to Beijing that will occur in 1997.

As a result, the emergence of Greater China remains an indeterminate process, the final dimensions of which are not yet clear. But the trends in the discussion may give a preliminary clue to what lies ahead. Increasingly, analysis is focusing on less formal and institutionalized mechanisms of economic and political integration. Federalism is emerging as the dominant formula for political unification, and the "economic circle" is replacing "common markets" and "free trade areas" for economic interaction.

In addition, discussions of the economic and cultural interactions among ethnic Chinese are becoming much less exclusive in tone. The most recent analysis of economic trends foresees the development of several different economic regions, each of which would link segments of the transnational Chinese economy to economic systems where ethnic Chinese do not play the dominant role. Similarly, discussion of cultural matters is increasingly acknowledging that Chinese living outside mainland China will probably develop and maintain a multi-layered cultural identity, viewing themselves both as Chinese and Taiwanese, or as Chinese and American, rather than as Chinese alone.

The rest of the world has viewed the prospect of a Greater China with both fascination and considerable alarm. Some see it in benign terms, as a dynamic common market which provides growing opportunities for trade and investment. More frequently, however, there has been concern that the combination of economic and military resources available to a Greater China will pose a significant threat to the commercial vitality and the strategic stability of the rest of the world. There is also the worry that the process of cultural integration will produce a neo-Confucianism whose authoritarian tendencies will pose an ideological challenge to the West.[57]

The trends outlined above, however, suggest that some of the alarmist interpretations of Greater China have been severely overdrawn, largely because they focus only on the integrative forces at work and overlook the centrifugal tendencies. It is unlikely that a single central government will be able to gain firm control of the economic and military resources of the mainland, Taiwan and Hong Kong. Without such a centralized political will, Greater China will not evolve into a strategic superpower of the magnitude many envisage. Similarly, it seems improbable that the various Chinese economies will form a closed economic bloc, buying primarily from themselves while seeking to export to others. And the cultural interaction within the global Chinese community is marked by sharp debate between proponents of democracy and advocates of state

57. See Samuel P. Huntington, "The clash of civilizations?" *Foreign Affairs*, Vol. 72, No. 3 (Summer 1993), pp. 22–49.

control, rather than by consensus on the desirability of authoritarian solutions. The international implications of greater cultural, economic and political interactions among ethnic Chinese will doubtless be significant, but they may not be either as great or as dire as some have suggested.

# The Foreign Relations of Greater China*

## Michael Yahuda

Greater China refers in the first instance to the close economic ties of trade, technology transfers and investment that have emerged since the second half of the 1980s linking Taiwan and Hong Kong with the rapid development of southern China. But it also suggests that the economic links are buttressed by familial, social, historical and cultural ties of a peculiarly Chinese kind. These ties and links have developed between different Chinese communities whose political divergences had until recently precluded such a development. Consequently the emergence of Greater China poses new challenges and opportunities to the political identities of its three constituent members and to the conduct of relations between them. Greater China and its possible future trajectory affects and is also affected by the rest of the Asia-Pacific region including the major powers of the United States and Japan as well as those in the immediate vicinity of South-east Asia.

The economic and social nexus of Greater China lacks any agreed institutional expression. Hong Kong, Taiwan and southern China are completely different political entities and have very different international identities. The former is a British colony preparing to develop the conditions to exercise a degree of political autonomy before sovereignty is transferred to Beijing. Taiwan is a *de facto* independent and sovereign Chinese state that is neither unified with the mainland nor a separate state that is in the process of developing from the practice of an authoritarian to a democratic political system. Southern China, or more narrowly the provinces of Guangdong and Fujian, enjoy relative and limited degrees of economic autonomy under the uncertain rule of Beijing and as such have no international personalities. Not only are there no formal ties that bind the three together, there are no agreed economic institutional rules that can be said to undergird what many see as the growing economic integration of this area.

Discussion of the foreign relations of Greater China must therefore begin with the appreciation that the three entities do not behave as if they are a single unit with a common purpose. At best they may be said to share certain interests especially in the economic sphere (but even in that area there are elements of competition and possibly conflict). There are no common institutions or diplomatic arrangements for the three to establish common positions amongst themselves, and still less for Greater China to conduct relations with other entities. Hong Kong, Taiwan and China differ in their political orientations, in their relations with each other, and in the ways their participation in Greater China affects their relations with the outside world.

*I would like to thank members of the *China Quarterly* conference on Greater China, and James Tang in particular, for their helpful comments in the discussion of a previous draft of this paper.

It is useful, therefore, to distinguish between what might be called Greater China's intramural from its extramural relationships. That is to say, how has the emergence of Greater China affected the political relations between Taiwan, Hong Kong and the Chinese mainland? Any change in these relations is necessarily reflected in changes in their political identities. The ways in which Hong Kong and especially Taiwan organize themselves politically and the basis on which they seek to have dealings with the outside world are directly linked to the character of their relations with China. In particular questions arise about those involving Taiwan. How are these being conducted and have they changed the established positions of both sides? How have they affected the evolution of Taiwan's political identity and the domestic political debates about its future? What has been the impact of Greater China upon Hong Kong whose future return to Chinese sovereignty had already been decided before the emergence of Greater China became evident? What is the role of Hong Kong in the triangular relationship that underpins Greater China?

The extramural relations of Greater China may be seen as involving primarily international economics and trade as these are the areas in which the impact of its emergence has been felt first and where the reactions of the outside world are perhaps more evident. But the focus here will be more on the political, diplomatic and strategic ramifications. The emergence of Greater China has coincided with the ending of the Cold War. And it is against that backcloth that the outside world has reacted to Greater China. Taipei and Beijing have each reacted to the changes in Eastern Europe and the replacement of the Soviet Union by 15 new states very much with the other in mind. The collapse of the Soviet threat and the anticipated decline of American force levels in the western Pacific have contributed to fears of renewed regional rivalries as arms expenditures have increased in the region as a whole. This is especially true of Beijing whose enhancement of its capacity to project naval and air force power has found a corresponding defensive reaction in Taipei, but this must also be seen within the larger picture of the littoral states of the seas of Eastern Asia. Issues involving Greater China are of immediate interest to Japan, the United States and the South-east Asian neighbours. The interests of the latter transcend traditional security concerns about territorial and maritime disputes in the South China Sea to include concern about the possible ramifications of Greater China for the local Chinese communities in their midst.

## The Intramural Relations of Greater China

*The formal and informal aspects.* The complex nexus of relations on which the economic ties of Greater China are based may be said to be those of family, or the long-standing social links between overseas Chinese and their ancestral villages and, more broadly, the networks of relationships (*guanxi*) that transcend bureaucratic barriers. In other words, the economic links are based less on those of legality and organizational rationality than on the traditional ascriptive ties between groups of people of similar ethnicity and customs that collectively may be called cultural in the anthropological sense. From the perspectives of the governments concerned and the international community at large the ties which bind together the different parts of Greater China may be said to be informal.

These may be contrasted with the formal relations of the international community that are based on the sovereign state. These formal ties are expressed in international law and in the various conventions and institutions associated with the international society of states that first emerged in Europe in the 17th century and which has since expanded to incorporate the whole world.[1] In that respect the emergence of Greater China may be seen as a re-adaptation of traditional Chinese patterns of association to the European inspired society of states. But it was not until the 1980s that the parties concerned relaxed sufficiently in their adherence to the formalities of international society to allow the informal aspects of their relations to develop.

The inter-relationship of what has been called here the formal and the informal is in fact highly complex. The co-existence of the two has been made possible by the connivance of the former in the operations of the latter. That is to say, the development of these ostensible economic relationships has required the tacit permission, if not the direct encouragement, of the established governments in primarily Taiwan and the Chinese mainland. The economic ties may therefore be understood as being part of a more extensive set of adaptations to changes in the various domestic and external environments of Taiwan, the Chinese mainland and Hong Kong. However all three centres have chosen in public to disregard their triangular relationship, preferring instead to depict it as no more than a set of bilateral relations between the Chinese mainland and each of the other two.

From the perspective of Beijing formal relations with Taipei and Hong Kong raise the highly emotive issues of sovereignty and the unity and territorial integrity of the Chinese state. Relations with Taiwan involve a rival claimant for the exercise of sovereign power and those with Hong Kong involve complex arrangements with an external state about the reversion of sovereignty which will take place by agreement in 1997. Beijing has been greatly concerned to keep these relations separate and exclusive. Much diplomatic effort has been devoted to excluding other parties in their management and in keeping their conduct within limits set by Beijing.

The very concept Greater China (*Da Zhonghua*) evokes a frisson of concern in official circles. Academics and businessmen in Taiwan, Hong Kong and Singapore have shown interest in it, but it is used most extensively in the United States. As used by American academics the

1. For an account of these see Hedley Bull, *The Anarchical Society* (London: Macmillan, 1977) and for an account of its spread to the rest of the world see A. Watson and H. Bull, *The Expansion of International Society* (Oxford: Oxford University Press, 1984).

connotation is principally economic.[2] But in Chinese usage whether as a "market" (*Jingji shichang*) or even more as a "commonwealth" (*lianbang*) the term evokes more than purely economic concerns as it necessarily touches on the sensitive issues of Chinese unity and the imprecise, but at times deeply felt, bonds that link together diverse Chinese communities through culture and/or ethnicity. Paradoxically it seems easier for outsiders to delimit the concept geographically than it is for the Chinese themselves. More is involved for Chinese than sheer practicalities in deciding whether to exclude Singapore or different parts of the mainland. Indeed if the criterion for inclusion were to be only the degree of economic interactions then the potential membership would continue to expand both within the mainland and outside it. Any Chinese attempt to spell out the geographical domain of Greater China would inevitably give rise to difficult political repercussions. Questions would arise about the basis of the political order that would apply among those who were included, and those Chinese who were left out would wish to know why. Meanwhile China's neighbours would not unreasonably be concerned as to what such an entity might portend for them.[3]

So far the term Greater China has not found great favour in any of the centres to which it applies. In the mainland there is concern lest use of the term might be seen as a weakening of the resolve to unify the country with Taiwan. In particular it is feared that it could be used by Taiwan to deflect the approach by Beijing to reunification. But at the same time the term is not rejected as worthless or malign. As Sun Xiaoyu, the Deputy Director of the Taiwan Office (of the State Council) noted, "it was not strange" that academics and business people in Taiwan, Hong Kong and Singapore should raise this concept of regional economic co-operation in response to changes in the international situation. However, he argued that "the most important question confronting Taiwan and the mainland was not Greater China, but the normalization of relations." He added, "without the acceptance of direct postal, transportation and commercial links across the Straits the idea of a Greater China or of a Greater China Commonwealth is nothing."[4]

In Taiwan too the concept has not received full endorsement by the government. Governmental officials are prepared to discuss something called a "Greater Chinese Common Market" (*Da Zhonghua Jingji Gongtong Shichang*), by which they understand the establishment of certain rules and procedures to facilitate economic exchanges that would be enforced separately by the different administrations in Taiwan and the

2. See for example the seven papers in the June 1992 Report, "American Economic Relations with Greater China: Challenges for the 1990s," by the American Enterprise Institute, Washington, D.C.

3. For an account of some of the proposals made by Chinese scholars in Hong Kong, Taiwan and the mainland see Charng Kao, "A 'Greater China economic sphere': reality and prospects," *Issues and Studies*, November 1992, pp. 49–64. The article also presents several economic arguments to demonstrate difficulties in formalizing the economic relationship in other than very loose terms.

4. Interview in Beijing, 10 August 1992.

mainland.[5] But they are very wary about the more explicit political dimensions. In principle, these could be accommodated with the officially approved idea of developing relations with the mainland on the basis of "one country two governments," but equally they could be in harmony with Deng Xiaoping's concept of "one country two systems." Meanwhile the term's use beyond the economic connotations could be electorally divisive and possibly damaging to the Kuomintang (KMT) in its electoral rivalry with the Democratic Progressive Party (DPP).

As an authority whose legality is based on Orders in Council in London the British appointed government of Hong Kong by definition cannot openly pronounce upon the issue. But since it has fallen to that government to prepare the ground for the development of a new political order able to exercise a high degree of autonomy after Hong Kong reverts to Chinese sovereignty in 1997, it has inevitably been involved in the practicalities of managing the implications for Hong Kong that have arisen from the emergence of Greater China. Ironically it is precisely because of the remaining British character of its rule, with the emphasis on freedom under the law, that Hong Kong has emerged as the main centre where questions about Greater China can be openly discussed among Chinese. Indeed it was Hong Kong's peculiar status that made it the ideal meeting point for senior representatives of Beijing and Taipei to sound each other out privately before taking up public positions on many questions regarding their relations.[6] Such meetings elsewhere might have risked embarrassing the host or invoking disagreement about such things as diplomatic status.

While the informal aspects of their relations may have facilitated the beginnings of what some have called the economic integration of Hong Kong, China and Taiwan, it is nevertheless clear that a full economic integration is impossible without addressing at least some of the more formal aspects. Taiwan, for example, can be expected to continue to resist allowing its economic trade with mainland China to exceed 10 per cent of its total trade as long as it fears becoming excessively dependent on the mainland. Such fears can be expected to persist until a more formal *modus vivendi* has been established between the two sides. Meanwhile a breakthrough of a kind was achieved when nominally non-governmental organizations from Beijing and Taipei met in Singapore in April 1993 and agreed on how to address some of the technical issues affecting the conduct of mainly economic relations across the Straits of Taiwan. Even more importantly, perhaps, it was agreed to conduct further meetings on a regular basis. This constituted the first formal agreement between the two sides since 1949. Its significance, however, should not be exaggerated as it was not found possible to reach agreement on how to guarantee Taiwanese investments on the mainland. Moreover, as the case of Hong

---

5. Interview with Jason Hu, Director of the Government Information Office, Taipei, 15 September 1992.

6. Vice-Director of the Taiwan Office, Sun Xiaoyu, for example, told me that on several occasions he had met senior officials from Taiwan in Hong Kong without this becoming public knowledge.

Kong illustrates, the difficulties in formalizing relations with Beijing should not be under-estimated even when the issue of sovereignty has been settled in Beijing's favour. Hong Kong, whose economy, in the view of many, has already been integrated with that of mainland China, may yet find that difficulties in formalizing the arrangements already agreed in principle under which sovereignty will revert to China in 1997 may fatally damage the whole exercise.

*Hong Kong and Greater China.* In many ways Hong Kong may be said to lie at the heart of the informalities that have characterized the development of Greater China. Its investments of around $10 billion account for 60 per cent of the total foreign direct investments (FDI) in the PRC and 80 per cent of that has been directed towards Guangdong province. More than 35 per cent of Hong Kong's industry has moved across the border. Re-exports in 1991 accounted for 70 per cent of total exports compared to 45 per cent in 1986. 22.5 million visits were made across the land border with the mainland. Hong Kong is China's most important trading partner accounting for 32 per cent of its trade. According to the London *Financial Times* of 20 November 1992, the relationship with Hong Kong in all its various ways accounts for 18 per cent of the value of China's GNP. Meanwhile China has become Hong Kong's largest outside investor with more than US$12 billion invested in real estate and other sectors.[7] It may be argued that Hong Kong has become even more important to China as a result of Deng Xiaoping's new strategy of accelerating the country's economic development that emphasizes the significance of Guangdong. Yet all this may still be at risk because of essentially political disagreements with Britain over Governor Chris Patten's proposals for the evolution of Hong Kong's electoral system in the run up to 1997.

The severity of the Chinese reaction to the Patten proposals might seem excessive in view of the enormity of the consequences that could arise from a collapse of confidence in Hong Kong. Not only would that endanger the economy and welfare of the 5.5 million people of the territory, but it would also damage the economy of Guangdong province and the Chinese economy as a whole. It could even threaten Deng Xiaoping's general strategy for the survival of the Communist Party by undermining domestic confidence in the ability of the leadership to provide increasing prosperity for the bulk of the people. Clearly, the reaction of China's leaders in risking so much over a territory that is due to be returned to their control in less than five years can only be explained in terms of their perceptions of what is at stake.

The Chinese leadership and Deng Xiaoping in particular have never believed British claims to be concerned for the welfare of the people of Hong Kong in their administration of the territory. Their consistent view has been that Britain's sole interest is in extracting as much money as

7. The figures are drawn from Pamela Baldinger, "The birth of Greater China," *The China Business Review*, May–June 1992, pp. 13–17.

possible. Moreover some have even believed that the British accentuation of the importance of the rule of law in Hong Kong (perceived as code words for human rights) and of the necessity of anchoring that after 1997 in a more democratic and accountable political system has been designed with the purpose of leaving disruption behind them that will be conducive to undermining Communist rule in China itself. In other words, from the outset British motives have been distrusted and their interests misunderstood.

At the same time China's leaders agreed in effect by the terms of the 1984 Joint Declaration to entrust the British administration in Hong Kong with the task of preparing the territory for the exercise of a high degree of autonomy by the time of the handover of sovereignty 13 years later. They acquiesced in the moves towards greater democracy by endorsing for the first time the principle of elections to the Hong Kong Legislature through functional constituencies in 1985. By the provisions of the Basic Law of 1990 it was agreed to extend the democratic principle by having 30 per cent of the seats in 1991 elected directly by the people of the territory and to increase progressively that number in the years to come. Although provisions were made for Sino-British consultations during the transitionary period, it was made clear that Britain would rule alone through the Hong Kong government. The negotiations at Chinese insistence were limited formally to representatives of the British and Chinese governments. A British proposal in 1983 to include Hong Kong representatives was rejected by the Chinese side as an attempt to introduce a "three legged stool" with the implication that the British would have two legs to the Chinese one.[8]

Central to the Chinese view was that the people of Hong Kong were compatriots who were already represented in Chinese organizations such as the National People's Congress (NPC) and the Chinese People's Political Consultative Conference (CPPCC). It was claimed that the Chinese side had ample opportunity to gauge other viewpoints in Hong Kong through the united front work carried out by the local Xinhua News Agency, as well as through the regular visits to the capital by Hong Kong entrepreneurs and others. Moreover it was axiomatic that no Chinese government, least of all this one, was prepared to concede to the British of all people that it did not enjoy a deep understanding of the true feelings of Chinese compatriots. The result of this ethnic and ideological arrogance has been to deny the Chinese government the opportunity to have full access to representative opinion in Hong Kong. The original British proposal was rejected out of hand rather than met by counter-proposals by the Chinese as to how Hong Kong representation could have been established on terms more acceptable to themselves.[9]

The vehemence of the Chinese response to the Patten proposals may

8. For a detailed account of the negotiations leading up to the Joint Declaration of 1984 see Robert Cottrell, *The End of Hong Kong, The Secret Diplomacy of Imperial Retreat* (London: John Murray, 1993).

9. The above analysis draws on the author's "Hong Kong's future: Sino-British negotiations, perceptions, organization and political culture," *International Affairs*, April 1993.

also be explained by the insecurities of a regime that faces an imminent succession problem in which it is feared that the survival of the Communist system itself may be in the balance. The collapse of Communism in Eastern Europe and the disintegration of the Soviet Union following hard on the heels of China's suppression of peaceful demonstrators have steeled the determination of Deng Xiaoping to resist at this stage pressures for political reform.[10] The Basic Law as endorsed by the NPC in 1990 included a clause specifically warning against "subversion" in Hong Kong. The pre-"Tiananmen" versions contained no such clause. The open manner in which Patten presented his proposals without prior consultations was deemed offensive as it ran counter to the traditional Chinese and Communist ways of conducting such business and it was certainly a departure from the way previous governors had negotiated with the Chinese side. Matters were not helped from the Chinese perspective by Patten's insistence that the ultimate authority for accepting or rejecting his proposals was the Legislative Council. Additionally, his popular and personable style of politics that has endeared him not only to people in Hong Kong but even more to people in Guangdong province, has profoundly upset the more hidebound Chinese Communist officials whom he has unwittingly up-staged.

The result has been that the British and Chinese sides have been cast into a trial of strength whose outcome is unclear. Although it is in the interests of both sides to reach agreement so as to avoid uncertainty, the collapse of confidence and possible disaster, the problem of reaching formal agreements presents them both with difficult dilemmas. The Chinese side must choose, on the one hand, between conceding to the British a greater degree of democracy and diminution of mainland control over Hong Kong, but ensuring a smooth transition of sovereignty in 1997, retaining confidence in the territory and benefiting from the continuation of rapid economic growth in southern China; and on the other holding out, without agreement if necessary, for effective control over Hong Kong in 1997 and beyond at the risk of possible disaster. The first course would accord with Chinese economic – and hence political – needs (as currently perceived by Deng Xiaoping) and the latter would satisfy nationalistic sentiments and fears of foreign subversion. The British dilemma is whether to proceed with arrangements to give Hong Kong the minimal terms necessary to enable it to continue to exercise the rule of law by embedding it in an independent legislature, at the risk of not reaching agreement with the Chinese; or whether an agreement should be reached with the Chinese, even if it provided something less than that, lest in the absence of an agreement the Chinese would pursue something worse after the reversion of sovereignty in 1997.

So far the emergence of Greater China has been based on what might

10. This was made abundantly clear at the 14th Party Congress held in Beijing as Patten was making his controversial proposals in Hong Kong on 7 October 1992. No reference was made in the Report to political reform such as the possible separation of Party and government envisaged at the previous Congress. Instead the emphasis was on the necessity of preserving Party dominance during a period of rapid economic change.

be called a version of "one economy two political systems" or a converging economy amid divergent polities. Hong Kong's significance for China has not rested solely on the economic factors of complementarity and the division of labour, in acting as entrepôt or in providing value added services – important as these are. It is also derived from Hong Kong's legal and political systems that enable it to operate as a successful financial centre of regional and global significance providing the range of services similar to those of the City of London. Its various freedoms (itemized in the Joint Declaration) ensure that it is able to operate as a hub for the information flows at the heart of operating a modern economy. One of the many paradoxes of Hong Kong is that it combines the traditional long-standing Chinese informal practices with those of the most advanced contemporary information technologies. The elderly leadership in Beijing may understand the former, but it shows few signs of recognizing the basis necessary for the operations of the latter. The legal system is an essential ingredient in the operation of the Hong Kong economy. At present it is perceived to draw its independence and integrity from the link with London; once that is cut in 1997 it risks being subject to the arbitrary pressures of Chinese politics unless it can be anchored in a local system of proper accountability. When the British Foreign Secretary, Douglas Hurd, made the point in Singapore (en route to meet his counterpart in Beijing in July 1993) that in this sense Hong Kong was a "political city" his remark drew oblique criticism from China's Foreign Minister, Qian Qichen. Deliberately or otherwise the Chinese side had misunderstood.[11]

Hong Kong has also played a critical role as a facilitator in the evolution of relations between Taiwan and the mainland. As noted earlier, it has been a convenient meeting place for politicians, officials and academics from the two centres. But, in the absence of direct shipping or air links between Taiwan and the mainland, it has also been the principal conduit through which exchanges between them have taken place. Starting with a few thousand in 1987, a million visits were made in 1991 by Taiwan people to the mainland via Hong Kong and nearly 900,000 such visits were recorded between January and July 1992. The value of China–Taiwan trade conducted principally via Hong Kong has shot up from US$0.9 billion in 1986 to US$5.8 billion in 1991 and is expected to reach US$7–8 billion in 1992. Investment from Taiwan in the mainland, estimated at US$2–3 billion, is also conducted largely through Hong Kong and, directed principally towards Fujian (the ancestral home of most people in the island), follows a pattern similar to Hong Kong.[12]

Of even greater significance from the perspective of Greater China is the development of ties between Hong Kong and Taiwan independent of their respective relations with the mainland. This became evident only in

11. For Qian's remarks see *Xinhua*, 9 July 1993 and for a more hard hitting response, *Ta Kung Pao* (Hong Kong) editorial, both in BBC, *Summary of World Broadcasts* (*SWB*), FE/1737, pp. A2/1–2.

12. Official figures cited by Baldinger, "The birth of Greater China," and by Angus Foster, "Bitter enemies become grudging partners," *Financial Times*, 13 November 1992.

1991 after the Taipei government had quietly dropped its objections to dealing with a Hong Kong that was to revert to Chinese sovereignty under Deng Xiaoping's scheme of "one country two systems." The Beijing government professed to see no harm at all in such relations provided that they were unofficial. Since the application of Deng's scheme to Hong Kong was meant as a forerunner to its application on even more "generous" terms to Taiwan, the Beijing leadership doubtless saw great benefits from Taiwan's implicit endorsement of Hong Kong's new position. In fact PRC representatives have sat alongside those of Hong Kong and Taiwan not only in the semi-official Pacific Economic Consultative Conference (PECC), but also in the inter-governmental Asia Pacific Economic Co-operation forum (APEC). They have done so on the grounds that qualification for membership is not restricted to sovereign states. Difficulties, however, arose after President Clinton suggested that the coming APEC meeting in Seattle due later in the year should also be a forum for the meeting of heads of government. Beijing immediately bridled at the suggestion, and Taipei, which presumably saw this as an unexpected opportunity to strengthen its international standing, responded by making two points: first that the Republic of China was a sovereign state; and secondly that APEC was "purely an economic, unofficial and consultative forum ... all of its members are independent economic entities, enjoying equal rights and obligations ... we resolutely oppose the Chinese Communist fallacy that we have no right to participate in the APEC summit's economic meeting."[13] Interestingly, the official Central Broadcasting System in reporting the Foreign Ministry's statement asserted that the refutation of Beijing's "fallacy" applied to Hong Kong too.[14] Meanwhile close economic ties had developed between Taiwan and Hong Kong as may be seen from the emergence in 1991 of Taiwan as Hong Kong's fourth largest trading partner and its largest source of overseas visitors, while Hong Kong has become Taiwan's second largest export market even though 40 per cent of the goods are re-exported to China.[15]

Nevertheless the Hong Kong–Taiwan ties are highly sensitive from the point of view of Beijing. The margins between their promoting and their undermining in practice the concept of "one country two systems" are very narrow. Any suggestion of inter-governmental relations between Hong Kong and Taiwan is regarded as unacceptable by Beijing. As Beijing's criticisms of Hong Kong Governor Chris Patten's meeting with a senior member of the KMT demonstrated, even links with the KMT under the guise of trade relations are suspect.[16] Yet ambiguities remain as Beijing has not objected to Taiwan's interests in Hong Kong being represented since September 1991 by John Ni, the former Director-General of the Industrial Development and Investment Centre in the Ministry

13. See Ministry of Foreign Affairs statement of 9 July 1993 in *SWB* FE/1739, p. A2/4.
14. *Ibid.*
15. Figures drawn from Baldinger, "The birth of Greater China."
16. *The People's Daily*, overseas edition, 16 November 1992. Xu Ping, "What is Chris Patten up to by meeting Hsu Sheng-fa?" *SWB* FE/1542, pp. A2/2–3.

of Economic Affairs in Taipei. Ni, the highest ranking official ever to represent Taiwan interests in the territory, is the head of the Chong Hwa Travel Agency, Taiwan's *de facto* representative office in the territory. His role is said to include keeping a watching brief on Taiwan's growing presence on the mainland.[17]

Despite (or rather because of) the fact that Deng Xiaoping and his colleagues regard the settlement of Hong Kong in 1997 as the model for the future re-unification with Taiwan, the British negotiators have been careful to avoid making references to the Taiwan factor lest they excite still further Beijing's suspicions about their true objectives. Given Chinese sensitivities about sovereignty and about the possible separation of Taiwan from the mainland the British have always felt that any formal linkage would fruitlessly provoke Beijing especially as it would go against the long-standing Sino-British understandings about limiting the activities in Hong Kong of Taiwanese representatives and their agents so that it could not become a base for them.[18]

Consequently Hong Kong's role in the triangle that makes up Greater China may be seen as a peculiar mix of formal and informal. Its significance as a major international financial and economic centre owes a good part to the formalities associated with its status under British auspices. This enabled it to enter into a wide range of international agreements and obligations buttressed by the respect for the probity of its legality and domestic administration. It can thus act as the great entrepôt for China and as the major quasi-external capitalist supplier of modernity to the vast hinterland of China. At the same time these formalities provide the framework within which the informal networks which really drive the economic dynamism of Greater China can operate. Clearly, the great unknown is whether the uncertainties of the transition to 1997 and the actual transfer of sovereignty of Hong Kong to the PRC will so change the formalities as to undermine them.

*Taiwan and Greater China.* Without devaluing the importance of Hong Kong, the key factor in the emergence of Greater China has been the growing role played by Taiwan especially from 1987 onwards. It was its burgeoning relationship with the mainland beginning with the relaxation of travel restrictions in 1987 that first paved the way and which has since continued to define the scope of the emerging community – if it can be so called. The relationship may be seen as trade-driven with its limits set by political considerations. Once begun, the economic relations developed at great speed, but it is not always appreciated that the politics of the situation were also highly dynamic. The political identities of the two domestic systems were in the process of change and development while at the same time the international environment was reflecting new uncertainties associated with the ending of the Cold War. But despite the dynamism inherent in the development of Greater China its potential has

17. Baldinger, "The birth of Greater China," p. 17.
18. See Dick Wilson, *Hong Kong! Hong Kong!* (London: Unwin Hyman, 1990), p. 196.

been limited by the long-standing impasse in the political relations between the PRC and the Republic of China on Taiwan (ROC). Backed by the threat of the use of force the former has all along refused to consider any future for Taiwan other than reuniting with the mainland under the sovereignty of the PRC. For its part the ROC on Taiwan has been locked into a situation in which it has refused to contemplate a long-term future for the island except as a part of China – but a China that is no longer under Communist rule. This impasse could only be broken by changes in the political identities of probably both sides.

The political identities of Taiwan and mainland China have become much more inter-related than ever before, and the evolution of Greater China poses ever more complex challenges to those identities. Political or state identity may be defined as the basic values which inform the domestic social and political arrangements of a state and which provide a basis for its appeal for recognition and support in the international community.[19] There are several important respects in which the separate state identities of the PRC and the ROC impinge differently on the question of Greater China. As seen by leaders of the PRC the importance of unification with Taiwan is a matter of finishing the civil war, completing a nationalist tryst with Chinese history and finally triumphing over the demeaning effects of past humiliations at the hands of Western powers. These considerations all mean more to the oldest generation of leaders than to their successors. Nevertheless, as an issue of national sovereignty, the question of re-unification with Taiwan is not something on which any of the succeeding generations of Beijing leaders can afford to be seen to temporize.

The issue for the government in Taipei has been starker still. It has been one of survival. As the government of the Republic of China it claims to represent China as a whole, of which Taiwan is only one province. Since the ROC is based in Taiwan it is possible to increase the influence and representation of local people in political affairs – as indeed is currently the case – without automatically challenging the government's credentials in theory to represent the interests of the Chinese people as a whole. But were the government to recognize what many regard as the realities of the situation and try to establish Taiwan as an independent state in name as well as in fact, it would not only risk an all-out attack by Beijing, but it would also undermine its own political legitimacy. Alternatively, were the Taipei leaders to warm to the blandishments of Beijing they fear being swallowed up in the embrace. Such is the holistic character of Chinese Communism as seen from Taipei that

19. The concept of state identity as used here is closely related to that of political culture on which there is a vast literature. As applied to international relations, reference may be made to Hedley Bull, *The Anarchical Society*, pp. 57–59 for a discussion of the basis of order within a modern state. More particularly, see Raymond Aron, *Peace and War, A Theory of International Relations* (London: Weidenfeld and Nicolson, 1966) pp. 99–104, for a discussion of the implications of the international system being "heterogeneous" – i.e., when states are characterized by different and competing principles of domestic legitimacy. See also the discussion by James Mayall, "The variety of states" in Cornelia Navari (ed.,) *The Condition of States* (Milton Keynes: The Open University Press, 1991) pp. 44–60.

it was claimed that any contact could not but erode the position of the KMT and the ROC. Conversely, any move away from the mainland could risk the development of a momentum towards separatism that would also threaten the survival of the KMT and the ROC. By the 1980s there was little sign of the imminent collapse of the Communist regime and still less of a revolt against Communist rule in favour of a return of the KMT. Consequently, the Taipei government had become boxed into a corner in which it had little hope of being able to reunite with the mainland on terms that it could accept and yet it was also opposed to any move towards establishing Taiwan as a separate state. The problem had been accentuated because of the authoritarian character of KMT rule.

The immobilism of the position of the Taipei government eventually gave way from the mid-1980s onwards as the result of a combination of several factors both domestic and external. At home the passage of time together with the social consequences of prolonged economic growth had left the KMT old guard marooned in a cocoon of the past. As frail aged men clung on to seats in the legislature won in elections held in the mainland in 1947 representing mythical constituents, a new middle class had emerged that demanded a greater say in public affairs.[20] Taiwan was perhaps fortunate at that point in its history to have the delicate and potentially highly divisive transition from tight authoritarianism to a more open, pluralistic and participatory system led by President Chiang Ching-kuo who, as Chiang Kai-shek's son and groomed successor, was able to command the personal allegiance of the old guard while preparing the ground for a gradual transfer of power to the new. Meanwhile Taiwan's external environment was changing rapidly: the Soviet threat to the region was diminishing as were Sino-Soviet tensions; and at the same time the effects of the deepening reforms in the Chinese mainland were increasing the economic ties of the mainland with Taiwan's economic partners and competitors in the Asia-Pacific. By this time the social and economic consequences of prolonged economic growth in the island had brought about a recognition that the character of Taiwan's comparative advantage in this respect was also changing. In short continuing with the status quo was becoming increasingly untenable.[21]

The PRC reforms had opened the country's economy and society to the rest of the Asia-Pacific in totally new ways as its foreign policy took on an omni-directional orientation. Taiwan was in danger of becoming even more isolated. The first public sign of change came in 1984 when two Chinese teams took part in the Los Angeles Olympics, the PRC and "Chinese Taipei" (*Zhonghua Taibei*). The formula was acceptable to both sides. Beijing objected to the designation of the Republic of China and Taipei did not wish to use the name Taiwan lest it evoke either a purely provincial identity or even possible independence. Taipei also objected to

---

20. For a full discussion of these trends on the eve of the development of ties across the Straits see T.B. Gold, *State and Society in the Taiwan Miracle* (New York: M.E. Sharpe, 1986).

21. For an excellent discussion of these issues see Peter R. Moody, *Political Change on Taiwan* (New York: Praeger, 1992), ch. 6, pp. 132–154.

the formula "China (*Zhongguo*) Taipei" as it may have connoted that it was a local Chinese government.[22] The indication of flexibility on an issue of such visibility prepared the ground for the development of unofficial economic relations with the mainland as Taiwan officials turned a blind eye to trade that was surreptitiously conducted through Hong Kong. Moreover some Taiwanese journalists took advantage of the new climate to break the rules by visiting the mainland and filing reports from there. The fact that these reports painted conditions on the mainland in such drab colours emboldened the authorities to break the taboo on allowing visits to the mainland.[23] One of the last major acts of President Chiang Ching-kuo before his death in January 1988 was to authorize on 15 October 1987 visits by Taiwan residents to the mainland for the purposes of family re-union. Although officially these were to be highly circumscribed a dam had been broken. What began as a small stream of several thousand visitors, as was noted earlier, soon swelled into hundreds of thousands to reach more than a million in 1991.

Beijing and Taipei interpreted the dynamics and implications of these events in very different and self-serving ways. Beijing has chosen to interpret these and the whole range of contacts and visits between the two sides as the result of the Taiwan authorities having to give way to an irresistible tide of pressure of compatriots seeking unity with the mainland.[24] But at the same time the leaders in Beijing have been anxious lest the increasing democratization in Taiwan might lead to increased votes for the Democratic and Progressive Party (DPP) which in their view translates into a growing demand for independence. Hence the then President Yang Shangkun went so far as to "sternly warn the handful of those actively advocating the 'independence of Taiwan': Do not misread the situation. Those who play with fire will be burnt to ashes."[25] The Beijing strategy in formal dealings with Taiwan has been to insist on some manifestation of the essential unity of Taiwan with China. But underlying that strategy is an analysis that depicts three political forces at work in Taiwan: first, the traditional KMT approach as represented by the former Prime Minister Hau Pei-ts'un that adheres to the necessity of unification with the mainland, but on anti-Communist lines; secondly, the DPP approach that under the guise of self determination favours independence; and thirdly, the intermediate KMT approach led by President Lee Teng-hui that favours the continuation of the status quo of *de facto* independence while ostensibly arguing for unity. This has been characterized as "neither independence nor unification."[26] Beijing is sympathetic to the first, hostile to the second and suspicious of the third. Meanwhile Beijing continues to remind the people and government in Taiwan of its readiness to use force should they opt for independence. While that threat may frighten potential voters from declaring in favour of the DPP and

22. *Ibid.* p. 136.
23. See the account in Simon Long, *Taiwan: China's Last Frontier* (London: Macmillan, 1991), ch. 9, esp. pp. 203–210.
24. Interview with Sun Xiaoyu.
25. *SWB* FE/1199, p. i.
26. Moody, *Political Change on Taiwan*, p. 133.

possible independence it can hardly endear the PRC to the Taiwan population. Indeed the effect of those threats especially in the light of Beijing's use of force to suppress the peaceful demonstrators on 4 June 1989 has been to consolidate the position of the KMT.[27]

The position of the Taiwan authorities perhaps may be best described as ambiguous. On the one hand the KMT government seeks to avoid the blandishments of Beijing, but on the other it opposes any moves towards independence. It approximates to the apocryphal English prayer, "Lord, make me good, but not yet." Thus the KMT government presents itself still as the true upholder of Chinese culture, the only legitimate representative of the Chinese people, that is waiting for the Chinese people finally to overthrow the Communist tyranny. It also has demanded that Beijing treat Taipei as an equal political entity – but so far without success as such a concession would undermine Beijing's position. Meanwhile Taipei has explained its tolerance of the growing economic interchange across the Taiwan Straits as evidence of its concern for the welfare and prosperity of the compatriots on the mainland. More broadly, it is hoped that in time that will contribute towards bringing about political change on the mainland. Nevertheless the KMT government is concerned to limit the economic engagement with the mainland lest its economy become too dependent on the PRC.[28] It has therefore aimed to steer a course that enables the island to retain mastery of its own destiny without being ensnared by Beijing's attempts to lock Taiwan into its schemes for unification, while at the same time leaving the door open for ultimate unification under different conditions in an undefined future. To this end for example, Foreign Minister Lian Chan proposed in April 1989 the idea of "one country two governments," *yiguo liang fu* (in opposition to Beijing's concept of "one country two systems"). The proposal, which had been rejected in Chiang Ching-kuo's lifetime as evoking a two China posture, is now regarded as similar to the old German formula of "one nation two states."[29] As advocated in 1989, the proposal could be seen not only as a counter to Beijing's formula, but also as a means of both deflecting the DPP demands for independence and of putting pressure on Beijing to treat Taipei as an equal partner. One of the consequences of the rise of the DPP has been to make the Beijing proposal of inter-party talks between the CPC and the KMT even more unacceptable in Taiwan. Lian Chan's formula of "one country two governments" envisaging a long-term co-existence between the two governments was predictably rejected by Beijing as "aimed at splitting China."

Such was the explosion of activity across the Straits engendered by the lifting of travel restrictions in 1987 that the ROC government decided by the end of 1990 to establish an organization that could negotiate the

27. See the discussion in Long, *Taiwan*, pp. 221–236.
28. See statements of alarm by the Mainland Affairs Council about capital outflow to the mainland of 17 May and 2 August 1993 in *SWB* FE/1693, p. A2/3 and FE/1760, p. A1/6 respectively. See also the caution by the Board of Trade of 29 April 1993 in FE/1676 A2/5.
29. For an interesting analysis see Gottfried-Karl Kindermann, "Recent ROC–PRC unification policies in the light of the German experience," *Issues and Studies*, Vol. 29, No. 5 (May 1993).

modalities of relations between the two sides. In less than three years two million people from Taiwan had visited the mainland, and more than ten thousand mainlanders had travelled to Taiwan on family visits or even to settle. The rapid expansion of trade which had surged from US$955 million in 1986 to $4.43 billion in 1990 and the widening scope of sporting, academic, cultural, religious and other exchanges were beginning to give rise to practical problems of what in other contexts would be regarded as of a consular kind. They included trade disputes, document authentication, illegal entries, marital relations, property inheritance and so on. In the absence of inter-governmental contacts Taipei established the Straits Exchange Foundation (SEF) in February 1991 as a technically non-governmental organization empowered to negotiate authoritatively over such matters. It received the legal endorsement of the ROC's Mainland Affairs Council in April 1991.[30] Beijing soon followed suit in establishing the Association for Relations Across the Taiwan Straits (ARATS) which also was technically a non-governmental body empowered with similar authority. Yet it was clear that the two bodies were unofficial only by name.

Interestingly, progress was made despite the fact that negotiations between the two soon got bogged down in procedural matters as ARATS and SEF sought a *modus operandi* that would not undermine the formal positions of each side or allow the other to score propaganda points. In the end a breakthrough was achieved when the leaders of SEF and ARATS, Koo Chenfu and Wang Daohan, held formal talks in Singapore on 27–29 April 1993. Agreement was reached about important technical matters necessary for the conduct of economic relations. These included the verification of documents, compensation for lost registered mail, arrangements for cultural and scientific exchanges and, most importantly, the establishment of regular channels of communication to discuss disputes over such things as fishing and smuggling. Although no agreement was reached about the protection of Taiwanese investments on the mainland, both sides declared the meeting to be a great success. Predictably, they disagreed about its significance. Beijing professed to see it as an important milestone on the way to eventual unification. Taipei saw it as demonstrating the equality between the two sides and as a boost to its own international standing. President Lee Teng-hui claimed the conduct of the talks and the ways the agreements were signed "showed it is an undeniable fact that we have equal status with Communist China."[31]

The closer working relations between mainland and island China should not be allowed to obscure the wide political gulf that still separates them, especially as that is bolstered by strategic and military considerations. Taiwan exists under a continual threat of Beijing's declared readiness to advance its claims by the use of force should it deem that necessary. Beijing has identified at least three conditions in which it

---

30. See *A Bridge for Chinese*, The Straits Exchange Foundation, Taipei, October 1991.
31. See Julian Baum, "China–Taiwan, tactical manoeuvres: participants differ over meaning of Singapore talks," *FEER*, 13 May 1993, p. 12.

would do so: if Taipei were to ally itself to the Soviet Union; if it were to seek independence; and if the continued separation of the island from the mainland were to endure for too long. The first has presumably lapsed, but perhaps remains as a warning against seeking an ally among Beijing's major or potential adversaries. The others remain, not only for the formalistic purpose of claiming the right to use force as part of the exercise of sovereignty, but as something to be invoked as a threat for the purpose of coercive diplomacy. Beijing's leaders regularly issue threats. These are often cited by the KMT perhaps as a way of reminding people of the dangers of voting for the DPP.[32] For its part the Taipei government and military has claimed all along to possess adequate forces to resist any military attacks from the mainland.[33]

These political and security tensions and conflicts which still lie at the heart of mainland–Taiwan relations may have been somewhat eased by the rapid development of economic ties, but they have not been dissipated. Since both sets of leaders and indeed the regimes themselves consider that their mutual relations are central to questions about their survival (which neither can take for granted), the politics of Greater China cannot be regarded as simply being driven by the requirements of trade and economics.

Moreover the political situation in both centres possesses its own dynamism that is continually changing the context within which the economics of Greater China operate. If the 14th CCP Congress of October 1992 ushered in yet a new line-up of managers of daily affairs in Beijing and of potential successors to the elderly leaders who wield ultimate power, the 19 December elections for the Legislative Yuan in Taiwan dramatically increased the representation of the DPP and deepened the divisions within the KMT.[34]

Interestingly, new political links have been forged between Taiwan and Hong Kong. Liberal independent legislators and members of the United Democrats of Hong Kong visited Taiwan at the invitation of the DPP. On their return they claimed that Beijing's harsh response to Governor Patten and his proposals for greater democracy in Hong Kong were a factor in increasing the votes for the DPP.[35] It is interesting that the Taipei government should have expressed support for his proposals at roughly this time, especially as Taipei a few years ago reversed its earlier hostility to the Sino-British Joint Declaration and thereby implicitly supported Beijing's concept of "one country two systems" – if only as applied to

32. See for example, Government Information Office, Taipei June 1991, *A Study of a Possible Communist Attack on Taiwan.* The pamphlet cites 69 statements by senior military and political leaders threatening the possible use of force issued between April 1975 and 13 December 1990.

33. See "Would Beijing dare invade?" *Newsweek,* 23 December 1991, p. 36, and the claim by Defence Minister Chen Li-an on 28 October 1992 that Taiwan's present air force could repel any mainland attack, reported by Central News Agency in *SWB* FE/1530, pp. B/16–17, 5 November 1992.

34. For analysis of the former see Tony Saich, "The 14th Party Congress: a programme for authoritarian rule," *The China Quarterly,* No. 132 (December 1992), pp. 1136–1160. For an account of the latter see Julian Baum, "The hollow centre: political result undermines President's power," *FEER,* 7 January 1993, pp. 14–15.

35. Author's interview with Legco member Huang Chenya of the UDHK, 21 August 1992.

Hong Kong. Clearly, in attempting to have itself recognized as *a* rather than *the* Chinese government, Taipei can take a more relaxed view of the Hong Kong situation and hope to benefit from the greater sense of plurality that is emerging among different centres of Chinese governance.

The emergence of the DPP as a potent political force in Taiwan has already affected relations across the Straits. Its significance seems set to grow. The DPP argues that its policy of "one China – one Taiwan" is no more than a reflection of existing reality and that the question is how to have that reality recognized more openly in the world at large. The DPP claims that sooner or later Beijing will have to come to terms with that too. The relations across the Straits therefore are not only dynamic but also uncertain as they depend in part on the degree to which the domestic political developments on each side involves changes in their respective political systems. Such a change would surely follow the DPP's accession to power in Taiwan; and it is difficult to conceive of the coming political succession on the mainland that did not entail some systemic change. Since consideration of such issues go well beyond the scope of this article, it may be useful at this point to look at the external ramifications of the Greater China question.

## The Extramural Relations of Greater China

The ending of the Cold War may be seen as having facilitated the emergence of Greater China. It removed superpower competition and Sino-Soviet rivalry from the context of the relations between mainland China and Taiwan. It marked the end of a direct strategic threat to China from Soviet forces deployed to the north and from its Pacific Fleet. It additionally had the effect of bringing to an end the so-called strategic great triangle in which China was of significance in the management of the global balance between the United States and the Soviet Union. As a result China lost its position as a quasi-strategic partner of the United States. By the same token, however, it became easier for Beijing to focus more on accentuating the economic dimensions of its foreign policy by developing from a policy characterized by independence from the super-powers to one that was better understood as being omni-directional with a strong regional bias towards the Asia-Pacific. But the region too was changing as its long-standing conflicts were also being detached from their embroilment with the conflicts of the global powers. The disengage-ment of the Soviet Union from the Korean and Indo-Chinese conflicts paved the way for treating them as local or at worst regional problems that for the first time were susceptible to solution. Throughout the region relations between former adversaries were improving with great emphasis being placed upon the development and expansion of economic relations. That established both a favourable context and an incentive to allow for greater interchange across the Taiwan Straits.

These developments, however, not only facilitated the emergence of Greater China but also encouraged the development of countervailing political tendencies. Taiwan was provided with greater opportunities to explore more independent and assertive policies known by the term "flexible diplomacy."[36] New opportunities arose in cultivating relations with the new regimes and states that emerged out of the disintegration of the former Soviet empire. Even Western powers were no longer reluctant to offend the sensibilities of the Beijing government and openly sent people of ministerial rank to Taipei. Beijing, to its chagrin, found that the diplomacy that in the 1970s and 1980s had been so effective in warning off Western governments from selling advanced weapon systems to Taiwan no longer worked in the 1990s. Moreover, since the Tiananmen killings of 4 June 1989 and the disintegration of Soviet Communism in the ensuing two years, the legitimacy problems of Beijing in seeking to combine unre-formed Communist political rule with rapid economic change of a more market orientation were having an adverse effect in Beijing's attempts to cultivate political unity with the other two elements of Greater China; and the Western world was being drawn into the problem.

*The Hong Kong question.* Since Hong Kong cannot be defended from the PRC it is in a different position altogether from Taiwan. There is no question of it acquiring independence or of it carrying out an exercise of self-determination. Although the conditions of its reversion to Chinese sovereignty in 1997 have been a matter for negotiation between the British and Chinese sides alone, aspects of foreign political relations impinge on the issue in many respects. Whether Beijing appreciates it or not, other Western countries in the region and beyond such as Australia, Canada and the United States have a close interest in the territory by virtue of history, demography and economics as well as from their commitments to uphold liberal values of the rule of law and democracy. Japan too has important economic interests and sees Chinese behaviour with regard to Hong Kong as a touchstone for evaluating Beijing's reliability as a partner in the Asia-Pacific. Further afield Germany and other West European countries are similarly concerned. Even within South-east Asia Beijing's treatment of Hong Kong is closely monitored and scrutinized for evidence of the PRC's adherence to moderation and to the norms of rational international behaviour. The fact that the American Congress in 1991 successfully passed into law a requirement that the Executive report on Beijing's adherence to the Sino-British agreements on Hong Kong may have particularly annoyed Beijing, but should not blind it to the fact that many others will be closely following these events whether or not they declare so in public. After all Beijing itself lodged a copy of the Joint Declaration with the United Nations as an international agreement. Its complaints about the alleged international-ization of the Hong Kong issue may be understandable, but they are not consistent with its own behaviour.

Moreover it can hardly assail the British appointed government of Hong Kong as unrepresentative of the Hong Kong people and their interests when the PRC representatives are content to sit alongside Hong

36. For a clear account see Michael Ying-mao Kau, "The ROC's new foreign policy strategy," in Denis Fred Simon and Michael Ying-mao Kau (eds.), *Taiwan: Beyond the Economic Miracle* (London & New York: M.E. Sharpe, 1992) pp. 237–255.

Kong government representatives in APEC or applaud their political lobbying in Washington on behalf of renewal of China's Most Favoured Nation legislative clause. However galling Beijing may find the support that Governor Chris Patten has garnered from Australia, Canada, the United States and albeit more cautiously from Japan, it should recognize that this is the price it has had to pay for interdependence. Were Beijing to coerce Hong Kong into abject submission it might risk not only "killing the goose that lays the golden eggs" in Hong Kong itself with incalculable consequences for the adjacent parts of the Chinese mainland and for its relations with Taiwan, but it would also damage its international reputation in highly significant ways. Perhaps the critical issue has less to do with Hong Kong *per se* than with Beijing's insecurities and the abiding fear of the Communist system being undermined by the process of "peaceful evolution."[37] As the Beijing-owned newspapers in Hong Kong have maintained on many occasions since Governor Patten made his proposals, the British are regarded as untrustworthy in not only seeking to denude the territory of capital, but also seeking to leave chaos behind them to destabilize Hong Kong, and beyond that to undermine Beijing in collaboration with the United States in particular. It is as if because of its foreign links and alien practices Hong Kong is regarded less as a minor place of great economic usefulness and more as a kind of cancerous growth on the Chinese body politic.

Yet Hong Kong possesses significant formal legal and economic capacity of considerable significance in international terms. As a sub-state unit,

the territory is more capable in administering its own affairs and providing political goods for its citizens than some other sovereign states. With a well-developed administrative machinery, a high degree of autonomy in managing its own political and economic affairs, an unparalleled degree of latitude in participating in international affairs among autonomous entities and a dynamic and open economy, Hong Kong's international capacity is by no means insignificant.[38]

Hong Kong has been an active member or associate member of many international or regional organizations including the Asian Development Bank (ADB), the GATT, the Customs Co-operative Council (CCC), the Economic and Social Commission for Asia and the Pacific (ESCAP), the PECC, APEC and the International Monetary Fund (IMF). Whether the growing importance of economics in international politics will lead Hong Kong to become more involved in world-wide political issues remains to be seen. But Hong Kong's role as an international city is vital to sustaining its present economic position and indeed to its capacity to be of such significance in the economic development of China itself. This relates to economic activities in the Asia-Pacific and in the world at large. Beijing's assertion that after 1 July 1997 Hong Kong's concerns will be

37. For an analysis of its role in PRC foreign policy-making see David Shambaugh, "Peking's foreign policy conundrum since Tiananmen: peaceful coexistence vs. peaceful evolution," *Issues and Studies*, November 1992, pp. 65–84.
38. James T.H. Tang, "Hong Kong's international status," *Pacific Review*, Vol. 6, No. 3 (1993), p. 209.

purely within the sovereign domestic affairs of the PRC is not only dangerously short-sighted, but it could also become a new source of conflict in China's foreign relations. If China is to reap the full benefits of the association with Hong Kong it should rephrase the question not as to whether Hong Kong should be internationalized, but rather as to what character that internationalization should take.

*The Taiwan foreign connection.* As long as each side of the Taiwan Straits claimed to be the only government of the whole of China other states had no alternative but to recognize one as the Chinese government. Their joint refusal to entertain any other arrangement such as "two Chinas," or "one China – one Taiwan," or even "one China – but not yet," combined with the absence of any acknowledged contacts between the two sides, served to solidify the status quo. Such formulae that each side had offered over the years to break the deadlock required the other (intentionally or not) to fulfil unacceptable conditions that would have undermined the viability of its existing system of government.[39] This position has been sustained militarily by the American pledge to defend Taiwan – a pledge that was renewed by the Taiwan Relations Act after the formal treaty was abrogated in 1979. The position has also found international legal expression by there being a division in the international community about which side to recognize as the legitimate sovereign representative of China. As was noted earlier, by late 1992 there were still 29 states that recognized the government in Taipei as the sovereign authority of the Republic of China. In other words the foreign connection has been necessary to the maintenance of the status quo.

The conditions (both intramural and extramural) that made the emergence of Greater China feasible also contributed to encouraging Taipei to find new ways in which to deepen its links with the international community. The increased connections with the mainland have had a dual and paradoxical effect on Taiwanese consciousness: they have encouraged a sense of economic complementarity and perhaps even interdependence; but at the same time have brought out a deeper appreciation of the differences between the two sides not only in levels of economic development but also in terms of culture.[40] External developments also impelled Taiwan towards increasing its international profile. The normalization of relations with Beijing in late 1978 led the United States to remove the last American military deployments from Taiwan and to distancing it somewhat from the Chinese civil war, which in any case scaled down in intensity. It meant that although the United States remained the main guarantor of Taiwan's security the island would have to become more self reliant in its own defence. The United States was legally committed to supplying arms to Taiwan, but it had become less

39. Lin Zhiling and Thomas W. Robinson, "Domestic and international determinants of Chinese reunification," *The Journal of East Asian Affairs*, Summer/Fall 1992, p. 430.

40. See the discussion by Edwin A. Winckler, "Taiwan transition?" in Tun-jen Cheng and Stephen Haggard (eds.), *Political Change in Taiwan* (Boulder & London: Lynne Rienner Publishers, 1992), pp. 221–259.

clear as to what precisely Washington might do in the event of attempts by Beijing to impose reunification by force. Not surprisingly, Taiwan sought to increase its visible weight in the international community as it realized that it could no longer rely on American protection alone. Curiously, Beijing's foreign policy in the 1980s facilitated Taiwan's new internationalism. The softening of its anti-Soviet line, the growing emphasis on the importance of economics in foreign relations, and the deeper levels of participation in international and regional organizations that were inherent in its omni-directional foreign policy all contributed to allowing Taiwan more room for international manoeuvre.[41]

The 1989 Tiananmen events did not fundamentally change the situation. On the contrary they served to intensify the trend of deepening economic and personal ties while simultaneously raising the levels of Taiwan's engagement with the international community. Tiananmen seemingly confirmed KMT propaganda about the character of the Communists and this made the Taipei government feel less concerned about a more sober-minded economic community in Taiwan dealing with the mainland. At the same time the KMT became less fearful of the appeal of the DPP and the independence cause now that the ruthlessness of the Communist leaders had been shown for all to see. The international reaction to Tiananmen ensured that Taipei would get an even better hearing for its claims. The subsequent collapse of Communism elsewhere had the beneficial effect from a KMT perspective of suggesting that perhaps after all time was on its side and that all it would have to do would be play its cards well while it waited for historical forces to bring the Communist system in the mainland to an end.

The rules of the competition between Beijing and Taipei for international recognition have been subtly changed by Taiwan's "flexible diplomacy." The earlier zero-sum game has been replaced by something that is altogether more adaptable. The most that Beijing had allowed since the 1970s in the relations between Taiwan and other countries was a technically non-official representation in each other's capitals that could handle economic, cultural and other exchanges. But as a result of Taiwan's new approach Beijing has had to give ground somewhat in practice even though it still formally adheres to the earlier rules. Beijing was most anxious to ensure recognition by the successor states to the old Communist order in Eastern Europe and the former Soviet Union along those lines. On the whole it was successful. But Taiwan secured something of a "coup" when it persuaded the Latvian government to grant an exchange of consulates despite the objections of Beijing.

In many ways this is a more important breakthrough for Taipei than being able to persuade two small West African states and a Central American one to forsake recognition of Beijing for that of Taipei. Taipei had simply bought their recognition with promises of aid that were notmatched by Beijing. With its enormous hard currency reserves that are second only to those of Japan and its economic muscle Taiwan has been

---

41. Lin and Robinson, "Domestic and international determinants," p. 431.

able to engage in what Beijing has called "dollar diplomacy." It is clearly that which has appealed to Latvia. The post-Communist regimes are obviously less in awe of Communist Beijing than many others and given their great economic needs they have a sharp and obvious view of their self-interests. Beijing has been able so far to keep the others "in line" by a mixture of economic incentives of its own and by stressing political and strategic concerns. This has worked with the neighbouring states and with the larger ones such as Central Asia, Russia and the Ukraine, and with Vietnam even though its largest investor is Taiwan.

Western states have upgraded the diplomatic status of those sent on leave to the technically unofficial missions in Taipei. Many have also allowed the unofficial Taipei representatives to enjoy diplomatic status, secure communication back home and access to government officials and even ministers. Beginning in 1991 Western trade and economic ministers have openly visited Taipei, including, in 1992, those from Britain, Germany and the United States. Taipei is actively seeking to build upon and extend these arrangements. To its chagrin Beijing is finding it increasingly difficult to stop what it clearly regards as an undesirable leakage. But Beijing's standing in world affairs is no longer what it was in the Cold War era despite its growing economic weight in the region and internationally. It is precisely its engagement with the international economy that makes Beijing's threats of unspecified retribution appear less credible; any exercise of such economic leverage that it may have would inevitably rebound against it and possibly damage its reputation as a reliable economic partner.

It is precisely in the critical security area that Beijing's reduced leverage is most evident. In 1981 it was able eventually to block the sale of submarines by the Netherlands to Taiwan. In 1992 by contrast it has found itself powerless to prevent separate agreements being signed by the United States and France to supply Taiwan with 150 F-16 and 30–50 Mirage-2000 aircraft that at a stroke increased the technological capability and defence capacity of Taiwan well beyond what is available to Beijing. Not only have these deals given even greater credibility to Taiwanese claims to be able to defend themselves successfully from attack by the mainland, but they also have profound implications for the management of the balance of power in the Asia-Pacific. Washington's willingness to back up its professed interest in regional stability through the supply of arms has to some extent answered any doubts about the American readiness to challenge a Chinese attempt to use its growing military power in pursuit of its claims for example in the South China Sea or across the Taiwan Straits. It is instructive that for the first time a European power was prepared to defy Beijing on an issue of this kind. It may be seen as an illustration of China's reduced leverage in the new post-Cold War era. The consequences of the diffusion of power and the fragmentation of polarity in the international system would appear to have confounded the expectations of China's leaders who thought that multipolarity would work to their advantage.

At the same time there is a danger that the leadership in Taiwan may overplay its international diplomacy, which is being increasingly driven by domestic factors that arise from the fragmentation of the KMT and the exigencies of electoral politics. A careful line has to be drawn between, on the one hand, easing into a position in which Beijing may gradually come to terms with a formula for unity that would allow Taiwan to enjoy in law the real independence which it currently enjoys in practice only, and on the other, making a unilateral move that would so provoke Beijing that whoever exercised leadership there would have no alternative but to take unilateral military countermeasures.

In the summer of 1993 the ROC government under pressure from the DPP launched a campaign to seek separate representation in the United Nations. Since the PRC can exercise a veto in the Security Council it would not be possible to gain membership without reaching an understanding with Beijing. The General Assembly refused to place the issue on its agenda in September 1993 even in the form of setting up a working party to study the question. Predictably, Beijing pronounced the issue dead and buried. President Lee Teng-hui, however, expressed his determination to raise it again. The new UN campaign which is pressed even more vigorously by the DPP has contributed to raising the international profile of Taiwan. It remains to be seen, however, whether it will proceed to deepen Taiwan's engagement with the international community by, for example, facilitating entry into UN affiliated bodies such as the World Bank and the IMF – perhaps along the lines of its membership of the Asia Development Bank. But what the campaign does illustrate is the facile logic of the argument that closer economic ties or even integration necessarily lead toward political integration.

*Conclusions*

The modalities of Greater China are driven by informal rather than formal institutions, but through the SEF and ARATS the two governments have found a way to provide what would otherwise be called necessary consular services. But the economic trends pointing to integration are not matched by their political counterparts. The foreign relations of Greater China point to a new capacity of Taiwan to accentuate its separateness from the mainland short of a formal declaration of independence. Hong Kong has been the main facilitator of the new arrangements, but notwithstanding its fundamental difference in status relative to the mainland and in its limited foreign relations, its treatment by the mainland both before and after 1997 will have profound implications for Taiwan and hence for Greater China.

Providing the affairs of Greater China are conducted with political prudence its future evolution would seem to depend on the continuing evolution of politics in the three centres. This would appear to be an example in international relations where modernity, prosperity and ultimately a new political order are best advanced by resisting the Weberian urge to formalize rules and regulations.

# Economic Integration within Greater China: Trade and Investment Flows Between China, Hong Kong and Taiwan*

## Robert F. Ash and Y. Y. Kueh

Economic integration is essentially a process of unification – the means whereby coherence is imposed upon previously separate, even disparate, geographical regions. It may be pursued as a domestic or international goal, although the simultaneous attainment of both may prove elusive. Recent efforts towards the creation of formal trans-national, regional economic identities, whether North American (NAFTA), European (EC) or Asian-Pacific (APEC), have sometimes been perceived as a threat to the establishment of a truly integrated *global* economy. By contrast, the remarkable degree of economic integration already achieved between southern China and Hong Kong (and, latterly, Taiwan) might ironically have a fissiparous effect on China's *domestic* economy. From this point of view, there is a danger that increasing economic integration within Greater China[1] could threaten China's national economic identity, or at least compel its re-definition.

Cultural and linguistic affinities have no doubt helped to facilitate the economic integration of China, Hong Kong and Taiwan. But international trade and foreign investment have been its most potent stimuli. The rapid development of trade has generated familiar static and dynamic gains, which have enhanced economic growth within the region. These have been complemented, especially for China, by the benefits of rapidly-expanding foreign investment. Overcoming their technological back-wardness is a cornerstone of developing countries' growth strategies and it is no coincidence that the Chinese government has increasingly used foreign investment to encourage productivity-enhancing technical pro-gress. After all, inflows of capital promise to obviate resource bottlenecks, especially capital shortages and skill deficiencies. China's willingness to accept such overseas participation, including foreign direct investment (FDI), in its domestic economic development is a measure of the real significance of its post-1978 open-door strategy.

The different resource endowments and levels of development of China, Hong Kong and Taiwan suggest how all stand to benefit from greater economic integration. Economic growth in Hong Kong and Taiwan has derived overwhelmingly from trade-orientated strategies,

* Some of the points raised at the workshop in Hong Kong in January 1993 have been incorporated into the revised version of this paper and we are grateful to participants, especially Joseph C. H. Chai, for their helpful observations. Y. Y. Kueh is also indebted to Yee-yen Chua, Li Fang and Sandy Chau for their assistance in obtaining valuable statistical materials relating to foreign investment.

1. For most purposes of this article we define "Greater China" in terms of the two southern provinces of Guangdong and Fujian, Hong Kong and Taiwan. Occasionally, however, our analysis extends to mainland China as a whole.

characterized by a decline in the export shares of resource-based goods in favour of those of labour and (later) capital-intensive products. Such developments have been accompanied by worsening shortages of land and labour, which have generated upwards pressure on rents and wages.

In China too the export sector, originally dominated by resource-based goods, has shifted towards the production of labour-intensive commodities. But land and labour remain plentiful and their accessibility has made the extension of Hong Kong and Taiwanese industrial facilities to the Chinese mainland an increasingly attractive proposition. For China, short of capital and technologically immature, such a relationship promises enormous benefits. This complementarity has generated an economic symbiosis between the constituent elements of Greater China.

Through their effects on resource allocation and their stimulus to technology transfer, the expansion of merchandise trade and investment has had a profound impact on the economies of Hong Kong, Taiwan and southern China. The same forces have generated new employment and production opportunities. They have also been the source of important structural changes, associated with the re-allocation of resources. Above all, they have caused accelerated economic growth, in recent times unmatched almost anywhere else in the world.

These considerations define the main themes of this article. In it we seek to assess, through an examination of the pattern and level of trade and investment flows, the extent to which Greater China has become economically integrated. We are also concerned to analyse some of the economic implications of this process. For reasons of convenience, trade and investment are treated separately. The reality is of course more complicated and less artificial. Each encourages and facilitates the other and it is the combined effect of both which makes their stimulus to economic growth so powerful.

*Merchandise Trade*

*Trade flows between China, Hong Kong and Taiwan.* The rapid expansion of China's foreign trade after 1978 is one of the most remarkable features of the impact of the reform programme (in this case, the open-door strategy). Between 1978 and 1991 China's merchandise trade grew, on average, by over 14 per cent per annum – almost twice as fast as global trade, marginally faster than Taiwan's, but a little more slowly than that of Hong Kong.[2] The outcome was that all three countries and regions dramatically increased their share of global trade during this period: China and Taiwan by almost 100 per cent each, and Hong Kong by almost 200 per cent. Imports and exports contributed about equally to

2. Global trade grew by 7.93% p.a., Taiwan's by 13.61%, Hong Kong's by 16.00%. See International Monetary Fund (IMF), *International Financial Statistics Yearbook, 1992* (hereafter *ISFY 1992*) (Washington, D.C.: IMF, 1992), pp. 108–115. Note that in 1992 China's merchandise trade expanded by a further 22% (State Statistical Bureau (hereafter SSB), *Zhongguo tongji zhaiyao 1993* (*Statistical Survey of China, 1993*) (Beijing: State Statistical Publishing House, 1993), p. 101.

Hong Kong's trade expansion, whereas the increasing contribution of China and Taiwan to world trade owed more to export expansion than to import growth.[3]

The historical context of the most recent (post-1978) expansion in Hong Kong's trade with China has been rehearsed elsewhere[4] and will not receive detailed consideration here. Suffice to say that between 1949 and the end of the 1970s, China's share of Hong Kong exports fell to a negligible level, although its role as an importer of Chinese goods remained significant. In the latter connection, it is worth recording that by the beginning of the 1970s Hong Kong's role as a channel for the re-export of Chinese goods had become insignificant.[5] In 1970, for example, the value of retained imports of Chinese products was 13 times higher than in the 1930s, whilst that of re-exported commodities was only 57 per cent more.[6] A striking feature of developments during the 1980s was a reversal of this position to one approximating that of the pre-war years.

Table 1 contains estimates of the average annual rate of growth of bilateral trade flows between 1980 and 1991. They highlight the process whereby Hong Kong and China have each become the other's most important trading partner.

Analysis of the data from which these estimates are derived suggests the critical contribution which China has made to Hong Kong's overall trade performance. For example, in 1978 exports[7] to China accounted for less than 1 per cent of Hong Kong's total exports. By 1983, the corresponding figure was 11.45 per cent, and by 1985 it had risen to 26.03 per cent. Thereafter, after a temporary decline, it remained (on average) in excess of 26 per cent. Without access to the Chinese market, Hong Kong's export growth in the 1980s would have been significantly slower,[8] although it would also have displayed a more sharply accelerating trend during the second half of the 1980s.

The symbiosis which has come to characterize the economic relationship between China and Hong Kong is highlighted in the British Colony's role as a re-distribution channel for goods passing through the territory.

3. IMF data for China reveal a reversal of the pattern of trade expansion in the first and second halves of the 1980s. In the earlier period, import growth sharply exceeded that of exports; latterly, the opposite was the case. In Hong Kong and Taiwan the second half of the decade witnessed an acceleration of growth of both exports and imports.

4. See, for example, Yun-wing Sung, *The China–Hong Kong Connection: The Key to China's Open Door Policy* (Cambridge: Cambridge University Press, 1991).

5. This role is a major complicating factor in compiling and interpreting trade statistics between China and the region. Goods flowing from (to) Hong Kong to (from) China comprise some which are part of a purely bilateral trade flow and others which have their origin or destination in a third country. It is important to distinguish between the two categories and to allow for a "re-export margin," added to goods which have passed through Hong Kong. In this article re-exported Chinese imports into Hong Kong are discounted on the basis of an assumed re-export margin of 25%; for commodities coming from other countries, a rate of 14% is thought more appropriate.

6. These estimates are derived from 1930s data, cited in Yun-wing Sung, *The China–Hong Kong Connection*, p. 19.

7. Including re-exports.

8. Calculations suggest that it would have declined by about 3 percentage points.

Table 1: **The Expansion of Trade Between Hong Kong and China (Average annual growth rate (%))**

| | HK exports to China | | | HK imports from China | | |
|---|---|---|---|---|---|---|
| | Total | Domestic | Re-exports | Total | Retained | Re-exports |
| 1980–91 | 31.86 | 32.03 | 31.79 | 23.57 | 8.96 | 32.98 |
| 1980–85 | 45.65 | 44.95 | 45.88 | 19.76 | 14.38 | 28.34 |
| 1985–91 | 20.36 | 21.26 | 20.06 | 26.74 | 4.44 | 36.83 |

*Sources:*
Hong Kong Census and Statistics Department, *Hong Kong Monthly Digest of Statistics*, various issues.

Domestic exports and re-exports from Hong Kong to China grew strongly, but in tandem throughout the period. By contrast, the global picture reveals slower export growth, but a differential performance in favour of re-exports. The share of re-exports in Hong Kong's total shipments to China remained stable at around 75 per cent throughout the 1980s, while the corresponding figure for countries other than China rose steadily from 30 to 70 per cent.[9]

Hong Kong's import profile shows that the growth of imports from China consistently outstripped that from the rest of the world.[10] Moreover, in contrast to the pattern of export growth, the expansion of imports – already strong during the first half of the 1980s – accelerated quite sharply after 1985. The increasing share of imports from China subsequently re-exported from Hong Kong is particularly striking. Between 1980 and 1985, this rose from 31 to 47 per cent; by 1991 it had reached an astonishing 86 per cent.[11] The true measure of this transformation is indicated by the changing ratio between re-exports of imports from China and from elsewhere: in 1978 it was 0.35:1.00, but by 1990 it had been reversed to 1.26:1.00.[12] Meanwhile, not only has the share of Chinese imports retained in Hong Kong declined, but – since 1988 – the absolute level of such shipments has also fallen.[13]

The growing importance of Hong Kong as a channel for the re-distribution of goods originating from, or destined for, China is the single most significant finding to emerge from Table 1. This fact, perhaps more than anything else, highlights the integration of the region into the southern Chinese economy.[14]

Between 1978 and 1983, Hong Kong's trade deficit vis-à-vis China

9. Hong Kong Census and Statistics Department, *Hong Kong Monthly Digest of Statistics* (hereafter *HKMDS*), January 1981, pp. 19–21, January 1987, pp. 19–22, and December 1991, pp. 19–22. By the beginning of 1993 re-exports accounted for 78% of Hong Kong's total exports (Hong Kong, *South China Morning Post* (hereafter *SCMP*), 14 May 1993, which also noted that "… the market in China for goods re-exported through Hong Kong is now almost double the size of the United States market …").

10. China's share of Hong Kong imports rose in every single year between 1978 and 1991, from 19% to 38%. *HKMDS*, January 1981, pp. 19–21, January 1987, pp. 19–22, and December 1991, pp. 19–22.

11. Re-exported imports to countries other than China showed a similar surge during the first half of the decade, but thereafter stabilized. *Ibid.*

12. To state it differently, in 1980 re-exports of Chinese imports accounted for 26% of all Hong Kong's re-exports; by 1990 the figure had risen to 56%.

13. The extent of the decline depends critically on assumptions made about the value of the re-export margin.

14. The very fact of such integration does, however, make interpretation of re-export data hazardous. Conventional practice regards any movement of goods across a border as trade. But cross-border shipments for processing purposes will lend an inflationary bias to measures of the volume of trade. Take the case of imported components from Taiwan, re-exported from Hong Kong to Guangdong, and subsequently shipped back in processed form (as Chinese exports) for re-export elsewhere (perhaps even to China itself!). Such a process will earn several separate entries in customs statistics, threatening to disguise the true value-added element embodied in each stage. The extent of the underlying interpretative problem is suggested by the finding that by 1991 the share of outward-processing trade in Hong Kong's gross imports from China had reached 67.6%.

increased from US$10.25 to 24.42 million.[15] A sharp but temporary reversal took place in 1984 and 1985 (the only post-1978 year in which Hong Kong enjoyed a bilateral surplus), but thereafter the deficit re-asserted itself and steadily increased to reach US$85.63 million in 1991. During the same period, Hong Kong consistently enjoyed a surplus in its trade with the rest of the world.[16] This was not always sufficient to nullify the bilateral deficit, the net result being that Hong Kong's global trade balance was sometimes in surplus, sometimes in deficit, without any clear pattern emerging.

Trade relations between Taiwan and the Chinese mainland were his-torically very close[17] and at the beginning of the 1930s, during the Japanese occupation of the island, its trade with the mainland accounted for half or more of total trade with countries other than Japan.[18] Such relations were interrupted after the removal of the Kuomintang govern-ment to Taiwan in 1949 and only officially resumed some three decades later. But as the estimates in Table 2 suggest, two-way trade subsequently expanded rapidly.[19]

The estimates leave no room for doubt about the dramatic nature of trade expansion across the Taiwan Straits during the 1980s and into the 1990s. At first it was subject to considerable instability, mainly because of strong annual fluctuations in Taiwanese exports to the mainland (only in 1985 did shipments in the opposite direction fail to record positive growth). Major increases between 1979 and 1981 gave way to absolute declines in 1982 and 1983, and recovery during 1984 and 1985 was again halted in 1986. In short, only since 1987 has relatively stable growth become apparent.

Until mid-1981 a no-tariff policy was a major incentive to Taiwan exporters to the PRC. But it also encouraged market saturation by inviting others to disguise their products as being of Taiwan origin. The sub-sequent abandonment of preferential treatment and imposition of stricter controls were the factors behind the negative growth of Taiwanese exports in 1982 and 1983. Recovery was, however, rapid and only momentarily interrupted in 1986, when import restrictions were

15. These and other estimates cited in this paragraph are derived from statistics in *HKMDS*.

16. It increased from US$1.11 to 72.54 million between 1978 and 1991.

17. In the early 18th century some 3,000 small-scale boats plied across the Taiwan Straits, carrying large quantities of sugar and rice to the mainland in exchange for cotton cloth, silk, paper and timber. See Zhou Shulian *et al.* (eds.), *Haixia liangan ji Xianggang jingji hezuo qianjing* (*Prospects for Economic Co-operation across the Taiwan Straits and with Hong Kong*) (Beijing: Economic Management Publishing House, 1991), p. 156.

18. *Ibid.* pp. 156–57.

19. The estimates are "suggestive" in the sense that they are derived from data which only show *indirect* trade between Taiwan and the Chinese mainland, conducted through Hong Kong. Such trade dominates transactions across the Taiwan Straits, but also underestimates their true extent by excluding indirect trade through other countries (for example, Japan and Singapore), as well as genuinely direct – but minor – trade with coastal mainland ports. See Gao Chang, Yan Zongda *et al.* (eds.), *Liangan jingji jiaoliu jin xiankuang ji fazhan chushi yanjiu* (*A Study of Economic Exchanges Across the Taiwan Straits: the Current Situation and Prospects for Future Developments*) (Taipei: Zhonghua Institute for Economic Research, 1992), pp. 14–16.

**Table 2: Changing Trends in Trade Between Taiwan and the Chinese Mainland: Indirect Trade Through Hong Kong**

| | Taiwan exports | | | Taiwan imports | | |
|---|---|---|---|---|---|---|
| | Annual growth rate of global exports (%) | Annual growth rate of exports to PRC (%) | Exports to PRC as % global exports | Annual growth rate of global imports (%) | Annual growth rate of imports from PRC (%) | Imports from PRC as % global imports |
| 1980–91 | 12.25 | 26.90 | 3.41 | 10.55 | 24.22 | 0.99 |
| 1980–85 | 8.78 | 28.08 | 1.61 | 0.36 | 7.79 | 0.48 |
| 1985–91 | 15.14 | 25.92 | 4.09 | 19.04 | 37.92 | 1.17 |

*Sources:*
HKMDS, various issues; and *IFSY 1992*, pp. 111 and 113.

introduced in an effort to halt the sharp decline in China's foreign exchange reserves.

For the post-1980 period as a whole, the average annual rate of growth of Taiwanese imports from the Chinese mainland almost matched that of exports to the PRC. However, legal restraints on such imports, especially during the early 1980s, were responsible for the much slower rate of expansion during the first half of the decade.

Table 2 also quantifies the increasing involvement of Taiwan and the PRC in each other's overall trade after 1980. At the start of the decade, mainland exports accounted for 1.22 per cent of Taiwan's global exports, the corresponding figure for imports being less than 0.5 per cent. By 1991 these figures had risen to 6.13 and 1.6 per cent respectively.[20] From the mainland's perspective, Taiwan's share in total exports rose more modestly from 0.43 to 1.57 per cent during 1980–91.

The indirect nature of trade between Taiwan and the PRC highlights the paramount role which Hong Kong has played in the evolution of bilateral trade relations. That it will continue to do this is suggested by the finding that in 1992 almost 49 per cent of shipments from Taiwan to Hong Kong were destined for the Chinese mainland, and 29.5 per cent of goods exported to Taiwan from Hong Kong originated in the PRC.[21]

Since 1980 Taiwan has maintained a favourable balance in its indirect trade with the PRC, the second half of the decade witnessing a consistent increase in its surplus. Indeed, between 1985 and 1991, Taiwan's cross-Straits surplus rose from 8 to 27 per cent of its global surplus.[22] Such estimates are one measure of the extent to which Taiwan's remarkable record in accumulating foreign exchange reserves has increasingly become linked to the expansion of trade with its neighbour.[23]

*Measuring trade intensity between China, Hong Kong and Taiwan.* Estimates of the trade intensity ratio (TIR) between two countries provide a formal measure of the changing strength of their trade relationship – the extent to which each is becoming more (or less) dependent upon the other.[24] A value of TIR greater than unity is significant in the sense that the share of country A's exports to country B in the former's export portfolio is higher than B's import share as a proportion of aggregated

20. Notice that in 1991 alone the PRC's share of all Taiwan's exports rose from 4.89% to 6.13%.

21. Hong Kong, *Ta Kung Pao* (*Ta Kung Daily*) (hereafter *TKP*), 30 December 1992.

22. Sources as in Table 4.

23. Since the late 1980s Taiwan's trade balance has also improved with ASEAN countries, but deteriorated against the United States. The changing pattern is not coincidental. On the one hand, growing American protectionism has forced Taiwan to diversify its export markets; on the other, increasing FDI by Taiwanese entrepreneurs in both the Chinese mainland and ASEAN countries has given added impetus to trade expansion with these countries.

24. TIR is given by the following formula:

$$TIR = X_{ij}/X_i \div M_J/M_W$$

where $X_{ij}$ are the exports of country i to country J; $X_i$ are the total exports of country i; $M_J$ are the total imports of country J; and $M_W$ are global imports.

Table 3: **TIR Estimates: China, Hong Kong and Taiwan**

|      | China–Hong Kong | | China–Taiwan | |
| --- | --- | --- | --- | --- |
|      | *With China as exporter* | *With Hong Kong as exporter* | *With China as exporter* | *With Taiwan as exporter* |
| 1978 | 24.43 | 0.62  | 0.53 | 0.0005 |
| 1980 | 20.92 | 6.23  | 0.43 | 1.20 |
| 1985 | 16.62 | 11.41 | 0.39 | 1.41 |
| 1989 | 17.68 | 13.21 | 0.64 | 2.24 |
| 1990 | —     | —     | 0.78 | 3.20 |
| 1991 | —     | —     | 0.90 | 3.48 |

*Sources:*
  *HKMDS*, various issues; *IFSY 1992*, pp. 111 and 113; United Nations, Economic and Social Commission for Asia and the Pacific, *Statistical Yearbook for Asia and the Pacific, 1991*, pp. 85 and 127–28.

global imports. The larger the value of TIR, the stronger the trade links between any two countries.

Table 3 sets out TIR estimates in selected years for China, Hong Kong and Taiwan in the twin contexts of Sino-Hong Kong and Sino-Taiwanese merchandise trade. The figures highlight some of the implications of China's implementation of an open-door strategy after 1978. They suggest that from a Chinese export perspective, trade with Hong Kong has remained "significant,"[25] albeit – especially in the early reform years – at a declining rate. From the Hong Kong perspective, the open-door policy had a marked impact, the TIR rising sharply up to the mid-1980s and then stabilizing somewhat.

If, however, re-exports of Chinese goods are excluded, the calculations show China's TIR to have fallen more sharply and consistently.[26] This would seem to suggest that an increasingly small proportion of exports to Hong Kong was retained in the territory. The results of similar calculations based on Hong Kong as the exporting region are much more closely in line with those in Table 3 and indicate an increasingly important role for the territory as direct and indirect supplier of goods to China after 1978.[27]

In the wake of the open-door strategy, China's trade ties with Taiwan rapidly assumed significance. But it is noteworthy that this process was driven more by the expansion of exports from Taiwan than from the PRC. With China (PRC) as the exporting country, the value of TIR has not yet reached unity, although if recent trends are maintained attainment of this level cannot be long delayed.[28]

25. That is, TIR $\geq$ 1. See above.
26. From 18.9 (1980) to 8.52 (1989).
27. By the end of the 1980s such shipments included a large proportion of goods destined for outward processing.
28. Also relevant are data cited in *TKP*, 31 May 1993.

*The changing composition of merchandise trade.* The export experiences of the countries in North-east Asia, including the constituent regions of Greater China, reveal a common pattern. In the early stages of economic development, exports derive largely from natural resource-based products. Only later is there an increasing role for labour-intensive manufactured goods – and ultimately for capital-intensive, high-technology commodities.[29]

The decline in the share of Chinese exports retained in Hong Kong is reflected in the changing structure of bilateral trade. One contributory factor has been the fall in food exports from the mainland, consequent upon rising per capita income.[30] More generally, Hong Kong consumers' perception of Chinese goods as cheap, but inferior in quality and design, has encouraged demand to shift towards other overseas sources of goods (especially manufactures).[31] Meanwhile, the share of re-exported Chinese goods has been rising. Between 1979 and 1987, for example, the ratios of retained to re-exported Chinese crude materials, chemicals and manufactures were reversed in favour of re-exports.[32]

Hong Kong's role as a direct supplier of goods to China has expanded markedly since 1978. The fact that domestic exports of producer goods (especially machinery and transport equipment) have outstripped those of consumer goods makes Hong Kong's trade with China unique and reflects the increasingly important role of Hong Kong-based industrial operations on the Chinese mainland.[33] Thus, the expanding share of Chinese imports of Hong Kong-produced machinery and components highlights the growing importance of outward-processing activities in southern China. This emerging pattern is further evidence of a cross-border economic symbiosis and growing regional integration.

Similar factors have determined the changing composition of Taiwan's exports to China. During 1985–90, for example, these were dominated by machinery, transport equipment and industrial materials for manufactur-

29. Between 1980 and 1991 the share of primary products in China's total exports fell from 50.2% to 22.5%, whilst that of manufactured goods (mainly produced by labour-intensive methods) rose from 49.8% to 77.5% (SSB, *Zhongguo shangye waijing tongji ziliao, 1952–1988* (*Statistical Materials Relating to China's Internal and External Trade, 1952–1988*) (hereafter *ZGSYWJTJZL*) (Beijing: State Statistical Publishing House, 1990), p. 430; and State Statistical Bureau, *Zhongguo tongji nianjian, 1992* (*Chinese Statistical Yearbook, 1992*) (hereafter *ZGTJNJ*) (Beijing: State Statistical Publishing House, 1992), p. 630). Since 1970 the share of labour-intensive manufactures in *Hong Kong's* exports has fallen steadily (e.g. from 75% to 55% during 1970–87) in favour of an expansion of capital-intensive goods (up from 21% to 41%) (data cited in Ross Garnaut, *Australia and the Northeast Asian Ascendancy* (Canberra: Australian Government Publishing Service, 1989), p. 54). The same period saw the simultaneous expansion of the export shares of labour and capital-intensive products in *Taiwan*, although it is only in recent years that the latter category has come to predominate (*ibid.*).

30. During the 1980s the proportion of total Chinese food exports retained in Hong Kong fell by more than half.

31. Ironically, more and more goods labelled "Made in China" have in fact been produced by subsidiaries of Hong Kong parent companies, sited in Guangdong.

32. Yun-wing Sung, *The China–Hong Kong Connection*, ch. 7.

33. A kind of technological complementarity is also evident. That Hong Kong's textile machinery does not embody the most up-to-date technology makes it appropriate for use in labour-intensive operations, such as China's resource-endowment favours.

ing purposes,[34] with the contribution of chemicals and related products also expanding rapidly.[35] These are precisely the goods needed by the subsidiaries of parent Taiwan companies, located in China. The simultaneous acceleration of exports and FDI from Taiwan to the Chinese mainland after 1987 suggests that the cross-Straits export expansion has been no less intimately related to investment considerations than in Hong Kong.

The composition of Chinese exports to Taiwan has been limited by government restrictions emanating from Taipei.[36] But available evidence points to the declining importance of agricultural products, fuels and raw materials at the expense of industrial materials for manufacturing, machinery and transport equipment, and miscellaneous manufactures.[37]

*The role of Guangdong and Fujian in trade integration within Greater China.* Hong Kong and Taiwan entrepreneurial activity has been heavily concentrated in Guangdong and Fujian provinces and the nature and level of the trade flows analysed above have been critically influenced by the process of economic integration between Hong Kong, Taiwan and southern China. This process has dictated the changing composition of shipments of goods to and from the Chinese mainland, not least as outward processing activities have come to dominate the operations of Hong Kong and Taiwanese manufacturers in China.[38]

The economic rationale of the integration of Greater China lies essentially in the complementarity of factor endowments throughout the region. In recent years, the continued economic expansion of Hong Kong and Taiwan has been constrained by shortages of land and labour – and associated pressures on rents and wages. In contrast to unemployment rates in these regions of well under 2 per cent,[39] the labour force in Guangdong and Fujian was growing, respectively, by 2.85 and 3.35 per cent during the second half of the 1980s.[40] Such figures mean access to

34. Although their relative importance did decline, in 1990 such products still accounted for 76.69% of Taiwan's exports to China.

35. The share of chemicals and related exports rose from 2.24% to 12.65% between 1985 and 1990.

36. See Maruyama Nobuo (ed.), *Kanan keizaiken: Hirakareta chiiki shugi (The South China Economic Region)* (Tokyo: Institute of Developing Economies, 1992), pp. 299–302 for a useful summary of cross-Straits trade policies emerging from Beijing and Taipei between 1977 and 1991.

37. As a proportion of total PRC exports to Taiwan, goods under SITC 0 and 2 fell from 74.93% to 31.85% (1985–90), whilst those under SITC 6, 7 and 8 increased from 13.39% to 54.26%.

38. Notice too that as Taiwan has become increasingly involved in southern China, its investment in Hong Kong has risen dramatically (in 1991 Hong Kong was the destination of 43% of all Taiwanese FDI in Asia). This sharp rise no doubt reflects the need to make appropriate servicing arrangements in Hong Kong for the operations of subsidiary companies in China.

39. See, for example, Alan J. Day (ed.), *The Annual Register, 1992* (Harlow, Essex: Longman Group, 1991), p. 360; and British Broadcasting Corporation, *Summary of World Broadcasts, Part 3: The Far East (Weekly Economic Report)*, FE/W0244, 19 August 1992, p. A/1.

40. SSB, *Quanguo gesheng zizhiqu zhixiashi lishi tongji ziliao huibian, 1949–89 (Compilation of Historical Statistics for Every Province, Autonomous Region and Directly-Administered Municipality in China, 1949–89)* (Beijing: State Statistical Publishing House, 1990), pp. 434 and 618. These figures imply an average addition of some 400,000

cheap labour and land for overseas entrepreneurs who are prepared to re-site their operations in southern China.

Guangdong and Fujian's trade growth after 1978 was significantly faster than that of China as a whole, and of Hong Kong and Taiwan.[41] Such rapid expansion was reflected in an increasing contribution by both provinces to China's overall trade, even though Guangdong's share of national exports only reattained the previous peak level (1970) in 1991.[42] Their contribution to China's trade balance throughout the 1980s was also positive and significant.[43] Meanwhile, one corollary of these regional developments was the spectacular decline of Shanghai's export role in domestic trade, its contribution to all exports falling from 23.55 to 7.98 per cent between 1980 and 1991.[44]

Such figures set the trade performances of Guangdong and Fujian in a national context. They do not, however, show the debt which they owed to evolving relationships with Hong Kong and Taiwan. Table 4 seeks to encapsulate these emerging trade relations. Between 1980 and 1991 Guangdong's exports to Hong Kong grew by 21.2 per cent annually – a performance which owed most to accelerated expansion after 1985.[45] The

---

*footnote continued*

(Fujian) and 800,000 (Guangdong) labour recruits each year. Notice too that secondary and tertiary-sector employment growth in both provinces has easily outstripped that of the primary sector (*ibid.*).

41. Guangdong recorded an average annual rate of growth of 20.27% during 1978–91 (Guangdong Provincial Statistical Bureau, *Guangdong tongji nianjian 1992* (*Guangdong Province Statistical Yearbook 1992*) (hereafter *GDTJNJ 1992*) (Beijing: State Statistical Publishing House, 1992), p. 342); the corresponding figure for Fujian was even higher (Fujian Provincial Statistical Bureau, *Fujian tongji nianjian 1992* (*Fujian Province Statistical Yearbook 1992*) (hereafter *FJTJNJ 1992*) (Beijing: State Statistical Publishing House, 1992)). Fujian's faster trade growth needs to be set against a much smaller base level than in Guangdong. Compare these figures with the estimates for Hong Kong and Taiwan presented earlier (see n. 2).

42. In 1970 Guangdong accounted for 19.2% of all China's exports; in 1991 the corresponding figure was 19.0% (*GDTJNJ 1992*, p. 342 and *ZGSYWJTJZL*, p. 502). Note that preliminary estimates indicate that Guangdong exports grew by a further 32% in 1992 (*TKP*, 1 January 1993).

43. To cite just one example: available evidence suggests that without Guangdong and Fujian, China's trade surplus in 1990 would have been reduced by 70%!

44. During the same period Shanghai's share of imports rose from 1.2% to 3.6%. By way of comparison, Guangdong's share of China's trade increased from 1.78% to 13.34% (imports), and from 12.11% to 19.03% (exports). The corresponding increases in Fujian were from 0.71% to 2.21% (imports), and from 2.01% to 4.07% (exports). (National data from *ZGSYWJTJZL*, pp. 432–33 and 438–39; Shanghai data from Shanghai Municipal Statistical Bureau, *Shanghai tongji nianjian 1992* (*Shanghai Statistical Yearbook, 1992*) (Beijing: State Statistical Publishing House, 1992), pp. 349 and 352. The sources for Guangdong and Fujian estimates are shown at Table 4, below. However, these figures conceal the fact that the shares of both Guangdong and Fujian in total exports declined between 1980 and 1985, thereafter rising in a spectacular fashion. Given the more consistent downward trend in Shanghai, it is clear that during the early 1980s the export performance of other parts of China outstripped that of all three regions. In this respect, it is noteworthy that in 1985 *Liaoning's* export share was the highest in the country (19.34%), even though just three years later its contribution had almost halved. Shandong was another province which experienced a significant relative decline (*ZGSYWJTJZL*, p. 510).

45. Average growth during 1985–91 was 27.94% p.a. The estimates show imports to have grown by 17.44% p.a. during 1985–91.

result was to raise Hong Kong's share in Guangdong's exports to so dominant a position that by 1991 such shipments constituted 85 per cent of total provincial exports and accounted for more than one-third of all exports from *China* to Hong Kong. This remarkable expansion also brought about a dramatic improvement in Guangdong's trade balance, the figures in Table 4 indicating that a minor deficit in 1985 was transformed into a healthy surplus by the end of the decade.[46]

Hong Kong also became an important destination for goods from Fujian during the 1980s. During the first half of the decade, exports to the British colony grew by almost 11 per cent p.a., but this figure accelerated to 28 per cent between 1985 and 1991.[47] This differential performance no doubt reflects the availability of new markets in Taiwan, as restrictions on cross-Straits trade were relaxed and entrepreneurs increasingly exploited new investment opportunities on the Chinese mainland. The same factors are no doubt responsible for the marked impact which Hong Kong and, latterly, Taiwan, had on Fujian imports. Taken at face value, the figures in Table 4 suggest that Hong Kong's share of provincial imports doubled between 1980 and 1985, but thereafter stabilized; by contrast, imports from Taiwan grew by more than 34 per cent annually during the next six years, their share rising almost three-and-a-half fold.[48]

The economic symbiosis inherent in integration counsels caution in interpreting these figures. Shipments of commodities between the Chinese mainland, and Hong Kong and Taiwan do not all derive from self-contained, indigenous activities. Rather, they have increasingly reflected the integrative impact of FDI and outward-processing operations. Such considerations make it desirable to distinguish between conventional merchandise trade and commodity movements related to FDI (*sanzi*[49]) or outward processing and compensation trade (*sanlai yibu*[50]). The significance of these distinctions is highlighted in Table 5.

These figures highlight the changing structural composition of the two provinces' exports and imports and thereby suggest the impact of regional integration with Hong Kong and Taiwan upon their foreign trade profiles. In the immediate wake of the new open-door policy, for example, virtually all Guangdong's exports remained conventional "merchandise exports" (*maoyi chukou*).[51] Their share fell from 96 to 83 per cent during the first half of the 1980s, but thereafter declined much more rapidly to

46. Guangdong's export surplus vis-à-vis Hong Kong almost doubled in two years, rising from US$2,960 to $5,290 million between 1989 and 1991.

47. For 1985–90 the corresponding figure is over 33% p.a.

48. Average annual growth of imports from Hong Kong was only 14.23% during 1985–91, compared with 42.90% during 1980–85.

49. This phrase (literally "three foreign-funded") refers to the activities of equity and contractual joint ventures and firms wholly under foreign ownership.

50. That is, processing operations based on the provision of raw materials, assembly operations based on the supply of components, and manufacturing based on supplied designs (*sanlai*); and exchange through the practice of compensation trade (*yibu*).

51. The difference between total exports and those associated with commissioned processing, compensation trade and FDI ventures provides a measure of merchandise exports.

Table 4: Trade Flows Between Guangdong, Fujian, Hong Kong and Taiwan

| | 1980 | | 1985 | | 1989 | | 1990 | | 1991 | |
|---|---|---|---|---|---|---|---|---|---|---|
| | Value US$ m. | % | Value US$ m. | % | Value US$ m. | % | Value US$ m. | % | Value US$ m. | % |
| *Guangdong* | | | | | | | | | | |
| Total exports | 2,194.72 | 100 | 2,952.67 | 100 | 8,167.67 | 100 | 10,560.24 | 100 | 13,687.87 | 100 |
| Hong Kong | 1,126.80 | 51.4 | 2,168.20 | 73.4 | 6,514.32 | 79.8 | 8,709.11 | 82.5 | 11,593.06 | 84.7 |
| Taiwan | — | — | — | — | 6.96 | 0.1 | 8.95 | 0.1 | 36.52 | 0.3 |
| Total imports | 356.12 | 100 | 2,426.64 | 100 | 4,831.21 | 100 | 5,748.88 | 100 | 8,510.09 | 100 |
| Hong Kong | — | — | 2,210.64 | 91.1 | 3,554.17 | 73.6 | 4,152.16 | 72.2 | 6,294.13 | 74.0 |
| Taiwan | — | — | — | — | 28.44 | 0.6 | 53.78 | 0.9 | 134.11 | 1.6 |
| *Fujian* | | | | | | | | | | |
| Total exports | 363.66 | 100 | 491.48 | 100 | 1,661.77 | 100 | 2,238.13 | 100 | 2,925.67 | 100 |
| Hong Kong | 116.76 | 32.1 | 200.76 | 40.8 | 761.69 | 45.8 | 1,065.35 | 47.6 | 1,075.58 | 36.8 |
| Total imports | 141.77 | 100 | 599.90 | 100 | 735.31 | 100 | 933.24 | 100 | 1,407.76 | 100 |
| Hong Kong | 37.25 | 26.3 | 318.23 | 53.1 | 373.23 | 50.8 | 459.94 | 49.3 | 747.23 | 53.1 |
| Taiwan | — | — | 13.20 | 2.2 | 20.41 | 2.8 | 41.58 | 4.5 | 103.84 | 7.4 |

*Note:*

The figures shown here are based on export and import trade statistics. Notice that a different set of estimates of Fujian's total exports and imports are available from "customs statistics," as follows: exports: 1989 – 1,828.36, 1990 – 2,448.82, 1991 – 3,147.46; imports: 1989 – 1,594.45, 1990 – 1,897.18, 1991 – 2,608.51.

*Sources:*

*Guangdong. GDTJNJ 1992*, pp. 343–45 (1980, 1985, 1990 and 1991); *GDTJNJ 1991*, pp. 303–305 (1989).

*Fujian.* Export and import trade statistics: *FJTJNJ 1992*, p. 330 (1980–85, 1989, 1990 and 1991) and pp. 332–33 (Hong Kong, exports and imports, 1980, 1985, 1989, 1990 and 1991; and Taiwan, imports, 1985, 1990 and 1991).

Customs statistics: *FJTJNJ 1991*, p. 314; *FJTJNJ 1992*, p. 337.

Table 5: FDI-Related Exports and Imports of Guangdong and Fujian Provinces

| | 1980 | | 1985 | | 1989 | | 1990 | | 1991 | |
|---|---|---|---|---|---|---|---|---|---|---|
| | Value US$ m. | % | Value US$ m. | % | Value US$ m. | % | Value US$ m. | % | Value US$ m. | % |
| *Guangdong* | | | | | | | | | | |
| Total exports | 2,194.72 | 100 | 2,952.67 | 100 | 8,167.67 | 100 | 10,560.24 | 100 | 13,687.87 | 100 |
| Commissioned processing | 82.33 | 3.8 | 272.50 | 9.2 | 578.17 | 7.1 | 583.32 | 5.5 | 799.72 | 5.8 |
| Compensation trade | 6.65 | 0.3 | 8.70 | 0.3 | 62.67 | 0.8 | 77.78 | 0.7 | 95.06 | 0.7 |
| FDI ventures | — | — | 221.16 | 7.5 | 2,276.71 | 27.9 | 3,723.83 | 35.3 | 5,327.48 | 38.9 |
| Total imports | 356.12 | 100 | 2,426.22 | 100 | 4,831.21 | 100 | 5,748.88 | 100 | 8,510.09 | 100 |
| FDI ventures | — | — | 336.56 | 13.9 | 1,950.92 | 40.4 | 3,297.44 | 57.4 | 4,513.02 | 53.0 |
| *Fujian* | | | | | | | | | | |
| Total exports | — | — | — | — | 1,828.36 | 100 | 2,448.82 | 100 | 3,147.46 | 100 |
| Commissioned processing | — | — | — | — | 178.07 | 9.7 | 208.54 | 8.5 | 293.31 | 9.3 |
| Compensation trade | — | — | — | — | 12.49 | 0.7 | 11.29 | 0.5 | 5.53 | 0.2 |
| FDI ventures | — | — | — | — | 687.14 | 37.6 | 1,115.52 | 45.6 | 1,376.95 | 43.8 |

Table 5: Continued.

| | 1980 | | 1985 | | 1989 | | 1990 | | 1991 | |
|---|---|---|---|---|---|---|---|---|---|---|
| | Value US$ m. | % | Value US$ m. | % | Value US$ m. | % | Value US$ m. | % | Value US$ m. | % |
| Total imports | — | — | — | — | 1,594.45 | 100 | 1,897.18 | 100 | 2,608.51 | 100 |
| Commissioned processing | — | — | — | — | 163.54 | 10.3 | 161.87 | 8.5 | 251.25 | 9.6 |
| Compensation trade | — | — | — | — | 9.90 | 0.6 | 4.20 | 0.2 | 5.04 | 0.2 |
| FDI ventures | — | — | — | — | 168.35 | 10.6 | 237.63 | 12.5 | 282.80 | 10.8 |
| Export processing | — | — | — | — | 584.25 | 36.6 | 895.97 | 47.2 | 1,278.55 | 49.0 |

*Notes:*

*Guangdong.* "Commissioned processing" is a translation of the Chinese phrase *lailiao jiagong*. It refers to the processing (*jiagong*) of materials from outside (*lailiao*) for re-export. This category usually includes assembly (*zhuanpei*) of product parts which have been similarly imported. Export through "compensation trade" (*buchang maoyi*) involves not only the provision of raw materials, semi-finished manufactures and/or parts, but also the supply of machinery and equipment, to be "compensated" for by reducing or relinquishing processing fees or land rents. Note that the term *sanlai yibu* embraces both *lailiao jiagong* and *buchang maoyi*. "FDI ventures" refer to the activities of the "three foreign-funded enterprises" (*sanzi qiye*): equity, contractual and wholly-foreign-owned ventures. Because of Chinese restrictions on domestic sales, the bulk of these enterprises' output is destined for the world market. A large proportion of exports generated through "commissioned processing" or "compensation trade" also involves FDI firms.

*Fujian.* "Export processing" translates the Chinese phrase *jinliao jiagong* (literally "imported materials for processing"). The term is clearly similar to *lailiao jiagong*, although it is not clear whether the activities under this heading constitute a broader category, which also embraces "commissioned processing." "FDI equipment" refers to imports via FDI of machinery and equipment as part of their investment.

*Sources:*

As Table 4. Estimates for Fujian are derived from customs statistics.

reach a mere 55 per cent in 1991. Initially, the role of exports generated through *sanzi* funding took second place to those facilitated by *sanlai yibu* activities. But under the impact of China's strategy of export-orientated foreign investment, this relationship changed dramatically during the second half of the decade. Increased capital inflows were reflected in a rapid growth of *sanzi* exports (on average, by 53 per cent p.a. between 1985 and 1991). As a result, by the beginning of the 1990s foreign sales of FDI-related products accounted for more than a third of all Guangdong's exports.[52] (On the import side the dominance of FDI-related activities emerges even more dramatically.) Although a detailed breakdown of Fujian's exports and imports is only available for the most recent years, the evidence points to the emergence of a similar pattern.[53]

The symbiotic economic relationship between the constituent parts of Greater China is well reflected in their trading position vis-à-vis the United States. Figure 1 seeks to illustrate this by showing the changing trade surpluses of Hong Kong, Taiwan and China (including Greater China) with the United States between 1981 and 1991.[54] It is clear that since the mid-1980s China's trade surplus with the United States has risen dramatically. By contrast, during 1987–91 the large surpluses enjoyed by Hong Kong and – especially – Taiwan declined no less significantly. There can be no doubt that these contrary trends precisely reflect the accelerated relocation, since the middle of the 1980s, of export-orientated Hong Kong and Taiwanese firms to mainland China (above all, the Pearl River Delta).[55]

The impact of the relocation of Hong Kong manufacturing activities in China, and associated "outward processing" operations for re-export through Hong Kong, is suggested by the estimates in Table 6. The figures reveal that between 1989 and the first half of 1992 some 71–77 per cent of Hong Kong's exports to China were destined for outward processing and related to FDI ventures. On the conservative assumption that the processing fee (including transport costs) constituted 20 per cent of the value of exports to China, the finished manufactures accounted, on average, for 68 per cent of Hong Kong's total exports to the United States during the same period. This clearly reflects the transfer of Hong Kong manufacturing enterprises to mainland China during recent years.

The evidence presented in this section suggests that the open-door

---

52. No doubt the figure would be even higher if provincial exports to Hong Kong alone were considered.

53. The available evidence also suggests that Taiwan's relationship with southern China has mirrored that of Hong Kong. Since shipments between Guangdong and Fujian, and Taiwan must formally pass through Hong Kong, the extent of Taiwan's linkages with the two Chinese provinces is partly concealed within the British Colony's own statistical records.

54. *TKP*, 1 January 1993, stated that China's trade balance with the USA had declined by 5% in 1992. However, another Hong Kong source subsequently revealed that the American deficit had further widened during the early months of 1993 (*SCMP*, 20 May 1993).

55. In the context of the accelerated re-location of manufacturing activity on the Chinese mainland, specific mention should be made of the Plaza Accord (1985), which forced Japan and Asian NIEs to appreciate their currencies against the U.S. dollar and thereby encouraged large-scale transfers of manufacturing operations within the Asia-Pacific Region.

Table 6: **The Implications of the Re-Location of Hong Kong Manufacturing Enterprises in China**

| | Hong Kong exports to China (US$ m.) | Hong Kong exports to China for outward processing (US$ m.) | % | Hong Kong exports to United States (US$ m.) |
|---|---|---|---|---|
| 1988 | 38,043 | — | — | 72,884 |
| 1989 | 43,272 | 32,262 | 74.6 | 72,162 |
| 1990 | 47,470 | 36,418 | 76.7 | 66,370 |
| 1991 | 54,404 | 40,369 | 74.2 | 62,870 |
| 1992 | | | | |
| Jan.–June | 28,499 | 20,323 | 71.3 | 28,038 |

*Source:*
*TKP*, 30 December 1992.

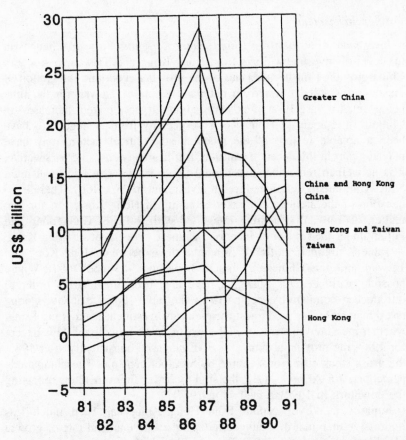

Figure 1: **Annual Trade Surpluses of Greater China with the United States 1981–91**

Sources:
1981–90: Ian K. Perkin, "Greater China trade area surplus with the U.S." in *SCMP*, 29 January 1992; Hong Kong and China 1991: *SCMP*, 21 February 1992; Taiwan 1991: *Taiwan Statistical Data Book 1992*.

strategy has facilitated the establishment of a framework to accommodate increasing involvement by Hong Kong and Taiwan entrepreneurs in the southern Chinese economy. The outcome has been to alter both the level and pattern of trade within Greater China. Especially striking are the changes which have taken place since the mid-1980s and which at present show no sign of abating. Such changes have of course had important implications for economic growth and structural change throughout the region. Before examining these implications in greater detail, however, further consideration must be given to the nature of investment flows from Hong Kong and Taiwan to Guangdong and Fujian.

*Foreign Investment*[56]

*Investment flows between China, Hong Kong and Taiwan.* Changes in the level of investment flows from Hong Kong and Taiwan to southern China provide a further measure of the growing economic integration of the region. Capital flows from mainland China to Taiwan for the time being remain largely non-existent, although accelerated increases in Chinese investment in Hong Kong – especially from Guangdong – have been a notable feature of the recent past. Political factors may have played a part in this recent expansion. But from an economic perspective, it is as well to remember that capital flows from Japan and the United States continue to dominate foreign investment in the colony. There is no question of the archetypal market economy of Hong Kong (or, for that matter, of Taiwan) becoming integrated with those of Guangdong and Fujian under the impact of increased Chinese investment in Hong Kong.

Table 7 summarizes trends in capital flows between Hong Kong and Taiwan and the Chinese mainland between 1985 and 1991. Where possible, estimates for Shanghai have also been included in order to introduce a comparative perspective. The table shows that Guangdong has remained by far the largest recipient of investment from Hong Kong, whether measured in terms of FDI flows or, more broadly, of AFI. Except for 1987, the provincial intake of FDI increased consistently after 1985, the gross stock rising on average by 51.2 per cent p.a. The comparable percentage for AFI was 47.1, the slightly lower figure perhaps reflecting the downturn in 1990 as well as in 1987.

Fujian's intake of capital from Hong Kong has been much less impressive than that of Guangdong (*cf.* an average annual rate of growth of AFI of 41 per cent). It is telling too that the cumulative level of AFI into Fujian from Hong Kong during 1985–91 was little more than half that received by the tiny enclave of Shenzhen Special Economic Zone (SEZ).[57] But Fujian's profile still compares favourably with most other FDI/AFI recipient provinces, including – see Table 4 – Shanghai.

After 1985 Hong Kong investment in China as a whole grew even more rapidly than in Guangdong.[58] Such a comparison is, however, misleading in at least one important respect. As a pioneer in the search for foreign capital, Guangdong was by 1985 already well-established as a recipient of investment from the British colony. Subsequently an increasing number of eastern coastal provinces emerged as competitors for the same pool of capital.[59] Even so, in 1991 Guangdong still accounted for

56. For a detailed analysis of quantitative trends in foreign investment and its distribution amongst "economically opened coastal areas" in China, as well as consideration of its impact on output and income growth, see Y. Y. Kueh, "Foreign investment and economic change in China," *The China Quarterly*, No. 132 (September 1992), pp. 637–690.

57. But in terms of AFI stock growth, Fujian and Shenzhen are almost identical.

58. The figures for investment in all China are 53.2% p.a. (FDI stock) and 55.2% p.a. (AFI stock).

59. For an elaboration of this point, see Kueh, "Foreign investment and economic change," pp. 652–55. See also *TKP*, 10 February 1993, which argues that although the Pearl River Delta remains the principal destination of Hong Kong investment, signs of a northward extension of capital flows (to Shanghai, Jiangsu, Zhejiang, etc.) are also in evidence.

Table 7: Shares of Guangdong, Fujian, Shanghai and All China in Realized Foreign Investment from Hong Kong and Taiwan, 1985–91 (US$ million)

| | 1985 | 1986 | 1987 | 1988 | 1989 | 1990 | 1991 | 1985–91 |
|---|---|---|---|---|---|---|---|---|
| *From Hong Kong* | | | | | | | | |
| Guangdong | | | | | | | | |
| FDI | 450.20 (47.11) | 622.65 (46.86) | 502.67 (27.79) | 836.54 (34.45) | 952.72 (40.68) | 1018.59 (48.08) | 1448.60 (54.42) | 5831.97 (42.75) |
| AFI | 845.63 (83.20) | 1095.45 (69.65) | 884.09 (42.28) | 1537.96 (49.46) | 1544.89 (53.04) | 1298.46 (53.40) | 1724.80 (58.97) | 8931.28 (55.61) |
| Shenzhen | | | | | | | | |
| FDI | 146.05 (15.28) | 328.87 (24.75) | 219.54 (12.14) | 225.61 (9.29) | 212.66 (9.08) | 177.99 (8.40) | 227.81 (8.56) | 1538.53 (11.28) |
| AFI | 272.42 (26.80) | 385.87 (24.53) | 256.32 (12.26) | 281.98 (9.07) | 287.29 (9.86) | 262.91 (10.81) | 323.75 (11.07) | 2070.54 (12.89) |
| Guangzhou | | | | | | | | |
| FDI | — | — | — | — | — | 125.71 (5.93) | 187.07 (7.03) | — |
| AFI | 136.63 (13.44) | 120.85 (7.68) | 49.72 (2.38) | 111.47 (3.58) | 104.16 (3.58) | 125.57 (5.16) | — | — |
| Fujian | | | | | | | | |
| FDI | 95.07 (9.95) | — | — | 80.56 (3.32) | 195.28 (8.34) | 160.91 (7.60) | 225.77 (8.40) | — |
| AFI | 141.97 (13.97) | 70.23 (4.47) | 36.67 (1.75) | 177.48 (5.71) | 204.23 (7.01) | 249.45 (10.26) | 225.77 (7.72) | 1105.80 (6.89) |

Table 7: Continued.

| | 1985 | 1986 | 1987 | 1988 | 1989 | 1990 | 1991 | 1985–91 |
|---|---|---|---|---|---|---|---|---|
| **Xiamen** | | | | | | | | |
| FDI | 58.83 (6.16) | — | — | 31.77 (1.31) | — | 45.08 (2.13) | — | — |
| AFI | * | * | * | * | 153.91 (5.28) | 107.27 (4.41) | — | — |
| **Shanghai** | | | | | | | | |
| FDI | — | — | — | — | — | — | 47.44 (1.78) | — |
| AFI | — | 31.30 (1.99) | 312.83 (14.96) | — | 178.96 (6.14) | — | — | — |
| **All China** | | | | | | | | |
| FDI | 955.68 (48.86) | 1328.71 (59.22) | 1809.05 (68.35) | 2428.05 (64.93) | 2341.77 (62.06) | 2118.48 (56.42) | 2661.81 (57.04) | 13643.55 (60.67) |
| AFI | 1016.37 (22.78) | 1572.85 (21.67) | 2091.24 (24.74) | 3109.44 (30.40) | 2912.78 (28.96) | 2431.68 (23.63) | 2924.96 (25.32) | 16059.32 (25.95) |
| *From Taiwan* | | | | | | | | |
| **Guangdong** | | | | | | | | |
| FDI | — | — | — | 3.24 | 22.72 | 70.33 (31.36) | 109.56 (23.32) | — |
| **Shenzhen** | | | | | | | | |
| FDI | — | — | — | 3.16 | 10.06 | 3.71 (1.65) | 2.16 (0.46) | — |
| **Guangzhou** | | | | | | | | |
| FDI | — | — | — | — | 4.37 | 22.69 (10.12) | 28.79 (6.13) | — |
| **Hainan** | | | | | | | | |
| FDI | — | — | — | — | — | 5.68 (2.53) | — | — |

## Table 7: Continued

| | 1985 | 1986 | 1987 | 1988 | 1989 | 1990 | 1991 | 1985–91 |
|---|---|---|---|---|---|---|---|---|
| **Fujian** | | | | | | | | |
| FDI | — | 0.57 | 0.72 | 11.01 | 106.66 | — | — | — |
| | — | — | — | — | — | — | — | — |
| **Shanghai** | | | | | | | | |
| FDI | — | — | — | — | — | — | — | — |
| | — | — | — | — | — | — | — | — |
| **All China** | | | | | | | | |
| FDI | — | — | — | — | — | 224.26 | 469.89 | — |
| | — | — | — | — | — | (5.97) | (10.11) | — |

*Notes:*

*The cumulative total AFI (1985–88) was US$240.46 million (3.09%).

FDI = foreign direct investment

AFI = all foreign investment (including FDI and loans)

Figures in brackets show the percentage share of total investment to China from Hong Kong and Taiwan, except for those under "All China," which show the share of Hong Kong and Taiwan in China's total intake for foreign capital. Some of the absolute US$ estimates for Hong Kong have been obtained by applying the FDI or AFI ratio to the total FDI or AFI intake for the relevant region. For example, Shenzhen's FDI (1991) is derived from the AFI ratio and total FDI (from Hong Kong and elsewhere). For some areas – notably Guangzhou (1985–88) and Shanghai (1986–87) – the ratio from the pledged, rather than realized, investment series has been used.

The figures for Taiwan are all from official mainland Chinese sources. For Fujian the estimates appear to constitute a complete series. The source from which they are taken (*FJTJNJ 1990*) also gives a cumulative total for 1979–89 as US$120.19 million. This is only marginally more than the US$118.96 million cited for 1986–89. It is curious that annual estimates for 1990 and 1991 are absent from the 1991 and 1992 editions of *FJTJNJ* – precisely when the national *Statistical Yearbook* made available such estimates for the country as a whole. The estimates for Shenzhen for 1988–91, which generate a cumulative total of US$19.09 million, seem to constitute another complete series, since the figure is almost identical to that given in *SZTJSC 1991* (p. 43).

*Sources:*

Hong Kong. Kueh, "Foreign investment and economic change," p. 674 and 682–83; *Guangzhou tongji nianjian 1992 (Guangzhou Statistical Yearbook 1992)* (hereafter *GZTJNJ*), p. 315; and *SHTJNJ 1992*, p. 358.

Taiwan. *GDTJNJ 1992*, p. 360; *Shenzhenshi qiwu shiqi guomin jingji he shehui tongji ziliao (1986–90) (National Economic and Social Statistical Material for Shenzhen Municipality during the Seventh Five-Year Plan Period (1986–90))*, p. 405; *Shenzhen tongji nianjian 1992 (Shenzhen Statistical Yearbook 1992)* (hereafter *SZTJNJ*), p. 397; *GZTJNJ 1991*, p. 305; *GZTJNJ 1992*, p. 315; *Hainan tongji nianjian 1991 (Hainan Statistical Yearbook 1991)*, p. 433; *FJTJNJ 1987*, p. 331; *FJTJNJ 1988*, p. 429; *FJTJNJ 1990*, p. 295; and *ZGTJNJ 1992*, p. 642.

more than half of total Hong Kong investment in China (54 per cent of FDI, 59 per cent of AFI). If Fujian were included (9 per cent of FDI, 8 per cent of AFI), the two provinces were in receipt of some two-thirds of foreign investment from the colony.

It is difficult to estimate with accuracy the level of Taiwanese investment in mainland China. The fragmentary data shown in Table 4 are all that can be found in official mainland publications. What is not in doubt is that Taiwanese investment in the two southern provinces has increased dramatically in recent years in the wake of informal contacts and, since 1991, the formal authorization by the Taipei government of "indirect investment" through third parties.[60] With US$469.89 million invested in 1991 (twice as much as in the previous year), FDI of Taiwanese origin accounted for some 10 per cent of China's total intake. Although this was far behind the contribution of Hong Kong, it placed Taiwan only marginally behind Japan as a supplier of FDI to the Chinese mainland. By the end of 1992, Taiwan had in fact overtaken Japan to rank second as a source of FDI to the PRC.[61]

Estimates of Fujian's intake of FDI from Taiwan in 1991 are apparently not available. But assuming that it was no smaller than the US$109.56 million invested in Guangdong, there can be little doubt that the combined share of the two provinces in FDI flows from Hong Kong and Taiwan was no less than 60 per cent – and cumulatively (1985–91) much more. Such figures demonstrate clearly the locational choice made by Hong Kong and Taiwanese entrepreneurs and signal the trend towards greater economic integration within Greater China.

There is, however, a qualification to be entered here. A survey conducted by the Ministry of Economic Affairs (MOEA) in Taipei in April 1991 suggested that the level of Taiwanese FDI in mainland China was more substantial than that indicated in official PRC sources. The survey, based on the responses of 2,503 firms which had voluntarily registered their investment interests with the government in Taipei, revealed a cumulative FDI stock of US$750 million.[62] Although it is impossible to

60. The momentum of Taiwanese investment in mainland China accelerated after an official government declaration (Taipei, November 1987) that Chinese from Taiwan would be allowed to visit relatives across the Taiwan Straits. The continued and active interest shown by Taiwanese entrepreneurs in seeking investment opportunities in the PRC eventually brought official approval (1991) of investment conducted "through a third country." For further details, see T.B. Lin, "Economic nexus between the two sides of the Taiwan Straits" (paper presented at Conference on the Economic Development of ROC and the Pacific Rim in the 1990s and Beyond: Taipei, 25–29 May 1992); and Charng Kao, "Economic interaction between the two sides of the Taiwan Straits" (paper presented at Conference on the Evolution of Taiwan within a New World Economic Order: Taipei, May 1993).

61. *TKP*, 2 June 1993.

62. See Charles H.C. Kao, Joseph S. Lee and Chu-chia Steve Lin, *Taiwan tupuo: liangan jingmao zhuizhong* (*An Empirical Study of Taiwanese Investment in Mainland China*) (Taipei: Taipei Commonwealth Publishing Company Ltd.), p. 12. The actual number of Taiwanese firms then operating in mainland China was thought to be between 3,000 and 3,500. Different estimates again are available in other Taiwanese sources. For example, the prestigious Chung-Hua Institution for Economic Research suggested that as of April 1993, some 2,700 Taiwanese firms were operating on the mainland with a total investment of US$3.7 billion (King Pei and Hsu Chia-xian, "Trends and prospects of economic interaction

Table 8: **Distribution of Cumulative FDI of Taiwanese Origin within Mainland China (as of April 1991)**

|  | FDI | | No. of firms | |
|---|---|---|---|---|
|  | US$ m. | % | Units | % |
| Guangdong | 342.6 | 45.7 | 1,253 | 50.1 |
| Shenzhen | 111.6 | 14.9 | 378 | 15.1 |
| Guangzhou | 55.9 | 7.5 | 146 | 5.8 |
| Fujian | 179.5 | 23.9 | 598 | 23.9 |
| Xiamen | 92.2 | 12.3 | 275 | 11.0 |
| Shanghai | 87.0 | 12.3 | 78 | 3.1 |
| Others | 140.9 | 18.8 | 574 | 22.9 |
| Total | 750.0 | 100.0 | 2,503 | 100.0 |

*Source:*
Kao, Lee and Lin, *Taiwan tupuo*, p. 12.

reconcile the statistical discrepancy, there is no doubt that a significant part of FDI flows to China from Hong Kong, Japan, the United States and South-east Asia reflect the activities of Taiwanese firms in disguise. It is unlikely, however, that such flows from places other than Hong Kong have exceeded the colony's own investment involvement and we are confident that the combined contribution of FDI from Hong Kong and Taiwan to mainland China (or Guangdong and Fujian) shown in Table 7 requires little modification.

In line with the findings of official PRC statistics, the MOEA survey reveals that accumulated FDI stock of Taiwanese origin was, as of April 1991, heavily concentrated in Guangdong and Fujian (see Table 8). On the basis of such evidence, the distribution of Taiwanese FDI between the two provinces seems less unbalanced than that of Hong Kong (see Table 7), although it remains heavily skewed towards Guangdong. In any case, current press reports indicate that new FDI from Taiwan continues to favour Guangdong ahead of Fujian.

---

*footnote continued*

between the two sides of the Taiwan Straits" (paper presented at a Symposium on the Current State of Economic Management in the Mainland, Taiwan and Hong Kong: Hong Kong, December 1991)). King and Hsu also give a cumulative total of US$100 million in Taiwanese investment in mainland China for 1979–87. This figure increased by US$300 million (1988) and 600 million (1989) (see Lin, "Economic nexus") to raise the cumulative total to US$1 billion. None of these figures is compatible with the official PRC statistics. The discrepancy is likely to reflect differences in the definition of FDI of Taiwanese origin (which may or may not include investment originating in Taiwanese firms based outside Taiwan – e.g. in Hong Kong or South-east Asia – and which have become detached from their parent companies). The cumulative total given in the MOEA 1991 survey (US$750 million) seems most reconcilable with the incomplete official PRC estimates shown in Table 7.

*Foreign Investment, Trade and Economic Growth*

It is difficult to estimate exactly how foreign investment from Hong Kong and Taiwan has translated into economic growth in Guangdong and Fujian provinces.[63] As a proxy, it is likely that Hong Kong contributed no less than 16 per cent of total fixed capital formation in Guangdong between 1985 and 1990 – and 28 per cent in Shenzhen. The comparable figure for Fujian is probably around 7 per cent.[64] Even more important is the fact that every dollar of foreign investment will generate a multiplier effect in terms of complementary domestic investment expenditure (expressed in *yuan*). In short, the overall level of investment associated with FDI and AFI has become very substantial.[65]

A summary of the growth performance of Guangdong and Fujian since 1980 is given in Table 9. For comparative purposes, data for Hong Kong, Taiwan and Shanghai are also included. Most foreign investment (FDI and AFI) has been directed towards high growth sectors and it is

Table 9: **The Growth Performance of Hong Kong, Taiwan and Selected Areas of China – Trends in gross domestic [national] product, 1980–91 (Average percentage annual rates of growth)**

|  | *1980–85* | *1985–91* | *1980–91* |
|---|---|---|---|
| Hong Kong | 5.60 | 7.20 | 6.47 |
| Taiwan | 6.71 [7.09] | 8.34 [8.63] | 7.69 [7.92] |
| Guangdong | 12.16 | 13.30 | 12.80 |
| Shenzhen | 54.54 | 25.95 | 38.22 |
| Guangzhou | 12.71 | 10.83 | 12.51 |
| Fujian | 11.91 [11.93] | 9.71 [9.96] | 10.71 [10.85] |
| Xiamen | 16.24 | 29.00 | 23.04 |
| Shanghai | 9.08 | 5.90 | 7.34 |

*Sources:*
  Hong Kong: *HKMDS*, September 1992, p. 10: Taiwan: *Taiwan Statistical Data Book 1992*, p. 25: Guangdong: *GDTJNJ 1992*, p. 83: Shenzhen: *SZTJNJ 1992*, p. 170, Guangzhou: *Guangzhou tongji nianjian 1992* (*Guangzhou Statistical Yearbook 1992*), p. 14 and p. 20. Fujian: *FJTJNJ 1992*, p. 20. Xiamen: *FJTJNJ 1992*, p. 447; Xiamen Statistical Bureau, *Fenjinde Xiamen* (*Advancing Xiamen*) (1989), p. 46. Shanghai: *SHTJNJ 1992*, p. 34.

63. For example, any attempt to estimate FDI's contribution to China's domestic capital formation and GNP growth should take account of possible distortions arising out of erratic exchange rate adjustments in converting foreign capital into *renminbi* (*RMB*) equivalent. See Kueh, "Foreign investment and economic change," p. 657.
64. These estimates were obtained by applying Hong Kong's shares (HKS) in the total intake of foreign investment of all kinds (FDI and capital borrowing) received by Guangdong, Shenzhen and Fujian to the respective percentage contributions of *all* foreign investments to total investment in fixed assets (CFA) in the corresponding areas. HKS are calculated from the absolute dollar figures shown in Table 7 and in Kueh, "Foreign investment and economic change," Appendix A, p. 683. CFA are given in *ibid.* p. 656.
65. For an elaboration of this point, see Kueh, "Foreign investment and economic change," p. 658.

reasonable to suppose that the impressive GNP growth recorded in Guangdong and Fujian (including Shenzhen, Guangzhou and Xiamen) after 1985 owed much to capital contributions from Hong Kong and Taiwan. The contrast between Hong Kong and Taiwan – both, after all, mature economies with a sustained record of high growth – and the two southern Chinese provinces is less significant than that between those same provinces and Shanghai. It is no coincidence that Shanghai has fallen far short of Guangdong and Fujian as a recipient of foreign capital. The data in Table 9 thereby suggest the influence of overseas involvement in the Chinese economy and its impact upon domestic growth.

*Trends Towards Economic Integration*

The factors which have led Hong Kong and Taiwanese firms to re-locate their manufacturing activities to mainland China are already the subject of a considerable literature. The most familiar argument is that against the background of high indigenous wage costs and land rents, entrepreneurs have sought increasingly to transfer their labour-intensive operations across the border, or Taiwan Straits, in order to take advantage of an abundant supply of cheap labour and land. The accelerated appreciation of the NT Dollar against the U.S. dollar since the mid-1980s has been a further contributory factor, prompting many Taiwanese firms to move to the mainland in an attempt to reduce export costs. More stringent government legislation to control pollution, as well greater self-awareness and even militancy on the part of the labour force, have been further reasons for the accelerating trend, especially amongst Taiwanese entrepreneurs.

In an attempt to measure the impact of the transfer of manufacturing activities from Hong Kong and Taiwan to the Chinese mainland, estimates of sectoral contributions to national income and employment in all three countries and regions, as well as of labour productivity, are set out in Tables 10A, 10B and 10C. There is no doubt that the re-location of manufacturing operations from Hong Kong and Taiwan to the Chinese mainland has been a catalyst in effecting remarkable structural changes in national income and employment within the constituent economies of Greater China. In 1991, for example, Hong Kong investors were reported to be employing some 3 million workers in Guangdong (especially in the Pearl River Delta).[66] This constituted a labour force about four-and-a-half times greater than the colony's own manufacturing workforce. Transferring industrial activities across the Shenzhen River meanwhile resulted in a decline in manufacturing employment in Hong Kong in both absolute and relative terms. Table 10A shows that the employment share of the industrial sector (including building construction) fell from 50 per cent

66. K.Y. Tang, "Outward processing in China and its implications for the Hong Kong economy" (paper presented at Symposium on Asian Newly-Industrializing Economies: Past Success and Future Challenge: Hong Kong, May 1991).

(1980) to 44 per cent (1985) to a mere 36 per cent (1991), whilst that of services rose from 48 to 54 to 63 per cent.

The corresponding changes in Taiwan's employment structure appear at first glance to have been less spectacular. But the reality is that employment in many branches of light industry (notably electrical engineering, footwear, plastics and textile production) has fallen dramatically as a result of the transfer of such labour-intensive activities to the PRC. Indeed at times the government in Taipei has expressed its concern about a "hollowing out" of the island's industrial structure.

The re-location of manufacturing firms to China has also been accompanied by striking changes in the structure of output in Hong Kong and Taiwan. Table 10A shows that the service sector's share in Hong Kong GDP increased by almost 8 per cent between 1980 and 1991, mostly at the expense of industrial activity. Similar structural "upgrading" has apparently taken place in Taiwan, although the smaller scale of its FDI involvement may mean that the principal reason for this lies elsewhere. The more significant consequence for Taiwan may have been in terms of changes in its *intra*-industrial structure. According to the Head of the Industry Bureau in Taipei, the large-scale transfer of "sunset industries" to the PRC has more than anything else accounted for the rapid increase of heavy industry's share in total manufacturing output in recent years (from 47 to 56 per cent between 1986 and 1991).[67]

There is no doubt that Guangdong and Fujian have benefited most from the increased economic integration of Greater China. As a result of accelerated GDP (GNP) growth and more rapid industrialization, the structure of output and employment in both regions – but above all in sub-provincial units such as Guangzhou, Shenzhen and Xiamen – has changed markedly. This process of structural change has been characterized by gains for the industrial and service sectors at the expense of agriculture, and by a reduction in inter-sectoral relative levels of labour productivity (Tables 10B and 10C). The significance of the latter achievement is highlighted by the experience of China's pre-reform era, when – accelerated industrialization notwithstanding – agriculture carried almost the entire burden of absorbing increases in labour supply, thereby exacerbating inter-sectoral productivity differentials.[68]

The tertiary sector's increased share of total output and employment since 1980 has been a noteworthy feature of the recent development experience of both Guangdong and Fujian.[69] This no doubt reflects the increased provision of banking, insurance and financial services, transport and telecommunication facilities, and expertise in processing export and import orders. An expansion of tourism and rise in real estate transactions also underlie the same trend. The growing contribution of the tertiary

67. Kao, Lee and Lin, *Taiwan tupuo*, pp. 90–91.

68. See Y. Y. Kueh, "The Maoist legacy and China's new industrialization strategy," *The China Quarterly*, No. 119 (September 1989), pp. 422–24.

69. Shenzhen seems to be the only exception, its tertiary share in GDP having fallen from 45% (1980 and 1985) to 35% (1991). This decline was offset by a rapid increase in industry's GDP share (from 26% to 60%, 1980–91).

Table 10A: Measuring the Impact of Re-locating Manufacturing Activities to the Chinese Mainland – The changing contributions of agriculture (A), industry (I) and services (S) to Gross Domestic Product and Employment in Greater China, 1980–91 (%)

| | 1980 | | | 1985 | | | 1991 | | |
|---|---|---|---|---|---|---|---|---|---|
| | A | I | S | A | I | S | A | I | S |
| *GDP* | | | | | | | | | |
| Hong Kong | 1.0 | 31.8 | 67.2 | 0.7 | 29.6 | 69.7 | 0.3 | 24.9 | 74.8 |
| Taiwan | 7.7 | 45.7 | 46.6 | 5.8 | 46.3 | 47.9 | 3.7 | 42.3 | 54.0 |
| Guangdong | 33.8 | 41.1 | 25.1 | 31.1 | 40.8 | 28.1 | 23.4 | 42.1 | 34.5 |
| Shenzhen | 28.9 | 26.0 | 45.1 | 7.9 | 46.8 | 45.4 | 4.6 | 60.2 | 35.2 |
| Guangzhou | 10.9 | 54.5 | 34.6 | 9.7 | 52.9 | 37.4 | 7.3 | 46.5 | 46.2 |
| Fujian | 37.2 | 41.5 | 21.3 | 35.7 | 38.0 | 26.3 | 31.2 | 39.8 | 29.0 |
| Xiamen | 21.1 | 58.6 | 20.3 | 12.7 | 56.3 | 31.0 | 10.4 | 53.7 | 35.9 |
| Shanghai | 3.2 | 75.7 | 21.1 | 4.2 | 69.8 | 26.0 | 4.0 | 64.3 | 31.8 |
| *Employment* | | | | | | | | | |
| Hong Kong | 2.0 | 49.6 | 48.3 | 1.8 | 43.8 | 54.4 | 1.0 | 35.9 | 63.1 |
| Taiwan | 19.5 | 42.4 | 38.1 | 17.5 | 41.4 | 41.1 | 12.9 | 40.1 | 47.0 |
| Guangdong | 73.7 | 13.9 | 12.5 | 60.1 | 21.3 | 18.6 | 51.0 | 25.9 | 23.1 |
| Shenzhen | — | — | — | — | — | — | 6.1 | 69.8 | 24.1 |
| Guangzhou | 40.2 | 33.6 | 26.2 | 31.3 | 37.7 | 31.1 | 27.6 | 36.8 | 35.6 |
| Fujian | 73.0 | 11.8 | 15.2 | 61.5 | 19.4 | 19.0 | 57.8 | 20.9 | 21.3 |
| Xiamen | — | — | — | 46.6 | 26.8 | 26.6 | 42.4 | 28.8 | 28.8 |
| Shanghai | 29.6 | 48.7 | 22.1 | 16.6 | 57.9 | 25.5 | 10.7 | 60.0 | 29.3 |

Table 10B: Relative Product per Worker, 1980–91

| | 1980 | | | 1985 | | | 1991 | | |
|---|---|---|---|---|---|---|---|---|---|
| | A | I | S | A | I | S | A | I | S |
| Hong Kong | 0.50 | 0.64 | 1.39 | 0.39 | 0.68 | 1.28 | 0.30 | 0.69 | 1.19 |
| Taiwan | 0.39 | 1.08 | 1.22 | 0.33 | 1.12 | 1.17 | 0.29 | 1.05 | 1.15 |
| Guangdong | 0.46 | 2.96 | 2.01 | 0.52 | 1.92 | 1.51 | 0.46 | 1.63 | 1.49 |
| Shenzhen | — | — | — | — | — | — | 0.75 | 0.86 | 1.46 |
| Guangzhou | 0.27 | 1.62 | 1.32 | 0.31 | 1.40 | 1.21 | 0.26 | 1.26 | 1.30 |
| Fujian | 0.51 | 3.52 | 1.40 | 0.58 | 1.96 | 1.38 | 0.54 | 1.90 | 1.36 |
| Xiamen | — | — | — | 0.27 | 2.10 | 1.17 | 0.25 | 1.86 | 1.25 |
| Shanghai | 0.11 | 1.55 | 0.95 | 0.25 | 1.21 | 1.02 | 0.37 | 1.07 | 1.09 |

Table 10C: **Total Inequality Amongst Sectors**

| | 1980 | 1985 | 1991 |
|---|---|---|---|
| Hong Kong | 0.37 | 0.30 | 0.24 |
| Taiwan | 0.24 | 0.24 | 0.18 |
| Guangdong | 0.80 | 0.58 | 0.55 |
| Shenzhen | — | — | 0.22 |
| Guangzhou | 0.59 | 0.43 | 0.41 |
| Fujian | 0.72 | 0.52 | 0.53 |
| Xiamen | — | 0.68 | 0.64 |
| Shanghai | 0.54 | 0.25 | 0.14 |

*Sources:*
Hong Kong: Census and Statistics Department, *Estimates of GDP, 1966–1991*, p. 38; *Hong Kong Annual Digest of Statistics* (1991 edition), p.34; Yin-ping Ho, *Trade, Industrial Restructuring and Development in Hong Kong* (London: Macmillan Press, 1992), p. 36. Taiwan: *Taiwan Statistical Data Book, 1992*, p. 17 and p. 41. Guangdong: *GDTJNJ 1992*, p. 85 and p. 142. Shenzhen: *SZTJNJ 1992*, pp. 161 and 182; *Shenzhenshi guomin jingji he shehui tongji ziliao, 1979–85 (National Economic and Social Statistical Data for Shenzhen Municipality), 1979–85)*, pp. 10–11; *SZTJNJ 1992*, pp. 168–69; *Shenzhenshi qiwu shiqi guomin jingji he shehui tongji ziliao, 1986–90*, p. 21. Guangzhou: *Guangzhou tongji nianjian 1992*, p. 28 and p. 358. Fujian: *FJTJNJ 1992*, p. 15 and p. 53; *Fujian shehui tongji ziliao, 1986 (Fujian Social Statistics, 1986)*, p. 43. Xiamen: *Fenjinde Xiamen*, p. 44; *FJTJNJ 1992*, p. 447; *Fujian shehui tongji ziliao, 1986*, p. 48; *Xiamen jingji tequ nianjian, 1990 (Xiamen SEZ Yearbook, 1990)*, p. 171. Shanghai: *SHTJNJ 1991*, pp. 34 and 72; *SHTJNJ 1992*, pp. 33 and 86.

sector in the southern Chinese economy is of course paralleled in the experience of other industrializing countries.

### The Economic Integration of Greater China: Issues, Problems and Prospects

The experience of economic integration in Greater China differs significantly from that which has occurred elsewhere in the world. For example, the EC and ASEAN are two economic groupings which have sought to create a single common market, designed to enhance the free movement of goods and factors of production to members' mutual advantage. By contrast, the establishment of closer ties between Hong Kong, Taiwan and the Chinese mainland is the result of the international-ization of manufacturing production, based on joint production and/or the division of labour and geared towards third-party countries (rather than member countries themselves). A large proportion of output so generated has been destined for overseas locations and most inputs similarly derive from abroad. The movement of factors of production, as well as of finished products, within Greater China meanwhile remains limited; and much Hong Kong and Taiwanese FDI is still heavily concentrated in SEZs, geographically isolated from the rest of the PRC. Backward and forward linkages have thereby been minimized.[70]

The creation of closer trade and investment ties between Hong Kong, Taiwan, Guangdong and Fujian and the process of economic integration which it has facilitated are in any case not free of risk. An example is that associated with the vulnerability of the Hong Kong and southern Chinese (especially Guangdong) economies to their export dependency on Amer-ican markets. From this perspective, an increase in export tariffs following cancellation of China's MFN status would have serious conse-quences for both regions. It has, for example, been estimated that the loss to Hong Kong could be as much as US$15.7 billion in overall trade and 60,000 jobs; re-exports from China might meanwhile fall by US$4.6–6.2 billion, leading to massive job losses in Guangdong.[71] Such data highlight the importance to China *and Hong Kong* of a resumption of Chinese membership of GATT. They also suggest how failure to resolve trade issues between China and the United States could undermine the very process of regional economic integration by leading investors to lessen their involvement in the southern Chinese economy and re-direct their investment elsewhere (say, to other countries in South-east Asia).

If the rapid expansion of cross-Straits trade has boosted Taiwan's export growth, it has also led to increasing dependence on Chinese markets. This has obvious dangers in a situation in which cross-Straits

70. We are grateful to Joseph C.H. Chai for raising the points outlined in this paragraph.
71. These are the Hong Kong government's own estimates, made in March 1992 in the wake of the annual U.S. review. The same report predicted that China's loss of MFN status would reduce Hong Kong's GDP growth in 1992 (forecast at 5%) by half. See *SCMP*, 14 March 1992; also *The China Business Review*, May–June 1992, p. 14. For consideration of the impact on the USA of a decision to revoke China's MFN status, see *SCMP*, 23 May 1993.

political relations remain uncertain. Meanwhile, Taiwanese enterprises must face up to increased competition from their overseas subsidiaries, now sited in southern China. Other things being equal, the access to cheaper land and labour which such firms enjoy should enable them to produce cheaper goods and may thereby threaten parent firms' competitiveness in international (and even local) markets.[72]

Nevertheless, as the estimates in Table 11 suggest, there also remains considerable scope for even closer economic integration within Greater China. The marked economic differences between Hong Kong, Taiwan and southern China in terms of the major measures shown above suggest that before full integration and equalization of per capita income, productivity and degree of industrialization[73] can be achieved, many economic and political barriers to cross-border labour mobility will have to be removed. However, the political unification which such an outcome would seem to demand is clearly far beyond anything conceivable within the foreseeable future.

The data in Table 11 indicate that within China, only Shenzhen can lay claim to approaching the advanced standards of Hong Kong and Taiwan in terms of per capita income, productivity and degree of industrialization. But even that gap remains considerable and in any case Shenzhen SEZ can perhaps be more usefully regarded as a "satellite town" of Hong Kong than an integral part of Guangdong.[74] If the SEZ's "second line," north of the enclave, replaced the Shenzhen River as the border with Hong Kong, no doubt economic equalization would rapidly come about. Whether or not this would be to the benefit or detriment of the British colony is an open question.

In any case, with or without Shenzhen, Hong Kong has now become inseparable from the economy of Guangdong. With the tertiary sector now contributing about three-quarters of GDP (see Table 10A), its process of "de-industrialization" seems to have reached a point at which it has become irreversible. The most unequivocal evidence of the two regions' inseparability are the estimates of the potential economic impact of a withdrawal by the United States of China's MFN status, cited earlier.

If Hong Kong has wholly succumbed to the principle of comparative advantage in pursuing regional economic specialization, Taiwan has adopted a more cautious approach vis-à-vis the Chinese mainland. Various econometric studies have been undertaken in an attempt to assess the security implications of its closer trade and investment relations with the PRC. One of these suggests that against the background of increased exports to mainland China in recent years, an embargo by the authorities in Beijing would, on average, have reduced Taiwan's GDP and total employment by 1.46 and 3.42 per cent respectively (1987–91).[75] Such

72. But see also below.
73. The capital/labour ratio provides one measure of the extent of industrialization.
74. See Yin-ping Ho, *Trade, Industrial Restructuring and Development*, ch. 10.
75. Yuh-jiun Lin and Chin-shu Huang, "Development of trade and investment between the two sides of the Taiwan Straits" (paper at Conference on Global Interdependence and Asia-Pacific Cooperation: Hong Kong, 8–10 June 1992), pp. 8 and 10.

# Table 11: Economic Disparities Within Greater China, 1991

| | Population (m.) | GNP (US$ m.) | Per capita GNP (US$) | GVIO US$ m. | Per capita GVIO (US$) | Capital/labour ratio (US$) | Trade volume (US$ m.) | Trade/GNP ratio |
|---|---|---|---|---|---|---|---|---|
| Hong Kong | 5.82 | 81,157 | 13,945 | — | — | 4,339 | 107,439 | 1.32 |
| Taiwan | 20.56 | 180,270 | 8,815 | 155,000 | 7,546 | 4,832 | 139,035 | 0.77 |
| Guangdong | 63.49 | 33,452 | 527 | 47,422 | 747 | 2,597 | 22,198 | 0.66 |
| Shenzhen | 2.39 | 3,284 | 1,491 | 5,303 | 2,223 | 4,951 | 5,967 | 1.82 |
| | (1.20) | (2,546) | (2,306) | — | — | — | — | — |
| Guangzhou | 6.02 | 7,265 | 1,214 | 10,887 | 1,808 | 3,998 | 5,382 | 0.74 |
| | (3.62) | (5,977) | (1,660) | — | — | — | — | — |
| Fujian | 30.39 | 10,480 | 340 | 12,378 | 402 | 1,761 | 4,334 | 0.41 |
| Xiamen | 1.15 | 1,169 | 1,016 | 1,936 | 1,683 | — | 2,406 | 2.06 |
| Shanghai | 13.40 | 16,114 | 1,203 | 36,583 | 2,730 | 2,822 | 8,044 | 0.50 |

*Notes:*

Bracketed figures are for Shenzhen and Guangzhou cities "proper," i.e. excluding the outlying counties.

*Population:* the estimates for Shenzhen embrace "temporary" and "permanent" residents.

*GNP:* the figures for Hong Kong, Shenzhen, Guangzhou and Xiamen are measures of GDP. Per capita GDP estimates for Shenzhen and Guangzhou are given independently in Chinese sources and are slightly different from figures which can be obtained from the estimates of population and GDP shown in Table 11.

*GVIO:* gross value of industrial output.

*Capital-labour ratio:* this refers to capital stock (K) per industrial employee (L). For Hong Kong and Taiwan K means, respectively, to gross domestic capital formation and gross fixed capital formation. For China, K is the net value of fixed assets (i.e. net of depreciation); and K/L refers to industry in general in Guangdong, Fujian and Shanghai, but only those enterprises which have an independent-accounting (*duli hesuan*) identity in Shenzhen and Guangzhou.

*Trade volume:* this embraces only domestic exports and imports (i.e. it excludes exports originating from, and imports destined for, other places). However, the data for Xiamen appear to include re-exports.

*Exchange rates:* US$1.00 is assumed to equal HK$7.80 (under the linked system), NT$25.75 (interbank closing rate, December 1991) and *RMB* 5.323 (official annual average, 1991).

*Sources:*

Hong Kong: Hong Kong Government Census and Statistics Department, *Estimates of GDP, 1966–1991*, p. 10; *HKMDS*, August 1992, p. 105 and September 1992, pp. 1–2 and 19. Taiwan: Council for Economic Planning and Development, *Taiwan Statistical Data Book, 1992*, pp. 1, 17, 49 and 192. Guangdong: *GDTJNJ 1992*, pp. 68, 183 and 341. Shenzhen: *SZTJNJ 1991*, p. 2; *SZTJNJ 1992*, p. 163; and *GDTJNJ 1992*, pp. 81, 93 and 105. Guangzhou: *GDTJNJ 1992*, pp. 91, 93, 104, 138 and 199; *Guangzhou tongji nianjian 1992*, p. 307. Fujian: *FJTJNJ 1992*, pp. 8–9, 53 and 146. Xiamen: *FJTJNJ 1992*, pp. 444–48; Y. Y. Kueh, "Foreign investment and economic change," pp. 689–690. Shanghai: *ZGTJNJ 1992*, p. 79; *SHTJNJ 1992*, pp. 33, 86, 112, 144 and 349.

losses would have to be regarded as fairly minor in their impact. By contrast, another study has argued that the reduction in Taiwan's GDP consequent upon reduced domestic capital formation might offset FDI-related exports to the PRC to generate a significant net income loss. To those who would use such estimates to highlight the threat posed by Taiwan's allegedly increasing dependency, it has, however, been argued that in the absence of investment opportunities on the Chinese mainland, Taiwanese entrepreneurs would merely have directed their funds elsewhere. Nor could there be any guarantee that the funds involved would have been used for productive purposes on Taiwan itself.[76]

Clearly, it is not easy to estimate the economic costs and benefits associated with Taiwanese investment in mainland China. But it would be surprising if the government in Taipei were not to act prudently to safeguard its security. To this extent, it is significant that when "indirect investment" to the PRC was officially sanctioned in 1991, it was deliberately restricted to 3,679 product categories. It was also specified that such investment should only involve labour-intensive undertakings to which the PRC could contribute necessary raw materials and in areas which, in terms of the domestic Taiwanese economy, had low inter-industrial linkages; and should embrace the production of goods which might enjoy a competitive advantage against Taiwanese exports.[77]

Whether Taiwanese investors will be able to overcome what are essentially political restrictions on their activities as successfully as they circumvented earlier restraints on investment contacts with mainland firms – and if so, how – remains to be seen. What is not in doubt, however, is the potentially explosive nature of the current situation, should continuing embargoes on direct commercial, navigational and postal links (the *santong*) be lifted. If this were to happen, a dramatic realignment of investment and trade flows within Greater China would certainly result. Such a prospect may at present seem remote. But it behoves the government and business community of Hong Kong to be on constant alert and ready to adjust their plans in anticipation of such an eventuality.

The various problems outlined in this final section suggest that the undoubted benefits of closer economic integration within Greater China are not to be taken for granted. The experience of the 1980s is evidence enough of the substantial gains to be derived from closer economic – and by implication, political – relations. But many obstacles remain to be overcome if the growth and structural benefits are to be sustained. To the extent that the economic well-being of Guangdong and Fujian determines the economic direction and health of the rest of the Chinese economy, resolving these issues assumes the greatest urgency in China itself.

76. See Kao, Lee and Lin, *Taiwan tupuo*, p. 42.
77. *Ibid.* p. 65.

# Direct Investment and Economic Integration in the Asia Pacific: The Case of Taiwanese Investment in Xiamen

## Qi Luo and Christopher Howe

The Asia–Pacific region, and particularly its East Asian core, has achieved an impressive record of growth, export expansion and regional economic integration that now spans more than three decades and a wide variety of world economic environments. A key indicator of these achievements is the changing level of intra-regional foreign trade. This indicator is positive for the region as a whole over the period, although trends since 1980 are quite sensitive to the precise definition of the region employed. However, for the NICs (Hong Kong, Taiwan, South Korea and Singapore) and the ASEAN group (Thailand, Malaysia, Indonesia, Philippines and Brunei) in isolation, intra-regional trade increased by approximately 25 per cent over the decade 1980–90.[1]

Trade within the Asia–Pacific as a whole has been driven by the exceptionally diverse endowments of the region's constituent economies in terms of natural resources, relative labour–capital proportions and technological capabilities. These complementarities have been far more important than regionally-biased policy factors or institutionalized preferential arrangements although, in the case of Japan, the intensity of regional trade is also a reflection of Japan's export credit and aid policies.

Within the Asian sub-group, the patterns of trade have become even more interesting and complex since the mid-1980s. As incomes have risen and development deepened, new patterns of increasing specialization have led to a distinct rise in intra-industry trade. Initially, this was a result of a deepening division of labour between Japan and neighbouring economies; more recently there have been signs of a growth in intra-industry trade both between and within the NIC and ASEAN groups. A major stimulus to these changes has been the combination of Japanese trade liberalization and exchange rate changes consequent upon the upward valuation of the yen against the U.S. dollar. While this change involved only the dollar and the yen at first, leaving the NICs in an exceptionally favourable competitive position, under pressure the NICs have been forced to appreciate their currencies strongly against the dollar (with the exception of Hong Kong which is tied to the dollar for political reasons), and this has helped to open their markets to other, new Asian industrializers.

Apart from trade, the major factor in Asian–Pacific integration has

---

1. Valuable surveys of these trends are in FAIR, *Interim Report of Asia Pacific Economic Research* (Tokyo, 1989) and Koichi Ohno (ed.), *Regional Integration and its Impact on Developing Countries* (Tokyo: Institute of Developing Economies, 1993, Part 1). An excellent survey of the development of south China with a valuable chapter and data survey on Taiwan–Fujian relations is Maruyama Nobuo (ed.), *Kanan keizaiken* (*The South China Economic Region*) (Tokyo: Ajia Keizai Kenkyujo, 1992).

been the cross flow of foreign direct investment (FDI). Prior to 1980, there were some substantial flows of investments from Japanese firms seeking to secure reliable supplies of raw materials, access to protected markets, or locations where pollution-intensive industries would find lower costs and less political opposition than was the case in Japan. However, during the course of the 1980s, a series of developments accelerated FDI flows and transformed their impact on trade structures.

First, Reaganite policies took the dollar to levels that forced American-based multinationals to seek low cost locations from which output could be re-exported back to the United States and to other markets. The Asian NIC group, with relatively low wages, well-educated labour forces and strongly motivated business environments, was an ideal solution to this problem. In addition, American multinational FDI flows were accompanied by technology flows to Asia which enabled local producers to take advantage of the opportunities created by the newly favourable cost and exchange rate levels. As a result, the American share of NIC exports expanded from 25 per cent in 1980 to 40 per cent in 1984 – an extraordinarily rapid change.

Secondly, between 1985 and 1988 the revaluation of the yen, designed to alleviate U.S.–Japan trade frictions, profoundly affected Japanese corporate attitudes to FDI. Faced with a rapid reduction in the value of the dollar from 250 to 125 yen by 1988, Japanese businessmen were taking the view that they must plan their business strategies on the assumption of a rate of 100 yen to the dollar. Although this level was never quite reached, the shift in resources was enormous. Between 1984 and 1989 world-wide Japanese FDI rose from US$10 billion to US$70 billion.[2] Of this, in the years 1986–90, more than a third was for investment in manufacturing and 12 per cent of the total went to Asia. The Asian share may seem small, but in relation to the size of some of the favoured Asian economies, the flows were large.

The impact of these flows on the economies of the NICs has been striking, and strongly supported by the slow upward adjustment of their exchange rates against the yen and their consequent gain in competitiveness vis-à-vis Japan. As a result, output, employment, exports and prices increased rapidly, providing strong incentives for government-supported upgrading of domestic and trade structures. In the cases of Taiwan, South Korea and Singapore, upgrading policies were reflected in a significant jump in R & D expenditures. In Hong Kong, where no appreciation against dollar was permitted by the dollar-link system, adjustment mainly took the form of a sharp increase in domestic prices and a rapid relative increase in the size of the service sector. In industry, although official Hong Kong policies had hitherto been strongly against any form of industrial policy, a shift of attitude could also be detected.

Rapidly rising labour and land costs in the NICs had important consequences for ASEAN, which found itself the beneficiary of further

---

2. All references in dollars ($) in this paper are, unless specified otherwise, to United States dollars (US$).

restructuring FDI, sourced not only from Japan and the United States but also from the NICs themselves. Data problems make the quantification of these changes difficult, but according to Japanese estimates, in 1988 FDI accounted for no less than 48.5 per cent of total ASEAN fixed capital formation, and flows of direct investment to Asian regional partners accounted for about half of all Asian investment outflows. These trends have begun to transform ASEAN trade structures. Traditionally primary producers, the ASEAN group have diversified into industrial exports, with Thailand as a striking example of development that has reached the stage where such exports are predominant. Further, since 1990 there have been signs that a new group, including Vietnam and the Philippines, is moving into the circle of FDI-led development. The overall strength of these recent changes has been so strong that while world-wide inflows of direct investment fell by 28 per cent between 1990 and 1992, total Asian inflows actually rose by 51 per cent.[3]

As for the Greater China economies, it is clear that while Hong Kong and China are to some extent special cases, Taiwan fits precisely into this analysis. An archetypal NIC, Taiwan has grown at about 9 per cent per annum for 40 years and during this period it has become the 14th largest trading economy in the world. A major factor in Taiwanese growth has been an active policy to encourage inflows of direct investment – especially from the United States and Japan. In recent years, moreover, Taiwan has been a major recipient of technology flows unrelated to investment in physical capital.

The events of the past five to six years have required a major re-evaluation of Taiwanese economic strategy. Wages and land prices have risen, exchange rate trends have been adverse, and ASEAN economies have become serious competitors in the more labour-intensive and less technologically demanding industries. As a result, Taiwan has been forced to make major efforts to upgrade its economic structure. This has been reflected not only in the massive plans for infrastructure investment, but also in a sharp rise in R & D expenditure. At the same time, Taiwan's exceptional trade surpluses have reflected the macro-economic shift to a rich and mature surplus savings stage of development. This has been evident since 1981. According to estimates by the Ajia Keizai Kenkyujo (Tokyo), the average gap between savings and investment as a percentage of national product during 1981–91 inclusive was an astonishing 11 per cent. These savings have provided the resources to attempt further economic restructuring through outflows of FDI. By investing abroad, Taiwanese companies can combine their own competitive advantages in management, trading and technology with the lower land and labour costs of neighbouring Asian economies. In addition, the impact of these flows on visible trade means that some of the surpluses that are an embarrassment for Taiwan vis-à-vis the United States can be shifted to those economies in which the Taiwanese companies locate.

The data on the size of the outflow of direct investment from Taiwan

3. Bank for International Settlements, *63rd Annual Report* (Basle, 1993), pp. 90–91.

are very imprecise. Taiwanese companies only report a part of their activities and a great deal of the flow goes through intermediary companies (often located in Hong Kong, where capital flow data is unavailable anyway). However, the general level of estimates suggests that between 1987 and 1992 Taiwan directly invested $25 billion abroad. Of that, $12 billion went to local Asian economies and about $6 billion (indirectly) to the PRC. Although the general level of outflow has been falling off, the flow to the PRC increased to flood levels in 1992/93, so that the accumulated stock of investment grew by about 50 per cent in a single year.[4]

The development of Hong Kong and China does not precisely fit this pattern for several reasons. In China's case, the critical difference is that its behaviour as a recipient of direct investment is strongly affected by the nature of the domestic administrative system, planning and legal arrangements, the nature of its industrial enterprises, and its political problems. All these tend to limit FDI from market economies and modify its impact. In Hong Kong's case, the impending reunification in 1997 creates many forces unique to that economy.

This article, therefore, will examine the effects of Taiwanese investment on the PRC economy, through a case study of the Xiamen Special Economic Zone (SEZ). This will throw light on ways in which Taiwanese FDI flows may influence the *overall pattern* of economic integration in the Asia–Pacific Region. These are issues of interest to both the PRC and Taiwan, as well as to scholars, traders and industrialists who have invested, or are planning to invest, in the PRC. After outlining the trend and characteristics of Taiwanese investment in Xiamen, the major effects of Taiwanese investment on the Xiamen economy are analysed and the problems and wider issues arising from the utilization of Taiwanese capital in the PRC discussed. The article ends with some conclusions on the prospects of the PRC–Taiwan relationship and implications for the formation of the so-called "Greater China Economic Community" within the Asia–Pacific region. It is hoped that the underlying issues can be revealed, in spite of the fact that FDI data are scarce and unreliable, and that changes in the policies and measures of the PRC and Taiwanese authorities are so frequent that research is often outdated before publication.

## The Special Features of Taiwanese Investment in Xiamen

The upsurge of Taiwanese investment has been one of the most prominent developments in PRC foreign economic relations in recent years. According to official Chinese sources, by the end of 1992 about 10,000 contracts had been concluded, calling for Taiwanese commitments

---

4. These estimates are based on figures quoted in *The Far Eastern Economic Review* (*FEER*), *China Daily* and the *Asian Wall Street Journal*. According to some commentators, all official numbers should be doubled. Judging by the discoveries made in the UK when serious enquiries were made into illicit post-war direct investment flows from the UK, this view should be taken quite seriously.

of more than $8 billion.[5] In 1992 alone, Taiwanese capital accounted for 13.19 per cent of total FDI projects in China, 9.54 per cent of total foreign capital commitments.[6] As a result, Taiwan has now surpassed Japan and the United States and become the second largest investor, behind Hong Kong, in the PRC.

Most Taiwanese projects are concentrated in the south-eastern coastal areas, with Fujian province accounting for nearly 65 per cent of the total. The Xiamen SEZ in southern Fujian has emerged as the front runner in attracting Taiwanese capital in the country, accounting for approximately a fifth of total projects and half of total pledged and invested capital.[7]

The Xiamen SEZ was opened in 1980 as one of China's five Special Economic Zones. The city faces Taiwan across 140 nautical miles of the Taiwan Straits. It has close historical, political, economic, social and lineage ties with Taiwan. Taiwanese and southern Fujianese speak the same dialect (*Minnanhua*), share the same culture and customs, and have an intimate historical relationship. Merchandise trade between southern Fujian and Taiwan was active as early as the 16th century and, with fluctuations, continued to thrive until 1949. Thereafter the Nationalists severed all links with the Communist mainland.

Today, Xiamen is a typical, small industrial city, containing an under-developed but all-embracing industrial system with some 620 largely outmoded enterprises. With the growing influx of Taiwanese investment, the SEZ authorities have attempted to transform their old industries as their top reform priority. According to the Eighth Five-Year-Plan (1991–95) for Xiamen, Taiwanese firms will generate almost 55 per cent (or 12 billion *yuan*) of total GNP (22 billion *yuan*) by 1995.[8] Thus, the significant involvement of, and the crucial role played by, Taiwanese investment in Xiamen's economic development clearly merit a detailed analysis.

The large-scale influx of Taiwanese capital into mainland China did not start until 1988. The political relaxation in Taiwan and, in particular, the removal of the ban on its citizens on travel to the mainland, triggered a steady stream of visitors to the PRC, especially to Xiamen.[9] Many combined private visits with a search for business opportunities. In response to this new development, the Xiamen authorities, apart from promulgating a series of laws, regulations and rules to encourage Tai-wanese investment, opened up three investment zones (*Haicang*, *Xinglin* and *Jimei*) and one high-tech park (*Yazhou*) exclusively for the Tai-wanese. As a result, the inflow grew at a staggering speed. The total annual investment amount peaked in 1989 ($454.15 million) and the number of projects in 1990 (172). More significantly, in 1989 the Taiwanese projects accounted for 76.62 per cent of all FDI projects and

5. BBC, *Summary of World Broadcasts*, FE/W00278, 19 May 1993, p. 7.
6. *Guoji maoyi (Intertrade)*, April 1993, p. 58.
7. *Beijing Review (BR)*, 27 January–2 February 1992, p. 17.
8. *Ibid.* p. 18.
9. It was estimated that the number of Taiwanese visitors to Xiamen had exceeded 1.3 million by the end of 1992.

87.06 per cent of all foreign committed capital in Xiamen (see Table 1). Today, Taiwanese projects play an increasingly important role in the development of export-oriented activity in Xiamen, with more than $300 million invested and over 200 projects under operation. These produce about one-fifth of the SEZ's total gross value of industrial output (GVIO) and nearly 15 per cent of total exports.[10] Without doubt, once direct communication, transport and business links with Taiwan commence, Xiamen will be the beach-head for further Taiwanese investment in the PRC.

## Motives

There are several important reasons for the recent flows of Taiwanese capital to the PRC. First, as noted above, is the consistent and steady appreciation of the New Taiwan dollar (NT$). Over the last decade this has seriously weakened Taiwan's export competitiveness. Since 1985 the NT$ has appreciated by more than 40 per cent against the US$ to NT$25 to $1 at mid-1992.[11] As the majority of exporters in Taiwan are small and medium-sized manufacturing firms, selling standardized products in highly competitive conditions, the rise of the NT$ has left them un-profitable or, at best, only marginally profitable.

Secondly, other production costs have risen sharply in recent years. Manufacturing wages have been increasing by about 15 per cent per year, pushing the latest minimum wage up to NT$12,365 ($494.6) per month, equivalent to NT$51.5 ($2.06) per hour.[12] This rate, which applies to both native and foreign workers in Taiwan, is about 13–14 times higher than that prevailing in most parts of the PRC.[13] Rising land cost adds another problem and pollution-control expenses have also gone up steeply.[14] All this has made the manufacture of labour-intensive products no longer competitive.

A third factor has been the deterioration of social order in Taiwan in recent years. Violent political demonstrations, various forms of public disorder and, especially, gangland extortion of businessmen by threats of kidnapping or other criminal actions, have all contributed to business-men's lack of confidence in the local investment environment.[15]

Fourthly, many Taiwanese firms are following the strategy of using FDI to expand their exports by opening up the mainland market, potentially

10. *Jingji ribao* (*Economic Daily*) (*JJRB*), 8 January 1992, p. 4.
11. *Free China Journal* (*FCJ*), 18 August 1992, p. 3. According to Osman Tseng, there are four reasons for the continued appreciation. The large surplus generated by Taiwan's foreign trade, its extraordinarily large sums of foreign exchange reserves and its higher interest rates have all created a growing demand for the NT$. Also, the economic recession in the U.S. has weakened the US$ and thus further raised the NT$. For more details, see Osman Tseng, "Unappreciated appreciation," *Free China Review* (*FCR*), February 1992, pp. 40–43.
12. *Ibid.*
13. The average wage in the mainland is only about one-tenth of that prevailing in Taiwan. For a typical Taiwan operation in the mainland, wages account for about 11% of the total production costs while in Taiwan it is about 36%. See *Jingji daobao* (*Economic Report*) (*JJDB*), No. 9 (9 March 1992), p. 33.
14. *FCR*, June 1990, p. 60.
15. *FCJ*, 6 October 1992, p. 7.

Table 1: **Development of Taiwanese Investment in Xiamen (1983 to September 1992)**

| | 1983–87 | 1988 | 1989 | 1990 | 1991 | 1992 (Jan.–Sept.) | Total |
|---|---|---|---|---|---|---|---|
| No. of contracts signed | 16 | 57 | 154 | 172 | 94 | 105 | 598 |
| % of total FDI contracts | 5.42 | 31.67 | 76.62 | 65.65 | 44.13 | 39.92 | 42.29 |
| Capital committed by Taiwan investors ($m.) | 21.50 | 82.19 | 454.15 | 370.00 | 195.68 | 204.21 | 1,327.73 |
| % of total foreign capital commitments | 4.19 | 52.80 | 87.06 | 67.40 | 37.65 | 27.73 | 44.25 |

*Sources:*
1983–87: *Xiamen tongji (Xiamen Statistics)*, No. 8 (1990), p. 23. 1988: Xiamen Statistical Bureau (XSB), *Xiamen tongji nianjian 1989 (Almanac of Xiamen's Statistics 1989)* (Xiamen: Xiamen tongji ju, 1989), p. 362. 1989: XSB, *Xiamen jingji tequ nianjian 1990 (Almanac of the Xiamen Special Economic Zone 1990)* (Beijing: Zhongguo tongji chubanshe, 1990), p. 329. 1990: ACE Editorial Board, *Zhongguo jingji nianjian 1991 (Almanac of China's Economy 1991)* (Beijing: Jingji guanli chubanshe, 1991), p. IV–89. 1991–September 1992: XSB, *Tongji jianxu (Statistical Summary)* (Xiamen: Xiamen tongji ju, 1992), p. 13.

the largest in the world. Expressing the general mood of the Taiwan business community, Wang Chien-shien, Taiwan's former Finance Minister, was quoted as saying: "the mainland is a market for Chinese people, and Chinese people from Taiwan should not lag behind Japanese and Koreans in penetrating the mainland market."[16]

A fifth factor is that in industries subject to heavy international restrictions, some Taiwanese businessmen try to make use of PRC export quotas, especially to the North American and EEC markets.[17] Finally, although Taiwanese appear to have been the leading NIC investors in ASEAN (especially Malaysia and Thailand), the very predominance of these investments has meant that they have not only served to raise local wage costs making them less attractive, but have also caused anti-Taiwanese "frictions" that have encouraged diversification to China and Vietnam.

### Special Features

The basic pattern of Taiwanese investment in Xiamen is that investors provide capital, technology and management expertise while Xiamen supplies cheap and abundant labour and land. However, in contrast to other investors in Xiamen, Taiwanese investors prefer wholly owned ventures to other forms of investment and, in many cases, emphasize their independence by supplying their own raw materials and export markets.

*Predominance of wholly owned ventures.* There is a growing tendency for Taiwanese investors to set up wholly owned ventures in Xiamen, instead of joint equity ventures or contractual management projects. Table 2 shows that the share of wholly owned ventures in the total number of Taiwanese firms climbed steeply, from 37.50 per cent in 1983–87 to a peak of 85.47 per cent in 1990, with an average percentage of 77.52 for the whole period 1983–91. Investment in wholly owned ventures amounted to nearly $1 billion, making up 90 per cent of the total Taiwanese investment in Xiamen.[18] Such a high proportion is unusual in the history of FDI in developing countries.

*Predominance of labour-intensive and light industries.* Because most Taiwanese investors go to the mainland to take advantage of the low labour costs there, the industries they bring in tend to be those producing light industrial/consumer goods, with low capital/technology-labour ratios. About 75 per cent of Taiwanese firms in Xiamen use only simple and, in many cases, second-hand machines imported from Taiwan, manufacturing goods such as footwear, clothing, toys, umbrellas, handicrafts,

---

16. *Ibid.* 18 August 1992, p. 3.

17. *Yuanjian (Global Views) (YJ)*, May 1992, p. 47. According to a survey report published in Taiwan in 1992, the export prices for the products manufactured by the Taiwanese firms in the mainland, i.e. those "made in China," are estimated to be 10% cheaper than those "made in Taiwan." See *ibid.* p. 44.

18. *BR*, 27 January–2 February 1992, p. 17.

Table 2: **Shares of Wholly Owned Ventures in the Total Number of Taiwanese Firms in Xiamen (1983–91)**

|  | 1983–87 | 1988 | 1989 | 1990 | 1991 (Jan.–Nov.) | Total |
|---|---|---|---|---|---|---|
| No. of wholly owned ventures | 6 | 32 | 125 | 147 | 59 | 369 |
| Total no. of Taiwanese firms | 16 | 57 | 154 | 172 | 77 | 476 |
| Share (%) | 37.50 | 56.14 | 81.17 | 85.47 | 76.62 | 77.52 |

*Sources*:
No. of wholly owned ventures: *Xiamen tongji*, No. 8 (1990), p. 26 and *Jingji ribao* (*Economic Daily*), 8 January 1992, p. 4. Total number of Taiwanese firms: Table 1.

luggage and sports equipment.[19] Indeed, some Taiwanese firms even used *less* capital per unit of labour than their local state-owned counterparts.[20]

*Prominence of chemical industry.* Relocation is crucial for Taiwanese chemical manufacturers because many of their customers have moved to the PRC.[21] Thus it is not surprising that Xiamen, as the focus of Taiwanese investment in the mainland, has a strong presence of chemical projects, including plastics and textile processing branches. As shown in

Table 3: **Composition of Taiwanese Firms in Xiamen by Industry (1990)**

|  | No. of projects | % | Amounts involved ($ million) | % |
|---|---|---|---|---|
| Chemical | 48 | 17.27 | 284.70 | 48.76 |
| Paper and stationery | 67 | 24.10 | 69.44 | 11.89 |
| Sewing and leather | 49 | 17.63 | 66.88 | 11.45 |
| Electric machinery | 26 | 9.35 | 61.89 | 10.60 |
| Textile | 21 | 7.55 | 38.41 | 6.58 |
| Building material | 23 | 8.27 | 30.03 | 5.14 |
| Food processing | 20 | 7.19 | 13.37 | 2.29 |
| Electronic | 10 | 3.60 | 10.91 | 1.87 |
| Engineering | 14 | 5.04 | 8.25 | 1.41 |
| Total | 278 | 100.00 | 583.88 | 100.00 |

*Source:*
*Xiamen tongji*, No. 8 (1990), p. 24.

19. *Xiamen tongji* (*Xiamen Statistics*), No. 8 (1990), p. 25.
20. One of the findings of the field visit in Autumn 1991. This is particularly true in umbrella and luggage manufacturing.
21. The plastic footwear industry is a good example. The total number of factories in Taiwan dropped from a peak of 1,400 to only 700 in 1990, primarily because of moves to the mainland. See *FCR*, June 1990, p. 60.

Table 3, although they make up only 17.27 per cent of all Taiwanese manufacturing projects in Xiamen in 1990, the amount involved ($284.70 million) accounts for a remarkable 48.76 per cent – nearly 37 per cent ahead of its closest rival, the paper and stationery industry. At the beginning of 1992 it was still at 40 per cent.[22]

*High ratio of export.* As most Taiwanese firms' finished goods are placed by their parent corporations in Taiwan, they tend to have very high ratios of export.[23] For example, in 1990 Taiwanese firms exported 86.12 per cent of their total output valued at 799.83 million *yuan*, in contrast with only 35 per cent for non-Taiwanese FDI firms in the same period.[24] The exports from Taiwanese firms accounted for 22.65 per cent of Xiamen's total exports. About three-quarters of these went to Europe and North America and 10 per cent to Japan.[25] A survey carried out in 183 Taiwanese firms in 1990 reveals that 107 of them (58.47 per cent) exported more than 80 per cent of their outputs, and that only eight (4.37 per cent) exported less than half (see Table 4).

Table 4: **Composition of Taiwanese Firms in Xiamen by Export Ratio (1990)**

| Export ratio (%) | Number of firms | Share (%) |
|---|---|---|
| 100 | 56 | 30.60 |
| 80–99 | 51 | 27.87 |
| 50–79 | 68 | 37.16 |
| Below 49 | 8 | 4.37 |
| Total | 183 | 100.00 |

*Source:*
Hu Peizhao *et al.*, "Report on the Taiwan investment in Xiamen," *Zhongguo jingji wenti* (*China's Economic Problems and Issues*), April 1990, p. 16.

*Diversification of investment structure.* Taiwanese investment in Xiamen tends to concentrate on manufacturing industries producing light industrial/consumer goods. In 1990, for example, 86 per cent of Taiwanese firms were engaged in manufacturing operations, making up 78 per cent of the total Taiwanese investment funds. Since 1991, however, service industries, particularly real estate, have become the new focus of Taiwanese investment. At present, they account for 12 per cent of all

22. *BR*, 27 January–2 February 1992, p. 18.
23. Caves argues that foreign investors having a competitive edge in overseas marketing are likely to play an active role in the export marketing of their subsidiaries. See R. E. Caves, "International corporations: the industrial economics of foreign investment," *Econometrica*, No. 149 (February 1971), pp. 1–27.
24. Kong Zhang, "Assessment of Taiwan investment in Xiamen," *Gang-Ao jingji* (*Hong Kong and Macau Economies*), June 1991, p. 34.
25. Xiamen Statistical Bureau (XSB), *Xiamen jingji tequ nianjian 1991* (*Almanac of the Xiamen Special Economic Zone 1991*) (Beijing: Zhongguo tongji chubanshe, 1991), p. 58.

Taiwanese projects and 20 per cent of investment capital. Indeed, real estate has become the second largest investment sector, after the chemical industry.[26] Two-thirds of property developers are known to come from Taiwan, and they, together with thousands of contracted builders, have created a booming property business in Xiamen.[27]

*Growing average size of investment.* Before mid-1988, Xiamen did not have a single Taiwanese project involving more than $10 million and average capitalization was only $736,355 per project.[28] Most were the same scale as local rural or township enterprises. Since the second half of 1988, however, the situation has changed as a result of the political initiative taken by the Taiwanese authorities. More than half of Taiwan's Top 100 Companies (including the Formosa Plastic Group) have sent delegations to Xiamen to explore the possibility of investment. As a result, a total of 11 big contracts involving $10 million each had been signed by the end of 1990, with the largest investment worth $200 million.[29] This has increased the average capitalization to $3.469 million per project, compared with only $1.35 million for the non-Taiwanese FDI projects.[30]

Furthermore, many existing Taiwanese firms have expanded their operations in Xiamen by re-investing their profits. For instance, the Sandexing Industry Co. Ltd., set up in 1985, has increased its production capacity 11-fold and is planning to build a new industrial park housing 16 other Taiwanese firms. The Xianglu Chemical Co. Ltd., in addition to considering the establishment of weaving projects, has asked to build new plants to produce related high-pressure packaging containers.[31]

Taiwanese investors have shown increased willingness to extend the length of their investment term. Table 5 shows that from July 1987 to June 1989 the shares of the firms having an investment term of over 20 years increased substantially, while those below dropped sharply. By the beginning of 1992 some firms had extended their investment terms to 70 years.[32]

Thus a new investment pattern seems to be emerging. It is gradually shifting from single investments in manufacturing made by small or medium firms to joint investments (or developments) in both manufacturing and service industries by several companies, company groups or even conglomerates. There has also been a shift from renting workshops or buildings to buying them and, more recently, to leasing or buying a piece of land to develop it into an exclusive Taiwanese investment zone or industrial park.

26. *BR*, 27 January–2 February 1992, p. 18. The total Taiwan investment in mainland real estate stood, at the beginning of 1992, at $100 million. See *ibid.*

27. Xu Caixue, "Xiamen builds her dream on Taiwan," *YJ*, February 1992, p. 121.

28. Hu Peizhao *et al.*, "Report on the Taiwan investment in Xiamen," *Zhongguo jingji wenti (China's Economic Problems and Issues)*, April 1990, p. 14.

29. *BR*, 27 January–2 February 1992, p. 17.

30. Zhang Fenqing, "Analyses of Taiwan investment in the Xiamen SEZ," *Duiwai maoyi yanjiu (Research on Foreign Trade)*, p. 3.

31. *BR*, 27 January–2 February 1992, p. 18.

32. *Ibid.* p. 17.

Table 5: **Composition of Taiwanese Firms in Xiamen by Length of Investment Term (July 1987–June 1989)**

| Length (year) | July 1987–June 1988 | | July 1988–June 1989 | |
|---|---|---|---|---|
| | No. of firms | % | No. of firms | % |
| Over 30 | 9 | 12.68 | 45 | 36.00 |
| 20–29 | 17 | 23.94 | 35 | 28.00 |
| 10–19 | 43 | 60.56 | 45 | 36.00 |
| Below 10 | 2 | 2.82 | 0 | 0.00 |
| Total | 71 | 100.00 | 125 | 100.00 |

*Source:*
Hu Peizhao, "Report on the Taiwan investment in Xiamen," p. 16.

*Generally good performances.* In contrast to the less satisfactory situation in all FDI projects, the financial performance of Taiwanese firms appears good.[33] Since many of them are small, light and self-equipped manufacturing ventures, they have the flexibility to plan for short gestation periods, and are normally able to sign contracts, go into operation and get returns within a year. According to a sample survey carried out by the Chinese Academy of Social Sciences, about 95 per cent of Taiwanese firms in Xiamen were profitable.[34] This ratio is considerably higher than the 53 per cent for the non-Taiwanese FDI firms. The footwear factories, for example, were reported to make 10–15 per cent more profits in Xiamen than in Taiwan.[35] Because of good performance, many firms start to play an important role in their parent corporations or their fields. Cankun Electric Appliance Co. Ltd. now produces two-thirds of the total output value of its general corporation,[36] while the Sandexing Industry Co. Ltd. has become the world's second largest manufacturer of conductive rubber.[37]

## Major Effects of Taiwanese Investment on the Xiamen Economy

Since it was opened as an SEZ in 1980, Xiamen's economy has grown rapidly, fuelled mainly by the inflow of FDI. In 1992 the SEZ's GDP rose to 7.8 billion *yuan*, a 5.1-fold increase over 1980. Exports hit $3.53 billion, jumping by 53 per cent over 1991 – the largest increase among all the SEZs. The overall indicator of economic efficiency was 5.4 percentage points higher than the national average.[38]

33. However, the scale of losses in all FDI projects in the PRC is rising, and, in some areas, about 50% of FDI firms are reported to run at a loss. This has already become the focus of attention both within and outside China. See *JJDB*, 6 April 1992, p. 18.
34. *Jing bao* (*The Mirror*), January 1992, p. 79.
35. Kong Zhang, "Assessment of Taiwan investment," p. 34.
36. *BR*, 27 January–2 February 1992, p. 17.
37. Xu Caixue, "Xiamen builds her dream," p. 120.
38. *Renmin ribao* (*People's Daily*) overseas edition, 14 April 1993, p. 1; *JJRB*, 20 February 1993. p. 3.

Taiwanese investment, as the largest source of FDI in Xiamen, has played a crucial role in its economic development in recent years. The most evident contributions made by Taiwanese firms to Xiamen seem to be the creation of employment, increase in exports and expansion of tourism.

*Reducing importance of the state-owned sector.* As in other parts of China, Taiwanese firms in Xiamen grow much faster than local Chinese enterprises, especially state-owned ones (SOEs). At present, there are several Taiwanese firms producing more than $30 million worth of GVIO monthly.[39] As a result, the share of the state-owned sector in the economy has declined steadily, while the private sector (including Taiwanese and other foreign-owned firms) has risen. By the end of 1991, for example, the GVIO and exports of some 200 Taiwanese firms in Xiamen accounted respectively for one-fifth and 22.65 per cent of the SEZ's totals.[40] Together with all other FDI firms, they make up about 52 per cent of the SEZ's total GVIO and 80 per cent of its exports.[41] It is thus clear that the role played by the state-owned sector in Xiamen's economy has diminished significantly. Facing stiff competition from Taiwanese and other foreign firms, some inefficient local enterprises, especially SOEs, find it hard to survive. For instance, the Xiamen Mechanical Engineering Plant, one of the leading SOEs in the SEZ, was forced to close down in 1991.[42]

*Over-riding local industrial development plan.* In the 1985–2000 Socio-economic Development Plan, the Xiamen authorities (like their counterparts in other SEZs) decided to put the development of the electronic industry as their top priority in the hope that it would, through FDI, become the leading industrial sector by 1995. This decision was made on the grounds that "the electronic industry will pioneer Xiamen's industrial transformation through its extensive linkage effects."[43] However, the growing influx of Taiwanese capital since 1988 has swept the plan aside. As shown in Table 3, Taiwanese investment in Xiamen is dominated largely by the chemical industry (48.76 per cent of total investment), and the share of electronics is almost negligible (1.87 per cent). Thus the structure of Taiwanese investment does not coincide with Xiamen's own industrial transformation plan. Faced with this divergence, the Xiamen authorities apparently abandoned their original goal and declared petrochemicals to be their new "investment emphasis."[44] Indeed, a great deal of work has been done to accommodate more and bigger chemical projects from Taiwan.

39. *JJDB*, 16 March 1992, p. 10.
40. *JJRB*, 8 January 1992, p. 4; *BR*, 27 January–2 February 1992, p. 17.
41. *JJDB*, 1 January 1992, p. 28.
42. Xu Caixue, "Xiamen builds her dream," p. 120.
43. Research Office of Development Strategy of the Xiamen SEZ Government, *Xiamen jingji shehui fazhan zhanlue 1985–2000* (*The Strategy of Xiamen Socio-Economic Development 1985–2000*) (Xiamen: Lujiang chubanshe, 1989), p. 139.
44. *BR*, 27 January–2 February 1992, p. 19.

*Linkage effects.* Most Taiwanese firms are characterized by what local people call the "five self-responsibles" (*wuge ziwofuze*), that is, they are responsible for their own capital, technology, raw materials, management and export markets. This means that, apart from making use of cheap labour and land in Xiamen, all other inputs are brought from Taiwan. For example, more than three-quarters of all raw materials, components and parts needed by Taiwanese firms in Xiamen come from Taiwan, and about 85 per cent of their finished products are exported to existing overseas markets. Some midstream factories have even invested with upstream and/or downstream factories, and formed a self-sufficient, self-sustained operational system, almost wholly independent of the local economy.[45]

Moreover, as most of the ventures are wholly owned (77.52 per cent, see Table 2), top and middle-level managerial personnel are normally sent from their parent corporations in Taiwan and control all aspects and stages of their operations in Xiamen. Xiamen employees with low-level management responsibilities account for less than 30 per cent of the total number of managerial staff and play only a minor role in the decision-making process.[46]

Clearly, these enclave operations have little linkage effect (forward or backward) or demonstration effects on the local economy. As a result, the plan to make use of Taiwanese investment to transform local industrial enterprises and to stimulate the development of other related industries is still far from being reality.

*Technology transfer.* As already shown, many Taiwanese firms are small-scale and labour-intensive enterprises, producing light industrial/consumer goods. Thus in most cases the technologies employed are simple, mature and standardized. A considerable amount of their capital equipment is second-hand, imported from factories in Taiwan. Of the 200 identified technologies introduced so far, "very few" could really be regarded as sophisticated.[47]

On the other hand, according to another survey, about 65 per cent of technologies introduced by the Taiwanese are judged as appropriate to Xiamen's conditions. The Taiwanese shoe-manufacturing technology in Xiamen, for example, has been carefully studied and then copied by the Fujian Mechanical Engineering Bureau, with a view to equipping all the mainland shoe-making factories with the same technology. Also, several Taiwanese firms have brought in some practical technical know-how and/or Western manufacturing standards, such as the American "UL," Canadian "CSA," Japanese "JIS" and German "RDEF-TUV," to manufacture products with well-known brands such as "Philips" and "Esars."[48]

45. *Xiamen tequ yanjiu* (*Research on the Xiamen SEZ*) (*XMTQYJ*), March 1991, pp. 17–18; Kong Zhang, "Assessment of Taiwan investment," p. 34.

46. *XMTQYJ*, March 1991, pp. 17–18.

47. *China–Britain Trade Review*, January 1992, p. 14; Yan Zhiping, "The constraints on and counter-measures for Taiwan investment in Xiamen," *Fujian jingji* (*Fujian Economy*), p. 28.

48. Yan Zhiping, "Constraints and counter-measures," p. 34.

*Increasing employment.* The total number of people working in Taiwanese firms is now around 45,000. Many more are self-employed in the
service industries which flourish in the periphery of the enterprises. The
Xiamen authorities spent only 140 million *yuan* on facilitating these
employment opportunities. It was estimated that if the jobs had been
created solely by the authorities it would cost them at least 700 million
*yuan*.[49]

*External effects.* As well as taxes, rents and charges paid to the local
authorities, Taiwanese investment has had a number of advantageous
effects. First, it has stimulated real estate business and greatly improved
the utilization of local infrastructure. Before 1988 only about 50 per cent
of a large number of standard factory buildings (which cost the authorities 420 million *yuan* to build) had been leased out. Since then, however,
all the empty buildings have been rented to or bought by the Taiwanese.
Many late arrivals had to settle in makeshift buildings or rent empty space
in local factories. As a result, the authorities claim to have recovered all
the buildings' construction costs by 1989, and to have achieved a rate of
return of 162 per cent.[50]

Secondly, Taiwanese investment has created a desirable social effect
on Xiamen and the neighbouring areas by generating employment. The
average annual salary for a worker in a Taiwanese firm is about 5,000
*yuan*, which is four times higher than the local annual living costs (1,250
*yuan*). Thus a worker employed in a Taiwanese firm can support another
three people in his or her family, compared with only 0.87 people in the
case of a worker employed by a local Chinese factory. As 80 per cent of
the 45,000 employees came from poorer rural regions around Xiamen, the
income effects created by Taiwanese firms are far-reaching.[51]

Thirdly, it has promoted the development of tourism in Xiamen.
During 1989–90, the number of foreign tourists visiting the PRC dropped
sharply because of the Tiananmen Square violence. In Xiamen, however,
the number of Taiwanese "tourists," many actually looking for business
opportunities, reached record highs of 73,000 in 1989 and 136,000 in
1990.[52] Indeed, Xiamen hotels had unusually high occupancy rates at that
time. Tourist numbers continued to grow in 1991 and 1992, when taxes
paid by the tourist industry to the SEZ authorities were reported to have
"climbed to new heights."[53]

Finally, it has induced investment from more than 30 Japanese firms,
business partners of Taiwanese firms currently operating in Xiamen.[54]

However, the massive influx of Taiwan capital and personnel has also
brought some unwelcome changes to the local population and economy.
First, it has contributed to inflation and social dualism. In 1988 and 1989,

49. Kong Zhang, "Assessment of Taiwan investment," p. 34.
50. Hu Peizhao, "Report on the Taiwan investment in Xiamen," p. 17.
51. Kong Zhang, "Assessment of Taiwan investment," p. 34.
52. XSB, *Xiamen jingji tequ nianjian 1990* (*Almanac of the Xiamen Special Economic
Zone 1990*) (Beijing: Zhongguo tongji chubanshe, 1990), p. 333.
53. Xu Caixue, "Xiamen builds her dream," p. 121.
54. *Ibid.* p. 120.

the price index of living costs for local people rose by 28.9 and 24.0 per cent respectively, leading to the deterioration of living standards for 17 per cent of families in Xiamen.[55] Thus while families benefiting from Taiwanese investment have greatly improved their welfare, some outside this group have clearly lost.

Secondly, the growing number of immigrants working in Taiwanese firms has exerted great pressure on housing, city-wide transport, school-ing and entertainment facilities. It has also led to an increase in crime and other illegal activities in Xiamen. This problem has been aggravated by the fact that many Taiwanese investors by-passed the local Labour Management Bureau to employ even cheaper labour from the rural areas around Xiamen. Taiwanese real estate speculation has also pushed up property prices to an unduly high level.

In addition, the perceived superiority of employment in Taiwanese firms has seriously affected the morale (and hence probably the produc-tivity) of employees in local Chinese enterprises, particularly SOEs. The wages and salaries of the former are about 2.14 times higher than those of the latter. As a result, many talented professionals and skilled workers have left their Chinese units for Taiwanese firms, leaving the local ones in decline.[56]

In short, the effects of Taiwanese investment on the Xiamen economy are profound, but they are by no means as influential and indeed crucial as those of Hong Kong investment on the Shenzhen SEZ, where a close economic integration between the two economies is taking place. Despite the achievement of attracting a greater inflow of Taiwanese capital, Xiamen seems to have failed to integrate Taiwanese investment into its economy, in particular to establish extensive economic and technological links between Taiwanese and local firms to transform its old, outmoded industry.

## Taiwanese Investment and the PRC Economy

Taiwan is the PRC's second largest source of foreign investment, so its impact on the PRC economy as a whole is significant. The scale of the investment is growing and its structure is becoming more diversified. More importantly, the capitalization per project in 1992 rose from $560,000 to $781,000, up by nearly 40 per cent over 1991.[57] According to a survey report released recently in Taiwan, Taiwanese-funded firms made up 19 of 500 top foreign-funded firms on the mainland in 1991. Professor Kao An-pang of Taiwan's National Chengchi University esti-mates that Taiwanese capital accounts for $8.6 billion of the mainland's GNP and $7.2 of its per capita income.[58] Another report, released by Taiwan's Council for Economic Planning and Development (CEPD)

55. XSB, *Xiamen tongji nianjian 1989* (*Almanac of Xiamen's Statistics 1989*) (Xiamen: Xiamen tongji ju, 1989), p. 352; XSB, *Xiamen jingji tequ nianjian 1990*, p. 305.

56. Kong Zhang, "Assessment of Taiwan investment," p. 35.

57. *FCJ*, 4 September 1992, p. 3.

58. *Ibid.* 30 November 1992, p. 3.

indicated that a 0.28 per cent increase in Taiwan's trans-shipment to the mainland would lead to a growth of one percentage point in mainlanders' per capita income.[59]

Perhaps the most important contribution of Taiwanese investment to the PRC economy has been its impact on exports. As most Taiwanese firms in the PRC have very high export ratios, they play an important part in boosting PRC exports.[60] Indeed, as a result of this investment, the PRC is increasingly becoming a foreign trade rival to Taiwan, especially in the American market. In 1991, Taiwan's market share in the United States rose by only 0.1 per cent from 1990's 4.6 per cent. The PRC, on the other hand, closed the gap by increasing its share markedly from 3.1 to 3.9 per cent.[61] In 1992, PRC exports rose to a staggering $165.6 billion, outstripping Taiwan's $153.48 billion.[62] Thus 1992 will go down in history as the first year the PRC out-traded Taiwan, which has long been praised for its successful, export-oriented economy. The Taiwanese authorities attributed the growth to Taiwanese investment, especially in labour-intensive, light industrial sectors. For example, mainland toy exports hit $810 million with an annual growth rate of 41 per cent, while footwear exports expanded at a speed of 44.3 per cent per year to $2.31 billion.[63]

### Problems and Wider Issues

In spite of the positive effects above, several serious problems and issues have emerged from the utilization of Taiwanese capital in the mainland, and these are now considered.

*Conflict between the structure of Taiwanese investment and the mainland plan of industrial transformation.* China's present industrial priority must now be to raise the technological level through, *inter alia*, the development of the engineering and electronic sectors. At the micro-level, it is crucial to improve the performance of tens of thousands of SOEs through radical reform programmes (including privatization). The role of FDI should be to assist the development of the industries which have extensive linkages to other manufacturing sectors, including machine tools, motor, iron and steel, heavy chemical, new material, equipment and instrument, and non-ferrous metal industries.

However, it is clear from the previous sections that the level and structure of Taiwanese investment generally do not match this strategy. In

59. *Ibid.* 20 November 1992, p. 3.
60. Trade between the PRC and Taiwan is growing sharply. Total trade volume with the mainland accounts for 4.6% of Taiwan's global trade (exports account for 7.3% and imports for 1.6%). See *FCJ*, 30 October 1992, p. 3. The same CEPD report also reveals the close trade linkage between the two in the sense that when PRC total exports expand by HK$1 million, Taiwan's exports to the PRC increase by 0.02%; while a decrease of $1 million in the PRC foreign exchange reserves result in a 0.01% drop in Taiwan's trans-shipments. See *ibid.*
61. *Ibid.* 24 July 1992, p. 3.
62. *Ibid.* 2 April 1993, p. 3.
63. *Ibid.* 18 September 1992, p. 3.

Xiamen's case, as has been seen, there is a conflict between the main interest of Taiwanese investment (chemical industry) and the local development priority (electronic industry). As well as the motives of investors, the policy of the Taiwanese authorities is also responsible for this conflict. According to the MOEA's new proposal, Taiwanese businessmen are automatically allowed to invest indirectly (via a third place) in 3,764 labour-intensive, low-tech products in the PRC. Applications for investment in some of the more capital/technology-intensive industries such as petrochemicals, cement and industrial parks will be considered on individual merit.[64] The authorities still firmly ban investment in what they see as high-tech products, projects "related to Taiwan's defence or economic security." A new law now requires that Taiwanese firms register their mainland operations with the authorities in order to facilitate "effectively guiding and ensuring the soundness of Taiwan investment on the mainland." Those failing to comply are subject to fines ranging from $115,000 to $576,000 and will be ordered to close down their project(s).[65]

Thus the role played by Taiwanese investment in the PRC economy is quite limited, despite the lower-level functions of increasing Chinese employment and exports. To rely on Taiwanese investment to restructure local industry and develop high-technology sectors, as Xiamen hopes, is, at least for the moment, unrealistic.

*Small-scale and enclave-type operations.* One of the legacies of the Maoist economy is the compartmentalization of industry by tens of thousands of local, small, self-sufficient enterprises. The current industrial reform has tried to eradicate this problem by reorganizing enterprises along economic lines, by mergers and by the formation of horizontal economic associations. As a result, many large enterprises, such as enterprise groups, are appearing. It is therefore essential for the PRC to integrate into the economy some advanced foreign multinationals which have extensive links with these enterprises.

However, the Taiwanese authorities' policy toward Taiwanese investment in the mainland is a major obstacle to this plan. Kao Koong-lian, a vice-chairman of Taiwan's Mainland Affairs Council, was recently quoted as saying that Taipei is "certainly not willing to see too many large firms go across the Straits."[66] It is reported that they wanted to use the indicator of output value as the criterion of approving investment projects. Thus a private firm will be allowed to invest in the mainland only if its output value per person per year is *below* Taiwan's average level by a certain margin. The standard set for 1992 is $50,000. Later, seven qualitative criteria were laid down to define the industries as labour-intensive, linkage-free, utilizing mainland resources, non-competitive, non-energy-consuming, non-polluting and achieving an appropriate

64. *Ibid.* 4 September 1992, p. 3.
65. *Ibid.* 21 July 1992, p. 8; 4 June 1993, p. 3; 15 June 1993, p. 3.
66. *Ibid.* 1 December 1992, p. 3.

ratio of local sales.[67] More recently, the authorities require manufacturers to retain part of their businesses, or "leave roots," in Taiwan. In other words, their mainland investments "cannot exceed a designated proportion of their domestic investments."[68] Taiwan's Investment Commission has already suspended approval of applications by ten companies listed on the island's stock market.[69] Without doubt, all these measures are intended to prevent or restrict large Taiwanese companies from investing in the mainland and thus to minimize the possibility of enhancing the mainland's industrial competitiveness.

*Regional limitation.* At present, Taiwanese investment is largely confined to China's south-eastern coastal areas, especially Fujian province, which reflects the economic and political considerations of both parties. One consequence of this high concentration, however, is severe overlapping of investment in the region. For example, a small rural town in Jinjiang county, southern Fujian, overwhelmed by 19 Taiwanese shoe-making factories has been dubbed as the "Taiwan shoe town." Indeed, the whole of southern Fujian will soon become a Taiwanese export processing zone.

In fact, with Taiwanese investment becoming larger and more diversified, other places in the Chinese interior may prove to be more suitable for Taiwanese investment. The MOEA's survey shows that Taiwanese firms situated in North-east China, Jiangsu and Zhejiang are the most profitable, followed by those in the Xiamen SEZ and Shanghai, while those in Fujian, Guangdong and the Shenzhen SEZ are the least.[70] Indeed, locations such as Shanghai, Tianjin, Liaoning, Jiangsu, Hubei and Sichuan are certainly better locations in terms of attracting large-scale or capital/technology-intensive industrial projects. Since these regions are generally more developed than South-east China, economic co-operation between the two sides will be at a higher and more sophisticated level. It will also be easier for Taiwanese investors to build up linkages with the local economy.

*Dual economy.* The expansion and, especially, enclave-type operation of Taiwanese investment has resulted in some dualistic phenomena in the PRC economy. It has become almost commonplace in some parts of Fujian, for example, to see fast-growing, capitalist Taiwanese firms coexisting side by side with stagnant or even declining socialist local enterprises.

From the national point of view, the influx of Taiwanese investment has aggravated the disparity of economic development between the south-eastern coastal areas and the inland regions. Since the PRC started to implement the open-door policy in the late 1970s and the early 1980s,

67. *JJDB*, 1 June 1992, p. 31.
68. *FCJ*, 4 September 1992, p. 3. As more than 90% of Taiwan firms are small and medium-sized, few have the ability to conduct simultaneous investment on both sides of the Taiwan Straits.
69. *Ibid.* 15 June 1993, p. 3.
70. *YJ*, May 1992, p. 44.

the economic growth in the south-east has persistently and substantially outpaced that inland, owing largely to the huge injection of foreign investment. As a result, the country is now divided by the more marke-tized, export-oriented economy in the south-east and the more centralized, inward-looking one in the vast hinterland. Both GNP and national income per capita of the former region are more than double those of the latter,[71] which has caused a large-scale migration from the poor inland to the more affluent south-east, destabilizing the inland economy. The inequality has already given rise to strong opposition from certain factions within the CCP leadership, as well as widespread resent-ment on the part of the inland authorities and people.

Clearly, these phenomena are potential causes for social unrest. If the Chinese authorities do not take action to narrow the divergence, they will soon face serious economic, social, cultural and, eventually, political consequences.

*Opening domestic market and attracting high-tech investment.* The PRC and Taiwan do have some high-technology industries which are complementary to each other. For example, the PRC is strong in space technology, micro-biology, medicine, optics and nuclear engineering, while Taiwan has computer manufacture, information technology, avi-ation, motor industry and electrical appliances. The PRC's strengths, coupled with its mighty heavy industrial base, could serve Taiwan's objective to upgrade its industries, while those of Taiwan, together with its experiences in industrialization, seem to suit the PRC's priority to develop electronic, automation, telecommunications and engineering industries.

Despite the fact that Taiwan, together with another 23 countries/ regions, has been chosen by the PRC as a partner for high-technology co-operation, the general technology level of Taiwanese investment attracted so far is, as shown above, disappointingly low. As well as the above-mentioned factors of the investment environment and Taiwan's official policy, the PRC's so-called Special Policy toward high-technol-ogy investment should be blamed. The policy has not been backed by effective tax, price and financial mechanisms and hence has had little influence on Taiwanese investors.[72] The PRC authorities ought to under-stand that insistence on export quotas for FDI may be inappropriate for high-technology investment, at least in the short term. In fact, those investors carrying advanced technologies or new products tend to take a longer-term view and are hence more interested in opening a new market in the PRC. Although the authorities have gradually come to realize the importance of "exchanging domestic markets for advanced foreign tech-nology," no specific policy measures have been worked out.[73]

71. *JJDB*, 15 June 1992, p. 12.
72. *Ibid.* 24 February 1992, p. 16.
73. Recently, the PRC offered to help Taiwan dispose of waste from its three atomic energy plants, which the PRC will not normally do for a "foreign" country. In exchange, Taiwan was to

*Funding of Taiwan firms.* Like other FDI firms on the mainland, Taiwanese firms suffer from the difficulty of raising local funds. The mainland banks, all owned by the state, lend most of their money to SOEs, in many cases to prop up the inefficient ones. Hence there is little left for Taiwanese firms. In addition, because of the lack of mortgage law in the PRC, it is very hard for a newly-established Taiwanese company (without credit record) to obtain a loan there. This situation has been exacerbated by the non-existence, up till now, of Taiwanese banks on the mainland and by the prohibition of foreign banks in the PRC to lend or deposit money in PRC currency.

Thus Taiwanese firms have to raise most, if not all, of their funds from outside the mainland.[74] According to a recent survey conducted by Taiwan's Chung-Hua Institution for Economic Research, 72.25 per cent of Taiwanese firms on the mainland get their funds from Taiwanese financial institutions, 17.2 per cent from mainland banks, 7 per cent from banks in a third country, and only 1.45 per cent from foreign banks operating on the mainland.[75] It was reported that, in the first five months of 1993 alone, Taiwan's capital outflow to the mainland soared to 700 per cent annual growth to a total of $511.4 million. This figure exceeds, for the first time, Taiwan's outward investment in all other sites.[76]

In the light of this, the Taiwanese authorities have recently reaffirmed their ban on Taiwanese banks setting up branches or directly financing Taiwan firms across the Straits.[77] A warning has been issued to banks involved in such financing that they will not receive support from BOT, the central bank, if they suffer from a shortage of funds.[78] At the same time, the authorities still ban direct remittances between the two sides and, instead, ask investors to remit their funds to a third place first in order to be considered as "indirect investment."[79] Moreover, they again ruled out the use of the NT$ and RMB *yuan* in any operation involving banks from both sides. Obviously, all these measures are designed to curb the outflow of Taiwanese capital and therefore will do nothing to ease the difficulty of raising funds or to cut costs of operation for Taiwanese firms on the mainland.

The PRC authorities, to encourage FDI, should relax their restrictions

---

*footnote continued*

co-operate in high-technology areas. At the same time, influential people in Taiwan made the suggestion that Taiwan should use its foreign exchange resources to buy the mainland's technology to support high-technology researches there. See *FCJ*, 28 August 1992, p. 3. Plans have reportedly been made to co-operate in such areas as aerospace, superconductivity and computers. See *ibid.* 6 October 1992, p. 7.

74. Some mainland scholars maintain that the acute difficulty of raising funds in the mainland is one of the major reasons why Taiwanese entrepreneurs prefer wholly owned ventures to mainland–Taiwan joint ventures. See Yan Zhiping, "Constraints and counter-measures," p. 29.

75. *FCJ*, 3 August 1992, p. 3.

76. *Ibid.* 15 June 1993, p. 3.

77. *Ibid.* 18 August 1992, p. 3; *Jiushi niandai (The Nineties)*, September 1992, p. 67.

78. *Ibid.* 14 August 1992, p. 8.

79. *Ibid.* 1 September 1992, p. 3.

on issuing loans to Taiwan firms, promulgate mortgage and other related laws as soon as possible, and consider allowing foreign banks in the PRC to handle their businesses in RMB *yuan*.

*Host policy.* Driven partly by long-term political considerations and partly by compatriot emotion, the PRC authorities offer more financial incentives to Taiwanese than to non-Taiwanese foreign investors. In addition, local authorities compete fiercely with each other in offering even more concessions to the Taiwanese, in order to boost the quantity of FDI in their regions. This has two consequences: first, as shown above, an unusually large number of low-level or "sunset" projects were attracted, many of which are overlapping; and secondly, the double standards have not only created confusion in the incentive policy but, more importantly, seriously damaged the prospect for non-Taiwanese foreign investors, particularly those from the industrialized West or with advanced technology, to come to the PRC. In fact, it is not necessary to offer extra financial concessions to Taiwanese investors. Many of them would rather see an increase in the ratio of local sales, relaxation of credit controls, and/or opening more sectors to them.[80]

## Prospects and Implications

In the light of the levels of economic development on both sides of the Taiwan Straits, it appears to be an ideal combination if Taiwan and the mainland's south-eastern coastal areas can restructure, at least partly, their economies and form a vertical economic integration, with the former focusing on R & D and design of products, manufacturing technologies, business management and international marketing, and the latter on massive production, especially of labour-intensive, light industrial exports. At present, both sides seem to work hard to maximize benefits from investment links and avoid negative impacts on their economies and states. At the same time, they try to achieve political ends by economic means. The failure to sign a bilateral investment protection agreement in the historic Singapore Talks earlier this year is a good case in point.

By actively promoting close economic links and interdependence across the Taiwan Straits, Beijing clearly hopes to achieve two political objectives: to counterbalance the growing tendency in Taiwan toward independence, and, eventually, to force the Taipei authorities to come to the negotiating table on Beijing's terms, if necessary by cutting off, or threatening to cut off, the linkages. On the other hand, by allowing the development of Taiwan businesses in the PRC, Taipei, too, could achieve two political gains: it could create powerful interests in certain groups of mainlanders and certain parts of the mainland which want to avoid the use of force against their business partners, and it could introduce "Taiwan experiences" and the culture of Asian capitalism to the mainland to expedite the process of "peaceful evolution."

80. *JJDB*, 25 May 1992, p. 22.

Of course, Taiwan has to prevent its economy from becoming too dependent on the mainland's, which, in a different context, is now the fate of Hong Kong and Macau. Taipei's view is that it must not give Beijing undue leverage in its dealings with Taiwan. It has made it clear that it will allow trade and investment links to develop more freely only when Beijing shows "gestures of goodwill" towards Taiwan. Based on this principle, Taiwan's CEPD has urged the government to implement a policy which would encourage trade with, instead of investment in, the mainland.[81] Clearly, Taipei is using economic assistance in the political bargaining process with Beijing.

Thus, how far and how fast PRC–Taiwan economic links will develop seems to depend more on political than economic factors. The persistent refusal by both to meet the other's demands has become the major obstacle to close economic integration. There is very little prospect, at least in the foreseeable future, of either changing their stance. It is this uncertainty in PRC–Taiwan political relations which will overshadow the development of economic links for a considerable time. Indeed, it also casts doubt on the formation of the so-called "Greater China Economic Community," comprising mainland China, Hong Kong (and Macau) and Taiwan.[82]

Among the three inter-relationships, the PRC–Hong Kong one has no really insurmountable problem from Hong Kong's impending return to the PRC's sovereignty. In fact, the two economies are already in a process of integration. There can be no doubt that after 1997 this process can only be faster and smoother. With regard to the Hong Kong–Taiwan relationship, as they have reasonably compatible economic systems, linkage between them should not be more difficult than that between any two market economies.[83] It is the PRC–Taiwan relationship which stands out as the most problematic and decisive of the three.

However, whatever happens in PRC–Taiwan political relations in the future, the economic ties between them will continue to grow in some form, because the structural conditions favouring co-operation are so powerful. It is possible that market forces may yet drive the economic links across the Taiwan Straits to an extent that neither Beijing nor Taipei can control the pace of development. If so, the formation of the "Greater China Economic Community" will come about in spite of the political obstacles.

Against this rather popular view, two points should be borne in mind. First, the future of Taiwan–China regional links will depend on global shifts in the pattern of trade liberalization and regional protection and integration. Thus, if the global shift is to greater regional and bi-lateral arrangements, this will tend to reinforce the PRC–Taiwan links within

81. *FCJ*, 4 June 1993, p. 3.

82. The World Bank, referring to the three entities as the "Chinese Economic Area," predicts that the area's economic boom will continue, making it the world's fourth growth pole. See *ibid.* 20 April 1993, p. 1.

83. In fact, the PRC–Taiwan relationship could affect Hong Kong's ties with Taiwan since the bulk of trade between the mainland and Taiwan goes through Hong Kong.

the broader framework of the regional arrangements. Secondly, the commercial case for Taiwan to avoid too much reliance on China is as strong as the political one. China has benefited precisely from the Taiwanese diversification away from other Asian locations and, given China's record of economic and political instability, no rational investor will become too dependent on it, either as a market or as a location for direct investment. Hong Kong's lack of room for flexibility on this issue is its major problem of economic strategy; Taiwan is fortunate in that it can enjoy strong benefits from its natural links with China, while retaining significant options to integrate its economy in other directions.

# Beijing and Taipei: Dialectics in Post-Tiananmen Interactions

## Chong-Pin Lin

The brutality of the 4 June 1989 Tiananmen Square crackdown ordered by Beijing quickly checked the former growing "mainland fever" among the inhabitants of Taiwan. It seemed that, with their aspiration to reunify with the People's Republic of China shattered forever, Taiwan's expanding non-governmental interactions with the mainland would cease indefinitely. Yet, on 5 July, 76 Taiwanese businessmen crossed the Taiwan Strait to attend an export commodities fair in Dalian. There, one Taiwanese visitor even made an investment of US$5 million.[1]

Half a year after the Beijing carnage, Taiwanese pop singers Lin Chung and Huang Lei celebrated the incoming Year of the Horse on stage in that same city.[2] Earlier, on 16 December 1989, Taiwan's then Foreign Minister Lien Chan announced that his government intended to end open animosity toward Beijing and would abandon such appeals as "Han Chinese (Taipei) tolerate no coexistence with invading bandits (Beijing)."[3] These post-Tiananmen developments – economic, social, and political – between Taiwan and the mainland carried goodwill and suggested an eventual integration. They unfolded, however, alongside parallel events portending conflict and persistent disintegration.

In mid-November 1989, glaring headlines in at least one leading Taiwanese newspaper pointed to a Hong Kong report that China's then Chairman of the Central Military Commission, Deng Xiaoping, had spoken to the high command of the People's Liberation Army in late August or early September, relaying the following message:

Do not always resort to a smiling face in dealing with Taiwan…. On this issue, we cannot exclude the use of force…. The purpose of building up the Army is to fight wars. These days, one possible war … is that with Taiwan. Incorporate the Taiwan issue on our timetable contingent upon: when Taiwan claims independence; when Taipei treats us with a "discourteous face"; and when Taiwan's "black hand" continuously interferes in our domestic affairs."[4]

---

1. All following monetary figures in U.S. dollars. "Commentary views Taiwan investment on mainland," Beijing *Zhongguo Xinwen She*, 29 December 1989, in *Foreign Broadcast Information Service* (*FBIS*), 8 January 1990, p. 51.
2. "Taiwan gexing Lin Chung, Huang Lei zai Jing canjia dianshi lianhuan hui" ("Taiwanese singers Lin Chung, Huang Lei participated in a Beijing TV gala"), *Shijie ribao* (*World Journal*, New York), 19 January 1990, p. 32.
3. "State to end open animosity toward mainland," *China Post*, Taipei, 17 December 1989, in *FBIS*, 26 December 1989, p. 55.
4. "Deng Xiaoping shuo hen hua: Taiwan du qilai jiuyao da" ("Deng Xiaoping spoke bold words: if Taiwan claims independence, we will strike"), *Zhongyang ribao* (*Central Daily News*, Taipei), 17 November 1989, p. 1.

As might be expected, the prospect of China invading Taiwan – often a hot topic among Taipei's intelligentsia – also evoked intense debate at public forums there, such as the 23–27 December 1989 Civilian Conference on National Issues (*minjian guojian hui*) which was attended by 250 Taiwanese elite and enjoyed President Lee Teng-hui's personal attention.[5]

These developments have outpaced commonly-held post-Tiananmen expectations for Taiwan–mainland relations in terms of the possibilities for both growing accommodation and increasing animosity. The multifariousness of these events, therefore, renders more pertinent than ever the question of whether relations between Taiwan and China will evolve towards a rapprochement, maintain the status quo, or even gravitate towards armed confrontation. Addressing this issue requires examination of the trends – political, economic, socio-cultural and strategic – in Taiwan–China interactions. The first major shift in these trends occurred a decade before the 1989 Tiananmen Square incident.

## Political Trends

On 1 January 1979, the routine and symbolic bombardment of Taiwan's offshore islands, Jinmen and Mazu (Quemoy and Matsu), was stopped, as Beijing's National People's Congress Standing Committee sent a message to Taipei calling for peaceful reunification of China. A series of similar proposals from Beijing followed in the next seven years (see Appendix), while Taipei adhered to its policy of the "Three Nos" (no contact, no negotiation, no compromise). On 14 October 1987, Taiwan's first official initiative on its mainland policy was taken by the ailing, yet anxious, President Chiang Ching-kuo who lifted the ban on ROC citizens visiting their relatives on the mainland. His death on 13 January 1988 occasioned the condolences of Chinese Communist Party General Secretary Zhao Ziyang to Taipei the next day.

The year 1988 saw an acceleration of peaceful overtures between Taiwan and China, especially after 9 July, when Zhao Ziyang congratulated Lee Teng-hui, acting Chairman since January, on becoming the official Chairman of the Kuomintang at its 13th Party Congress. One highlight among these activities occurred on 14 July when KMT senior statesman, Chen Li-fu, leading 34 colleagues, put forward the proposal of reunifying China through traditional culture; on 15 July, Zhao Ziyang reciprocated by stressing that both sides share a foundation in politics, economics and cultural tradition. Two months later, Beijing discontinued the policy established in 1962 of offering a monetary reward to Taiwanese defecting with military ships or aircraft. Three days after that, on 14 September, Taipei reduced the reward, delivered since 1959, to mainland pilots defecting with warplanes of less advanced models.

5. Taiwan President Lee Teng-hui listened to the summaries of the Conference discussions while receiving the key participants on 26 December 1989. Also see for examples: *Zhongguo shibao* (*China Times*, Taipei), 25 December 1989, p. 2; *Zili Zaobao* (*Independence Morning News*, Taipei), 25 December 1989, p. 2.

The continuing momentum of constructive political interaction seemed to culminate in the spring of 1989, one month before the Tiananmen tragedy. On 1 May, not only did Taiwan's first official delegation since 1949 attend the Asian Development Bank's annual meeting in Beijing, but the delegation led by Finance Minister Shirley Kuo also stood up for the playing of the PRC national anthem.

The Tiananmen shock to Taipei, seemingly ineradicable at the time, began to dissipate sooner than expected. One month after ROC Foreign Minister Lien Chan's announcement ending open animosity toward Beijing in December 1989, Taipei further relaxed its mainland travel policy by allowing low-level government officials to visit their relatives across the Strait.[6] In the first half of 1990, Taipei further lifted a series of visitation restrictions allowing elected and appointed ROC officials to call on mainland relations in a private capacity, and permitting mainland cultural and athletic celebrities to visit Taiwan.[7] On 18 September 1990, Red Cross officials from Taiwan and China, ostensibly non-governmental but indirectly representing each government, having secretly met on Jinmen Island – still heavily fortified by Taiwanese forces against possible PRC invasions – jointly announced that they had signed an agreement on repatriation procedures for illegal immigrants from either side.[8] One day earlier, Taiwan athletic teams had arrived in Beijing to participate in the Asian Olympic Games under the name "Chinese-Taipei."[9] In August 1991, two mainland journalists and two mainland Red Cross officials visited Taiwan, this being the first time in 42 years that personnel commissioned by Beijing had set foot on the island.[10] In addition, quasi-governmental co-operation between Taiwan and China developed beyond their immediate geographical confines. In early August 1990, more than 100 Taiwanese engineers and technicians succeeded in evacuating from Kuwait after the Iraqi invasion under assistance offered by the PRC embassy.[11] In late October, Beijing accused Tokyo of encroaching on China's sovereignty by allowing the installation of navigational lights on the controversial Diaoyutai (Senkaku) Island after Japanese warships dispelled the protesting Taiwanese fishermen earlier

6. "Diceng gongwu renyuan tanqin zhunle" ("Visitations of mainland relatives by low-level government officials approved"), *Shijie ribao*, 17 January 1990, p. 8.

7. "Chronology-pragmatic adaptations," *Free China Review* (Taipei), January 1991 p. 15.

8. Li Yu, "Xin tupo: liangan Jinmen tanpan de lishi yiyi" ("A new breakthrough: the historical significance of the Quemoy negotiation between two sides of the Taiwan Strait"), *Shibao zhoukan* (*China Times Weekly*, New York), 29 September–5 October 1990, pp. 8–10.

9. "ROC team gets warm welcome: Peking kicks off Asian Games," *Free China Journal*, 20 September 1990, p. 1.

10. "Liangan fenge sishier nian hou, shoupi dalu jizhe lai Tai" ("The first group of mainland journalists arrived in Taiwan after 42 years of separation") *Zhongyang ribao*, 14 August 1991, p. 1; "Mainland Red Cross officials to arrive 21 August," CNA, Taipei, 20 August 1991 in *FBIS*, 20 August 1991, p. 69.

11. Jing Shixiu, "Taiwan zai Keweite de gongzuo renyuan xiang Zhonggong qiuyuan" ("Taiwanese workers in Kuwait requested the assistance of Communist China"), *Shibao zhoukan*, 25–31 August 1990, pp. 26–27.

that month.[12] Although both incidents slightly embarrassed the Taipei government, which passively witnessed the developments, positive interactions across the Strait reached new dimensions. On 27–28 April 1992, a milestone conference in Singapore between the Straits Exchange Foundation (SEF) from Taiwan and the Association for Relations Across the Taiwan Straits (ARATS) from the mainland produced four agreements on functional matters such as registered mail delivery. Although unofficial in name, both organizations were headed by former officials closely tied to the Taipei and Beijing leadership respectively.

The trends of accommodation and integration in post-Tiananmen political interactions between Taipei and Beijing have, however, been accompanied by currents of a contentious and disintegrative nature. At least five such currents have become prominent, and not all were foreseeable in June 1989. First, a diplomatic contest between Beijing and Taipei has intensified, increasingly highlighting their irreconcilable positions regarding the status of Taiwan: "a province of China" according to Beijing, or, according to Taipei, "one of the two governments of China" therefore deserving "international living space" such as representations in foreign capitals and international organizations. As Taipei shifted from ideology-bound inflexibility to a "pragmatic diplomacy" (*wushi waijiao*), Beijing condemned this "dangerous" trend as it cultivates internationally the "deplorable" status quo of "two Chinas" or "one China, one Taiwan."[13] The effort to solidify the separation between Taiwan and the mainland, Beijing warned, would arouse "the fire of anger smoldering in the bosom of the Chinese people."[14]

Aided by its accumulated wealth, Taipei gained between July 1989 and July 1991 recognition by Grenada, Liberia, Belize, Lesotho, Guinea-Bissau, Nicaragua and the Central African Republic. Within weeks of each event Beijing withdrew its embassy from the country in question. In early 1990 Taipei began furthering the pursuit by broadening its diplomatic agenda to improve, under Beijing's strong protests or silent suspicion, substantive ties with Western countries (France, Canada, Australia, New Zealand), Eastern bloc countries (Poland, Czechoslovakia, Hungary), socialist Third World countries (Vietnam, North Korea), and even the then Soviet Union and its subsequently derived independent republics.[15] In February 1992, Beijing withdrew its embassy from Latvia

12. "Sovereignty over islands viewed," Beijing in Japanese to Japan, in *FBIS*, 22 October 1990, p. 7.

13. "Zhonggong Xinhuashi fabiao Taiwan zhengqing huigu" ("Chinese Communist Xinhua News Agency published annual report of Taiwanese politics"), *Zhongyang ribao*, 21 January 1990, p. 1.

14. "Liaowang views 'disasters' of independence," *Liaowang*, Beijing, 19 March 1990, pp. 12–14, in *FBIS*, 17 April 1990, pp. 51–53.

15. For Beijing's reactions, see for example, Liu Guofeng, "Taiwan dangju dui Sulian zhengce cuoshi de yixie bianhua" ("Changes in Taiwanese authority's policy towards the Soviet Union"), *Liaowang* (*Outlook*, Beijing), 26 November 1990, p. 23; "Interview with spokesman of Chinese Foreign Ministry on French Industrial Minister's visit to Taiwan," Xinhua, Beijing, 23 January 1991, in *Newsletter, The Embassy of the People's Republic of China*. For Taiwan's broadened diplomatic activities, see for example, Lena H. Sun, "China opts to maintain ties to Eastern Europe: Beijing fears political inroads by Taiwan," *Washing-*

following the establishment of consular relations between the latter and Taiwan, thus revealing a new dimension of Beijing's objection to Taipei's diplomatic expansion. Taiwan's unexpected application on 1 January 1990 to join GATT under the name "the customs territory of Taiwan, Penghu, Jinmen and Mazu," instead of the title "Republic of China" demonstrated its determination with operational flexibility to join international organizations, an approach Beijing found unacceptable.[16] On 31 August 1993, Beijing issued a White Paper in six languages condemning Taipei's effort to enter the United Nations. Shortly afterwards, the follow-up SEF–ARATS talks broke down, and only 17 per cent of Taiwan's people, down from 50 per cent at the conclusion of the ice-breaking Singapore conference in late April, still believed in China's friendliness toward Taiwan.[17]

In spring 1990, Beijing launched a diplomatic counter-offensive to salvage its Tiananmen-damaged international image with the apparent effect of containing the rapid expansion of Taipei's governmental and substantive global presence.[18] By late 1992, Beijing had not only resumed diplomatic relations with Indonesia, improved relations with former enemies such as Moscow, New Delhi and Hanoi, and established embassies in Namibia, Republic of the Marshall Islands, Israel, Saudi Arabia, Singapore and South Korea – the latter three being once staunch allies of Taipei – but also had begun extending China's influence in Asia, Latin America and the Middle East, and strengthening weakened diplomatic connections with Eastern Europe.[19] On 11 February 1991, Beijing dispatched its Deputy Foreign Minister, Yang Fuchang, to the Middle East just one week before his counterpart from Taipei, Chang Hsiaoyen (John Chang), went there too to seek improvement of relations with the

---

*(footnote continued)*

*ton Post*, 19 February 1991, p. A16; "Taiwan daibiaotuan siyue fang Beihan" ("Taiwanese delegation to visit North Korea in April"), *Shijie ribao*, 21 January 1990, p. 1; "Zhong Yue guanxi huo zhongda tupuo" ("Major breakthrough in Taiwan–Vietnam relations"), *Zhongyang ribao*, 10 January 1991, p. 1; "Zhong Niu hang quan tanpan xiazhou zai Tai juxing" ("Taiwan–New Zealand talk on establishing direct flight to be held in Taipei next week"), *Shijie ribao*, 1 February 1991, p. 10; "Taibei jiang zai Wuotaihua she zhengfuxing banshi chu" ("Taipei to establish governmental office in Ottawa"), *Shijie ribao*, 4 November 1990, p. 1; "Taibei jiang zai Ganbeila she jingji wenhua zhongxing" ("Taipei to establish economic-cultural centre in Canberra"), *Shijie ribao*, 29 January 1991, p. 2.

16. Frances Williams and Jonathan Moore, "Taiwan's GATT application angers Peking," *Far Eastern Economic Review*, 1 February 1990, pp. 36–37.

17. Julian Baum, "Divided nations", *Far Eastern Economic Review*, 16 September 1993, p. 10.

18. For Beijing's post-Tiananmen diplomatic counter-offensive beginning in spring 1990, see for example: "Recent diplomatic activities of CPC viewed," *Da Gong Bao*, Hong Kong, 10 May 1990, in *FBIS*, 21 May 1990, p. 1; "Zhonggong jiaqiang longluo disanshijie, Yang Shangkun Wu Xueqian pupu fengchen" ("Communist China to strengthen ties with the Third World: Yang Shangkun, Wu Xueqian travel abroad"), *Shijie ribao*, 14 May 1990, p. 2; "More reportage on Li Peng's four-day Moscow visit," Xinhua, Beijing, 24 April 1990, in *FBIS*, 26 April 1990, p. 11.

19. Chen Wenying and Chen Xiaochun, "China's noticeable diplomacy of 1990," *Beijing Review*, 24–30 December 1990, pp. 12–13; Lena Sun, "China, S. Korea establish full relations," *Washington Post*, 24 August 1992, pp. A10–A18.

region.[20] The European tour of PRC Foreign Minister Qian Qichen in February and March 1991 was perceived internationally as yet another attempt to circumvent future diplomatic advancement of the Taiwan authorities.[21] One month after Taipei and Canberra agreed to solidify their diplomatic relations, Beijing heralded on 28 February 1991 Australia's decision to restore ties with China.[22] The post-Tiananmen diplomatic competition between Beijing and Taipei had grown more intense than generally expected.

Secondly, advocacy for "Taiwan independence" became a more prominent issue, which Beijing condemned as a movement "against the fundamental interests of the Chinese nation" and "a road to disaster."[23] On 7 October 1990, Taiwan's major opposition – the Democratic Progressive Party (DPP) – adopted a resolution entitled "Taiwan's Sovereignty Power Reaches Not the People's Republic of China and the People's Republic of Mongolia," which Beijing denounced for attempting to "split China."[24] During its annual conference on 13 October 1991, the DPP became committed by its charter "to build a Taiwanese republic with independent sovereignty."[25] The next day, Beijing reiterated President Yang Shangkun's 9 October warning to Taiwanese independence advocates that "those playing with fire will burn themselves to ashes."[26]

Thirdly, with respect to the post-Tiananmen pro-democracy movement, Taipei surprisingly reversed its attitude from ambiguous timidity in June to assertive support by December 1989. At the year's end, more than 100 pro-democracy leaders in exile arrived in Taipei and were greeted with

20. Yang visited Syria, Turkey, Yugoslavia and Iran. According to Taipei, Chang's trip enhanced relations with Saudia Arabia, Kuwait, Iran and Israel. "Beijing fuwaizhang Yang Fuchang fang si guo" ("Beijing's Deputy Foreign Minister Yang Fuchang visits four countries"), *Shijie ribao*, 11 February 1991, p. 1; "Chang Hsiaoyien 19 ri Fu Sha fangwen" ("Chang Hsiaoyien visited Saudia Arabia on 19 February), *Shijie ribao*, 19 February 1991, p. 9; "Enhanced relations with Mideast South," CNA, Taipei, 28 February 1991, in *FBIS*, 5 March 1991, p. 77; "Saudia Arabia substantive ties to be maintained," "Government exchange offices with Israel," "Trade, economic ties with Iran strengthened," "Representative office in Kuwait reopen," all CNA, Taipei, 28 February, 2, 3 March 1991 in *FBIS*, 5 March 1991, p. 78.

21. Lena H. Sun, "China opts to maintain ties to Eastern Europe: Beijing fears political inroads by Taiwan," *Washington Post*, 18 February 1991, p. A16; also see Asashi Shimbun, 20 January 1991, reported in "Qian Qichen Ouzhou xing" ("Qian Qichen's European tour"), *Shijie ribao*, 11 February 1991, p. 12.

22. "Taibei jiangzai Ganbeila" ("Welcomes Australia's 'positive attitude'") Xinhua, Beijing, 28 February 1991, in *FBIS*, 28 February 1991, p. 2.

23. "Liaowang views 'disaster' of independence," p. 53.

24. Zhu Xianlong, "Zhi zai fenlie Zhongguo de 'Taiwan zhuquan' jueyi an" ("Aiming to split China: the resolution 'Taiwan's sovereignty Power'"), *Liaowang*, 5 November 1990, p. 20. Also see a less formal report from Hong Kong: "PRC leaders shocked by Taiwan independence bill," *Zhengming*, No. 157 1 November 1990, pp. 18–19, in *FBIS*, 7 November 1990, pp. 55–56.

25. Julian Baum, "Opposition party opts for independence: one China policy," *Far Eastern Economic Review*, 24 October 1991, pp. 20–21.

26. "Jing gao 'Taidu' fenzi wanhuo bi zifen" ("'Taiwanese independence' advocates be warned: those playing with fire will burn themselves to ashes"), *Renmin ribao*, 15 October 1991, p. 1.

receptions in their honour and offers of financial backing.[27] Ever since, visits of mainland dissidents – many seeking monetary assistance – have become regular events in Taiwan.[28]

Fourthly, Beijing has announced, at a seemingly accelerated pace, the arrests of "spies" commissioned by Taiwan for the purpose of social sabotage and intelligence gathering. At least fourteen such announcements have been made since June 1989.[29] Finally, by mid-January 1990, Taipei appeared to have adopted a policy of continuing its support for the political liberalization of Hong Kong, even after 1997.[30]

In the eyes of PRC leaders, certain trends emanating from Taiwan reinforced each other in irritating and threatening Beijing. The PRC charged, first, that the KMT was responsible for the escalation of the Taiwanese independence movement, largely as a result of the party's "appeasing and indulgent" attitude and probably even "tacit encouragement."[31] Secondly, they argued that foreign forces led by the United States and Japan in pursuit of their own "strategic interests" sought to perpetuate "splitism" of the Chinese nation by "supporting overtly or covertly" the bottom-up Taiwanese independence movement (*Tai du*) or, "in a disguised form," the top-down "independent Taiwan" (*du Tai*) policy characterized by Taipei's "elastic and silver bullet diplomacy."[32] To deter external powers from seizing Taiwan and internal elements from splitting it, Beijing therefore could not promise to forego the use of force over Taiwan.[33] Thirdly, they claimed that Taipei's efforts to foment social unrest on the mainland through supporting exiled dissidents and sending

27. Xia Yun, "Guofu dalu zhengce jiang angshou kuobu?" ("KMT government's mainland policy will advance in strides?"), *Shibao zhoukan* (*China Times Weekly*, New York), 6–12 January 1990, p. 15.

28. See for example, "Visit by four mainland dissidents approved," CNA, Taipei, 26 June 1990 in *FBIS*, 27 June 1990, p. 52; "He Shang, zhuyao zhuangao zhe Su Xiaokang zaidu fang Tai" ("Chief author of River Elegy, Su Xiaokang revisits Taiwan"), *Shijie ribao*, 2 June 1990, p. 8.

29. See "Zhonggong xuancheng puohuo Taite an" ("Chinese Communists announced breaking Taiwanese spy ring"), *Shijie ribao*, 14 January 1990, p. 1; "Taiwan tewu an di er li xuan pan" ("The second case of Taiwanese spies reaching judgement"), *Lianhebao*, (*United Daily News*, Taipei), 5 January 1990, p. 10; "Taiwan spies discovered in Yunnan," Kunming Yunnan Provincial Service, 31 January 1989, in *FBIS*, 2 February 1989; "Beikong wei Tai huiji qingbao" ("Accused for spying for Taiwan"), *Shijie ribao*, 5 February 1990, p. 2; "Zhonggong shengcheng panchu wumin Taiwan jiandie tuxing" ("Chinese Communists announced the sentencing for imprisonment of five Taiwanese spies"), *Zhongyang ribao*, 3 March 1990, p. 4; "Zhonggong zai Guangxi, Tianjin ji Shandong puohuo sanqi Taite anjian" ("Chinese Communists broke three Taiwanese spy rings in Guangxi, Tianjin and Shangdong"), *Shijie ribao*, 16 May 1990, p. 2; "Shangdong Yantai yi nanzi beibu" ("Man in Shangdong Yantai arrested"), *Zhongyang ribao*, 18 May 1990, p. 4; "Two Taiwan 'spies' arrested in Hunan," Changsha Hunan Provincial Service in Mandarin, in *FBIS*, 20 August 1990.

30. "Li Huan tan jiu qi hou Tai Gang guanxi" ("Li Huan talked about Taiwan–Hong Kong relations after 1997"), *Shijie ribao*, 17 January 1990, p. 1; "Beijing upset over support," *South China Morning Post*, Hong Kong, 17 January 1990, p. 8 in *FBIS*, 18 January 1990, p. 55.

31. "Li Peng chongshen fandui Tai du" ("Li Peng reiterated condemnation on Taiwan independence"), *Zhongyang ribao*, 1 February 1990, p. 4.

32. "Liaowang views 'disaster' of independence," p. 52.

33. "Jiang Zemin chongshen bu fangqi wuli jiejue Taihai wenti" ("Jiang Zemin reiterates not to renounce the use of force in resolving the Taiwan Strait problem"), *Shijie ribao*,

secret agents to the provinces increased tensions on both sides of the Strait.[34] In the eyes of ROC leaders, Beijing's criticism of Taipei for applying "silver dollar diplomacy," which the PRC had engaged in even more, was annoyingly unjustified; and Beijing's diplomatic containment of Taipei and its non-renunciation of the use of force against Taiwan were tantamount to "threatening with machine guns on three sides, leaving exit on one" toward submission.[35]

On 16 January 1980, Deng Xiaoping said in his "Speech to the 10,000 Cadres" that "the return of Taiwan to the motherland" was one of the CCP's three major tasks.[36] Since then more than a decade has elapsed, during which time "opposing hegemony" and "economic construction," the other two major tasks, have borne impressive results; reunification of China, however, remained even more remote after 4 June 1989. Even before then, Beijing had demonstrated a growing sense of urgency on this issue by adding to its State Council Taiwan Affairs Office two similar departments specializing in socio-cultural and economic affairs.[37] In September 1990, PRC President Yang Shangkun admitted publicly that the unresolved issue of reunification brought the increasingly anxious geriatric leaders in Beijing "long nights ... fraught with dreams."[38] Since the 1989 Tiananmen incident, however, the PRC government's eagerness for expanded bilateral interaction has become mixed with suspicion and circumspection. For example, despite the July 1989 announcement that its policy on Taiwan remained unchanged,[39] Beijing began restricting the activities of Taiwanese journalists on the mainland two months later, according to PRC Foreign Minister Qian Qichen.[40]

While the Beijing government initiated political interaction and led the PRC economic and social sectors in exchanges with Taiwan, Taipei's

---

*(footnote continued)*

29 June 1990, p. 1; "Yang Shangkun on China's reunification," *Beijing Review*, 26 November–2 December 1990, pp. 15–16.

34. "Taiwan tewu jiguan chashou dalu dongluan zongshu" ("Summary of the involvement of Taiwanese spies in mainland unrest"), *Liaowang*, 7 August 1989, pp. 4–6. "Zhonggong gongji maotou zhuan xiang liuwang haiwai yiyi renshi" ("Chinese Communists turned criticism at exiled dissidents"), *Lianhebao*, 3 August 1989, p. 9.

35. "Chien Fu zhi Beijing cai zhengge shi 'Kaizi Waijiao' " ("Fredrick Chien points out that Beijing applies the real 'silver dollar diplomacy' "), *Shijie ribao*, 29 December 1990, p. 2; "Ma Yingjiu zhi Zhonggong dui Tai zhengce ren shui ye nanyi jieshou" ("Ying-jeou Ma held that Communist China's policy towards Taiwan is intolerable to anyone"), *Zhongyang ribao*, 13 November 1990, p. 1.

36. Willen van Kemenade, "Proposal for a book with the working title: One China but when?," to be published by MacMillan, London.

37. "Zhonggong guowuyuan Taibanshi zhizhang gongbu zhihou de shengshi" ("Observations on the announcement of responsibilities of Communist China State Council Taiwan Affairs Office"), *Zhongyang ribao*, 3 February 1989, p. 2.

38. Yang said, "Mr Deng Xiaoping has proposed that it is better for both the mainland and Taiwan to establish contacts and realize the goal of the country's reunification when the senior leaders of the CPC and KMT in Taiwan are still alive." See "Yang Shangkun on China's reunification," p. 17.

39. "Policy on Taiwan unchanged," *Beijing Review*, 10–16 July 1989, p. 12.

40. "Zhonggong tiaozheng dui Tai guanxi" ("Communist China adjusted its relations with Taiwan"), *Shijie ribao*, 16 September 1989, p. 1.

government at first merely reacted passively and followed the lead of Taiwan's non-governmental forces in the developments. Then, with extreme caution, Taipei gingerly edged toward an increasingly more flexible and forward-looking mainland policy based on the separation of affairs between the government and the people in the economic, academic, cultural and athletic spheres. The five principles reiterated by Taiwan's Government Information Bureau Director, Shaw Yu-ming, on 13 October 1988 were, "security, non-governmental contacts, no direct contacts, contact limited to civic affairs and gradual progress," which were characterized by Beijing as "peace but no talks, communication but no unification, contention but no war, and division but no separation."[41] In such a process, Taiwan's non-official political elite often functioned as the vanguard in breaking the restrictions decreed by Taipei's government on contact with the mainland, as did National Assembly Deputy, Wu Che-lang, in July 1988,[42] and Legislator Hu Chiu-yuan in October of the same year.[43] Even university professor Li Ching-hua, the son of the then Premier Li Huan, had suggested in May 1988 the need to revise the ossified "Three Nos" policy.[44]

After the Tiananmen incident, Taipei surprisingly not only continued the thawing of its mainland policy but also, after a while, proceeded at an accelerated pace. After Lee Teng-hui was elected President on his own merit in March 1990, he began pushing towards more active political interactions with Beijing. By spring 1991, Lee had established three organizations for co-ordinating mainland affairs including the "non-governmental" Strait Exchange Foundation (SEF) for direct contact with the PRC, enunciated "guidelines for national unification," and announced the end of the ROC's technical state of war with the PRC effective from 1 May 1991 (see Appendix).[45] Although Beijing criticized Taipei's

41. Li Jiaquan, "More on reunification of Taiwan with the mainland," *Beijing Review*, 16–22 January 1989, p. 28.
42. "Tupo Guomindang bu zhunxu gongzhi renyuan wangfang jinji" ("Breaking the KMT's restrictions on mainland visitation by government employees"), *Huaqiao ribao*, (*China News*, New York), 20 July 1988, p. 1.
43. "Zishen liwei Hu Qiuyuan dalu tangqin" ("Senior Legislator Hu Qiuyuan visits mainland relatives"), *Huaqiao ribao*, 9 September 1988, p. 1.
44. Li Qinghua, "Dui xian jieduan dalu zhengce de ji dian jianyi" ("A few suggestions on the current mainland policy"), *Zhongguo shibao* (*China Times Daily*, Taipei), 10 May 1988.
45. The three organizations include the National Unification Council (a consultative body for the President, established on 17 October 1990), the Mainland Affairs Council (a policy planning agency of the Executive Yuan, established 18 October 1990), the Strait Exchange Foundation (a non-governmental organization for implementing Taipei's policy while dealing with the mainland, established 21 November 1990). The "guideline for national unification" was formally enunciated by President Lee on 7 March 1991. On 25 December 1990, he announced that Taipei would terminate the "Period of Mobilization for Suppression of the Communists Rebellion by the ROC" by May 1991. See Li Jiangrong, "Shutu tonggui de dalu zhengce jigou" ("Mainland policy agencies have different functions but same objectives"), *Shibao zhoukan*, 27 October–2 November 1990, pp. 28–29; Wang Zaixi, "Zhongzhi 'Kanluan' dui Taiwan zhengju he liangan guanxi de yingxiang" ("Impact of terminating 'rebellion suppression' on Taiwan and interactions across the Strait"), *Liaowang*, 28 January 1991, pp. 8–9; "Coordinating mainland affairs," *Free China Journal*, (Taipei) 25 February 1991, p. 1; "Guojia tongyi gangling quanwen" ("Guidelines for national unification: the full text"), *Zhongyang ribao*, 7 March 1991, p. 1.

"national reunification programme" for demanding that PRC leaders change the mainland's current political and economic systems and for persisting in the "attempt to counter-attack the mainland,"[46] Beijing reciprocated on functional terms. On 16 December 1991, the PRC founded the Association for Relations Across the Taiwan Straits (ARATS) – a "non-governmental" but "authoritative organization" – as the counterpart of Taipei's SEF.[47]

In sum, the post-Tiananmen political interactions across the Strait have contained a mixture of unexpected movements towards co-operation and integration, as well as both lingering and emerging signs of contention portending conflict and disintegration.

## Economic Trends

In early February 1990, both Taipei[48] and Beijing[49] announced that for 1989 indirect trade between Taiwan and China amounted to $3.7 billion, up from $2.6 billion in 1988.[50] This record increase (see Table 1) invalidated the general expectation of a Tiananmen-traumatized Western public. Rather unexpectedly, the total of Taiwan–mainland indirect trade and mainland-bound Taiwanese investment in the latter half of 1989, as handled by Chase Manhattan Bank's China branch, more than doubled that in the first six months.[51] Also, most of the 1989 Taiwanese investment in the mainland was made after June, according to one Hong Kong report.[52] As of February 1990, the accumulated total of Taiwan–mainland indirect trade was $10 billion[53]; Taiwanese businessmen had initiated at least 500–600 investment projects on the mainland with a total capital investment of over $1 billion, an increase of more than 100 per cent over 1988[54]; and Taiwanese entrepreneurs had applied for some 2,000 trade-marks and 500 patents.[55] In Fujian province alone, which faces Taiwan across the Strait, 1989 saw the establishment of more than 200 new

46. "Article views mainland–Taiwan relations," *Renmin ribao*, 6 February 1991, p. 4 in *FBIS*, 7 February 1991, pp. 57–58; "National People's Congress: Li Peng delivers report at 25 March session," Beijing Domestic Service, 25 March 1991, in *FBIS*, 27 March 1991, p. 33.

47. Yang Yuanhu and Li Dahong, "Promoting exchanges across the Taiwan Straits," *Beijing Review*, 3–16 February 1992, pp. 30–33.

48. "Two-way trade with mainland increased in 1989," CNA, Taipei, 3 February 1990, in *FBIS*, 6 February 1990, p. 41.

49. "Liangan jianjie maoyi zong'e qunian zengzhi 37 yi meiyuan" ("Indirect trade across the Straits increased to $3.7 billion last year"), *Shijie ribao*, 10 February 1990, p. 31.

50. "Two-way trade with mainland," p. 41.

51. "Huaqi yinhang jinbannian yewu beizeng" ("Chase Manhattan Bank's business in the second half of 1989 more than doubled"), *Shijie ribao*, 16 February 1990, p. 8.

52. "Xiamen-Taiwan de ling yige jiagong chukou qu" ("Xiamen-Taiwan's additional special manufacture export district"), *Zhongyang ribao*, 6 February 1990, p. 1.

53. "Commentary on developing trade ties with Taiwan," *Zhongguo xinwen she*, Beijing, 20 December 1989, in *FBIS*, 4 January 1990, p. 65.

54. "Commentary views Taiwan investment on mainland," p. 51.

55. Li Dahong, "Weile cujin liangan," p. 22.

Table 1: **Indirect Trade Between Taiwan and Mainland China (US$m.)**

| Year | Trade turnover |
| --- | --- |
| 1978 | 47 |
| 1979 | 77 |
| 1980 | 321(a) |
| 1981 | 467 |
| 1982 | 298 |
| 1983 | 265 |
| 1984 | 553(b) |
| 1985 | 1,104 |
| 1986 | 925 |
| 1987 | 1,516 |
| 1988 | 2,600(c) |
| 1989 | 3,700(d) |
| 1990 | 4,043 |
| 1991 | 5,793(e) |
| 1992 | 7,410 |

*Notes:*
(a) $450 million according to Ralph N. Clough, "The Republic of China and the world," in Hungdah Chiu and Shao-Chuan Leng (eds.), *China: Seventy Years after the 1911 Hsin-hai Revolution* (Charlottesville, Virginia: University Press of Virginia, 1984), p. 539.
(b) $1,130 million according to the source for 1978.
(c) $2,717 million according to the source for 1979–87.
(d) $3,483 million according to the source for 1979–87.
(e) $7,500 million according to Jiang Lingzhi, "Haixia liang an jingmao guanxi de xin zhuanzhe" ("The new turning point of the economic and trade relations across the Taiwan Strait"), *Liaowang*, 1 June 1992, pp. 22–23.

*Sources:*
1978: "Mainland trade mania shows," *Free China Journal*, 30 March 1989, p. 8; 1979–87: Hong Kong Census and Statistics Department Figures cited in Chung Chin, "Trade across the Straits," *Free China Review*, January 1991, p. 43: 1988–89: "Two-way trade with mainland increased in 1989," CNA, Taipei, 3 February 1990, in *FBIS*, 6 February 1990, p. 4; 1989–90: "Indirect trade with mainland hits high in 1990," CNA, Taipei, 21 February 1991, in *FBIS*, 21 February 1991, p. 52; 1991: "Liangan maoyi chuang wu xiang jilu" ("Trade across the Taiwan Strait set five records"), *Shijie ribao*, 8 March 1992, p. 6; 1992: "Cross-Strait trade expected to top $10 billion," *China Daily*, Beijing, 3 April 1993, in *FBIS*, 5 April 1993, p. 54.

Taiwanese enterprises with investment totalling over $400 million, representing more than 200 per cent in annual growth.[56]

In 1990, despite the ROC government's effort to slow down economic

56. Xie Xiangru, "Min-Tai mingjian jialiu xiang zongshen fazhan" ("Scope of Fujian–Taiwan civilian exchanges deepens"), *Liaowang*, 22 January 1990, p. 22.

Table 2: **Taiwanese Investment in Mainland China (US$m.)**

| Year | Accumulated investment |
|------|------------------------|
| 1988 | 600 |
| 1989 | 1,000 |
| 1990 | 3,000 |
| 1991 | 5,000 |
| 1992 | 5,700 |
| 1993 (June) | 7,000 (9,000) |

*Sources:*
    1989: "Commentary views Taiwan investment on mainland,"
*Zhongguo Xinwen She*, Beijing 29 December 1989, in *FBIS*, 8 January 1990, p. 51; 1990: "Most cross-Strait investors keep roots in Taiwan," *CNA*, Taipei, 12 August 1992 in *FBIS*, 12 August 1992; 1991: "Qu nian Taizi liu Dalu gaoda 50 yi meiyuan" ("Last year's capital flow from Taiwan to mainland reached $5 billion"), *Shijie ribao*, 15 January 1992, p. 1; 1992: Contracted Taiwanese investment – see Central Intelligence Agency, *China's Economy in 1992 and 1993; Grappling with the Risks of Rapid Growth* (Washington, D.C.: Central Intelligence Agency, 1993), pp. 14–15; Taipei's Ministry of Economic Affairs put the estimate at more than US$4 billion in late 1992 – see "Taiwan: investment in China," *Far Eastern Economic Review*, 26 November 1992, p. 67; 1993: the estimate varies between Taipei's US$7 billion and Beijing's US$9 billion – see "Some 8,000 firms register Mainland ventures," CNA, Taipei, 4 June 1993 in *FBIS*, 7 June 1993, p. 73.

exchange with the mainland in the summer, indirect trade across the Strait grew even further to $4.04 billion, increasing 9 per cent over 1989; and in 1991, the volume jumped by 43 per cent to $5.79 billion, or by 86 per cent to $7.5 billion according to Hong Kong sources.[57] By early 1991, Taiwanese businessmen had established on the mainland from 1,600 to over 2,000 enterprises with a total investment from $2 billion to over $5 billion, representing a growth of 100 to 400 per cent since 1989.[58] Continuing to grow, Taiwanese mainland-bound investment reached between $7 billion and $9 billion by June 1993[59] (see Table 2). Contrary to

57. Mainly due to Taiwan's problems of capital flight, declining export, and collapsing stockmarket, Taipei announced in July 1990 an effort to "cool off the mainland (economic) fever." See Gan Changqiu, "Ruhe kandai Taiwan dangju 'lengque Dalu re' " ("How to view Taiwan authority's efforts to 'Cool off the mainland fever' "), *Liaowang*, 8 October 1990, pp. 26–27; and "Efforts to slow down mainland trade viewed," CNA, Taipei, 17 September 1990, in *FBIS*, 17 September 1990, p. 55.

58. The higher figures came from Beijing and the lower, Taipei. See "Taishang zai bi an touzi yi yu 15 yi mei yuan" ("Taiwanese businessmen have invested over $1.5 billion across the Strait"), *Shijie ribao*, 24 January 1991, p. 2; "Taishang touzi dalu chuxian xin reliu" ("Taiwanese businessmen are investing on the mainland with renewed enthusiasm"), *Renmin ribao*, 4 January 1991, p. 5; "Liangan zhuankou maoyi jinnian jiang da sishi yi meiyuan" ("Indirect trade across the Strait reach $4 billion this year"), *Shijie ribao*, 28 December 1990, p. 10.

59. The estimate varies between Taipei's $7 billion and Beijing's $9 billion. See "Some 8,000 firms register mainland ventures," CNA, Taipei, 4 June 1993, in *FBIS*, 7 June 1993, p. 73.

prevailing views that the 4 June Tiananmen massacre had a long-lasting effect on the flow of Taiwan merchants across the Strait, the influence was transient. Taiwanese investors did hesitate immediately after the incident in Beijing, but not for long.

Visits such as that of the Taiwan business delegation to Dalian on 1 July, an oddity at the time, soon became commonplace. From August to October 1989, Taiwan manufacturers transferred to the mainland more than 50 production lines for making shoes, umbrellas and furniture. Over 500 Taiwan businessmen attended a Guangzhou export commodities fair in the autumn of 1989, more than ever before.[60] On 16 December 1989, an unofficial Taiwan delegation led by legislator Chang Ping-chau, and an obviously semi-official mainland group led by the former Minister of Commerce, Zhen Hongye, signed an agreement in Hong Kong to establish an organization – the Association for Co-ordination of Trading and Commercial Affairs Across the Strait (ACTCA) – for promoting and mediating economic and technological exchanges between the two sides.[61] In early 1990 Wang Yung-ching, head of Taiwan's largest conglomerate, Formosa Plastics, and the 15th wealthiest man in the world, made an investment reconnaissance trip to the mainland where he discussed the prospects of investing $3.5 billion.[62]

Why the economic interaction across the Strait has manifested such resilience and momentum may be attributed to the following factors. First, the economic compatibility of the two sides remains strong, and may, in fact, have increased in the post-Tiananmen period. Taiwan's abundant capital and advanced technology match well with China's ample resources and low cost of production. The cost of labour on the mainland was 5 to 10 per cent of that in Taiwan, and the cost of land only 0.5 per cent, according to Wang Yung-ching after his trip across the Strait.[63]

Secondly, the deteriorating investment environment in Taiwan compelled its entrepreneurs to look for opportunities outside. In 1989, the number of Taiwan's emigration applicants – more than 90 per cent of them wealthy businessmen capable of investing $20–40 million abroad – grew three times from that of 1988 to about 10,000 families. Of these, 50 to 70 per cent cited as their main concern insecurity under a rapidly deteriorating social order: where extorting well-to-do businessmen had become prevalent; where kidnapping and murder were in the news almost

60. "Commentary views Taiwan investment on mainland," p. 52.

61. Li Dahong, "Weile cujin liangan shuangxiang jiaoliu" ("For promoting two-way exchanges across the Strait"), *Liaowang*, (*Outlook*, Beijing), 8 January 1990, pp. 21–22; "Commentary on developing trade ties with Taiwan," *Zhongguo xinwen she*, Beijing, 20 December 1989, in Daily Report on China, *FBIS*, 4 January 1990, pp. 64–65.

62. Wang Yung-ching and family's net worth was estimated at $4 billion and, owned, in addition to Formosa Plastics Group, 14 plants in the U.S. "The billionaires," *Fortune*, 11 September 1989, p. 76. "Businessman's mainland trip, intentions detailed," *Hong Kong Standard*, 1 February 1990, p. 6, in *FBIS*, 2 February 1990, p. 56; Fu Yijie, "Wang Yung-ching toushi wen lu" ("Wang Yungching threw a stone to probe his path"), *Shijie ribao*, 18 February 1990, p. 1.

63. "Wang Yung-ching baozheng ba gen liu zai Taiwan" ("Wang Yung-ching guaranteed to leave roots in Taiwan"), *Shijie ribao*, 28 January 1990, p. 6.

daily; where "contagious" and violence-prone protest movements spread from political dissidents to environmentalists, from farmers embittered by imported American agricultural products flooding the market to veterans dissatisfied with their military retirement compensations; and where the government was perceived as impotent because of its inability to arrest the erosion of social conditions.[64] A common complaint was the corrosion of labour's previously admirable work ethic by widespread gambling fever and stockmarket mania, which had reduced the respectable acronym of the ROC to that of the "Republic of Casino."[65] The considerable appreciation of the Taiwan dollar against the American dollar, which was the highest among world currencies and amounted to 45.5 per cent from 1984 to 1989, also added increasing pressure for Taiwan businessmen to divest at home and invest abroad.[66]

Thirdly, both China's widely recognized market potential and its easily underestimated productivity potential were attractive to Taiwan investors. During the Tiananmen aftermath, China's productivity in light industry proved to be more vigorous than expected. In 1989, textile exports exceeded $13 billion, replacing Taiwan's as number three in the world in this category[67]; and exports to the United States, consisting largely of light industry products, amounted to $11 billion, growing 44 per cent from 1988.[68]

Fourthly, the Beijing government continued and even escalated its efforts to attract Taiwan investors after 4 June 1989. During July and August 1989, approved by China's State Council, Fujian province opened up a new special economic zone in Xiamen, Xinglin and Haicang for Taiwan capital which began to arrive within two months.[69] After PRC Premier Li Peng announced the lifting of martial law on 11 January 1990, the mainland-bound flow of Taiwan merchants grew even further.[70] Despite its grave financial difficulties, Beijing decided in late January 1990 not to collect newly-added taxes from enterprises with foreign, including Taiwanese, investments in the coming year with the obvious aim of enticing investors.[71]

64. "Ni luan wo zou! Fuweng yiwofeng yimin" ("When chaos arrives, one leaves! The rich swarmed to emigrate"), *Lianhebao*, 4 January 1990, p. 4. See for example, Lincoln Kaye, "Capital fright: Taiwan plans tough law to combat crime and labor unrest," *Far Eastern Economic Review*, 7 December 1989, pp. 52–53.

65. Chen Ziyan, "Taiwan shi Yazhou piaofu ducheng?" ("Is Taiwan the Asian floating casino?"), *Zhongguo shibao*, 27 January–9 February 1990, p. 71.

66. "Qunian gegou huobi dui meiyuan huilu, taibi shengzhi fudu shijie diyi" ("Taiwanese currency was number one among other currencies in appreciation rate against U.S. dollars"), *Shijie ribao*, 13 February 1990, p. 1.

67. "Dalu fang pin chukou er chaoyu Taiwan" ("Mainland textile export value surpassed Taiwan's"), *Shijie ribao*, 3 February 1990, p. 31.

68. "Dalu huo su Mei wei shou liu si yingxiang" ("Mainland export to the U.S. unaffected by 4 June"), *Shijie ribao*, 18 January 1990, p. 2.

69. Xie Xiangru, "Min–Tai mingjian jiaoliu."

70. "Taiwan da qiye qiu shengcun fen du hai wang dalu touzi" ("Large Taiwanese enterprises busily crossed the Straits to invest in the mainland to survive"), *Shijie ribao*, 24 January 1990, p. 32.

71. "Xiyin waishang touzi sanzi qiye bu zheng xin sui" ("To attack foreign investment three foreign enterprise types pay no new taxes"), *Shijie ribao*, 24 January 1990, p. 32.

Finally, Taipei's government, although officially still upholding the "Three Nos" principle, demonstrated growing tolerance in its practices toward economic exchanges across the Strait. In mid-January 1989, the ROC National Trade Bureau Director indicated that his government would no longer verify the final destination of exported goods so long as they were not directly shipped to the mainland. This policy simply recognized the growing dependence of Taiwan's economy on the mainland market which had become the fourth largest for the island's exports in 1988 with an 80 per cent growth from 1987 to over $2 billion.[72] At the same time, bilateral direct trade – outlawed by Taipei – expanded before and after the Tiananmen incident with the blessing of the deliberate ignorance of the Taiwanese government. One captain of a Taiwan merchant ship anchored at Xiamen observed in September 1989 that the Nationalist patrol boats no longer interfered in his activities.[73]

Examination of the economic interactions across the Strait points to several noteworthy trends. At the non-governmental level, expanding Taiwanese investment on the mainland, which has become more prominent than the growing trade across the Strait, has exhibited the following traits: the amount of investment has increased, with the average Taiwanese enterprise growing from $1 million in 1988 to $2 million in 1989; the term of investment has lengthened from two or three to ten to 20 years; its scope has widened from manufacturing (processing and assembly) to include architectural, agricultural and service industries (finance, tourism and real estate); increasing numbers of investors have exported to the mainland new and full sets of equipment rather than used and incomplete ones; the typical investor has evolved from an individual businessman to financial groups, and Taiwanese investments with little or no mainland participation have grown in number.[74] In 1989, 74 per cent of Taiwanese-funded enterprises in China consisted of independent investment, and investment regions have been expanded from the coast inland.

At the governmental level, Taipei has gradually but continuously relaxed restrictions on bilateral economic interaction, less in response to Beijing's appeal for full-scale exchanges than in recognition of the fast-evolving reality shaped largely by the economic initiatives of Taiwanese citizens. By 1990, Taipei's commercial policy of the "Three Nos" (no direct shipping, no direct communication and no direct trade) existed in name only. In mid-January 1990, the then Taiwan Economics Minister, Chen Li-an, indicated that his government should not regulate economic relations (trade and investment) by means of restrictions, and that his

72. "Taiwan dui liangan maoyi guan jin bu guan chu" ("Taiwan's policy on trade across the Straits is check import not export"), *Huaqiao ribao*, 17 January 1989, p. 2.
73. "Taihai zhijie maoyi shizhi jinxing" ("Direct trade across the Taiwan Straits advanced substantively"), *Zhongyang ribao*, 9 September 1989, p. 2.
74. "Commentary views Taiwan investment on mainland," *Zhongguo xinwen she*, Beijing, 29 December 1989, in *FBIS*, 8 January 1990, p. 52. "Tai shang dalu touzi zhuan xiang changqi xing" ("Taiwanese investment in mainland shifts to long-term commitment"), *Shijie ribao*, 7 February 1990, p. 31. Xie Xiangru, "Min–Tai mingjian jiaoliu."

ministry would reconsider its current policy of banning direct investment on the mainland.[75]

Among the prevailing trends toward further co-operative interactions are minor signs which foreshadow conflict. Concerns for Taipei include the danger of Taiwan's growing economic dependency on the mainland, the possibility that Taiwanese investment on the mainland could eventually strengthen China's overall commercial competitiveness to the detriment of Taiwan's economy, and that mainland-bound Taiwan investors could form an interest group susceptible to the manipulation of Beijing.[76] Concerns for Beijing include the fear that greater presence of Taiwanese economic power on the mainland might weaken people's confidence in their government, compared to Taipei's success in development, and that a network of Taiwan investors might defy Beijing's control.[77]

In sum, the post-Tiananmen economic interaction across the Strait has manifested unexpected momentum, and trends towards co-operation and integration seem more numerous and significant than those auguring conflict and disintegration.

## Social Trends

The post-Tiananmen interactions between the societies across the Taiwan Strait have shown noteworthy trends at least in the following areas.

*Travel and communication.* In 1988, 450,000 Taiwanese visited mainland China[78]; in 1989 – the year of the Tiananmen incident – this had grown to 500,000[79] (or even 550,000 according to PRC Vice-Premier Wu Xueqian on 19 February 1990)[80]; and in 1990, 1991 and 1992, the annual total swelled to over 900,000, 940,000 and 1,500,000 respectively.[81] In 1988, Fujian residents made 130,000 telephone calls to Taiwan; in 1989 the number increased to 450,000[82] and in 1990 it was

75. "Government may increase pace of mainland trade," CNA, Taipei, 17 January 1990 in *FBIS*, 29 January 1990, pp. 52–53.

76. See "Direct trade with mainland still forbidden," *Taipei International Service*, 28 January 1990, p. 53; Louise Ran, "Dangxin, wu guoyu yixiang qinyuan" ("Be careful, do not think wishfully") *Zhongguo shibao*, 10–16 February 1990, p. 30.

77. For example, see "Zhonggong liyao Tai shang touzi, que you fangfan bici lianluo" ("Communist China actively invited Taiwan investors but prevented them from networking"), *Shijie ribao*, 9 February 1990, p. 31.

78. "Taibao tangqin luyou jingshang jinnian renshu chaoguo qunian" ("Number of Taiwan compatriots visiting relatives, touring, and doing business exceeded that of last year"), *Shijie ribao*, 15 December 1989, p. 32.

79. "Residents in Beijing discuss direct contacts," *Xinhua*, Beijing, 18 January 1990, in *FBIS*, 29 January 1990, p. 53.

80. "Wu Xueqian jiejian Taiwan tongmeng fangtuan" ("Wu Xueqian received Taiwan's reunification alliance visiting delegation"), *Shijie ribao*, 19 February 1990, p. 1.

81. "Tai nian waichu luyoujing sanbaiwan ren ce" ("Taiwanese abroad were nearly three million"), *Renmin ribao* (overseas edition), 14 January 1991, p. 5; *China Daily*, 1 March 1992; Julian Baum, "Dirty linen: turf war over China policy goes public," *Far Eastern Economic Review*, 1 July 1993, p. 21.

82. "Fujian gua wang Taiwan dianhua qunian da sishiwuwan zhang" ("Telephone calls from Fujian to Taiwan reached 450,000 in number last year"), *Shijie ribao*, 17 January 1990, p. 32.

1,009,000.[83] In 1989, letters crossing the Taiwan Strait in both directions totalled 13 million, a 350 per cent jump from the 1988 volume,[84] and in 1990 the amount grew to 21 million.[85] The adverse effects of 4 June 1989 on Taiwan–mainland social interaction, at least in westward visits and bilateral communication, were unremarkable.

*Entertainment.* In April 1989, Taiwanese gymnasts competed with Asian athletes in China for the first time in four decades. By February 1990, 12 Taiwan sports teams had followed suit despite the distaste left by the Tiananmen incident. To prepare for the 11th Asian Olympics in September 1990, the Taiwan ping-pong team even invited mainland coaches for training in Hong Kong.[86] In late January 1990, at the same time as the Beijing performance of Taiwanese pop singers Lin Chung and Huang Lei, crews from all three Taiwan television stations shot footage of the celebration of the Spring Festival, or Chinese New Year, in Beijing.[87] In early February 1990, it was confirmed that representatives from both China and Taiwan would compete for the title of "Miss Model Universe" in Taipei.[88] Similar integrative trends continued in still other avenues of social exchanges.

*Culture.* Half a year after the Tiananmen incident, arrested academic exchanges moved forward again. In early February 1990, some 100 scholars from both sides of the Strait exchanged views on their common cultural heritage at the "Conference on Novels from Ming and Qing Dynasties."[89] Meanwhile, two groups of Taiwanese scholars from the "Mainland Research Association" and the "National Taiwan University Professors Association" visited major universities on the mainland.[90] During the same period, Chen Che-nan, a KMT legislator in Taiwan, met mainland representatives in Hong Kong to initiate the establishment of 30 "sister schools" across the Strait, at the risk of being disciplined by his party.[91] The momentum of cultural exchange was also manifested in

83. "Fujian sheng zhibo Taiwan dianhua" ("Direct telephone calls from Fujian to Taiwan"), *Shijie ribao*, 26 December 1990, p. 11.
84. "Liangan hu xie xinjian da yiqianwuwan jian" ("Letter correspondence across the Straits reached ten million in number"), *Shijie ribao*, 12 February 1990, p. 31.
85. "Liangan tongyou de huigu yu zhanwang" ("Postal exchanges across the Strait: reviews and prospects"), *Liaowang*, 18–25 February 1991, p. 37.
86. Bao Jifu, "Haixia liangan tiyu jiaoliu huode lishixing tupuo" ("Historical breakthrough in athlete exchanges across the Straits"), *Liaowang*, 12 February 1990, p. 40.
87. "Mainland, Taiwan conduct cultural exchanges," Xinhua, Beijing, 30 December 1989, in *FBIS*, 8 January 1990, p. 51.
88. "Dalu daibiao lai ding le" ("Mainland representatives will arrive for sure"), *Shijie ribao*, 7 February 1990, p. 8.
89. "Liangan yantao Ming-Qing xiaoshuo" ("Two sides of the Straits conferred on Ming-Qing novels"), *Shijie ribao*, 3 February 1990, p. 32.
90. "Jiaoshou fangwentuan yu tigai hui zuo tan" ("Professors of visiting delegation met with system reform committee"), *Shijie ribao*, 3 February 1990, p. 3.
91. "Wei liangan tijie jiemei xiao Chen Chenan ganmao dangji chufen" ("For establishing sister schools across the Straits, Chen Chenan would rather risk being disciplined by Party"), *Shijie ribao*, 1 February 1990, p. 7.

publications. For example, a volume entitled *Zhongguo wenhua yanjiu nianjian* (*Chinese Cultural Research Chronology*), compiled by mainland scholars was published in Taiwan in May 1990 with jointly-compiled sequels to follow.[92]

*Religion.* Mainland-bound religious activities from Taiwan have proceeded despite governmental restrictions and seem little affected by the Tiananmen crisis. In April 1989, PRC President Yang Shangkun even indicated his willingness to consider the release of the renowned dissident Wei Jingsheng – an effect that pressure from Washington had failed to achieve – only if Taiwanese Buddhist leader Xing Yun were to press the point once more during his visit in Beijing.[93] In the following month, 19 Taiwanese fishing boats carrying pilgrim worshippers of the Goddess Matsu sailed directly to Her birthplace in Meizhou, Fujian, defying Taipei's ban on direct visits across the Strait.[94] All through 1989, streams of Taiwan pilgrims poured into Fujian. In late February 1990, a record size religious excursion of some 300 believers opened the season of celebration for the Goddess's 1,030th anniversary in April[95] heralding a year unmatched to date of Strait-crossing Taiwanese pilgrims totalling 80,000.[96] By October 1991, the cumulative number of Taiwanese pilgrims had reached 300,000.[97]

*Law.* In response to the increased social interaction across the Strait, the need for co-operation arose in dealing with marital and inheritance disputes and criminal extradition. Bound by the "Three Nos" policy, Taipei in most cases reacted with reservation to Beijing's appeal for joint action. In February 1989, in an unprecedented move, Beijing extradited Yang Min-chung, charged for murder in Taiwan, via Singapore to Taipei.[98] A year later, mainland public security agencies arrested 17 gun smugglers from Taiwan along with 25 from the mainland and one from Hong Kong, all members of a network that had allegedly flooded Taiwan

92. "Wenhua yanjiu nianjian ji zai Tai chuban" ("Culture research chronology will soon be published in Taiwan"), *Shijie ribao*, 22 January 1990, p. 2.

93. "Qiu qing shifang Wei Jingsheng Zhongguo bu maizhang, Yang Shangkun cheng Xing Yun shi liwai" ("China submits to no pressure for releasing Wei Jingshen, Yang Shangkan considered Xing Yun exception"), *Huaqiao ribao*, 24 April 1989, p. 2.

94. "Yilan Meizhou jinxiang hongdong quansheng" ("Yilan–Meizhou pilgrimage electrified the entire province"), *Huaqiao ribao*, 1 May 1989, p. 3.

95. "Taiwan xintu chusan fu Meizhou jinxiang" ("Taiwan worshippers sailed to Meizhou in pilgrimage on the third of the lunar new year"), *Shijie ribao*, 16 January 1990, p. 32.

96. Fujian provincial government released the annual number of Taiwanese pilgrims. See "Min–Tai guanxi shida xinwen chulong" ("Top ten news of Fujian–Taiwan relations released"), *Shijie ribao*, 11 February 1991, p. 12.

97. "Wu nian lai da sanshiwan ci" ("The number reaches 300,000 in five years"), *Shijie ribao*, 21 October 1991, p. 11.

98. "Mainland said to agree on criminal extradition," *Taipei International Service*, 13 February 1989, in *FBIS*, 13 February 1989.

with 1,600 pistols and 40,000 bullets made in the PRC.[99] While Beijing suggested on 4 February 1990 that the 17 be extradited to Taiwan in exchange for Wu Dapeng, who was wanted by the PRC and had been arrested in the ROC, Taipei requested on 5 February, through the Paris-based International Criminal Police Commission, that the 17 be returned to Taiwan without mentioning Wu.[100]

The strong momentum of co-operative social interactions across the Strait which continued despite the trauma of Tiananmen coexisted with certain developments which foreboded conflict. In 1989, illegal firearms confiscated by the Taiwan police amounted to about 10,000 (mostly made in the PRC and bearing consecutive serial numbers), up from 2,400 in 1988.[101] In late December 1989, Taipei government spokesman Shaw Yu-ming attributed the recent drastic deterioration of public security in Taiwan to the gun smuggling across the Strait, facilitated by a "conniving" Beijing government.[102] Furthermore, another form of smuggling which originated on the mainland also troubled Taiwanese society. The Institute for National Security Policy Research, a non-governmental think-tank in Taipei, reported in November 1989 that at least 5,000 to 6,000 mainland drifters had illegally arrived in Taiwan by infiltrating the coastline on fishing boats under night cover, and that among these "guestworkers" and "imported prostitutes" were commissioned agents engaging in sabotage and espionage.[103] Since spring 1990, additional frictions have occurred between the two societies from unforeseen developments such as the illegal profiteering and lecherous behaviour of Taiwanese businessmen and fishermen causing increasing resentment among the mainland populace, the growing number of mainland pirates preying upon Taiwanese fisherman, and the tragic deaths of mainland drifters during extradition voyages supervised by Taipei.[104]

On balance, the social interaction across the Strait exhibited greater integrative than disintegrative trends, and the mainland-bound movements far exceeded the reverse. At least three factors may account for

99. "Liangan bufa fengzi goujie zousi heiqiang, Zhonggong jue qisu shiqi ming Taiwan heidao" ("Criminals from both sides of the Straits co-operated in gun smuggling, Communist China decided to prosecute 17 Taiwan lawbreakers"), *Shijie ribao*, 4 February 1990, p. 1.

100. "Beijing asked to return local arms traffickers," CNA, Taipei, 5 February 1990, in *FBIS*, 6 February 1990, p. 41.

101. "Lian hao heixin hongxin shouqiang cong chi" ("Proliferation of "Blackstar" and "Redstar" pistols bearing consecutive serial numbers"), *Zhongyang ribao*, 6 November 1989, p. 1.

102. "Shaw condemns mainland arms smuggling," CNA, Taipei, 29 December 1989, in *FBIS*, 29 December 1989, p. 54.

103. "Chang Rungfa jijinhui guoce yanjiu zhongxin tichu jing gao" ("The Institute National Policy Research of Chang Rungfa Foundation publicized warnings"), *Shijie ribao*, 5 November 1989, p. 1.

104. "Taibao piaoji, Dalu fangan" ("Taiwanese visitors frequent prostitution houses, mainland populace resentful"), *Shijie ribao*, 1 June 1992, p. 32; "Taibao bu guiju zi re mafan" ("Taiwanese visitors behave badly and invite troubles"), *Shijie ribao*, 14 June 1990, p. 32; "Dalu dongnan yanhai 'xiandai haidao' siyi hengxing" (" 'Modern pirates' roam mainland's south-east coast"), *Zhongyang ribao*, 2 July 1990, p. 1; "Dalu haidao xuexi Jilong yuchan" ("The bloodbath of Keelung fishing boat by mainland pirates"), *Shijie ribao*, 28 February 1991, p. 10; "Qianfan toudu renshi fasheng liangqi canju" ("Extraditing drifters led to two tragic accidents"), *Shijie ribao*, 22 August 1990, p. 1.

such developments. First, Beijing's efforts at fostering goodwill among Taiwanese people never slackened. For example, on 4 February 1990, the PRC government dispatched People's Liberation Army vehicles to rescue 17 Taiwanese tourists from a snowstorm in Zhangjiajie, Hunan while leaving some Hong Kong tourists still stranded at the location.[105]

Secondly, the Taipei government has maintained since 1988 its relaxation, however limited, of restrictions on non-governmental contact and communication across the Strait. In April 1988, written correspondence between the two sides began passing through a transfer station in Hong Kong administered by the International Red Cross.[106] As described by Tao Pai-chuan, Taipei's Adviser on National Policy, in October 1988, the emerging but tacit stance taken by his government was "communication by letter but no postal exchanges, ... interflow but no contact ...."[107]

Finally, nationalistic sentiments rooted in cultural and familial bonds proved to be an unstoppable force for social interaction between the two sides. Even Chen Yin-chen, a Taiwanese author with no relations on the mainland, publicly expressed his sense of urgency for reunification based on the "warmth towards compatriots and profound concerns for the bones and flesh of his mainland brothers and sisters" when the Taiwan civilian delegation led by him, "China Reunification Alliance," landed in Beijing on 15 February 1990.[108] After the worst flood in a century struck southern China in the summer of 1991, Taiwan donated $6 million in rescue funds, far exceeding the $25,000 from the United States and $300,000 from Japan.[109]

*Strategic Trends*

Both Taipei and Beijing have expressed an intention to co-operate militarily with each other in the defence of the Spratlys.[110] As previously mentioned, in October 1990 Beijing accused Tokyo of violating China's sovereignty after Japanese naval vessels harassed Taiwanese fishing boats near Diaoyutai (Senkaku) Island. But apart from these rare occasions of mutual support, most of the post-Tiananmen interactions between Beijing

105. "Gaogan pai junche zhi zhu Taiwan tuan" ("High-ranking cadres dispatched military vehicles to rescue only Taiwan tourists"), *Shijie ribao*, 5 February 1990, p. 31.

106. "Taiwan Hongshizihui zhengshi xuanbu liangan tong xin fang shi shouli reqi" ("Taiwan Red Cross formally announced the date for handling correspondences across the Straits"), *Huaqiao ribao*, 18 April 1988, p. 1.

107. Tao's comment, referred to as "five nos and five yeses," in its entirety is: "Communication by letter but no postal exchanges, exchange of goods but no trade, interflow but no contact, dialogue but no negotiation, and relaxation but no compromise." See Li Jiaquan, "More on reunification of Taiwan with mainland," *Beijing Review*, 16–22 January 1989, p. 28.

108. "Tonglian dalu fangwentuan sheng min" ("Reunification alliance's announcement for visiting mainland"), *Shijie ribao*, 16 February 1990, p. 21.

109. "Gang Tai dali zhenzai" ("Hong Kong and Taiwan offer great help in disaster relief"), *Shijie ribao*, 24 July 1991, p. 10.

110. "Rear Admiral on co-operation with Taiwan navy," *Voice of Pujiang*, Shanghai, 30 January 1989, in *FBIS*, 2 February 1989, p. 73; "Taipei ban haijun Nansha xunyi shouze" ("Taipei decreed naval guidelines for patrolling the Spratlys"), *Huaqiao ribao*, 12 April 1988, p. 2.

and Taipei in the strategic arena have manifested distrust and friction despite the growing accommodations in economic, social and, to a lesser extent, political exchanges across the Taiwan Strait.

Four contentious trends have become prominent in mainland–Taiwan strategic interactions. They are Taipei's apprehensive reactions to Beijing's military rhetoric, the tension-causing activities of the mainland fishing flotilla, Taipei's alarmed perception of Beijing's intimidating military operations, and the mini-arms race across the Taiwan Strait.

*Beijing's militant rhetoric.* Beijing has mentioned repeatedly that it will not renounce the use of force in achieving reunification, while Taipei, vigilantly recording these "verbal threats," has noted that their frequency has increased and their tone has toughened since the 1989 Tiananmen incident. According to Taipei's Government Information Office, Beijing issued five such statements in 1989 and 22 in 1990.[111] In October 1991, Taipei's Mainland Affairs Council Director Huang Kun-hui reported that Beijing had reiterated more than 70 times in one year its non-renunciation of using force against Taiwan.[112] In May 1992, PRC President Yang Shangkun turned down Taipei's proposal that the mainland and Taiwan sign a non-aggression treaty.[113]

On 27 May 1990, Yang Shangkun, while receiving overseas Chinese during his visit to Argentina, reiterated Beijing's non-renunciation of force against Taiwan with a reminder that "we [Beijing] have nuclear warheads, ballistic missiles, submarines, many submarines...."[114] Bordering on nuclear blackmail, such statements coming from the leader of a country that claimed never to use nuclear weapons against a non-nuclear neighbour were unprecedented. On 10 June 1991, PRC State Council Taiwan Affairs Bureau Chief Wang Zhaoguo commented to a visiting delegation that "if Beijing merely launches a blockade, Taiwan can not endure it."[115] Beijing's belligerent rhetoric reached a new height four months later. Publicly denouncing the escalating Taiwanese independence movement, Yang stated on 10 October 1991: "A small number of separatists be warned. Do not misjudge the situation. Those who play with fire will perish by fire."[116]

111. Government Information Office (Taipei), *A Study of a Possible Communist Attack on Taiwan* (Taipei: Good Earth Printing Company, 1991), pp. 30–61.
112. "Zhonggong yinian lai tan wuli dui Tai" ("Communist China's mentioning of the use of force against Taiwan last year"), *Shijie ribao*, 7 October 1992, p. 2.
113. "Yang Shangkun ming biao ju tan liangan hu bu qinfan tiaoyue" ("Yang Shangkun clearly indicated his refusal to discuss the non-aggression treaty across the Taiwan Strait"), *Shijie ribao*, 30 May 1992, p. 1.
114. Yang was denouncing both the Taiwanese independence movement and Taipei's insistence on having an equal status when talking to Beijing on a government-to-government basis. See "Yang Shangkun fan Taidu kouqi qiangying" ("Yang Shangkun sounded tough in opposing Taiwanese independence"), *Shijie ribao*, 8 June 1990, p. 1.
115. "Zhonggong jianchi tongyi zhuzhang" ("Communist China insists on re-unification"), *Zhongshi wanbao* (*China Times Express*, Taipei), 12 June 1991, p. 1.
116. Yang was commemorating the 80th anniversary of the 1911 revolution led by Sun Yat-sen whose wish to see China reunified "remained unfulfilled." See "Yang Shangkun Zhuxi de jianghua" ("The Speech by President Yang Shangkun"), *Remin ribao*, 10 October 1991, pp. 1–3.

Beijing has frequently explained that its non-renunciation of using force against Taiwan was meant for foreign, not Taiwanese, consumption in order to deter certain international powers from taking Taiwan away from China forever, because "for Chinese to fight Chinese makes no sense."[117] However, Taiwan's apprehension of the mainland threat has not decreased as a result. An October 1991 opinion poll conducted in Taiwan showed that those who fear a PLA invasion of the island if Taiwan were to announce independence amounted to 60.6 per cent of the respondents.[118] One month after the April 1993 Koo–Wang Conference in Singapore – a landmark event of growing goodwill across the Taiwan Strait – 67 per cent of college students in Taiwan foresaw a blockade by Beijing upon Taipei's declaration of independence, according to one survey.[119] Expanded activities of mainland fishing boats and movements of the People's Liberation Army have also contributed to the contentious strategic interactions between the mainland and Taiwan.

*Mainland fishing flotilla.* In November 1989, Taipei's official newspaper described the hydrographical survey around Taiwan by PRC boats allegedly connected with Beijing's National Defence, Science, Technology and Industry Commission as "obviously having ulterior motives against us."[120] In recent years, Taipei has observed with growing unease the broadened mainland fishing flotilla operations, ranging from harassing offshore islands to invading Taiwanese coastal waters and ports. For example, waves of mainland civilian vessels encroached on the waters around Jinmen and Mazu islands in the spring of 1990. The ROC Defence Ministry reported that from 25 April to 23 May 1990, troops stationed on those offshore islands had to fire 5,556 bullets and 143 artillery shots to drive away 6,574 sorties of mainland fishing boats at an average of 227 a day.[121] Formations of mainland boats have often lingered enigmatically off Taiwanese waters, such as on 9 April 1991, 26 September 1991 and 1 April 1992 when groups numbering around 50, 200 and 100 vessels respectively were sighted near Taoyuan and Penghu.[122]

117. In August 1987, Yang Shangkun said to Taiwanese Americans then visiting Beijing: "Our talk of applying armed forces against Taiwan is for the American audience. We will not actually apply force against Taiwan." Ma Feibai, "Deng Xiaoping kaishi bu naifan le!" ("Deng Xiaoping has begun to be impatient!"), *Xin Xinwen (The Journalist*, Taipei), 26 December–1 January 1989, p. 79; also see " 'Talk' ridicules Taiwan invasion fears," Beijing in Mandarin to Taiwan, 27 February 1991, in *FBIS*, 5 March 1991, p. 72.

118. *Shijie ribao*, 28 October 1991, p. 9.

119. "Daxuesheng 64% bu zancheng taidu" ("64% of college students disapproved Taiwanese independence"), *Zhongyang ribao*, 8 June 1993, p. 3.

120. "Chunli shouji Taiwan chuandao shuiwen ziliao" ("Gathering hydrographical data of entire Taiwan with all capabilities"), *Zhongyang ribao*, 24 November 1989, p. 1.

121. "Zhonggong chuanzhi xu saorao Jinma" ("Chinese Communist vessels continue to harass Jinmen and Mazu"), *Shijie ribao*, 26 May 1990, p. 7.

122. "Wushi yi dalu chuan bijin Taiwan linhai" ("Some 50 mainland boats near Taiwan's territorial waters"), *Shijie ribao*, 10 April 1991, p. 8; "Jin liangbai sou dalu chuan jijie Taoyuan waihai" ("About 200 mainland boats gather outside the territorial waters near Taotuan"), *Shijie ribao*, 6 September 1991, p. 8; and "102 Sou dalu yuchuan jijie Penghu haiyu" ("102 mainland fishing boats gather in territorial waters of Penghu"), *Shijie ribao*, 12 April 1992, p. 5.

According to one study, mainland fishing boats, some fortified with armour, attacked Taiwanese civilian and naval vessels on 14 different occasions from 5 November 1990 to 9 April 1991, killing several sailors and kidnapping a few patrolling soldiers.[123]

These incidents have reinforced Taipei's suspicion that some mainland civilian vessels are in fact units of the coastal militia which comprise up to 300,000 men, and 32,000 merchant and fishing boats. In Taipei's view, their missions include probing weaknesses of Taiwan's defence, gathering intelligence reports, delivering infiltrating agents, and even assisting the PLA Navy by diverting the ROC Navy's attention during an armed conflict.[124] Taipei therefore decided to toughen its posture. In March 1990, the Taiwanese government allowed its patrol boats to fire shots more than just for warning, directly at mainland vessels if necessary.[125] In April 1991, the government decided to intensify patrols and to destroy, if necessary, mainland Chinese vessels that refuse to leave waters off Taiwan.[126]

After March 1990, Taiwanese shots at mainland vessels resulted in injuries and deaths, and hostility among mainland fisherman towards the Taiwanese navy and coastal police rose steadily.[127] Taipei saw this as part of a media campaign conducted by PRC officials aimed at mainland fisherman.[128] One New China News Agency dispatch from Fuzhou on 18 October 1991 stated that Taipei "mobilized naval ships to rob mainland fishing boats and to shoot to death fishermen from Fujian province, which has caused one's hair to stand on its end out of anger."[129] Apparently in retaliation, PRC coastal patrols began shooting at Taiwanese fishing boats in April 1991, further aggravating the situation.[130] In 1992, at least 19 Taiwanese fishing boats were harassed or robbed by mainlanders and at least five mainland boats were shot by the Taiwanese navy, which

123. Ji Yinghuan, "Liangan guanxi de yi gu anchao" ("A dark current in the relations across the Taiwan Strait"), *Shibao zhoukan*, 20–26 September 1991, p. 25.

124. See for example, "Zhonggong guangshou Taishi yu chuan, juxin buze" ("Chinese Communists mass purchase Taiwanese-styled fishing boats with unfathomable motives"), *Shijie ribao*, 15 March 1991, p. 9.

125. "Taiwan jisi jian zhiqin buzai zhiyu shijing" ("Taiwan's anti-smuggling patrol ships no longer restricted to firing warning shots"), *Shijie ribao*, 24 March 1990, p. 5.

126. "Navy to intensify patrols to protect fisherman," Taipei, CNA, 3 April 1991, in *FBIS*, 4 April 1991, p. 83; "Intruding mainland vessels may be destroyed," Taipei, CNA, 9 April 1991, in *FBIS*, 8 April 1991, p. 65.

127. See, for example, a report dispatched from Fujian, "Min yanhai yumin dui guofu junjing chongman diyi" ("Fisherman from Fujian coast harbour strong hatred against Taiwanese Navy and coastal police"), *Shijie ribao*, 10 October 1991, p. 8.

128. "Troops kidnap, torture mainland fisherman," Beijing in Mandarin to Taiwan, 24 March 1990, in *FBIS*, 26 March 1990, p. 53. "Zhonggong qitu zhizhao dui Tai buman qing xu" ("Chinese Communists attempt to create anti-Taiwan sentiments"), *Shijie ribao*, 9 September 1991, p. 8.

129. "Junjing jie yuchuan" ("The Navy and the coastal patrol held up fishing boats"), *Shijie ribao*, 19 October 1991, p. 8.

130. "Dalu gong an chuan sheji Taiwan yuchuan" ("Mainland public security ships shoot at Taiwanese fishing boats"), *Shijie ribao*, 18 April 1991, p. 8.

resulted in recurrent protests from both Taipei and Beijing against each other.[131]

*Beijing's military operations.* Taipei has perceived a growing security threat in the PLA's post-Tiananmen movements. Beijing has never made explicit that its military exercises are threatening to Taiwan, but they have often coincided in timing with its official denunciations of the Taiwanese independence movement and of Taipei's effort to expand its international presence (see Table 3). Typically, these operations occurred in areas not distant from Taiwan, and simulated air, sea or amphibious battles – conditions similar to Beijing's possible military actions against the island and its offshore territories. For example, an operation in the South China Sea in October 1990, described by Beijing as "a parachute-landing exercise on an island for the first time" by the PLA,[132] caused grave concern across the Strait and was seen by Taiwan's Defence Ministry as a rehearsal for an assault against Taiwan.[133]

*The Mini-Arms Race.* In recent years, Taiwan has made impressive progress in its defence capability, emphasizing improvement in quality over expansion in quantity. Such efforts continued and probably accelerated after the 1989 Tiananmen incident. The 1989 budget for Taiwan's armed forces, about one-tenth the size of the PLA, was $6.84 billion, exceeding the $6.67 billion of the 1989 PLA budget. The Taiwanese defence budget grew 27 per cent to $8.69 billion in 1990, and 7 per cent to $9.29 billion in 1991, surpassing the published PLA budget every year.[134]

By February 1991, Taipei had completed the ten-year "Chiashan Project," an underground airforce base east of the Central Mountains, from which 200 stored fighter planes could taxi to nearby Hualien Airport.[135] Meanwhile, in 1990, the construction of eight other underground military bases, dispersed around Taiwan and to be operational by 1993, had begun.

While the United States continued to sell Taiwan arms (such as the first three of ten anti-submarine helicopters delivered in July 1991, the 68

131. The sources include: *Renmin ribao*, 20 April 1992, p. 1; 24 June 1992, p. 5; *FBIS*, 3 June 1992, p. 54; 13 July 1992, p. 60; 30 July 1992; *Shijie ribao*, 22 May 1992, p. 9; 22 July 1992, p. 1; 27 July 1992, p. 6; 7 August 1992, p. 7; 5 October 1992, p. 8; 13 November 1992, p. 9; *Far Eastern Economic Review*, 6 August 1992, p. 12; *Zhongyang ribao*, 13 July 1992, p. 1.
132. "Airborne units conduct island paratroop exercise," *Jiefangjun bao*, 5 November 1990, p. 1 in *FBIS*, 21 November 1990, p. 27.
133. "Paratroops carry out practice drop on island," *Wen Wei Bao*, Hong Kong, 6 November 1990, p. 1, originally carried by *Jiefangjun bao*, 5 November 1990 in *FBIS*, 9 November 1990.
134. *The Military Balance 1991–1992* (London: The International Institute for Strategic Studies, 1991), pp. 150, 180.
135. "Tunnel links air force bunkers to Hualien Airport," Taipei Domestic Service, 12 February 1991, in *FBIS*, 19 February 1991, p. 59. "Shanfu wakong ke tingfang zhanji liangbai jia" ("Excavated mountains can store 200 fighters"), *Zhongyang ribao*, 14 February 1991, p. 1.

Table 3: Post-Tiananmen PLA Exercises Perceived as Invasion Simulations by Taiwan

| Time | Nature of exercises | Original sources |
|---|---|---|
| *1989* | | |
| Early May–mid-September | East Sea Fleet in the West Pacific Ocean and South China Sea | *Renmin ribao* 21 September 1989 |
| July–September | Nanjing Military Region at Jiulongjiang near Jinmen | *Shijie ribao* 17 November 1989 |
| Autumn | Nanjing Military Region in waters near Penghu | *Shijie ribao* 17 November 1989 |
| October–December | East China Sea Fleet in open seas beyond the littoral zone | *Jiefangjun bao* 21 November 1989 |
| *1990* | | |
| 9–12 March | South-east coast of China with Jian-8 fighters | Taiwan intelligence *Shijie ribao* 12 March 1990 |
| April | Naval reconnaissance and Marine troops in amphibious operations on coral reef islands (probably in South China Sea) | *Wen Wei Bao* 18 April 1990 |
| Late September | Shengyang Military Region naval militia in an exercise of transporting troops and arms under battle conditions | *Jiefangjun bao* 13 October 1990 |
| 20 October | Airborne exercises on a South China Sea island | *Jiefangjun bao* 5 November 1990 |

| *1991* | | |
|---|---|---|
| 8 February | Navy's airforce exercises including "unprecedented scenario in training" such as low penetration flights | *Renmin ribao* 8 February 1991 |
| March | Nationwide military exercises in a magnitude "rarely seen in recent years" | *Renmin ribao* 19 March 1991 |
| July | Navy seafaring, combined arms exercises in the Yellow Sea and Bohai Sea | *Jiefangjun bao* 5 July 1991 |
| 28–30 September | China's first post-Tiananmen military parade after an exercise in Guangdong with PLA reserves | *Shijie ribao* 29 September 1991 |
| 26 September–1 October | Guangzhou and Nanjing Military Regions | *Shijie ribao* 3 October 1991 |
| October | Exercises along the Yangzi River | *Renmin ribao* 25 October 1991 |
| October–November | Army exercises in Fujian | *Zhongyang ribao* 1 December 1991 |
| 17 November | Airforce exercises over the Yellow Sea | New China News Agency 10 November 1992 |
| December | Airforce exercises in East China | New China News Agency *Shijie ribao* 16 December 1991 |
| 25 December–1 January | Nanjing and Jinnan Military Regions | *Dongxiang* (Hong Kong) 14 March 1992 |

combat helicopters that Washington may transfer to Taiwan by December 1995, and 150 F-16 fighters deliverable after 1996[136]) Taipei became increasingly active in indigenous development of armaments and in diversification of weapon suppliers. Taiwan's first jet fighter (IDF), which is comparable to the American F-16, made its public debut in October 1989 and entered mass production virtually on schedule in April 1992.[137] Taiwan has also developed tactical missiles such as the long-range ship-to-ship Heroic Wind (Hsiung Feng) II missile deployed in 1991, the surface-to-air Sky Bow (Tien Kung) I and II missiles deployed by 1991, and the air-to-air Sky Arrow (Tien Chieng) missile to be deployed in the early 1990s.[138] In October 1991, Taiwan's first self-built missile frigate was launched, with seven more to follow by the year 2000,[139] and Taiwan's first locally-produced Brave Tiger (Meng Hu) tank was deployed in April 1990.[140]

In September 1991, the French government, despite Beijing's protest, authorized the sale of 16 frigates worth $4.8 billion to Taiwan, with deployment scheduled in four years.[141] In November 1992, Paris decided to sell 60 Mirage 2000-5 fighters to Taipei, ignoring Beijing's objection.[142] By 1991, Taipei had expanded its non-American arms sources to more than 20 countries, including most notably the Netherlands who had sold Taiwan two attack submarines. Besides items such as Belgian missile generators and German torpedoes, Taiwan also acquired Israeli weaponry.[143] Despite Tel Aviv's then-ongoing unofficial ties with Beijing, Israel exported more than $1 billion worth of "aerospace equipment," much of it military, to Taiwan in 1990 alone.[144] In July 1991, Taipei even

136. "Mei shou Tai fan qian zhishengji" ("The U.S. sold Taiwan anti-submarine helicopters"), *Shijie ribao*, 28 July 1991, p. 1. "Mei ning shou Tai 68 jia zhishengji" ("The U.S. about to sell Taiwan 68 helicopters"), *Shijie ribao*, 3 April 1992, p. 2. Julian Baum, "A foot in the door," *Far Eastern Economic Review*, 17 September 1992, p. 12.

137. "Taiwan's IDF bid," and "Taiwan's new fighter enters production," *Aviation Week and Space Technology*, Vol. 136, No. 17 (27 April 1992), pp. 7, 38–44. "Taiwan jet blows tire at its debut," *Milwaukee Sentinel*, 30 October 1989, p. 11.

138. "Sky bow makes formal bow," *Free China Journal*, 28 September 1989, p. 2. "Fazhan duan chang cheng dui kong feidan" ("Developing short and long-range air-to-air missiles"), *Shijie ribao*, 27 January 1991, p. 2. *The Military Balance 1991–1992*, p. 180.

139. "Navy launches first Taiwan-built missile frigate," CNA, Taipei, 7 October 1991, in *FBIS*, 8 October 1991, p. 76.

140. " 'Brave Tiger' tank roars," *Free China Journal*, 19 April 1990, p. 1.

141. "New missile frigate to upgrade naval forces," CNA, Taipei, 3 October 1991, in *FBIS*, 3 October 1991, p. 56. "Sale of French frigates to Taiwan protested," Xinhua, Beijing, 28 September 1991, in *FBIS*, 30 September 1991, p. 22.

142. "Gou zhi 60 jia huanxiang zhanji Zhong Fa jin qian heyue" ("Taiwan and France sign agreement today on sale of 60 Mirage fighters"), *Zhongguo shibao*, 17 November 1992, p. 7.

143. Liu Jiansheng, "Taiwan junhuo cong nali lai?" ("Where are Taiwan's weapons from?"), *Jiushi niandai yuekan* (*The Nineties Weekly*, Hong Kong), May 1991, pp. 68–72; *Military Balance 1991–1992*, p. 180; "Bilishi shou Tai huojian fadongji" ("Belgium sold Taiwan missile generators"), *Shijie ribao*, 19 May 1991, p. 1; "Haijun tianshou jingmi yulei" ("Navy acquired sophisticated torpedoes"), *Shijie ribao*, 4 August 1991, p. 4; Liu Jiansheng, "Taiwan junhuo," pp. 71–72.

144. "Israeli trade, aerospace purchases reported," CNA, Taipei, 7 September 1991, in *FBIS*, 10 September 1991, p. 71.

considered Moscow's initial offer to sell Mig-31 interceptors.[145] By 1992, Taiwan's arms build-up had begun to promise a point of equilibrium in the military balance across the Taiwan Strait.

Parallel to Taipei's defence build-up, the PLA escalated its efforts in arms acquisition after the Tiananmen incident. Reversing a declining trend since 1979, China's defence budget has grown continuously since 1989 with an increase of 13 per cent in that year, 15.5 per cent in 1990, 12 per cent in 1991, 13.8 per cent in 1992, and 14.9 per cent in 1993.[146] Despite its quantitative reduction of forces, the PLA has become more active in procuring new weapons to boost its projection force which, in Taipei's perception, will inevitably affect the strategic balance across the Taiwan Strait.

As a result of Beijing's incessant efforts to reach out diplomatically, the post-Tiananmen international sanctions on China did not succeed in restricting Beijing's foreign supplies of military technology for long. By the autumn of 1990, France had decided to upgrade two Chinese Luda-class destroyers with air defence missiles and search radars.[147] A year later, Moscow sold Beijing three IL-76TD military transport planes and considered helping China develop Yak-141 fighters capable of short take-offs and vertical landings.[148] By spring 1992, Israel had reportedly transferred to China, among other materials, technology for re-fuelling in mid-air and even American "patriot" missile technology for use in China's new KS1 surface-to-air missile.[149]

In September 1990, Beijing negotiated with Moscow to purchase state-of-the-art Sukhoi SU-27 jet fighters, which would be the first significant arms transfers since the 1950s. At the time, observers expected only a small number of the aircraft to be sold and saw in the deal already "a quantum leap in the firepower of China's air force, as well as a shift in the balance of military power in Asia."[150] By April 1992, China had purchased from the Russian Republic 24 high-performance SU-27

145. "Yi qian beiwang lu" ("The memorandum has been signed"), *Shijie ribao*, 30 July 1991, p. 1.

146. Robert Delfs, "Premier Li calls for austerity, sacrifice: tighten your belts," *Far Eastern Economic Review*, 30 March 1989, p. 10. See also, "Gongjun 'piluan' you gong" ("The PLA was rewarded for quelling the rebellion"), *Shijie ribao*, 22 March 1990, p. 31; "Increased military spending," *South China Morning Post*, Hong Kong, 25 March 1991, in *FBIS*, 26 March 1991, p. 14; "Zhonggong bennian junshi yusuan ju zeng" ("Communist China's military budget this year grows noticeably"), *Shijie ribao*, 23 March 1992, p. 2; and "Ri juece Zhonggong zai fabiao guofang baipishu" ("Japan decides to urge China to publish defence White Paper"), *Lianhebao*, 24 May 1993, p. 1.

147. Ted Hooton, "French to upgrade Chinese Luda destroyers," *International Defense Review*, August 1990, p. 920.

148. Henry Dodds, " 'Hokum' takes to the air: Yak-I41 may find role with air force," *Jane's Defense Weekly*, 28 September 1991, p. 551; "Zhonggong xiang Sulian caigou sanjia junyong yunsu ji" ("Communist China purchases three military transport airplanes from the Soviet Union"), *Zhongguo shibao*, 27 September 1991, p. 10.

149. Jin Zhaofu, "Youtairen he Zhonggong wuqi susong" ("The Israeli–Chinese arms transfer"), *Shijie ribao*, 9 April 1992, p. 36; "Beijing fazhan KS1 feidan" ("Beijing develops KS1 missile"), *Shijie ribao*, 18 January 1992, p. 10; and Christopher F. Foss, "Phased array for China's KS1 SAM," *Jane's Defense Weekly*, 11 January 1992, p. 39.

150. "Purchase of Soviet jet fighters considered," *AFP*, Hong Kong, 29 October 1990, in *FBIS*, 29 October 1990, pp. 7–8.

fighters reportedly with an additional 48 to follow.[151] Moreover, according to its Foreign Ministry, Moscow would even transfer the manufacturing technology of SU-27 to Beijing by 1996.[152]

Meanwhile, Beijing strived to realize its long-standing aspirations of acquiring an aircraft carrier, which Western observers previously considered too costly and therefore impracticable for the PLA. By June 1990, the conversion of roll-on roll-off amphibious ships to helicopter carriers had begun, which resulted in the inauguration of the PLA Navy's first ship-based aircraft unit in January 1991.[153] In 1992, Beijing became noticeably active in shopping for an aircraft carrier from Ukraine or Russia.[154]

In addition to widening foreign sources of military hardware, Beijing has increased its efforts to upgrade its domestically-produced arsenal. By late 1991, the PLA had deployed more than ten varieties of self-developed guided missiles on most naval ships, and some 30 types of such missiles at air defence bases.[155] The PLA Navy tested a new C-34 torpedo over the Taiwan Strait in early 1990 and announced late last year the successful development, interestingly with extra-budgetary and non-governmental funds, of another torpedo called "China's Sturgeon."[156] Most of these events attracted Taipei's nervous attention. So did an October 1990 report that the PLA was secretly manufacturing a new landing vessel.[157]

In sum, post-Tiananmen strategic interaction between Beijing and Taipei has heightened tensions resulting from mutually distrustful perceptions and reinforced by the increasingly unfriendly, if not hostile, strategic behaviour of each party. In Taipei's view, the June 1989 Tiananmen crackdown indicated that violence from Beijing, however unlikely, can never be ruled out. In Beijing's view, the imperialist forces, forever intent on splitting Taiwan away from the motherland, have expanded their assistance in Taiwan's defence build-up since the break-up of the former Soviet Union; and Beijing must not renounce the use of

151. "Beijing qiagou Sulian xianjin zhangji" ("Beijing arranges the purchase of advanced Soviet fighters"), *Shijie ribao*, 30 October 1990, p. 2; Jin Zhaofu, "Zhonggong damai Erluosi jingmi wuqi" ("Communist China purchases many hi-tech Russian weapons"), *Shijie ribao*, 23 April 1992, p. 40.

152. Pin Kefu, "Zhonggong goude Sulian zhanji weili dazeng" ("Communist China obtains Soviet fighters greatly increasing its capabilities"), *Zhongguo shibao zhoukan*, 19–25 April 1992, pp. 16–17.

153. Barbara Starr, "China considers carrier plans," *Jane's Defense Weekly*, 16 June 1990, p. 17; "Navy's first ship-based aircraft unit inaugurated," *Renmin ribao*, 9 January 1991, p. 4, in *FBIS*, 16 January 1991, p. 46.

154. "China: fighting back," *The Economist*, 7 March 1992. Sheryl WuDunn, "China browses for tanks, aircraft and carrier in ex-Soviet lands," *New York Times*, 7 June 1992, p. A20.

155. "Zhonggong yanzhi chenggong duozhong zhanshu daodan" ("Communist China succeeded in developing many tactical missiles"), Xinhua, Beijing, 10 October 1991, in *Shijie ribao*, 11 October 1991, p. 10.

156. "Torpedo developed using nongovernmental funds," *Jiefangjun bao*, 25 October 1990, p. 1, in *FBIS*, 13 November 1990, p. 36; "Zhonggong shishe xinxing yulei" ("Communist China tests new landing vessels"), *Shijie ribao*, 8 October 1990, p. 31.

157. "Zhonggong bimi zhizao xinxing dengluting" ("Communist China secretly manufactures new landing vessels"), *Shijie ribao*, 8 October 1990, p. 31.

force to achieve reunification in order to deter foreign intervention over the issue of Taiwan, "a province of China." As Beijing's non-renunciation of the use of force has further aggravated Taipei's misgivings toward Beijing, Taipei feels compelled to accelerate its military self-strengthening. For its part, Beijing's concern that Taipei may soon achieve military sufficiency to deny Beijing's credibility in its strategic threat to Taipei has pushed Beijing further along in its own weapons acquisition programmes.

## Conclusions

Examination of post-Tiananmen trends in political, economic, social and strategic interactions between Taiwan and the mainland suggest the following conclusions. First, the Taiwanese people's mainland-bound economic and social activities after the Tiananmen incident expanded at a rate unexpectedly greater than before the incident, except for a transient wait-and-see period in June and July of 1989.

Secondly, the mainland's Taiwan-bound economic and social activities both before and after the Tiananmen incident have grown at a minimal rate, limited by the Taipei government's caution and resistance towards Beijing's persistent initiatives for communication, contact and negotiation. Despite the Tiananmen incident, however, it is expected that such activities will grow as Taipei has begun, and may accelerate, relaxation on restrictions of non-governmental exchanges.

Thirdly, it is not unlikely that Beijing and Taipei, driven by different motives, will manage to achieve direct political contacts in the foreseeable future. PRC gerontocrats wish to realize reunification within their lifetime. Taiwan leaders may have conceived a grand strategy of "soft-offensives," combining the economic, social, and even political movements toward the mainland to change eventually the nature of the PRC state and society, and to encumber Beijing's use of force against Taiwan.

Fourthly, the post-Tiananmen era has seen the dialectical coexistence of two opposite sets of trends in Taiwan–mainland relations, both developing at a rate faster than anticipated in the public perception while neither cancelling out the impetus of the other. One is the set of accommodating trends which manifest most strongly in economic and social interactions, less in political and rarely in strategic interactions. The other is a set of contentious trends which manifest most strongly in strategic, slightly less so in political, and the least in socio-economic interactions. While the accommodating trends promise integration, the contentious trends portend conflict. In addition, the accommodating trends have stemmed primarily, though not entirely, from non-governmental forces. Political powers may slow down or speed up, but can no longer reverse these trends. The long-term, cumulative effects of such trends will be formidable.

Finally, the contentious interactions have resulted largely, but not wholly, from the governmental forces. As both the Taipei and Beijing governments evolve, their rivalry rooted in the past will probably weaken.

Although in the short term, the possibility of rising tension or even hostile operations across the Taiwan Strait cannot be ruled out, the probability of such a prospect is diminishing because of the cross-Strait interactions outlined in this article.

Appendix

**Chronology: Taiwan–China Interactions**

*1979*

1 January     Beijing sends message of peaceful reunification of China to Taiwan and ceases bombardment of Jinmen and Mazu (Quemoy and Matsu).

*1981*

29 March      Kuomintang's (KMT's) 11th Party Congress in Taipei passes the resolution on the reunification of China under the Three People's Principles.

30 September  Ye Jianying puts forward nine proposals on the reunification of China, including exchange of mail, trade, air and shipping services.

7 October     Chiang Ching-kuo calls for unification of China based on the Three People's Principles and states that "we shall never negotiate with the Chinese Communists."

*1982*

10 June       Taiwan's Premier Sun Yun-hsun says that when mainland living standards approach that of Taiwan, reunification will be a matter of course.

*1983*

26 June       Deng broadens the areas in which Taiwan would be autonomous.

*1984*

February      Taipei officially allows its citizens to contact mainland citizens abroad on occasions of a non-political nature. Later in the year, mainland and Taiwan athletes compete in the Los Angeles Olympics.

20 February   Deng Xiaoping enunciates the concept of "one country, two systems," to be implemented after reunification.

26 September  The Sino-British Accords on the Future of Hong Kong contains the "one nation, two systems" formula which the PRC intends to apply to Taiwan as well.

*1986*

17 May        Beijing's Civil Aviation Administration of China and Taipei's Taiwan China Airline (CAL) reach an agreement in Hong Kong concerning the release of CAL's jet plane which landed in Guangzhou on 3 May.

*1987*

May           Taipei tacitly approves indirect shipment of Taiwanese goods to China.

1 July        Taipei lifts martial law.

| 15 September | Two journalists of Taiwan's *Independent Evening Post* visit the mainland, defying the ROC government's regulations. |
| | Taiwan's *Independence Evening News* journalist visits Beijing. |
| 14 October | Taipei lifts ban on Taiwan inhabitants visiting mainland relatives. |
| 27 October | A Taiwanese journalist questions Chinese Communist Party (CCP) leaders at the CCP's 13th Party Congress. |

*1988*

| 14 January | Zhao Ziyang, CCP General Secretary, sends Taipei condolences over the death of Chiang Ching-kuo, Chairman of the Kuomintang. |
| April | Taiwan and China delegates attend Asian Development Bank 21st meeting in Singapore. |
| 4 May | Taipei returns a hijacked Boeing 737 to China. |
| 9 July | Zhao Ziyang congratulates Lee Teng-hui on becoming the Chairman of the KMT. |
| 14 July | KMT senior statesman, Chen Li-fu, proposes reunification of China through Chinese culture. |
| 15 July | Zhao Ziyang responds that both sides of the Straits share foundations in politics, economics and cultural tradition. |
| September | Taipei unprecedentedly sends Academia Sinica scholars to attend the 22nd International Science Congress in Beijing. |
| 11 September | Beijing discontinues the 1962 reward policy for Taiwanese defecting with military ships or aircraft. |
| 14 September | Taipei reduces the reward established in 1959 for certain categories of defecting mainland pilots. |
| 9 November | Taipei begins issuing entry permits, with some conditions, to mainlanders visiting ailing relatives or attending funerals in Taiwan. |

*1989*

| February | Beijing deports the first Taiwan criminal via Singapore to Taipei. |
| 17 April | Taiwan gymnasts participate in an international competition held in China. |
| | Taiwan officially allows its journalists to report news from China. |
| 1 May | Taiwan's Finance Minister Shirley Kuo leads its first official delegation since 1949 to China, attending the Asian Development Bank's annual meeting. |
| 10 May | Taipei lifts the ban on postal communication with China. |
| 4 June | Tiananmen Square incident. |
| 11 September | Taipei allows mainland pro-democracy movement leaders to settle in Taiwan. |
| November | Beijing strongly condemns the Taiwanese independence movement. |

| | |
|---|---|
| 23 November | Taipei allows Taiwanese who arrived on the mainland before 1949 to return and settle in Taiwan. |
| 16 December | Non-governmental delegations from Taipei and Beijing establish a trade co-ordination committee in Hong Kong. Taiwan's Foreign Minister Lien Chan announces an end to open animosity toward China. |

*1990*

| | |
|---|---|
| January | Y. C. Wang of Formosa Plastics Corporation visits China to explore opportunities for investment. |
| 11 January | China's Premier Li Peng announces the lifting of martial law imposed on 20 May 1989. |
| 16 January | Taipei allows low-level government employees to visit mainland relatives. |
| 30 April | Taipei allows elected officials to make private visits to the mainland during holidays and recesses. |
| 20 May | Taiwanese President Lee Teng-hui in his presidential inaugural address calls for opening "channels of communication" with the mainland and for ending the state of war. |
| 25 June | Taipei allows government officials to visit sick relatives or attend funerals on the mainland. |
| | Taipei allows mainland cultural and athletic celebrities to visit Taiwan. |
| 18 September | Red Cross officials from both Taipei and Beijing on Jinmen Island sign an agreement on procedures for the repatriation of illegal immigrants. |
| 22 September | Taiwan athletic teams participate under the name "Chinese Taipei" in the Asian Olympic games held in Beijing. |
| 24 September | Taipei's Ministry of Economic Affairs approves indirect ROC exports to the mainland. |
| 6 October | Taipei establishes the National Unification Council (NUC) in the Presidential Office. |
| 7 October | Taiwan's Democratic Progressive Party adopts a resolution not recognizing that Taiwan's *de facto* sovereignty reaches the mainland. |
| 18 October | Taipei establishes the Mainland Affairs Council (MAC) in the Executive Yuan. |
| 21 November | Taipei establishes the Straits Exchange Foundation (SEF) for making "unofficial" contact with Beijing. |

*1991*

| | |
|---|---|
| 9 March | Taipei's SEF begins its operation. |
| 11 March | Taipei proclaims the Guidelines for National Unification, passed by the MAC on 23 February 1991 and by the NUC on 18 December 1990. |
| 22 March | Taipei allows government-run enterprises to import raw materials from the mainland. |

| | |
|---|---|
| 29 April | A delegation of Taipei's SEF visits Beijing's Taiwan Affairs Office, signifying the first contact between the two governments in 42 years. |
| 1 May | ROC President Lee Teng-hui proclaims an end to the Period of National Mobilization for Suppression of the Communist Rebellion and upgrades Beijing to a "political entity." |
| 27 June | Taipei officially allows mainland journalists to visit Taiwan without renouncing their Chinese Communist Party membership. |
| 29 July | Beijing allows Taiwan, as a special administrative district, to retain its armed forces and purchase from other countries weapons considered necessary but not detrimental to the national interests of a reunified China, according to Beijing's ten-point proposal stated in *Liaowang* overseas edition. |
| 22 August | Two mainland Red Cross officials arrive in Taiwan, marking the first such visit of personnel commissioned by Beijing in 42 years. Two accompanying mainland journalists are the first to see Taiwan in 42 years. |
| 27 September | France announces its approval of the sales of unarmed frigate hulls to Taiwan, which Beijing's Foreign Ministry terms "very regrettable." |
| 7 October | The ROC Navy launches the first Taiwan-built missile frigate (Cheng Kung) which will carry two anti-submarine helicopters. |
| 9 October | PRC President Yang Shangkun warns the independence advocates in Taiwan that "those who play with fire will be burned to ashes." |
| 13 October | Taiwan's main opposition, the Democratic Progressive Party, commits in its charter "to build a Taiwanese republic with independent sovereignty" at its annual conference. |
| 16 December | Beijing establishes the Association for Relations Across the Taiwan Straits (ARATS). |

*1992*

| | |
|---|---|
| 25 February | Beijing's Standing Committee of the National People's Congress passes the law on territorial waters and contiguous zones, which enables Beijing to exercise control over Taiwan and its offshore islands. |
| May | Russia begins delivering 24 Sukhoi-27 fighters to China. |
| 24 August | China and South Korea establish diplomatic relations; and Seoul withdraws recognition of Taipei. |
| 2 September | United States President Bush decides to allow the sale of 150 F-16 fighter planes to Taipei. |
| 17 November | France decides to sell 60 Dassault Mirage 2000-5 fighters to Taiwan. |

*1993*

27–28 April     C. F. Koo of Taipei's SEF and Wang Daohan of Beijing's ARATS meet in Singapore and agree to routine consultations, registered mail transactions and document verification.

August          Beijing issues policy paper on reunification during follow-up SEF–ARATS meetings, which break down shortly afterwards.

# Political Change on Taiwan: Transition to Democracy?

## Shao-chuan Leng and Cheng-yi Lin

Samuel P. Huntington categorized Taiwan's path to democracy as "transformation," by which he meant that "the elites in power took the lead in bringing about democracy." The ruling Kuomintang (KMT) would agree with this explanation, although the opposition Democratic Progressive Party (DPP), which was established in 1986 in defiance of martial law, would argue that Taiwan's liberalization and democratization was carried out through a process of transplacement, in which "democratization resulted largely from the joint action by government and opposition groups."[1]

A brief examination of the political system of the Republic of China (ROC) will provide the background for Taiwan's transition to democracy. In 1947, two years before retreating to Taiwan, the ROC government had its Constitution adopted by the popularly elected National Assembly. Its five-power system of government may well be called Sun Yat-sen's constitutional democracy with Chinese characteristics. To the Western separation of power system of the executive, legislative and judicial branches, he added the Control Yuan and the Examination Yuan to continue respectively the traditional Chinese censorate institution to check the bureaucracy, and civil service examination system to recruit civil servants. Although organized on the model of the Leninist Party, the Kuomintang was committed by Sun's teachings to move progressively from one-party rule to the final stage of constitutional government.[2]

In the midst of full-scale civil war, in April 1948 the first National Assembly adopted Temporary Provisions to provide the ROC President with emergency powers during the "period of Communist rebellion."[3] On the basis of these provisions, martial law in Taiwan was declared in May 1949. In 1966 the National Assembly amended the Temporary Provisions to give the President additional powers, including the establishment of the

1. Samuel P. Huntington, *The Third Wave* (Norman, Oklahoma: University of Oklahoma Press, 1991), pp. 113–14; Alfred Stephen, "Paths toward redemocratization: theoretical and comparative considerations," in Guillermo O'Donnel, Philippe C. Schmitter and Laurence Whitehead (eds.), *Transitions from Authoritarian Rule: Comparative Perspectives* (Baltimore: The Johns Hopkins University Press, 1986), pp. 64–84. For the role of Taiwan's opposition in the transition to democracy, see Alexander Ya-li Lu, "Political opposition in Taiwan: the development of the Democratic Progressive Party," in Tun-jen Cheng and Stephen Haggard (eds.), *Political Change in Taiwan* (Boulder: Lynne Rienner Publishers, 1992) pp. 121–146; Yangsun Chou and Andrew J. Nathan, "Democratizing transition in Taiwan," *Asian Survey*, Vol. 27, No. 3 (March 1987), pp. 277–299.

2. See Shao-chuan Leng and Norman D. Palmer, *Sun Yat-sen and Communism* (New York: Praeger, 1961), pp. 93–94; Sidney Chang and Leonard Gordon, *All Under Heaven . . . Sun Yat-sen and His Revolutionary Thought* (Stanford: Hoover Institution Press, 1991), pp. 109–113.

3. "Constitution of the Republic of China," in A. Blaustein and G. Flanz (eds.), *Constitutions of the Countries of the World* (Dobbs Ferry, NY: Oceana, 1981), pp. 45–47. Subsequently, the Temporary Provisions were amended in 1960, 1966 and 1972.

National Security Council, a major decision-making organ not accountable to an elected body.

During the early 1950s the ROC government began to institute local
and provincial elections on Taiwan, but members of the three national
representative institutions (the National Assembly, the Legislative Yuan
and the Control Yuan) elected on the mainland in 1947–48 were allowed
to serve indefinitely.[4] While the presence of these senior members might
symbolize the ROC government's continuity and claim to the Chinese
mainland, it undercut the representative nature of the institutions on
Taiwan and became the target of criticism and ridicule. Elderly members
were derided as "the 10,000-year delegates" and "old thieves."

There is no question that the Temporary Provisions, martial law and
the senior members of parliamentary bodies were among the factors
retarding political change in Taiwan. On the other hand, socioeconomic
modernization and the growing strength and maturity of the opposition
(*dangwai*) in the mid-1980s created favourable conditions for Taiwan to
move from a "soft authoritarianism" to democracy. Fortunately President
Chiang Ching-kuo responded to the changing environment by starting the
transition process. In July 1987 he lifted martial law and removed the ban
on organizing new political parties, and in December 1987 he announced
a plan to reform parliamentary bodies. According to Andrew Nathan and
Helena Ho, internal pressure within Taiwan, influence from the United
States and the threat of the PRC all affected Chiang's decision. His health
and succession, political values and sense of mission may also have been
important factors. In transitions to democracy, Taiwan's experience is
comparable to Spain's, in the model of Alfred Stepan's "Path 4a"
("redemocratization [*sic*] initiated by the civilian or civilianized political
leadership"). However, Nathan and Ho point out that Taiwan's case
differs from that of Spain in several ways: the existence of the China
mainland factor, the starting of the transition by the leader of the old
regime, and a much less serious potential challenge to reform by the
military.[5]

After Chiang's death in January 1988, his successor, Lee Teng-hui,
pledged to carry out his policies of reform and democratization. In
January 1989 President Lee promulgated the Civil Organizations Law
setting rules for the formation of new political parties. In February 1989
the Legislative Yuan revised the Election and Recall Law to lift many

4. In January 1954 the Council of Grand Justices rendered a constitutional interpretation
(No. 31) to permit senior members of these bodies to continue to serve "pending a new
election." Hungdah Chiu, "Constitutional development and reform in the Republic of China
on Taiwan," *Issues & Studies*, Vol. 29, No. 1 (January 1993), p. 20. Between 1972 and 1989
a small number of additional members were elected in "supplementary elections" to the three
representative bodies. They were subject to re-election every six years (National Assembly
and Control Yuan) or every three years (Legislative Yuan). *Ibid.* pp. 21–22.
5. See Andrew Nathan and Helena V. S. Ho, "Chiang Ching-kuo's decision for political
reform," in Shao-chuan Leng (ed.), *Chiang Ching-kuo's Leadership in the Development of the
Republic of China on Taiwan* (Lanham: University Press of America, 1992), ch. 2. For a
detailed discussion of the ROC's transition, see Hung-mao Tien, *The Great Transition: Political and Social Change in the Republic of China* (Stanford: Hoover Institution Press, 1989).

restrictions on campaign activities. In early 1990 Lee survived the political crisis resulting from factionalism that split the KMT over the presidential election. He demonstrated great skill in restoring consensus and was elected as President by the National Assembly in March 1990.[6] He was also able to diffuse the tensions and calm down emotions in dealing with the DPP and student demonstrators by promising and holding a national affairs conference in the summer of 1990. In April 1991 the KMT leadership had the National Assembly pass constitutional amendments to provide for a total renewal of the three parliamentary bodies. The election for the National Assembly was to be at the end of 1991, the Legislative Yuan at the end of 1992, and the Control Yuan in early 1993.

During the campaign for the National Assembly election on 21 December 1991, the KMT stressed "reform, stability and prosperity" while the DPP ran on a platform of Taiwan's independence. A total of nine million voters went to the polls. The result was a KMT landslide victory. They captured 71.17 per cent of the popular votes and 254 seats (including at-large national and overseas seats) while the DPP won only 23.94 per cent of popular votes and 66 seats. Only one of the 15 minor parties achieved 3 seats and just two independent candidates were successful. The election was hailed by the American press as the most democratic one ever held in China.[7] The KMT claimed the outcome as an impressive vote of confidence by the people, and the DPP blamed its defeat on the KMT's ability to buy votes. Neutral observers, however, tend to attribute the results to a number of factors. Among them were the DPP's counter-productive tactics, appeal to a narrow constituency and advocacy of Taiwan independence, and the KMT's ability to change the size of electoral districts (58), manipulate the media, appeal to the popularity of President Lee, and use its superior party machine and greater financial strength to support its candidates.[8]

All things considered, Taiwan had a good start in the transition to democracy. Much, however, remains to be done before the process is completed. Despite some progress, government policy-making is not yet fully vested in the hands of elected officials. This prompts a comment that the first full-scale elections for the National Assembly (1991) and the Legislative Yuan (1992) by an all-Taiwan electorate would "not necessarily produce a surrender of power from the ruling elites to a democratically elected civilian government," as has occurred in other regimes.[9] The

6. For details, consult Ts'ai Ling and Ramon H. Myers, "Surviving the rough-and-tumble of presidential politics in an emerging democracy: the 1990 elections in the Republic of China," *The China Quarterly*, No. 129 (March 1992), pp. 123–148.

7. In an editorial, for instance, *The Washington Post*, 30 December 1991, p. A12, called the elections "the closest thing to free elections in 40 years."

8. For a well-balanced assessment of the election, see Tao-tai Hsia and Wendy Zeldin, "The December 1991 National Assembly Elections on Taiwan," Appendix 9 to *Hearings on Taiwan before Subcommittee on Asian and Pacific Affairs on the Committee on Foreign Affairs*, House of Representatives, 102nd Congress, first session (1991), pp. 103–120.

9. Yun-han Chu, *Crafting Democracy in Taiwan* (Taipei: Institute for National Policy Research, 1992), p. 46, 97–98. For details of electoral competition in Taiwan, see Teh-fu Huang,

purpose of this study is to explore the prospects of Taiwan's democratization by focusing attention on such issues as the constitutional revision, presidential election formula, rising role of the Legislative Yuan and national identity crisis.

### Constitutional Reform

Constitutional reform was one of the items at the top of the agenda of the six-day National Affairs Conference from 28 June to 4 July 1990. This had no statutory power but served to defuse popular resentments about the KMT's political reforms.[10] Of the 142 delegates, including representatives from the entire political spectrum, 93 favoured revision of the 1947 Constitution, while 32 voted for drafting a new one adapted to Taiwan. According to Article 27 of the Constitution, the National Assembly was the body empowered to initiate constitutional amendments or decide on amendments submitted by the Legislative Yuan. However, National Affairs Conference delegates differed over how their proposed revision of the Constitution should be carried out. As many as 39 out of 89 polled delegates favoured allowing the Legislative Yuan to initiate constitutional amendment proposals which would then be submitted to the National Assembly, while a constitutional convention to be summoned by the President through the exercise of his emergency power was preferred by 15 delegates. There was no support at all for a two-stage constitutional reform.[11] However, the KMT government opted for allowing the National Assembly to revise the Constitution in two stages.

The first stage of the revision procedure took place in April 1991. The surviving members of the First National Assembly elected in 1947 and those members elected in the 1986 supplementary election amended the Temporary Provisions governing the power of the President and elections of central government officials. With the completion of this first stage and the adoption of ten amendments, President Lee Teng-hui announced the termination of the Period of National Mobilization for Suppression of Communist Rebellion on 30 April 1991.

In June 1990, the Council of Grand Justices of the Judicial Yuan had made a new interpretation of the Constitution (Ruling 261) calling for members of the First National Assembly elected on the mainland in 1947 to resign by 31 December 1991. The second stage of constitutional

---

*footnote continued*

"Electoral competition and democratic transition in the Republic of China," *Issues & Studies*, Vol. 27, No. 10 (October 1991), pp. 97–123.

10. For significance and results of the National Affairs Conference, see Harvey J. Feldman (ed.), *Constitutional Reform and the Future of the Republic of China* (Armonk: M. E. Sharpe, 1991), pp. 22–47.

11. *Guoshi Huiyi shilu* (*Faithful Record of the National Affairs Conference*), Vol. 1 (Taipei: Secretariat of the National Affairs Conference, 1990), pp. 1350–51. See also Jaushieh Joseph Wu, "Politics of constitutional reform in the Republic of China: problems, process, and prospects," Paper delivered at the Sino-American-European Conference on Contemporary China, Institute of International Relations, National Chengchi University, Taipei, 16–22 August 1992, pp. 13–14.

revision was entrusted to the newly-elected Second National Assembly, plus members of the first Assembly who had been elected in 1986, a total of 403 delegates. Of these, 318 (78.91 per cent) were KMT members – more than the three-quarters needed to pass a constitutional amendment (Article 174). During the extraordinary session of the Second National Assembly held from 20 March to 27 May 1992, the two major factions of the DPP, Formosa and New Tide, though differing over the question of Taiwan independence, jointly supported a separation of power among the three branches of government and the direct election of the President. Because of its numerical inferiority in the National Assembly (75 against the KMT's 318), the DPP resorted to the tactics of filibustering, name-calling, rallies and demonstrations to air their frustrations. Unable to reach any agreement with the KMT, the DPP deputies pulled out of the session on 4 May as a protest, followed by six independents on 20 May. The constitutional process was thus left entirely in the hands of the KMT deputies, who adopted on 27 May their Party Central Standing Committee's version of constitutional revision in the form of eight additional articles.[12]

Articles 5 and 6 of the 1991 amendments provided the legal basis for the election of the Second National Assembly. Extra-constitutional institutions, such as the National Security Council and the National Security Bureau, prescribed by the Temporary Provisions effective during the "Period of Communist Rebellion," were provided for the President to make major policy decisions in Article 9. Though the law of Emergency Orders prescribed by Article 43 of the ROC Constitution was not enacted, the President's emergency powers were provided for in the Temporary Provisions. These were retained, though in a restricted form, in Article 7 of the amendments:

The President may, by resolution of a council of the Executive Yuan, issue emergency orders and take all necessary measures to avert an imminent danger to the security of the state or the people or to cope with any serious financial or economic crisis, without being subject to the restrictions prescribed in Article 43 of the Constitution. However, such orders shall, within ten days of issuance, be presented to the Legislative Yuan for confirmation. Should the Legislative Yuan withhold confirmation, the said emergency orders shall forthwith cease to be valid.[13]

Even though President Lee Teng-hui promised to use his emergency powers cautiously, those who favoured a parliamentary democracy criticized the incorporation of this amendment and the retention of the National Security Council under the President, fearing that it might lead to a presidential system of government to continue the legacy of the strong-man rule.[14]

12. *Free China Journal*, 29 May 1992, p. 2; Julian Baum, "Taiwan: machine politics," *Far Eastern Economic Review*, 18 June 1992, p. 23.
13. *Republic of China Yearbook, 1991–92* (Taipei: Guanghua Publishing Company, 1991), p. 581. For details of ROC emergency power practices, see Tao-tai Hsia with Wendy Zeldin, "Laws on emergency powers in Taiwan," in Shao-chuan Leng (ed.), *Coping with Crises: How Governments Deal with Emergencies* (Lanham: University Press of America, 1989), pp. 178–79.
14. *Zhongyang ribao* (*Central Daily News*), 25 April 1991, p. 1.

The focus of the second stage of constitutional revision was supposed to be the method of electing the President. The KMT was again split between supporters of direct and indirect election, just as it was in the 1990 presidential election between the "mainstream" faction supporting Lee Teng-hui and his running mate Li Yuan-tsu and the "non-mainstream" faction supporting Lin Yang-kang and Chiang Wei-kuo.[15] In 1990 a consensus was restored and Lee was elected. This time the conflict within the KMT top leadership was too intense to allow a final decision to be reached. Leaders of both factions decided to put off this crucial part of the revision process until 1995, and they instructed KMT deputies not to bring up the issue during the extraordinary sessions of the Second National Assembly in 1992. Nevertheless, the President's power of nomination and the National Assembly's power of confirmation were expanded during the second stage of constitutional reform (see Table 1).

According to Article 91 of the ROC Constitution and Article 3 of the 1991 amendments, members of the Control Yuan are elected by provincial and municipal councils and the Chinese citizens residing abroad. The President and Vice-President of the Control Yuan are elected by and from among its members. In an effort to end vote-buying for Control Yuan seats in the Taiwan Provincial Assembly and the Taipei and Kaohsiung Municipal Councils, the third plenary session of the 13th KMT Central Committee decided to turn this highest watchdog agency into a quasi-judicial organization. The new Control Yuan had 29 members, all appointed by the ROC President with the consent of the National Assembly. This dramatic change was strongly resisted by the Taiwan Provincial Assembly, which called a recess of several weeks in protest.

On 15 January 1993 the National Assembly, without its DPP members, exercised its power of consent for the first time, approving 25 out of President Lee Teng-hui's 29 nominees for the Control Yuan. Chen Li-an, a former Defence Minister and son of a former Premier, was appointed as the Control Yuan President. The four rejected nominees were Chen Yung-hsing, a DPP National Assembly deputy; Chin Mao-sung, a KMT member of the Taipei City Council; Hung Chun-mao, a KMT member of the Kaohsiung City Council; and Hsu Kuo-liang, a KMT overseas representative from the Philippines.[16] Even though its future status is still subject to change, the National Assembly has already proved itself more than a rubber-stamp body.

The Control Yuan has been deprived of its power to confirm the appointment of high-ranking officials in the Judicial and Examination Yuans, but its powers of impeachment, censure and audit were largely kept intact. In the old Control Yuan, a proposal to impeach a central or local government functionary or a member of the Judicial or Examination Yuans could be made by a single member. Article 15 of the 1992 amendments, however, stipulates that such a proposal must now be made by two or more members of the Control Yuan. Restrictions like this raise

15. Ts'ai and Myers, "Surviving the rough-and-tumble," pp. 129–145.
16. *Zhongguo shibao* (*China Times*), 17 January 1993, p. 2.

Table 1: **Confirmation of Heads of ROC Central Government Branches**

| | ROC Constitution 1947 | | 1992 amendments | |
| | Nominated by | Confirmed by | Nominated by | Confirmed by |
|---|---|---|---|---|
| Judicial Yuan | | | | |
| President/Vice-President; Grand Justices | President | Control Yuan | President | National Assembly |
| Examination Yuan | | | | |
| President/Vice-President; members | President | Control Yuan | President | National Assembly |
| Control Yuan | | | | |
| President/Vice-President; members | — | — | President | National Assembly |

Table 2: **Requirements for the Control Yuan to Initiate Impeachment**

|  | ROC Constitution 1947 | 1992 Amendments |
| --- | --- | --- |
| Public functionaries; personnel of the Judicial/Examination Yuans | 1 or more members | 2 or more members |
| President or Vice-President | One-quarter of the Yuan members | Half the Yuan members |

doubts as to whether the President-appointed Control Yuan would be prepared to impeach the President or Vice-President (see Table 2).

Even though there was no decision on how to elect the President, the KMT Central Standing Committee (CSC) decided that the National Assembly would be convened annually. Article 11 of the 1992 amendments stipulates that "When the National Assembly convenes, it shall hear a report on the state of the nation by the President, discuss national affairs and offer counsel." Fearing that the Assembly would lose the right to elect the President and Vice-President, certain members of the Second National Assembly were eager to appoint a permanent speaker and to have the Assembly act as a check on the Legislative Yuan. They failed in this effort to create a bicameral parliament but did succeed in forestalling the attempt to downgrade or even abolish the National Assembly. Members even overruled the KMT CSC's original plan to extend legislators' terms from three to four years.[17] Some National Assembly members, specialists in constitutional law, succeeded in establishing a Constitutional Tribunal under the Judicial Yuan to "adjudicate matters relating to the dissolution of unconstitutional political parties."[18]

On 4 January 1993, President Lee Teng-hui delivered the ROC's first-ever state of the nation address to the National Assembly, after which he listened to suggestions from the deputies. However, his absence from the reminder of the suggestion session from 5 to 7 January (his place was taken by Presidential Secretary-General Tsiang Yien-si) provoked the majority of National Assembly members to fury.[19] In April 1993, the National Assembly exercised its confirmation power once again, this time over the nomination of Chiu Chuang-huan as President of the Examination Yuan, Mao Kao-wen as Vice-President, and the nominees for the four vacant Control Yuan seats. Even though the DPP has demanded a single-chamber parliament and the abolition of the Control Yuan and the National Assembly, the Assembly continues to compete with the Legislative Yuan. It exerts its power of supervision over the President just as the assertive legislature does over the Executive Yuan.

17. *Zhongyang ribao*, 23 May 1991, p. 1.
18. *Zhongyang ribao*, 22 April 1992, p. 2.
19. *Zhongguo shibao*, 6 January 1993, p. 1; 8 January 1993, p. 4.

*Conflict over the Presidential Election Formula: Direct Popular Vote vs. Direct Election by Delegates*

Almost all the 142 delegates of the National Affairs Conference agreed that starting from the next (ninth) term the President should be elected by the people.[20] However, the delegates could not agree whether this election should be direct or by proxy through an electoral college. The DPP insisted on direct popular election. One-on-one contests are easier for the DPP, as the results of past mayoral and county magistrate elections indicate. At first, the KMT seemed to favour an electoral college. The party's Constitution Revision Planning Group studied both proposals, but decided to recommend the electoral college system to the CSC in February 1992. However, after consultations with opinion leaders, Lee Teng-hui, who is ROC President and chairman of the KMT, insisted that both proposals be put before the CSC.[21] This dramatic reversal of policy was a political bombshell to liberals and conservatives in the KMT. President Lee's unpredictable decision-making once again became an issue, as his critics remembered how he had hand-picked his running mate Li Yuan-zu without consulting Li Huan, then Premier, and Hau Pei-tsun, then Minister of National Defence, in February 1990.[22]

The heated island-wide debate over the formula for electing the ROC President dominated newspaper headlines in March 1992. Taiwan's two most influential pro-KMT newspapers, *Zhongguo shibao* (*China Times*) and *Lianhebao* (*United Daily News*), were pitted against each other, with the former supporting and the latter opposing direct popular election.[23] Local politicians also took sides with one faction or the other. All public opinion polls indicated that those supporting direct popular election outnumbered those favouring direct election by proxies (see Table 3).

The KMT hierarchy (the CSC and the entire Central Committee) was also split over the presidential election issue. The 29 participants of the CSC special meeting on 9 March 1992 could reach no conclusion after a seven-and-a-half hour discussion. Fourteen CSC members supported direct popular election, ten were against, and the five who were undecided favoured placing both methods before the third plenary session of the KMT's 13th Central Committee. The four observers, when asked by Chairman Lee Teng-hui to express their opinion, favoured direct election (see Table 4). Although there was a small majority favouring direct presidential election, Chairman Lee Teng-hui decided to postpone a decision on this controversial issue. The battlefield went to the KMT Central Committee.

At the third plenary session of the KMT's 13th Central Committee

---

20. *Guoshi huiyi shilu*, Vol. 1, pp. 1339, 1342; *Free China Journal*, 9 July 1990, p. 1.
21. President Lee Teng-hui's remarks to the KMT Second National Assembly Deputies, see *Lianhebao* (*United Daily News*), 26 March 1992, p. 3.
22. Ts'ai and Myers, "Surviving the rough-and-tumble," p. 132.
23. *Zhongguo shibao*, 6 March 1992, p. 3; *Lianhebao*, 13 March 1992, p. 2.

Table 3: **Public Opinion Poll on Presidential Election Formula**

| Survey conductor | Direct popular election (%) | indirect election (%) |
|---|---|---|
| 1. ROC Public Opinion Poll Association | 37.1 | 16.5 |
| 2. Lianhebao | 35.0 | 17.0 |
| 3. Lianhebao | 38.0 | 18.0 |
| 4. Public Opinion Research Foundation | 47.8 | 21.0 |

Sources:

1. Zhongyang ribao (Central Daily News), 8 March 1992, p. 2; 2. Lianhebao (United Daily News), 8 March 1992, p. 2; 3. Lianhebao, 13 March 1992, p. 2; 4. Zhongyang ribao, 23 March 1992, p. 2.

Table 4: **KMT CSC Members' Attitudes Towards Presidential Election Method**

| Vote | Name | Position |
|------|------|----------|
| Direct popular election | Lin Yang-kang | President of Judicial Yuan |
| | Huang Tsun-chiu | President of Control Yuan |
| | Wu Poh-hsiung | Minister of Interior |
| | Chien Fu (Frederick Chien) | Minister of Foreign Affairs |
| | Lien Chan | Governor of Taiwan |
| | Cheng Wei-Yuan | Senior Adviser to the President |
| | Koo Chen-fu | Senior Adviser to the President |
| | Hsu Shui-teh | Representative of Tokyo Office of Association of East Asian Relations |
| | Chao Tze-chi | President of World League of Freedom and Democracy |
| | Su Nan-cheng | National Policy Adviser to the President |
| | Chen Tien-mao | Speaker of Kaohsiung City Council |
| | Hsu-Sheng-fa | Chairman of China National Federation of Industry |
| | Hsieh Shen-shan | Legislator |
| | *Observers:* | |
| | Huang Ta-chou | Taipei City Mayor |
| | Chen Chien-shih | Speaker of Taipei City Council |
| | Wu Den-yih | Kaohsiung City Mayor |
| | Chien Ming-ching | Speaker of Taiwan Provincial Assembly |

**Table 4: Continued**

| Vote | Name | Position |
|---|---|---|
| Direct election by delegates | Hsieh Tung-min | Senior Adviser to the President |
| | Li Kwoh-ting | Senior Adviser to the President |
| | Yu Kuo-hwa | Senior Adviser to the President |
| | Lee Huan | Senior Adviser to the President |
| | Shen Chang-huan | Senior Adviser to the President |
| | Chiu Chuang-huan | Senior Adviser to the President |
| | Hau Pei-tsun | Premier |
| | Ho I-wu | Senior Adviser to the President |
| | Mao Kao-wen | Minister of Education |
| | Hsu Li-nung | Chairman of Vocational Assistance Commission for Retired Servicemen |
| Undecided | Ni Wen-ya | Senior Adviser to the President |
| | Soong Chu-yu (James Soong) | Secretary-General of the KMT |
| | Chen Li-an | Minister of National Defence |
| | Shih Chi-yang | Vice-Premier |
| | Tseng Kuang-shun | Chairman of Overseas Chinese Affairs Commission |
| Absent | Kuo Wan-rong (Shirley Kuo) | Chairman of Council for Economic Planning and Development |
| | Chang Chien-pang | Former Minister of Transport and Communications |

*Sources:*
*Lianhebao,* 10 March 1992, p. 3; *Zhongyang ribao,* 10 March 1992, p. 2.

(14–16 March 1992), the 180 members were also divided into two camps. Those in favour of an electoral college system argued that a President by a direct popular vote in Taiwan could give the impression of a "President of Taiwan," thus implying Taiwan independence. Supporters of direct popular election, on the other hand, pointed out such a system would be in keeping with recent popular trends demonstrating the people's desire to have more participation in the government.[24] Chiu Chuang-huan, a senior presidential adviser with presidential ambitions of his own, argued that the KMT should not follow the DPP and that a directly elected President could easily become a dictator. Chiu strongly advocated direct election by proxies because this formula would preserve the National Assembly and the ROC's five-power system of government. Under this formula overseas Chinese, who are represented in the Assembly, would still be able to participate in the ROC political process.[25]

A compromise resolution was worked out to avoid further dissension within the KMT, and this was announced to the plenary session by Lin Yang-kang, Judicial Yuan President and a possible future presidential contender. The consensus reached was that starting from the 1996 election, the ROC President "will be elected in free areas of the Republic of China," and that the method of election should be decided after "prudent studies" and should accord with public opinion.[26] The Central Committee also agreed that if the presidency and vice-presidency were vacated, the National Assembly would elect successors. They also decided to shorten the terms of the President and the National Assembly members from six to four years.

Facing insurmountable obstacles, President Lee Teng-hui reaffirmed that he had no intention of seeking re-election. He clarified his position in a speech to the KMT members of the Second National Assembly on 25 March arguing that a future directly elected President would not necessarily be "the President of Taiwan," nor would such a President imply Taiwan independence. To quell fears that direct election would exclude overseas Chinese from the political process, President Lee promised to improve the electoral system to guarantee overseas Chinese the right of political participation. In the meantime, the top KMT leaders reached a preliminary agreement that the method of presidential election would not be incorporated into the additional constitutional articles to be passed by the Second National Assembly but would be deferred until 1995.[27]

Even though the DPP tried to bring up the direct presidential election issue through street demonstrations and public debates, the work of constitutional reform during the 70-day extraordinary session of the Second National Assembly (March–May 1992) was dominated by the

24. *Free China Journal*, 17 March 1992, p. 1.
25. *China Post* (Taipei) 16 March 1992, p. 1.
26. *Zhongyang ribao*, 17 March 1992, p. 1; *China Post*, 17 March 1992, p. 1.
27. *Lianhebao*, 26 March 1992, p. 3.

KMT. The rules for presidential elections as contained in Article 12 of the 1992 constitutional amendments are as follows:

Effective from the 1996 election for the ninth-term President and Vice-President, the President and the Vice-President shall be elected by the entire electorate in the free area of the Republic of China.

The electoral method for the aforementioned election shall be formulated in the additional Article to the Constitution at an extraordinary session of the National Assembly to be convoked by the President before 20 May 1995.

Beginning with the ninth presidential term, the term of office for both the President and the Vice-President shall be four years. The President and the Vice-President may be re-elected for a second term; and the provisions in Article 47 of the Constitution shall not apply.

Recall of the President and the Vice-President shall be executed in accordance with the following provisions:

(1) By a motion to recall put forward by one-fourth of all delegates to the National Assembly, and passed with the concurrence of two-thirds of such delegates.
(2) By a resolution to impeach adopted by the Control Yuan, and passed as a resolution to recall by two-thirds of all delegates to the National Assembly.

Should the office of the Vice-President become vacant, the President shall nominate a candidate within three months and convoke an extraordinary session of the National Assembly to elect a new Vice-President, who shall serve out the original term until its expiration. Should the offices of both the President and the Vice-President become vacant, the President of the Legislative Yuan shall serve notice on the National Assembly to convoke an extraordinary session within three months to elect a new President and a new Vice-President, who shall serve out each respective original term until its expiration.[28]

The debate over the method of electing the ROC President has diverted attention from the issue of which type of regime is suitable for Taiwan. Juan J. Linz has argued that presidentialism could create difficulties in the process of democratization, and his arguments provided some ammunition to KMT opponents of direct presidential elections.[29] However, comparisons among presidentialism, parliamentarianism and mixed arrangements such as that of the French Fifth Republic and their possible adaptation to Taiwan were not the focus of the KMT-dominated constitutional reform.

### The Rising Role of the Legislative Yuan

Even though certain KMT members of the Second National Assembly have called for a bicameral parliament, the top echelons of the KMT and the DPP are united to forestall this. The DPP goes even further, insisting that there should be a single house, that is, the Legislative Yuan. Since the retirement of mainland-elected legislators, the Legislative Yuan has

28. *Free China Journal*, 23 June 1992, p. 7.
29. Juan J. Linz, "Transitions to democracy," *Washington Quarterly*, Vol. 13, No. 3 (Summer 1990), p. 153.

Table 5: **Proportion of Elected Supplementary Seats to the Total Seats in the Legislative Yuan, 1980–89**

| Number of seats | 1980 | 1983 | 1986 | 1989 |
|---|---|---|---|---|
| Elected members | 69 | 70 | 72 | 101 |
| Entire chamber | 406 | 368 | 324 | 287 |
| Percentage | 17.0% | 19.0% | 22.2% | 35.1% |

*Source:*
  Yun-han Chu, *Crafting Democracy in Taiwan* (Taipei: Institute for National
  Policy Research, 1992), p. 58.

taken on an increasingly important role in ROC government decision-making.

Article 2 of the 1991 constitutional amendments stipulated that "six members [of the Legislative Yuan] shall be elected from the Chinese citizens who reside abroad," and "30 members shall be elected from one nation-wide constituency." These two categories of legislators are elected by proportional representation from lists put forward by the various political parties. The amendments abolished occupational constituencies. The remaining 125 legislators are elected from 29 electoral districts. The election in December 1992 was aimed to result in a 161-member legislature truly representing the Taiwan electorate (see Table 5 for contrast).

According to Article 62 of the ROC Constitution, the Legislative Yuan is the highest legislative organ of the State. When mainland-elected legislators were in the majority, the executive branch could easily dictate to the Legislative Yuan through party channels. However, if other articles of the Constitution are fully implemented after the December 1992 election, the legislature will probably be able to exert a check on the power of the executive.

The Premier is nominated by the President with the consent of the Legislative Yuan (Article 55). The Executive Yuan is responsible to the Legislative Yuan through an annual policy statement and a report on the administration, while legislators have the right to interpellate the Premier, ministers and chairmen of Executive Yuan commissions (Article 57). The Legislative Yuan may also influence government policy through its "power to decide by resolution upon statutory or budgetary bills or bills concerning martial law, amnesty, declaration of war, conclusion of peace or treaties, and other important affairs of the state" (Article 63).

The increasing power of the Legislative Yuan has challenged the legitimacy of the Executive Yuan and the non-elected KMT leaders. The Legislative Yuan has become an arena for those who are critical of mainstream opinion in the KMT apparatus. Two major critics of the government, John Kuan (former deputy Secretary-General of the KMT), and Yung Wei (former Chancellor of the Sun Yat-sen Institute of Policy Research and Development) both won hotly contested KMT primaries in Taipei. The KMT has also attempted to curry favour with leading legislators by recruiting them into the KMT decision-making process; to

Table 6: **Senior and Outstanding Legislators (February 1993)**
A. Senior members of the Legislative Yuan

---

*Seven-term Legislators (3)*
Hsieh Shen-shan, KMT CSC Member, Deputy Secretary-General of the KMT
Liu Sung-pan, President of the Legislative Yuan (KMT)
Tsai You-tu, At-large legislator (KMT)
*Six-term Legislator (1)*
Wang Ching-ping, Vice-President of the Legislative Yuan (KMT)
*Five-term Legislators (6)*
Chou Shu-fu, At-large legislator (KMT)
Hung Chao-nan, Deputy Director, KMT Overseas Affairs Department
Hung Yu-chin, Director of Party and Parliament Co-ordination Committee
Li You-chi, At-large legislator (KMT)
Tsai Sheng-pang, Taipei County legislator (KMT)
Yao Ying-chi, Deputy Secretary-General of KMT
*Four-term Legislators (5)*
Chang Chun-hsiung, At-large legislator (DPP)
Huang Chu-wen, Taoyuan County legislator (KMT)
Liao Fuw-peen, KMT Legislative Caucus Whip
Luo Chwin-jinn, At-large legislator (KMT)
Wu Der-mei, Kaohsiung City legislator (KMT)
*Three-term Legislators (7)*
Jaw Shau-kong, Leader of New KMT Alliance
Chen Je-nan, Kaohsiung City legislator
Hsu Kuo-tai, Taoyuan County legislator (DPP)
Huang Cheng-i, Director of KMT Party Relations Working Committee in
    Legislative Yuan
Ju Gau-jeng, Chairman of Chinese Social Democratic Party (CSDP)
Tsay Chung-han, Legislator representing plains aborigines (KMT)
Yu Cheng-hsien, Kaohsiung County legislator (DPP)

---

*Notes:*
    Compiled by the authors. Jaw Shau-kong was re-elected in 1989 and 1992, but he served as head of the Environmental Protection Administration in 1990–92. Chen Je-nan was expelled from the KMT for publicly advocating "one China, one Taiwan" before the December 1992 election.

this end, the KMT Party–Executive–Legislative Principals Meeting has gradually taken the place of the KMT CSC in the policy-making process.[30] Legislators like Jaw Shau-kong and Chang Po-ya were recruited into the Cabinet.

The seniority system in the Legislative Yuan is far from taking root. In the 1989 election, for example, 88 out of the 130 victorious candidates were elected or, in the case of overseas representatives, appointed for the first time. In the result of 1992 election, 99 out of 161 legislators were freshmen. However, from the surveys in Table 6, one can see that most outstanding legislators are junior members and all except Liu Hsing-shan

30. *Lianhebao*, 28 September 1992, p. 4.

Table 6: **Continued**
B. Outstanding members of the Legislative Yuan

| | | |
|---|---|---|
| (i) | 1. | Chen Shui-bian (DPP, Taipei City) |
| | 2. | Pang Pai-hsien (DPP, Nantou County) |
| | 3. | Hsieh Chang-ting (Frank Hsieh) (DPP, Taipei City) |
| | 4. | Lu Hsiu-yi (DPP, Taipei County) |
| | 5. | Ting Shou-chung (KMT, Taipei City) |
| | 6. | Lin Chi-chia (KMT, Taipei County) |
| | 7. | Oung Chung-chun (KMT, Chiayi County) |
| | 8. | Liu Hsing-shan (KMT, defeated in 1992 election) |
| | 9. | Lee Ching-hsiung (DPP, Kaohsiung City) |
| | 10. | Wang Chin-ping (KMT, Kaohsiung County) |
| (ii) | 1. | Ting Shou-chung (KMT) |
| | 2. | Chen Shui-bian (DPP) |
| | 3. | Hsieh Chang-ting (DPP) |
| | 4. | Lin Chi-chia (KMT) |
| | 5. | Chu Feng-chih (KMT, Taoyuan County) |
| | 6. | Liu Hsing-shan (KMT) |
| | 7. | Lin Hsi-shan (KMT, Changhua County) |
| | 8. | Ju Gau-jeng (CSDP, Yunlin County) |
| | 9. | Lin Shou-shan (KMT, Kaohsiung City) |
| | 10. | Chen Kui-miao (KMT, Penghu County) |

*Sources:*
(i) Survey by Taipei's Society, a group of liberal scholars pushing for reforms of public affairs, based on the opinions of media reporters covering the Legislative Yuan, see *Chengshi baodao* (*Report of Taipei's Society*), No. 10 (December 1992), pp. 77–81.
(ii) Survey of the Parliament Watch Foundation, a Taiwanese version of Common Cause, based on the degree of fulfilment of campaign promises by legislators, see *Zhongguo shibao*, 7 December 1992, p. 3.

were re-elected in the 1992 elections. Since 1989, both the KMT and the DPP have employed a system of primaries for nominating candidates. In 1992, the KMT held primaries in 11 out of 29 electoral districts, while the DPP did so in seven electoral districts, as well as for its at-large seats. The result of the primaries is binding for the DPP but serves only as a reference for the KMT.[31] With campaign expenses sky-rocketing, legislators often seek financial backing from the business sector. However, business interests have now begun to endorse their own candidates, and 12 of the 98 formally nominated KMT candidates for the 1992 election were tycoons.[32]

The results of Taiwan's first fully democratic legislative elections, in which at least 400 candidates were competing for 161 seats, surprised

31. James A. Robinson, "Can primaries thwart democracy," *Free China Journal*, 21 August 1992, p. 7. For the results of the KMT and DPP primaries, see *Lianhebao*, 6 July 1992, p. 2; 16 August 1992, p. 2; 31 August 1992, p. 2.
32. *Lianhebao*, 17 September 1992, p. 3; Julian Baum, "Building the ballot," *Far Eastern Economic Review*, 1 October 1992, p. 14.

Table 7A: **The Percentage Share of Popular Vote of KMT, Tangwai/ DPP, and Independent Candidates in Legislative Yuan Elections**

| Party | 1980 | 1983 | 1986 | 1989 |
|-------|------|------|------|------|
| KMT | 73.64 | 72.86 | 69.06 | 60.6 |
| Tangwai/DPP | 8.28 | 16.68 | 22.22 | 28.2 |
| Independents | 18.09 | 10.46 | 8.72 | 11.2 |

*Source:*
Yun-han Chu, *Crafting Democracy in Taiwan*, p. 55.

both KMT and DPP leaders. When candidates affiliated to the KMT but running without party nomination were included, the KMT's proportion of the popular vote was 60.5 per cent. The DPP won 31.9 per cent of the vote, and independents and the CSDP won eight seats and 6 per cent of the vote. When the at-large seats had been distributed, the KMT ended up with 103 seats, the DPP with 50, and independents and CSDP eight between them (see Table 7B).

The 1992 election was conducted in a free and relatively fair manner. Vote rigging in Hualien county resulted in the defeat of Huang Hsin-chieh, the former Chairman of the DPP, and disgrace for the KMT government. In March 1993, the ROC Central Election Commission declared Huang Hsin-chieh the winner of the Hualien race after the Hualien District Court had ruled that the results of voting in eight polling

Table 7B: **Net Results of 1992 Legislative Yuan Election**

| Party | No. of candidates | Votes received | Total votes (%) | District seats won | At-large seats national/overseas |
|-------|------|------|------|------|------|
| KMT | | | | | |
| Nominees | 125 | 5,031,259 | 53.0 | 73 | 27/6 |
| Non-nominees | 43 | 710,203 | 7.5 | 7 | 0 |
| Total KMT | 168 | 5,741,462 | 60.5 | 80 | 19/4 |
| DPP | | | | | |
| Nominees | 59 | 2,944,195 | 31.0 | 37 | 16/3 |
| Non-nominees | 8 | 78,638 | 0.8 | 0 | 0 |
| Total DPP | 67 | 3,022,833 | 31.9 | 37 | 11/2 |
| CSPD | 22 | 126,213 | 1.3 | 1 | 0 |
| Other parties | 20 | 56,083 | 0.6 | 0 | 0 |
| Independents | 71 | 542,714 | 5.7 | 7 | 0 |
| Total | 348 | 9,489,305 | 100 | 125 | 30/6 |

*Source:*
*China Post* (Taipei), 21 December 1992, p. 16.

stations were invalid.[33] This decision brought the number of DPP seats in the Legislative Yuan up to 51, while KMT seats were reduced to 102.

Vote-buying is common in the ROC and the 1992 election was no exception. It is regarded either as a national trait or a personal "thank you" for getting to the polls. The non-mainstream faction of the KMT attacked the fairness of the party nomination process, and the DPP and general public also tended to perceive KMT candidates as wealthy ("golden oxen") and practitioners of money politics.[34]

Learning a lesson from the 1991 National Assembly elections, the DPP modified its campaign strategy. Along with substituting calls for Taiwan independence with the slogan "one China, one Taiwan," the DPP put special emphasis on practical issues, such as farm prices, social welfare, tax reduction, environmental protection and equal rights under law. In contrast to the KMT's unchanged slogan of "reform, stability and prosperity," the DPP appealed to the public with the "three antis" (opposition to military rule, privileges and money politics) and "three pros" (in favour of tax cuts, direct presidential elections and self-determination).[35]

The KMT emerged from the election with a much smaller majority than anticipated, while the DPP won nearly one-third of the seats in the Legislative Yuan. A number of factors have been suggested to explain the "surprising" outcome.[36] First, the KMT is believed to have lost touch with the public in this election. Its campaign strategy, centred around business and financial groups as well as local factional networks, alienated the middle and lower classes. Corruption scandals and socio-economic problems in the country further aggravated voters' dissatisfaction. The split within the KMT between the mainstream and non-mainstream factions (between the pro-President Lee Wisdom Coalition and the pro-Premier Hau Pei-tsun New KMT Alliance in the Legislative Yuan) also hurt the ruling party's cause.

The DPP, on the other hand, made a skilful appeal to the electorate by playing down the independence issue and focusing on social policy.[37] It attacked the KMT for alleged graft and corruption in government and close ties with "golden oxen," vote-buying, and other election irregularities. Despite the existence within the party of such middle groups as the Welfare State Front and Justice Alliance as well as the Formosa and New Tide factions, the DPP managed to portray itself as a well disciplined and

33. *China Post*, 18 March 1993, p. 1.
34. *Newsweek*, 21 December 1992, p. 38; *Financial Times*, 21 December 1992, p. 4; *Los Angeles Times*, 20 December 1992, p. A10.
35. *Free China Journal*, 11 December 1992, p. 7; 15 December 1992, p. 7.
36. For comments on this election, see "Great change in Taiwan's politics," *Shibao zhoukan* (*China Times Weekly*, U.S. edition), 3–9 January 1993, pp. 38–43; "Hsu Hsing-ling is elevated; Lee Teng-hui looks sad," *Xinxinwen* (*The Journalist*), 26 December 1992, pp. 20–24; "The KMT failed because of its poor mathematics," *Xinxinwen*, 27 December 1992–2 January 1993, pp. 31–34; "Editorial," *Lianhebao*, 20 December 1992, p. 2.
37. For DPP's Chairman Hsu Hsin-liang's expressed strategy, see Joseph Wu, "The ROC's Legislative Yuan election of December 1992", *Issues & Studies*, Vol. 29, No. 1 (January 1993), pp. 120–21; Michael Hindley, "KMT needs to learn from setback," *Free China Journal*, 12 January 1993, p. 7.

united party, badly needed in Taiwan to provide appropriate check-and-balance against the KMT's monopoly of power.

By and large, the most telling fact of the election is the growing maturity of the electorate in Taiwan and their preference for candidates' individual quality over connections to power or wealth. The voters wanted a change and sent a clear message through ballots. They were primarily interested in domestic issues, not those of independence or unification; they registered their disgust with political corruption and politics as usual. The setback of money politics in this election was underscored by the fact that many wealthy candidates lost and those who managed to win did only by narrow margins. Among those who lost were incumbent lawmaker Wang Ling-lin, vice-chairman of the powerful Rebar Group, and Legislative Yuan Vice-President Shen Ming-he, backed by Hualong and Huaxing business groups. Meanwhile, candidates who were change-oriented and anti-money-politics did very well. Jaw Shau-kong of the New KMT Alliance, who ran without the party's support, was the single highest vote-getter in the country (235,887 votes in Taipei country). His friend, former Finance Minister Wang Chien-shien, received the highest votes in Taipei city with 129,019. The anti-establishment-politics sentiment among the electorate also appeared to account for the defeat of most of the leaders of the pro-Lee Wisdom Coalition in the Legislative Yuan.[38]

The implications of the 1992 election are mixed. The DPP has proved itself a serious opposition party with the potential to become a ruling party before the end of the century. As DPP Chairman Hsu Hsin-liang declared on the night of the election, Taiwan no longer has a "party-and-a-half" system, but more of an institutionalized two-party one. With the DPP's strong showing, and a contingent of vocal non-mainstream KMT members in the Legislative Yuan, the legislature is likely to grow increasingly assertive in relation to the executive branch.

It has already caused new precedents to be set. First, Premier Hau and his cabinet were forced to resign by the pressure of the DPP and the KMT mainstream members in the Legislative Yuan. Secondly, President Lee succeeded in appointing Lien Chan, a mainland-born Taiwanese, as Premier. To senior members of the KMT CSC, such as Lee Huan, Lee Kwoh-ting, Hsu Li-nung, Shen Chang-huan and Hau Pei-tsun, KMT mainstream leaders acted "shamelessly" in not taking responsibility for the party's dismal electoral performance.[39] After the election, the KMT fell into further disarray over the resignation of Premier Hau and his replacement by Lien Chan, and the nomination of KMT Secretary-General James Soong as the new Governor of Taiwan Province. More upheavals are expected in the run-up to the party's 14th National Congress in autumn 1993.

38. The negative attitude of the electorate toward "golden oxen" and "vote-buying" is discussed in *Xinxinwen*, 20–26 December 1992, p. 24; *Zhongguo shibao*, 20 December 1992, p. 2; Allen Pun, "Fat cats deflated in election bids," *Free China Journal*, 22 December 1992, p. 7; Julian Baum, "The hollow centre," *Far Eastern Economic Review*, 7 January 1993, pp. 14–15.

39. *China Post*, 11 March 1993, p. 1.

The DPP, with one-third of all legislative seats, can form temporary alliances with either faction of the KMT depending on specific issues. If the KMT starts to treat the opposition party more seriously, Beijing is sure to feel uncomfortable. Beijing was careful not to provoke either voters or candidates with threats during the 1992 campaign. However, at least seven former political prisoners and a few overseas Taiwanese independence advocates were elected. Developments in Taiwan indicate that Beijing will be forced to modify its stance against making deals with the DPP. As one observer has remarked, the tripartite balance of forces which has taken shape in Taiwan is likely to make cross-Strait relations more complicated.[40] What Beijing seems most concerned about is the possibility that, as economic links between China and Taiwan grow closer, a democratic Taiwan will drift further and further from the mainland politically.

Factionalism has become an interesting phenomenon in the ROC Legislative Yuan. There are now four major factions of the DPP (Formosa, Welfare State Front, Justice Alliance and New Tide) in the Legislative Yuan, but they are united against the KMT. Before the 1992 election, there were at least six KMT factions in the Legislative Yuan: the Wisdom Coalition, the New KMT Alliance, the Reconstruction Research Club, New Idea Club, the Harmony Club and the Association for the Reform of the Parliament.[41] The Wisdom Coalition and the New KMT Alliance were the largest – the former supporting direct and the latter indirect election of the President. Certain members of the Wisdom Coalition were critical of Premier Hau Pei-tsun for his insistence on the "one China" principle, while the New KMT Alliance criticized President Lee Teng-hui for tolerating calls for Taiwan independence. KMT Central Party Headquarters was determined through the nomination process to purge the legislature of faction members critical of the party line, and demanded that key figures withdraw from factions.

The Wisdom Coalition did particularly badly in the 1992 legislative election, with ten of its members – including leading lights such as Lin Yu-siang, Wu Tzu, Liu Hsing-shan and Tsai Pi-huang – failing to achieve re-election. The New KMT Alliance turned out to be very successful with only one member not re-elected. Now joined by new legislators such as John Kuan and Lee Ching-hua, the Alliance is a bastion of non-mainstream forces. The division between it and the KMT mainstream faction in the legislature prompts the general observation that "there are two parties and three political groups" in the Legislative Yuan. Be that as it may, the new KMT Alliance is still a minority group. In March 1993, it applied to register as a political group with a platform based on "saving" the ideals of ROC founding father Sun Yat-sen and preventing the KMT and the country from falling into the grip of money politics. Alliance

40. Li Jiaquan, "Taiwan's political situation after legislative election," *Beijing Review*, 1–7 February 1993, p. 16.
41. Gunter Schubert, "Constitutional politics in the Republic of China: the rise of the Legislative Yuan," *Issues & Studies*, Vol. 28, No. 3 (March 1992), pp. 21–37.

leaders claim that they are not seeking to divide the KMT but to save it from further decline. They have set themselves the target of recruiting 100,000 members to prevent the DPP from gaining control of the government. The Alliance intends to mobilize enough public support to give it a decisive role in the KMT's 14th National Congress. However, as pointed out by a news journal, unless it can develop a public policy of constructive nature, slogans of generalities will not carry it too far.[42]

### Identity Crisis: Independence vs. Reunification

The end of the Cold War has brought the demise of Communism and the resurgence of separatism. Those who advocate Taiwan independence have been encouraged by the independence of the three Baltic states and other former Soviet republics and their later admission into the United Nations.

In its 1986 party platform, the DPP said that the future of Taiwan should be determined by all residents of the island. This principle of self-determination was crystallized into four preconditions for Taiwan independence – "if the KMT negotiates with the Communists, if the KMT sells out the interests of the people of Taiwan, if China attempts to take over Taiwan, or if the KMT fails to implement genuine political reform" – which were contained in a DPP special convention resolution of 17 April 1988.[43]

In September 1991, the DPP launched a campaign for United Nations membership under the name of Taiwan or the Republic of Taiwan. The New Tide faction also proposed that a clause calling for the establishment of a Republic of Taiwan be included in the party platform. At the DPP's fifth national convention in October, the Formosa and New Tide factions agreed to adopt a platform amendment which stated that "according to the principle of self-determination, the formation of an independent sovereign Republic of Taiwan with the establishment of a new constitution must be decided upon by all inhabitants of Taiwan through a plebiscite."[44]

The DPP's Taiwan independence clause triggered an explosion among top leaders of both the KMT and the Chinese Communist Party (CCP). On 10 October the President of the People's Republic of China (PRC), Yang Shangkun, warned Taiwan independence supporters on the island that "those who play with fire will be burned to ashes."[45] To defuse tension between the two sides of the Taiwan Strait, President Lee Teng-hui criticized the DPP, saying that "such a reckless and irresponsible move has completely disregarded the security of the nation and the

42. "New KMT alliance moves to become a de facto political party," *Shibao zhoukan*, 21–27 March 1993, p. 27.

43. Marc J. Cohen, *Taiwan at the Crossroads* (Washington, D.C.: Asia Resource Center, 1988), p. 399.

44. *Minzhu jinbudang dangzhang dangceng* (*Democratic Progressive Party Charters and Platforms*) (Taipei: Democratic Progressive Party, 1991), p. 13.

45. *Renmin ribao* (*The People's Daily*), 10 October 1991, p. 3.

well-being of all people."[46] The KMT government went further by launching a series of raids on the violence-prone Organization for Taiwan Nation-Building and the local branch of the New York-based World United Formosans for Independence. In the meantime, the Political Party Screening Committee under the Executive Yuan demanded that the DPP revise its party charter or face disbandment.[47] Confrontation between the KMT and the DPP over the Taiwan independence clause was mitigated by the election for the Second National Assembly, in which the DPP suffered a major setback in its popular vote. In the second stage of constitutional reform, the power to dissolve a political party was shifted from the Executive Yuan to the Constitutional Tribunal of the Judicial Yuan. In May 1992, the KMT government further revised Article 100 of the Criminal Code, also known as the sedition law, to exclude those who advocate Taiwan independence but stop short of active violence and coercive action. Revision of the ROC National Security Law in June 1992 meant that only those overseas Taiwan independence activists with a history of violence could be barred from entering the country. The KMT government's threat to dissolve the DPP for the Taiwan independence clause in its charter was finally removed when the Legislative Yuan revised the Law on the Organization of Civic Groups in July 1992.[48] As a result of the revision of the anti-sedition law, ROC's blacklists of dissidents denied entry to Taiwan are reported to have been reduced drastically from more than 800 to a mere five.[49] In March 1993 the Taiwan High Court acquitted Taiwan independence activist Chang Tsan-hung on charges of sedition. The founder and chairman of the World United Formosans for Independence was allowed to move his organization headquarters to Taiwan.[50]

The recent acts notwithstanding, the KMT government continues to adhere to the principle that there is but one China, and that China will eventually be reunified. In October 1990, the National Unification Council (NUC) was established under the Office of the President. Its main functions are "to further the goal of national unification, to assist the government in effectively planning the policy framework for achieving unification, and to integrate opinion at all levels of society and in all political parties concerning the issue of national unification."[51] The DPP's refusal to participate in the NUC under its present title reflects the party's rejection of the inevitability of unification.

In February 1991, the NUC adopted the Guidelines for National Unification which envisage a three-phase process of reunification, starting with exchanges and reciprocity, followed by mutual trust and co-operation, and finally consultation and unification. The guidelines state that

46. *Free China Journal*, 18 October 1991, p. 1.
47. *Free China Journal*, 8 November 1991, p. 2.
48. *Free China Journal*, 7 July 1992, p. 1; Julian Baum, "Easing up, somewhat," *Far Eastern Economic Review*, 28 May 1992, p. 18.
49. *Free China Journal*, 25 December 1992, p. 1.
50. *Ibid.* 23 March 1993, p. 1.
51. *Republic of China Yearbook*, 1991–92, p. 88.

"the timing and manner of China's unification should first respect the rights and interests of the people in the Taiwan area, and protect their security and welfare." It is clear from the Guidelines that the KMT's policy is actually "one China, but not now." For example, they state that "after an appropriate period of forthright exchange, co-operation and consultation conducted under the principles of reason, peace, parity and reciprocity, the two sides of the Taiwan Straits should foster a consensus of democracy, freedom and equal prosperity, and together build anew a unified China."[52]

Formulation and implementation of the government's policy towards mainland China is the responsibility of the Mainland Affairs Council under the Executive Yuan. The KMT government adopts a *quid pro quo* policy: no official contacts with the Chinese Communists unless Beijing renounces the use of force and its practice of isolating the ROC. In the absence of official contacts, therefore, a private but government-endorsed Straits Exchange Foundation was established to handle bilateral problems with its Chinese counterpart, the Association for Relations across the Taiwan Straits. The DPP plays a marginal role in Taiwan's mainland policy formulation process. Several DPP members have visited the mainland, but political calculations force its leaders to keep their distance from the Chinese Communists. Law and order in the Taiwan Straits, according to the DPP platform, should be regulated by international law, because the PRC is a foreign country.[53]

Confrontations between the KMT and the DPP over unification (*tong*) and independence (*du*) have also spread into the academic community and the mass media. KMT leaders including Lin Yang-hang and Hau Pei-tsun have openly called for a truce between *tong* and *du*, but the issue has haunted politicians, particularly at election time or when the KMT government has suffered a diplomatic setback. According to the public opinion polls conducted by the Taipei-based Public Opinion Research Foundation (PORF), around 20 per cent of the population support Taiwan independence (see Table 8), and almost 60 per cent of survey respondents believe that if Taiwan declares itself independent, the PRC will use force against the island.[54]

In fact, more and more people on the island are neither pro-re-unification nor pro-independence, as demonstrated by a survey conducted by the National Science Council in March 1991, in which 45 per cent of the respondents favoured the status quo. A similar result, of 50 per cent, was obtained in a KMT-sponsored survey in October 1991.[55] A June 1990 *Lianhebao* survey, in which respondents were asked whether they

52. Ying-jeou Ma, "The Republic of China's policy toward the Chinese mainland," *Issues & Studies*, Vol. 28, No. 2 (February 1922), pp. 1–10.
53. *Minzhu jinbudang dangzhang dangceng*, p. 13.
54. The survey was conducted by Public Opinion Research Foundation, see *Zhongguo shibao*, 21 October 1991, p. 3; *Zhongyang ribao*, 11 May 1993, p. 1. Until May 1993, less than 20% of those surveyed supported independence, but this was raised to 23.7% in the May survey following the Koo–Wang meeting in late April 1993.
55. *Lianhebao*, 1 April 1991, p. 4; 28 October 1991, p. 2.

Table 8: **Public Opinion on Taiwan Independence Movement**

| Date | Survey conductor | Approve/disapprove (%) |
|------|------------------|------------------------|
| November 1988 | PORF | 2/— |
| August 1989 | PORF | 16/— |
| December 1989 | PORF | 8.2/— |
| June 1990 | PORF | 12.5/67.0 |
| October 1990 | Lianhebao | 21/57 |
| December 1990 | PORF | 12.0/61.7 |
| June 1991 | PORF | 12.7/65.3 |
| September 1991 | Lianhebao | 18/54 |
| October 1991 | Lianhebao | 14/58 |
| October 1992 | PORF | 15.1/63.3 |
| October 1992 | Lianhebao | 16/51 |
| March 1993 | Lianhebao | 17/49 |
| May 1993 | PORF | 23.7/55.3 |

*Sources:*
*Mainland Policy: Selected Opinion Polls Conducted in Taiwan, 1988–92,* Mainland Affairs Council, The Executive Yuan, Taipei, Republic of China, August 1992, p. 6; *Zhongyang ribao,* 1 November 1992, p. 1; 11 May 1993, p. 1, data provided by the Public Opinion Poll Centre of the *Lianhebao.*

would support unification with a mainland still ruled by a Communist dictatorship, yielded a negative result, with only 11 per cent in favour of unification and 42 per cent for Taiwan independence. In the same survey, when asked what to choose if the CCP truly practises democracy and protects freedom on the mainland, 75 per cent of the respondents were in favour of unification and only 5 per cent for Taiwan independence.[56]

Despite their lack of official contacts, Taiwan and the Chinese mainland have been engaged in informal, people-to-people relations since 1987. The growth of tourism, economic interactions, cultural and sports exchanges is increasing rapidly. For example, residents of Taiwan are reported to have made over three million visits to the mainland between 1987 and 1992.[57] Bilateral indirect trade through Hong Kong reached $5.8 billion in 1991 and $7.4 billion in 1992. It is expected to hit $10 billion in 1993.[58] Taiwan's investments on the mainland increased annually at an average rate of over 100 per cent in the last three years. Today, the total amount is estimated to be around $10 billion.[59]

56. *Lianhebao,* 15 June 1990, p. 2.
57. *Shijie ribao (Global Journal),* 5 December 1989, p. 32; "Tourism," *Almanac of China's Foreign Economic Relations and Trade, 1992* (Beijing: Editorial Board of the Almanac, 1992), p. 417.
58. "Trade between Taiwan province and the mainland," *ibid.* p. 416; "Cross-Strait trade," *CNA,* 19 March 1993.
59. "Foreign investment in the PRC, 1991–92," JETRO, *China Newsletter,* No. 102, January–February 1993, p. 19; Julian Baum, "Taipei's offshore empire," *Far Eastern Economic Review,* 18 March 1993, p. 45; Jeremy Mark, "Taiwan and China fail to resolve investment dispute," *Wall Street Journal,* 29 April 1993, p. A10.

This impressive economic phenomenon is referred to by commentators as the emergence of Greater China, composed of mainland China, Hong Kong and Taiwan. Combining Taiwan's technology and financial power, Hong Kong's international marketing skills and China's vast resources and manpower, Greater China is said to be a "potential economic superpower," able to stand up to Japan.[60]

While some measure of economic interdependence is indeed developing between Taiwan and South China, the continuation of the ROC's "three nos" policy (no contacts, no negotiations and no compromise) does hamper its relations with the Chinese mainland. Beijing has pushed for direct postal, trade and transformation links, but Taipei would not open the "three links" unless the PRC ends the threat of force and recognizes the ROC as an equal political entity.[61]

There is, however, a growing pressure for the ROC government to adjust its mainland policy. First, businessmen in Taiwan want direct links to facilitate their activities in China. Secondly, Taipei authorities will want to keep access to Hong Kong after the return of the colony to Chinese rule in 1997. Thirdly, President Lee is believed to have a sense of mission to achieve a breakthrough in mainland relations while Deng Xiaoping is alive.[62] A couple of interesting signs have appeared lately. One was an agreement of both sides to schedule for late April in Singapore an unofficial meeting between Koo Chen-fu, chairman of Taiwan's Straits Exchange Foundation (SEF), and Wang Daohan, chairman of China's Association for Relations Across the Taiwan Straits (ARATS). The other was the appointment of President Lee's two close aides to important posts concerning mainland affairs. In early March 1993 Chiu Cheyne, deputy Secretary-General of the presidential office, was appointed as Secretary-General of the SEF, and Chiao Jen-ho, a bureau chief of the presidential office, was appointed as Vice-Chairman of the Mainland Affairs Council (MAC).[63]

On 19 March 1993 Chiu Cheyne expressed his "personal view" about the need to revise the "three nos" policy, and his position was echoed by an editorial of the *China Post*.[64] Nevertheless, MAC officials were quick to clarify any "misunderstanding" of Chiu's statement and made it clear that cross-Strait relations are still in the first phase of the ROC's Guidelines for National Unification, and that no official contacts will be possible until both sides treat each other on an equal footing in the second

60. Louis Kraar, "A New China without borders," *Fortune*, Vol. 126, No. 7 (5 October 1992), p. 125. See also David Chen, "The emergence of 'Greater China'," *Free China Journal*, 2 March 1993, p. 7.

61. Ralph Clough, "The ROC and international community in the 1900s," *Issues & Studies*, Vol. 29, No. 2 (February 1993), pp. 15–16.

62. Julian Baum, "Feeling their way," *Far Eastern Economic Review*, 1 April 1993, p. 19; "Lee Teng-hui's golden opportunity," *Xinxinwen*, 28 March–3 April 1993, p. 9.

63. *Zhongyang ribao*, 3 March 1993, p. 1. These two appointments are viewed as an indication that Lee personally is to take charge of the mainland policy. See "Lee Teng-hui's close aides come to the front," *Xinxinwen*, 7–13 March 1993, pp. 12–16.

64. "Revise policy of 'three nos'," *China Post*, 20 March 1993, p. 4.

stage.[65] Conflicting opinions between the SEF and MAC can be understood better if viewed from what they each represent. The SEF is a private intermediary organization reflecting the wishes of citizen groups and tends to get ahead of the government over relations with the mainland, while the MAC is a cabinet-level agency in the Executive Yuan with the responsibility of formulating and implementing the official mainland policy.[66] In the final analysis, all is under the control of President Lee Teng-hui, who cautioned people to be patient in "forging rapprochement with the mainland" and not to have too high expectations of the Koo–Wang meeting.[67]

On 7 April 1993 Chiu Cheyne went to Beijing to hold preparatory consultations with his Chinese counterpart, Tang Shubei of ARATS, to clear the way for the Koo–Wang "historical meeting" in Singapore later in the month. They succeeded in resolving a number of issues and agreed to consider the meeting as non-governmental, administrative, economic and functional in nature.[68]

The first high-level semi-official meeting of Koo and Wang held in Singapore on 27–29 April achieved accords in technical and exchange areas but failed to make a political breakthrough. Altogether four agreements were signed between SEF and ARATs. Three of them covered cross-Strait delivery of registered mail, verification of official documents and establishment of regular communication channels between the two organizations. The fourth was a joint statement issued at the end of the meeting which listed topics to be addressed by both sides in the future. These include crime, illegal immigrants, fishing disputes, copyright protection and judicial co-operation. The agreement also dealt with cross-Strait educational, cultural and scientific exchanges as well as joint exploitation of natural resources.[69]

Throughout the meeting some hard negotiations appeared to be taking place. Taipei wanted a formal agreement to protect Taiwan investors on the Chinese mainland, while Beijing called for direct links across the Taiwan Strait. Because of the political implications of the issues involved, neither side yielded to the demands of the other.[70] Nevertheless, in the circumstances the Koo–Wang meeting symbolized an important step forward towards establishing a framework for increasing contacts and exchanges and providing a regular, if unofficial, channel of communication across the Taiwan Strait. "The bridges we have built," Koo said, "mark a very important milestone for orderly and future relations between

65. *Free China Journal*, 23 March 1993, p. 1; 26 March 1993, p. 1.

66. For Lee's skilful use of SEF and MAC, see "Lee Teng-hui's left and right hands are playing two chess games simultaneously," *Xinxinwen*, 28 March–3 April 1993, p. 21.

67. *Zhongyang ribao*, 1 April 1993, p. 1.

68. Nicholas Kristof, "After four decades of bitterness, China and Taiwan plan to meet," *New York Times*, 12 April 1993, pp. A1, A5; *Zhongyang ribao*, 13 April 1993, p. 1; *Renmin ribao*, 12 April 1993, p. 1.

69. Nicholas Kristof, "Starting to build their first bridge, China and Taiwan sign four pacts," *New York Times*, 30 April 1993, p. A11; *Zhongyang ribao*, 30 April 1993, p. 1.

70. *Ibid.*; Jeremy Mark, "Taipei remains wary of political agenda," *Asian Wall Street Journal*, 30 April–1 May 1993, pp. 1, 6; "A dangerous warmth," *The Economist*, 1 May 1993, pp. 31–32.

the two organizations."[71] As was to be expected, the DPP attacked the meeting as a plot of the KMT to sell out Taiwan, and after its conclusion DPP observers in Singapore also condemned the signed agreements, saying that China had taken far more than it gave.[72]

### Other Factors Affecting Taiwan's Transition to Democracy

Edwin A. Winckler has argued that the Chiang Ching-kuo era in Taiwan saw a transition from "hard" to "soft" authoritarianism, and under President Lee Teng-hui Taiwan has liberalized its authoritarian system but not yet institutionalized democracy. Winckler also predicts that in Taiwan "a full transition from authoritarianism to democracy is likely to accelerate only in the mid-1990s and culminate in the first decade of the next century."[73] Liberalization and democratization measures have almost taken Taiwan across the threshold of a free society, according to a Freedom House cross-national survey (see Table 9).

There are several positive signs in Taiwan's transition to democracy. First, young leaders of both the KMT and the DPP are strongly committed to democratic values. Secondly, although it has a sizeable state-run sector, Taiwan basically has a free market economy which generates popular demand for further political reform. Thirdly, a civil society consisting of assertive social movements and civil organizations challenging the authority of the KMT government existed long before the political society emerged and has continued to broaden participation beyond the political realm.[74] Fourthly, the emergence of stable and broadly inclusive political parties, at least 66 of which have been registered besides the KMT and DPP, has made widespread political participation possible. Finally, regular elections for local and central representatives, and in the future the direct election of the Taiwan Governor and possibly the President of the ROC, allow meaningful political competition and the replacement of leaders without violence.

However, there are also certain unsatisfactory developments. Regular elections have stimulated political development in Taiwan but the rules are still unfair to non-KMT candidates. The election code discriminates against the opposition by allowing the KMT to have a larger percentage of seats than its percentage of the popular vote, while its monopoly of television and radio has proved effective. The KMT also has abundant

71. "China, Taiwan take first steps together," *Christian Science Monitor*, 30 April 1993, p. 6.

72. *AFP*, 29 April 1993; *Zhongyang ribao*, 30 April 1993, p. 2.

73. Edwin A. Winckler, "Institutionalization and participation on Taiwan, from hard to soft authoritarianism," *The China Quarterly*, No. 99 (September 1984), pp. 481–99; Edwin A. Winckler, "Taiwan transition?" in Cheng and Haggard (eds.), *Political Change in Taiwan*, p. 248.

74. Hsin-huang Michael Hsiao, "The rise of social movements and civil protests," in Cheng and Haggard (eds.), *Political Change in Taiwan*, pp. 57–72; Hung-mao Tien, "Social change and political development in Taiwan," in Harvey Feldman, Michael Y. M. Kau and Ilpyong J. Kim (eds.), *Taiwan in a Time of Transition* (New York: Paragon House, 1988), pp. 1–37.

Table 9: **Taiwan by Freedom Ratings**

|  | Political Rights | Civil Liberties | Freedom Ratings* |
|---|---|---|---|
| 1979 | 5 | 4 | 9 |
| 1980 | 5 | 5 | 10 |
| 1981 | 5 | 6 | 11 |
| 1982 | 5 | 5 | 10 |
| 1983 | 5 | 5 | 10 |
| 1984 | 5 | 5 | 10 |
| 1985 | 5 | 5 | 10 |
| 1986 | 5 | 5 | 10 |
| 1987 | 5 | 4 | 9 |
| 1988 | 5 | 3 | 8 |
| 1989 | 4 | 3 | 7 |
| 1990 | 3 | 3 | 6 |
| 1991 | 3 | 3 | 6 |
| 1992 | 3 | 3 | 6 |

*Comparisons of freedom ratings (1992):*

| | | | |
|---|---|---|---|
| South Korea | 5 | Japan | 3 |
| Indonesia | 11 | China | 14 |
| Malaysia | 9 | Vietnam | 14 |
| Philippines | 6 | Cambodia | 12 |
| Singapore | 9 | Laos | 13 |
| Thailand | 7 | | |

*Note:*
    *Partly free states (freedom ratings 6–10); free states (freedom ratings 3–5); not free states (freedom ratings 11–14).
*Sources:*
    Raymond D. Gastil (ed.), *Freedom in the World* (Westport, Connecticut: Greenwood Press, 1986); *Freedom at Issue*, January–February 1989, pp. 47, 52–53; *Freedom at Issue*, January–February 1990, p. 19; *Freedom Review* January–February 1991, p. 18; *Freedom Review*, January–February 1992, p. 18; *Freedom Review*, January–February 1993, pp. 15–16.

"access to public and private funds and assistance from administrative and security agencies."[75]

Robert Dahl has set seven requirements for a democratic state, many of which Taiwan fulfils. A crucial exception is that "control over government decisions about policy" has not been "constitutionally vested in elected officials."[76] Non-elected KMT officials play a much more impor-

75. *Country Reports on Human Rights Practices for 1991* (Washington, D.C.: Government Printing Office, 1992), p. 842.
76. Robert A. Dahl, *Dilemmas of Pluralist Democracy* (New Haven: Yale University, 1982), p. 10.

tant role in policy decisions than those elected. For example, the percentage of elected officials in the KMT central decision-making bodies such as the Central Committee was nominal before the 13th Party Congress in 1988 (see Table 10). However, improvement did occur in 1988, and more can be expected in the 14th Party Congress in 1993.

The task of separating the party from the state remains the biggest challenge facing the KMT, even though it adheres to the principle of further democratization.[77] The KMT has dominated the electorate, other political parties, the formation of governments and the public policy agenda in Taiwan for at least four decades. If it were to remain the ruling party it would act as a stabilizing factor, but whether it will pattern itself after the authoritarian Institutional Revolutionary Party of Mexico or Japan's more democratic Liberal-Democratic Party remains to be seen.[78]

The politicization of the military and the security apparatus is another impediment to the transition to democracy in Taiwan. The KMT authorities have taken a number of positive steps to check the power of the military-security establishment, such as lifting martial law in 1987, terminating the Temporary Provisions of the Constitution in 1991, and abolishing the Taiwan Garrison Command in 1992. Under pressure from the DPP members of the National Defence Committee of the Legislative Yuan, the KMT government has begun to institutionalize the Yuan's oversight of the military, and has taken up a recommendation to set up an Intelligence Committee to supervise the National Security Bureau.[79] Nevertheless, the military is still a force to be reckoned with in Taiwan politics; for example, the conservative Vocational Assistance Commission for Retired Servicemen (VACRS) endorses candidates running for National Assembly and Legislative Yuan seats. Even though the so-called iron vote of the military is no longer guaranteed, all 11 VACRS-endorsed candidates were elected in the 1992 elections.[80]

The DPP has consistently urged the "nationalization" of the armed forces, because the Constitution stipulates that "no political party and no individual shall make use of the armed forces as an instrument in a struggle for power" (Article 139) and "no military man in active service may concurrently hold a civil office" (Article 140). Despite these guarantees, it is suspected that the National Security Bureau was involved in taping and monitoring the activities of the DPP. The opposition further accused Chiang Wei-kuo, the Secretary-General of the National Security Council and Chiang Kai-shek's younger son, and Hau Pei-tsun, the then Minister of Defence, of leading the challenge against Lee Teng-hui's candidature for the presidency in 1990.[81]

---

77. Tun-jen Cheng, "Democratizing the quasi-Leninist regime in Taiwan," *World Politics*, Vol. XII, No. 4 (July 1989), p. 496.

78. T. J. Pempel (ed.), *Uncommon Democracies: The One-Party Dominant Regimes* (Ithaca: Cornell University Press, 1990), p. 4; Hung-mao Tien, *The Great Transition*, p. 12.

79. *Lianhebao*, 19 April 1992, p. 2.

80. *Duli zaobao* (*Independence Morning Post*), 20 December 1992, p. 3.

81. Ts'ai and Myers, "Surviving the rough-and-tumble," p. 137.

Table 10: **Background of KMT Central Committee Members**

| | 1952 | | 1957 | | 1963 | | 1969 | | 1976 | | 1981 | | 1988 | |
|---|---|---|---|---|---|---|---|---|---|---|---|---|---|---|
| | No. | % | No. | % | No. | % | No. | % | No. | % | No. | % | No. | % |
| Party | 9 | 28 | 20 | 40 | 32 | 43 | 25 | 25 | 34 | 26 | 34 | 23 | 27 | 15 |
| Administration | 6 | 19 | 3 | 6 | 7 | 9 | 22 | 22 | 29 | 22 | 48 | 32 | 60 | 33 |
| Military and security | 11 | 34 | 18 | 36 | 24 | 33 | 29 | 28 | 30 | 23 | 27 | 18 | 25 | 14 |
| Elected officials | 1 | 3 | 3 | 6 | 3 | 4 | 7 | 7 | 18 | 14 | 18 | 12 | 48 | 27 |
| Others | 5 | 16 | 6 | 12 | 8 | 11 | 18 | 18 | 19 | 15 | 23 | 15 | 20 | 11 |

*Source:*
Wu Nai-teh, "Consolidation of authoritarian regime in Taiwan," paper delivered at conference on the Post-Cold War Asia-Pacific and China–Taiwan Relations, sponsored by Japan Taiwan Research Association, Tokyo, 26–28 March 1992, p. 17.

Since 1988, the KMT has begun to remove its party organs from the military. Now the pace of change is being accelerated. Military personnel no longer pay party dues, nor attend small group meetings under party guidance. What still remains is the KMT's political education in the armed forces.[82]

The United States factor was apparent in Taiwan's democratization in the 1980s. For example, the United States Congress conducted numerous hearings on the KMT's human rights abuses and the continuance of martial law on the island. Since martial law was lifted and the KMT began tolerating dissident opinions, American influence on Taiwan's political development has become marginal.[83] Overseas Chinese participation in Taiwan politics has also been limited since the Constitution was amended. Articles 1 and 2 of recent amendments limited the number of overseas members of the National Assembly to 20 and of the Legislative Yuan to six. The New KMT Alliance has, however, found useful allies against the mainstream KMT among the overseas Chinese community, and the DPP has been supported by pro-independence groups living mostly in Japan and the United States.

Ironically, the largest overseas pressure group seeking to influence Taiwan's political development is the leadership in Beijing. By threatening to use force to stop Taiwan independence, Beijing has effectively limited Taiwan's options for the future. Communist Chinese leaders assumed a low profile during the 1992 legislature election in Taiwan, but have not hesitated to condemn any move toward independence. In his report to the Eighth National People's Congress in March 1993, Li Peng said that the PRC "will take all necessary drastic measures to stop any activities aimed at making Taiwan independent and splitting the motherland."[84] In an interview with *U.S. News & World Report* in February 1993, Jiang Zemin stated: "We advocate achieving national reunification as soon as possible through peaceful methods. But we do not promise not to use military force. This is absolutely not directed to the Taiwanese people. This is mainly directed against forces of Taiwanese independence and foreign interference."[85]

*Conclusion*

Constitutional democracy denotes separation of political power and limited government accountable to the electorate. Neither the direct nor indirect election of the ROC President will dramatically affect the transition to democracy on Taiwan. The method of election, however, would determine the type of regime, and the question of which system – presidentialism, parliamentarianism or a mixed arrangement – is most

82. *Xinxinwen*, 28 March–3 April 1993, pp. 12–13.
83. Cheng-yi Lin, "The U.S. factor in Taiwan's political development," in Jaw-ling Joanne Chang (ed.), *ROC–USA Relations, 1979–1989* (Taipei: Institute of American Culture of Academia Sinica, 1991), pp. 126–135.
84. *Renmin ribao*, 16 March 1993, p. 1; FBIS, *Daily Report–China*, 2 April 1993, p. 35.
85. "A conversation with Party leader Jiang Zemin," *U.S. News & World Report*, 15 March 1993, pp. 60–61.

suitable. The KMT dominated both stages of the constitutional reform process but failed to deal with relations among the President, the Premier and the Legislative Yuan. The emergence of the National Assembly with new powers of confirmation and the right to hear the President's report on the state of the nation add more confusion to the political system. There is neither historical tradition nor institutional need for a bi-cameral parliament.

Constitutional issues are usually contentious objects in countries going through the transition process to democracy. To build consensus in a functioning democracy, the majority party should welcome the minority party's constructive input while the latter should respect majority decisions. In any future attempt to revise the Constitution, both the KMT and DPP should show accommodating spirit and effort in order to reach some basic agreement to define clearly the ROC political system and solidify the rising importance of the Legislative Yuan.

On balance, Taiwan's political changes in recent years have been truly impressive. The last two general elections, the 1991 National Assembly election and the 1992 Legislative Yuan election, were praised by outside observers as open, free and fair. Human rights protection has been greatly enhanced. Not only is blacklisting of political dissidents a thing of the past, but some former political prisoners are now elected officials or legislators. In the areas of freedom of speech and freedom of the press, Taiwan's level of achievement is comparable to that of Japan. There is, of course, more to be done on the road to democratization. For instance, changes ought to be made in the electoral system to ensure its equitableness to all political parties. Regulations of lobbyist activities and the publicizing of financial assets of elected officials are needed to curb the abuses of "money politics." Depoliticizing the military-security establishment and separating the state and the party remain urgent tasks for the KMT government. While conservative elements in the KMT may offer resistance to slow down the transition process, KMT reformers on Taiwan, as in the case of Spain or Mexico, can invoke "backward legitimacy" and stress elements of continuity with the past,[86] with an appeal to Sun Yat-sen's ultimate goal of having his party "return the government to the people (*huanzheng yumin*)."

The 1992 legislature election ushered in a new era of political pluralism on Taiwan with an established and permanent two-party system. The emergence of a fully-fledged, assertive Legislative Yuan serves as an effective counterbalance to the executive branch of the government. A good example is its recent decision to shelve the two bills containing organization laws for the National Security Council and the National Security Bureau on the ground that they would increase the power of the President without supervision by elected representatives.[87]

86. Samuel P. Huntington, "How countries democratize," *Political Science Quarterly*, Vol. 106, No. 4 (Winter 1991–92), p. 599.
87. *Free China Journal*, 16 April 1993, pp. 1–2.

There is little question that recent elections have demonstrated the maturity of Taiwan's electorate to judge candidates more on individual merits than on party or factional affiliations. Both political parties should learn valuable lessons from them. To remain as a ruling party, the KMT needs to offer a clean and efficient government with a vigorous policy agenda, not to be too closely tied to financial magnates. The mainstream and non-mainstream factions should learn to co-exist and work for common goals. One way to promote party unity is for the KMT leadership to democratize the party structure as well as the election and decision-making processes. On the other side, the DPP needs to act responsibly as a legitimate challenger to the KMT. Street politics and violent behaviour will not enhance its image in the long run. Constructive policy alternatives are more likely to win votes than negative slogans and obstructive tactics.

One major problem in Taiwan's transition to democracy is the national identity crisis resulting from lingering suspicion and distrust between Taiwanese and mainlanders living on the island. This divisive issue of family origin has been aggravated and exploited by politicians for selfish gains. In a 10,000 word letter published recently, Wang Yung-ching, the renowned Taiwanese industrialist, made an appeal to all people to resolve disputes between different provincial groups. In his words, "we all are Chinese"; people both inside and outside the government should be broad-minded and handle matters according to conscience and fair play, not bound by the "sentimental knot of provincial origin."[88] In the same vein, a number of legislators from different political parties also agreed that public figures should not stir up the emotional issues of provincial origin as a political tool.[89]

Undoubtedly, a Taiwan-born leader like President Lee Teng-hui can do much to help bridge the gap between the two subethnic groups and promote their mutual trust through wise policy and impartial personnel selections. Taiwan's mainland policy is a case in point. On this issue, President Lee and his supporters have taken a centralist position between the extremes of independence and unification by maintaining the status quo and promoting peaceful coexistence and cultural and economic exchanges with the PRC. This policy is not only realistic and sound but also in full accord with the views of a large majority of Taiwan's residents as demonstrated consistently by public opinion surveys conducted in the ROC.

Economic interactions and cultural exchanges across the Taiwan Strait have recently been expanding rapidly. There is also a growing pressure from Taiwanese business interest for improving communications with the mainland. What the recent Koo–Wang meeting accomplished was the establishment of a quasi-official framework to facilitate more cross-Strait exchanges. It was an important step towards the further development of economic interdependence between Taiwan and the mainland and the

88. *Zhongyang ribao*, 2 February 1993, pp. 1, 3.
89. *Ibid.* 2 April 1993, p. 22.

continuing evolution of Economic Greater China consisting of China, Taiwan and Hong Kong.

Nevertheless, economic integration is one thing and political unification is another. It is unlikely that Taiwan–mainland relations will move in the foreseeable future to the stage of official contacts and political negotiations. The cautious, stage-by-stage approach seems to be the only policy option for Lee's government that reflects the current wishes of the people on Taiwan.

National unification is a long-term goal, and its ultimate realization depends upon a number of variables. Among them are the PRC's continued economic reform, its commitment to political change and Taiwan's further democratization. As contacts across the Taiwan Strait become more regular and expansive, one can expect the DPP to become more involved in Taiwan's mainland policy, seeking to play a "supervisory role." This will probably provide Taiwan with a bargaining chip to "separate economics from politics" when negotiating with the mainland. Until convinced that it is in their best interest to integrate with China politically, the overwhelming majority of people living on Taiwan will continue to want neither unification nor independence but the maintenance of the status quo. It is to be hoped that this fact may give the PRC more incentive for political change on the model of Taiwan.

# Political Change in Hong Kong*

## Brian Hook

On 1 July 1997, Hong Kong, the only significant remaining part of the British Empire, will revert to China. In the same year India, once the jewel in that crown and whose emancipation marked the beginning of the end, will celebrate the 50th anniversary of its independence. History will record that for the latter part of these five decades the economic development of Hong Kong was, compared to other former British territories, spectacular. Once Hong Kong had overcome the challenge of the mass influx of refugees following the Chinese civil war, which endured for almost two of the five decades, its subsequent development, measured in material terms, was exemplary. No matter what the challenge, the Hong Kong population rose to it. Yet, compared to India and other parts of the former empire, its government until the eve of the reversion remained, judged by recognized criteria, "undemocratic" and unrepresentative, executive-led, and based on a colonial form of constitution.

This is a striking paradox. The lack of a fully constituted representative government based on a universal franchise and direct elections did not lead Hong Kong people to seek to migrate. On the contrary, many Chinese citizens whose government was formed by the Communist Party of China, which claimed a large measure of democracy, constantly attempted to migrate to Hong Kong. Only when the date of reversion approached and certain local Chinese leaders (notably Xu Jiatun, then Head of the New China News Agency (NCNA), whose memoirs were serialized in a leading newspaper[1]) commented in ways that the Hong Kong people perceived to be minatory or when China was wracked by political and economic crisis, did they seek to leave.

*This article builds on my earlier study of the Hong Kong government which showed that political developments in the 1970s amounted essentially to change within tradition; see Brian Hook, "The government of Hong Kong: change within tradition," *The China Quarterly*, No. 95 (1983), pp. 491–511. An earlier version was presented at the China Quarterly Conference on Greater China held in Hong Kong in January 1993. I am grateful to John Burns, Byron Weng, and David Shambaugh for their constructive comments on it.

1. See Xu Jiatun, "Xianggang huiyilu" ("Hong Kong memoirs"), *Lianhebao* (Hong Kong) serialized from 9 May 1993, which provides a unique and fascinating insight into the perception of the former Head of the Hong Kong branch of the NCNA, of his relations with the Beijing leadership, his colleagues, certain members of the Hong Kong business elite, the Sino-British negotiations, and of attempts in Hong Kong to develop representative government. In addition, referring to the background to the negotiations, Xu claims that the former Governor of Hong Kong, Lord MacLehose, raised the question of the expiry of the lease on the New Territories with the Ministry of Foreign Affairs (MFA) during his visit to China in 1979. The MFA was unprepared and had to seek instructions. Having done so, the response was that "China would take back Hong Kong" ("Zhongguo yao shouhui Xianggang"). The MFA also indicated it was hoped he would not raise the matter with Deng Xiaoping. Nevertheless, the Governor did so, with the result that Deng told him unequivocally China would "take back sovereignty over Hong Kong at the appointed time" ("Zhongguo jieshi yiding yao shouhui Xianggang"). This claim begs the question as to whether the outcome of negotiations could have been any different had the MFA been given more time and had the issue not been put to Deng in 1979, as it had requested. In his memoirs Xu opines that the negotiations would have come later had the issue not been raised then. That option did not address the uncertainty felt in Hong Kong business circles at the time.

For 30 years from 1947 the Hong Kong authorities, the British government and, it would appear, significant sections of public opinion in Hong Kong, seemed reluctant to abandon a form of government developed from the traditional colonial pattern, for a modern democratic system that, arguably, would correspond to the level of social and economic development the territory had increasingly attained. This reluctance is a major feature of the political history of Hong Kong in the post-war period. For this reason the government and politics of Hong Kong (which in this study include not only the constitutional structure and the organs of government but also the level and nature of government-related political activity), the increasing politicization of the Hong Kong people and the overarching role of the Communist Party of China have attracted increasing attention since the signing of the Sino-British Joint Declaration (JD) in 1984.[2]

Despite the conspicuous and widely acknowledged ability of Hong Kong people to shoulder all the responsibilities of government, the absence of self-determination was, in itself, neither unexpected nor especially noteworthy. The eventual reversion of Hong Kong to China, for which the Chinese Nationalist authorities had manoeuvred in 1945 only to be thwarted by Winston Churchill, had been acknowledged implicitly by Britain since the early 1950s and stated explicitly by China in the early 1970s. Nevertheless, the possibilities for the evolution of the government and politics of Hong Kong up to and beyond the retrocession are of interest. Will the evolution, even allowing for the change in sovereignty, be within tradition or constitute a break with tradition? Will constitutional change and development further promote, and sustain in perpetuity, the ordered nexus of social values and relations that is implicit in the concept of civil society? In particular, will the promised high degree of autonomy, under the visionary concept of "one country, two systems" with Hong Kong people actually ruling Hong Kong, be exercised by newly-emerged Hong Kong leaders on the basis of full or a greatly enhanced degree of representative government, or will this remain, as in the past, politically unattainable?

These issues and related matters are the focus of this article, which attempts to elucidate and evaluate the degree of change that has brought Hong Kong to its present stage of political development. It addresses the impetus for political change; elite and popular reactions to the prospects of political change, that is reactions to the changing situation; and the impact of political change.

---

2. The JD provided the terms for an agreed *retrocession* of the territory, or, looked at through Chinese eyes, the restoration of the rightful sovereignty of China over Hong Kong. It therefore determined that the future government and politics of the territory would not be the same as that for other parts of the British Empire, normally for the territory to proceed from dominion or colonial status to independence. Instead the JD provided for the sovereignty over the entire territory under the administration of the Hong Kong government, both ceded and leased, to be restored to China on the expiry of the lease governing that part known as the New Territories at midnight on 30 June 1997. Thereafter it would become the Hong Kong Special Administrative Region (HKSAR). The text of the JD appeared in a White Paper published by the British government in London on 20 September 1984.

*Sources of Political Change: The Internal/External Nexus*

The impetus for political change in Hong Kong has come from two main sources, one indigenous and the other exogenous. The indigenous source is the exemplary pace and scope of economic development in Hong Kong since the 1970s. The exogenous source is to be found in the outcome of the Sino-British negotiations on the future of Hong Kong, in particular to the JD under the terms of which China subsequently enacted the Basic Law (BL) for the Hong Kong Special Administrative Region (HKSAR). The provisions of the BL include stipulations as to the political structure of the future HKSAR, to which any interim political change is expected to converge.[3]

Regarding the first impetus for change, as early as the mid-1970s when Hong Kong experienced the beginnings of prosperity, it was evident that a new middle class was emerging. The socio-economic growth that enabled Hong Kong to become one of the four "mini-dragons" simultaneously generated a middle class that demanded more political participation. The process of middle class politicization was particularly evident in the 1980s and early 1990s, but could also be perceived in the late 1970s. An early example is the incorporation of the Hong Kong Observers Ltd.,[4] a well-informed, liberal, reformist interest group from whose ranks some of the leading democratic political figures and commentators in contemporary Hong Kong have been drawn. The Hong Kong Observers (HKO) had among their objectives the promotion of a wider participation in the government of Hong Kong, of greater responsiveness by the government to the perceived needs of Hong Kong, and of research into issues of public interest and community welfare. In the late 1970s, the HKO contributed influential articles to the Chinese and English-language media in the colony.[5] The emergence of such a group generated by the new middle class, some of whose members had also been student activists (though not left-wing ones), was one of the earliest concrete signs that the Hong Kong middle class should be integrated more fully into the political system. The failure of the Hong Kong government to accommodate these new political forces at the time led to

3. The BL was adopted on 4 April 1990 by the Seventh NPC at its third session. The text used in this article was published by the Consultative Committee of the Basic Law of the HKSAR, Hong Kong in 1990. The concept of convergence was actually acknowledged by Britain in 1985 by the then Minister of State Timothy Renton shortly after the Director of the Hong Kong branch of the NCNA had implied that Britain would be departing from the JD if direct elections were to become an option in the 1987 constitutional review.

4. The business incorporation, which has been followed by other groups, avoided both the need to register as a society, and any breach of the law on assembly. Such matters were enforced by the police; business incorporation was within the purview of the Registrar General.

5. The information on the HKO is based in part on an interview with the Hon. Christine Loh Kung-wai, an appointed Legislative Councillor, in July 1993. There is a view that the HKO began as a pressure group/think tank and ended by being itself co-opted into the establishment. This it would deny, indicating its members were seldom, if ever, appointed to formal consultative bodies in the political system they sought to improve by reform.

what Ian Scott has referred to as a weakening of credibility and a crisis of legitimacy for the government of Hong Kong.[6]

The chief impediment to the timely integration of the Hong Kong middle class into the political system was the evident material success of the existing traditional system and an equally evident reluctance by its architects and beneficiaries to implement any change outside tradition.[7] The success of the system could be demonstrated by applying two criteria. First, Hong Kong had enjoyed sustained economic growth to which, in the view of the business and bureaucratic elites and a large section of the population, the policies of the government were closely linked. Moreover, the system was notable for an effective framework of law and order, the provision of infrastructure and an adequate delivery of social services on the basis of low taxes. Together with the cultural preferences of the majority expressed in terms of familism, patriarchy and avoidance of politics whenever possible, it did not engender substantial opposition. Secondly, sustained economic growth and its cultural context had enabled Hong Kong to avoid the syndrome identified by Samuel P. Huntington, namely the development of an intolerable gap between social mobilization and economic development, such as characterized the political instability of many developing countries.[8]

On the eve of the emergence by the new middle class in Hong Kong, the political system was characterized by a 20th-century version of the practice of synarchy[9] and by the sophisticated development of a process identified by Ambrose Yeo-chi King as the administrative absorption of politics.[10] The concept of synarchy, in its 19th-century context, produced a joint administration by British and non-British leaders. The administrative absorption of politics was achieved by the formal and informal absorption of Hong Kong Chinese civic and business leaders, who might otherwise have become foci of political activity, into the process of elite consensual government at various levels. Hong Kong thus maintained a minimally integrated social-political system in which the bureaucratic polity remained a dominant feature.

Lau Siu-kai noted in his study of society and politics in Hong Kong: "There is an emerging middle-income educated sector which is increasingly inclined to participate in public decision making and which is beginning to be disillusioned with the responsiveness thus far displayed by the Hong Kong government."[11] Lau cites a Hong Kong Government Home Affairs Department small-scale study conducted in the late 1970s

6. Ian Scott, *Political Change and the Crisis of Legitimacy in Hong Kong* (Hong Kong: Oxford University Press, 1989).

7. See Brian Hook, "The government of Hong Kong."

8. Samuel P. Huntington, *Political Order in Changing Societies* (New Haven: Yale University Press, 1968).

9. John K. Fairbank, "Synarchy under the treaties," in John K. Fairbank (ed.), *Chinese Thought and Institutions* (Chicago: University of Chicago Press, 1957), pp. 163–203.

10. Ambrose Yeo-chi King, "The administrative absorption of politics in Hong Kong: emphasis on the grass roots level," *Asian Survey*, Vol. 15, No. 5 (May 1975), pp. 422–439.

11. Lau Siu-kai, *Society and Politics in Hong Kong* (Hong Kong: The Chinese University Press, 1987), p. 187.

of a select group of well-educated middle income executives with an average age of 33. The study found they were unanimous in believing that there was a credibility gap between the public and the government; that the system of government by consultation had limitations; that the interests of the wider community were not safeguarded by "unofficials" (appointees from financial, real estate and industrial circles on consultative committees); that the unofficials on consultative committees did not speak out; and that the government needed to make much more effort in community relations.[12]

### Elite and Popular Reaction

Against a background of pressure arising from the objective need for political change in the early 1980s, the government embarked on a programme aimed at developing representative government in Hong Kong. The stages and content of the programme have already been analyzed by a number of scholars,[13] but it is important to note the outcome. First, despite significant interest in and support for change at the time of the 1987 constitutional review,[14] substantial reform, such as direct elections to the Legislative Council (Legco) (which would have broken with tradition and begun the integration of the middle class into the political system), was postponed until 1991. In the meantime, key elements of the Hong Kong middle class had become increasingly frustrated by their perception of a continued bilateral (British and Chinese) approach to the issue of retrocession, expressing the view that Hong Kong was being marginalized in the negotiations leading to the JD and to the key issues of the transition. It appears that this perception was justified, even though the Governor's closest advisers on the Executive Council had been privy to the process since its inception. The perception was engendered to some extent by the secrecy surrounding bilateral contacts, but most of all by the manifest success enjoyed by China in persuading Britain to concede to the principle that significant constitutional reform should converge with the future Basic Law. It has not been wholly dispelled by the presence of directly elected representatives in the legislature since 1991. Whether advancing direct elections to 1988, thus providing three additional years of experience at a key juncture in the transition, would have made a significant difference to the process will remain a matter of debate for some time.

Whatever the motivations for the limitations placed on the programme for developing representative government, the debate they engendered

12. *Ibid.* The note is drawn from "A problem of credibility," a mimeographed talk by John Walden, former Director of Home Affairs, given to the HKO on 13 February 1980.

13. See Scott, *Political Change and the Crisis of Legitimacy*; Norman Miners *et al.*, in Kathleen Cheek-Milby and Miron Muskat (eds.), *Hong Kong: The Challenge of Transformation* (Hong Kong: The Centre of Asian Studies, University of Hong Kong, 1989).

14. Ann Quon, "Support mounts for elections," *Sunday Morning Post*, 31 May 1987, noted in Scott, *Political Change and the Crisis of Legitimacy*, p. 291. Scott states "that all polls showed that at least a plurality and, in most cases, an absolute majority were in favour of direct elections in 1988...."

from 1984 to 1988 was responsible for politicizing Hong Kong and for the eventual development of a diverse range of political parties and groups which were to contest the 18 seats open for direct election to the 60-seat 1991–95 legislature. If the motivation was to retard politicization and the onset of confrontational politics, this was manifestly not achieved. Indeed, the outcome was quite the opposite: the indigenous impetus for political change from middle class activism was evident not only in challenges on major themes such as convergence and deferred direct elections but on a range of matters including livelihood and civil liberties issues.

Examples of such activism were the debates over the location of the joint-venture nuclear power plant at nearby Daya Bay and the revelation that a number of reinforcing bars had been omitted during a phase of its construction; and over the perception of an official wish to curtail the right to criticize legislators, to retain and, so it was argued, to facilitate the prosecution of the offence of publishing "false news," and to abolish the jury system in the trial of commercial crimes.[15] The most politicizing event, however, not only occurred outside Hong Kong but dragged it into the maelstrom of the internal politics of China – this was the military measures adopted to suppress the democracy movement of 1989. The tragic events in Beijing on 4 June 1989 provide an example of a concatenation of indigenous and exogenous factors in the impetus for political change in Hong Kong. Middle class political activism was at the core of the leadership of the mass movement in Hong Kong in support of mainland students. In turn, the support in Hong Kong for Chinese activists reinforced the view of the Chinese leadership that the resumption of sovereignty over Hong Kong must entail control over it, lest it serve as a base for subversion. This led to an increasingly restrictive interpretation of the concepts of "one country, two systems" and a "high degree of autonomy."[16]

The crisis in China in the early summer of 1989 occurred at a stage when Hong Kong middle class activists and their allies had become, by virtue of frustration over the postponement of direct elections and unsuccessful attempts to influence the drafting of the BL, a broadly based coalition. The question of the future of Hong Kong appeared linked to the future of a China where the demise of Communism in its present form seemed predictable. The Chinese Communist Party was on the defensive. International Communism was in retreat. The crisis in Beijing therefore appeared to some of the one million or so Hong Kong residents who took to the streets in peaceful demonstration as a harbinger of a new form of government. This was an opportunity to demonstrate opposition to the brutal manner in which the student movement in Beijing had been suppressed and to signal support for the movement.

In Hong Kong, activism in the domestic arena was thus boosted by

15. Scott, *Political Change and the Crisis of Legitimacy*, pp. 312–16.

16. Chen Xitong, "Guanyu zhizhi dongluan he pingxi fangeming baoluan de qingkuang baogao" ("Report on quelling the turmoil and counter-revolutionary rebellion"), *Renmin ribao*, 10 July 1989, p. 2.

politicization on a much wider scale during the crisis of 1989. The consequences of the frustration of middle class aspirations in the 1980s, empathy for the Chinese student demonstrators, and at the time an almost universal distrust of those who appeared to have been responsible for their suppression, were evident in the results of the 1991 direct elections for 18 seats in the Legco. Candidates identified with the movement for democracy enjoyed much greater support than those associated with conservative policies.[17] The stage was thus set for the political changes ushered in by the 1991 "new-look" Legco, on which the middle classes were significantly represented. The dominant party of Legco could logically expect to be represented on the Executive Council (Exco). In future, the Hong Kong government could no longer assume a certain majority for its policies.

### Exogenous Sources of Political Change: The Basic Law

The aim of retarding the programme for developing representative government was to allow time for drafting and enacting the BL (1985–90). This, achieved by a Basic Law Consultative Committee (BLCC), a Basic Law Drafting Committee (BLDC)[18] and the National People's Congress (so with no formal input from the British side) was to embody the provisions of the JD as interpreted by the Chinese side. Insofar as it was to impose political change, the BL provided for a political system in which the government remained executive-led, with a strong Chief Executive and an Exco not conspicuously fully accountable to Legco, and a Legco in which, of a 60 seat chamber (assuming 20 members would be directly elected in 1995), 24 would be directly elected in 1999 (the second term) and 30 in 2003. The remainder of the seats were to be occupied by 30 functional constituency representatives, and members returned by an Election Committee (ten in the 1995 elections when the composition of the election committee would be *de jure* in the hands of the British, and six in 1999). To proceed to a fully directly-elected

17. On a 39% turn-out the liberals (United Democrats, Meeting Point, Association for Democracy and People's Livelihood and the Hong Kong Democratic Foundation) gained 58% of the vote. Their 21 candidates won 15 seats; liberal independents won three seats with some 27% of the vote. The United Democrats with 12 of the 18 seats dominated the Legco. None of the five conservative candidates of the Liberal Democratic Federation who gained 5% of the vote, nor any of the Pro-China candidates (from the Federation of Trade Unions, New Hong Kong Alliance, Hong Kong Citizens Forum, Kwun Tong Man Chung Friendship Promotion Association) who gained some 8% of the vote, nor any of the other groups (The Reform Club, Civic Association and the Trades Union Council) who gained about 2% of the vote, won any seats. Hong Kong Government Gazette Extraordinary, No. 133 (41), 20 September 1991.

18. The Basic Law Drafting Committee was established by the NPC on 18 June 1985 with 59 members, 23 of whom were from Hong Kong. The PRC members represented the departments of the government and the CPC. Among the Hong Kong members were ten businessmen and financiers, three lawyers and a retired judge. The Basic Law Consultative Committee was formed through discussion and consultation (initially described as democratic consultation) from August 1985 onwards, on 18 December 1985, to seek views on the appropriate content of the BL. It had 180 members from eight categories in differing proportions.

legislature after 2007, the relevant annex to the BL would have to be amended by a two-thirds majority of all members and the consent of the Chief Executive, a procedure that would require a significant proportion of sitting functional constituency members to be convinced that their role could be performed better by directly elected members.[19]

The Hong Kong government was aware of the growing middle class pressure for change and also conscious of business, bureaucratic elite and Chinese preferences for a modified traditional system. It consequently introduced reforms that brought relatively minor developments at three levels of government. The 1982 elections on a broad franchise for a proportion of the seats on the District Boards contributed, however, to the establishment of a new pattern of district administration[20] and a precedent for closer involvement by citizens in government. Moreover, by 1985 District Board members, including some of the leading politicians in Hong Kong in the 1990s, generated nine members of the Regional Council (Regco) and ten members of the Urban Council (Urbco), the second tier of representative government, and, through an electoral college, ten of the 12 members of Legco to be so elected (the Municipal Council constituencies of the electoral college, Urbco and Regco electing the other two).

By 1985, one year after the signing of the JD, the Hong Kong authorities had therefore created a fairly integrated three tier system of representative government.[21] Furthermore, the informal selection of functional representatives for the Legco was, from 1985, replaced by the election of 12 members from nine functional constituencies. Although middle-class activists still saw the system as unrepresentative and undemocratic, at the level of the legislature, 24 of 56 members were now "elected." The issue of *direct* elections to Legco had been shelved, but the White Paper appeared to acknowledge that the traditional system had been optimally reformed and envisaged a very small number of directly elected members in 1988 and a significant number by 1997. Such a departure from tradition would be reviewed in 1987. For the present there would be no change that would fundamentally affect the relationship between the government and the legislature.

The Chinese authorities did not envisage any such development in 1988. Having signed the JD they did not, according to Xu Jiatun, anticipate fundamental structural change in the run up to 1997. On the contrary, their understanding was no change in the status quo (*xianzhuang bu bian*). Xu claims that the then senior unofficial member of Exco, Sir S. Y. Chung, appeared to understand that when China talked

19. The Decision of the NPC on the Method For the Formation of the First Government and the First Legislative Council of the HKSAR, third session of the Seventh NPC on 4 April 1990. The Basic Law of the HKSAR of the PRC, Annex II.

20. Green Paper, A Pattern of District Administration in Hong Kong, June 1980; White Paper, District Administration in Hong Kong, January 1981; both were published by the Hong Kong Government Printer.

21. Green (July 1984) and White (November 1984) papers: The Further Development of Representative Government in Hong Kong.

of no change for 50 years this was on the basis of the present state of affairs (that is, 1984) rather than no change from 1997. By the time he was reporting on the proposals in the 1984 White Paper to his superiors, Xu had evidently overcome the "coldness" of his initial reception by the Hong Kong and Macau Office of the State Council and had tackled the difficulties in a branch where six of the seven deputies were Cantonese. Xu reoriented the NCNA office workstyle, characterized by the Centre as "leftist and narrowly focused" (*yi zuo er zhai*).[22]

Xu himself relaxed the security strictures on members of the branch. He pursued a policy of establishing close links with local business elites, and he claims to have had social contact with political activists such as Lee Chu-ming (Martin Lee) and Szeto Wah. In retrospect Xu showed an acute appreciation of the composition and aspirations of the middle class in Hong Kong. Although his acquaintance with Hong Kong affairs was relatively brief, he claims to have been instrumental in breaking a deadlock during the negotiations over the establishing of the Joint Liaison Group (JLG).[23] Towards the end of the negotiating period Britain remained suspicious of the proposal to establish the JLG on the grounds that it could develop into a second power centre in Hong Kong, and lead to what Xu cited as a "lame-duck" Hong Kong government. To dispel this fear, Xu claims to have proposed that the JLG should remain until the year 2000. He put this successively to Hu Yaobang, Ji Pengfei and Zhao Ziyang (his closest colleagues) at Beidaihe in August 1984. Zhao then cleared it with Deng Xiaoping. Xu's argument was that while China had no intention of using the JLG as a second power centre, Britain's suspicions could be allayed by the willingness to allow the JLG to function after sovereignty had been returned to China. If China created difficulties in the JLG before 1997, Britain could do the same subsequently.

Following Xu Jiatun's report on the reforms mooted in the 1984 Green and White Papers, which he characterized as amounting to "13 years of great change and 50 years of no change" (*shisan nian da bian, wushi nian bu bian*) the Centre subsequently shifted its policy from not interfering in the programme to insisting on gradualism and the principle of convergence with the yet-to-be-drafted BL. Xu Jiatun claims he was instrumental in convening meetings of the departments concerned and in convincing them of what he perceived to be long-term implications of the programme for developing representative government.[24] These appear to be the basis for the conspiracy theory that envisages Britain as plotting to produce a way of continuing to rule Hong Kong after 1997 through proxies. The shift in policy from passively reporting on the reform programme to actively opposing it as a breach of the JD was eventually reflected in the weakening of British resolve on the future development

22. Xu Jiatun, "Xianggang huiyilu," section 50.
23. *Ibid.* section 29.
24. *Ibid.* sections 51 and 52. Xu Jiatun claims his views were supported by a number of Chinese and foreign business elites.

of representative government, despite this having been a major factor in advocating the acceptance of the JD. The British Minister of State for Hong Kong spoke of the need for convergence with the BL and in January 1986 following his visit to China, it was agreed the British and Hong Kong governments would consult China on political reforms.[25] The consequences of convergence as they affected the composition of the legislature are shown in Table 1. The implementation of the concept of convergence was not threatened until the announcement of the Patten proposals in October 1992.

The effect of "applied convergence" is clear in Table 1, first from the retarded introduction of directly elected members and secondly from the formulation of the 1988 proposals for Legco. According to the 1988 White Paper, in 1991 ten members would be elected from geographical constituencies that would, in effect, replace ten of the 12 seats generated by the electoral college, the other two being retained as special constituencies for Urbco and Regco. Once the BL had been drafted the government "converged" on its provisions, subsequently confirmed by the NPC, for the formation of the first government and first Legco of the HKSAR, which provided the link from the 1995 to the 1999 elections. The key to this link was the concept of the legislators riding the "through train." This was, in principle, mutually acceptable until the Patten proposals of 1992 which, in particular, affected the generation of functional constituency and electoral college legislators. In practice, the Chinese side had already introduced restrictions on serving legislators following the 1989 crisis, excluding those who had supported the democracy movement and limiting the proportion who held foreign nationality or right of abode abroad.

In effect, the BL was responsible not only for establishing the main contours of the political system for the post-1997 period but also for the speed of the pre-1997 development of representative government. Once the drafting process had begun, the programme initiated in Hong Kong in 1984 was subordinated by Britain to the concept of convergence and with it, to the continuity of the 1995 legislature until 1999 (the "through train"). Even the models for the composition of the legislature that emerged from the Office of Members of Executive and Legislative Councils (OMELCO) during the crisis period in 1989 reflected an unprecedented degree of unanimity between the various factions, one seeking the direct election of 50 per cent of Legco by 1997 and another the direct election of 30 members of a 60-seat Legco in 1995, with various arrangements for a fully elected chamber thereafter, but these swayed neither the Chinese authorities nor, it would seem, the British government.

The extremely cautious expansion of democracy by the Hong Kong authorities under the influence of the British government is one of the principal characteristics of elite reaction to the impetus for change. Instead of pushing ahead with a modest programme for developing

25. Scott, *Political Change and the Crisis of Legitimacy*, p. 24.

Table 1: **The Composition of the Hong Kong Legislature 1984–2003: Applied Convergence**

| | Appointed Members | | Elected Members | | | |
| | Officials | Unofficials | Functional constituency | Electoral college | Directly elected | Total |
|---|---|---|---|---|---|---|
| 1984 | 18 | 29 | 0 | 0 | 0 | 47 |
| 1985 | 10 | 22 | 12 | 12 | 0 | 56 |
| 1988 | 10 | 20 | 14 | 12 | 0 | 56 |
| 1991 | 3* | 18 | 21 | 0 | 18 | 60 |
| 1995 | 0 | 0 | 30 | 10 | 20 | 60 |
| 1999 | 0 | 0 | 30 | 6 | 24 | 60 |
| 2003 | 0 | 0 | 30 | 0 | 30 | 60 |

*Note:*

*Excludes the President, the Governor, who from 1991 could appoint a deputy to preside in his absence. Later in 1991 Legco elected its own President.

*Sources:*

The Green Paper of 1984, the White Papers published by the Hong Kong Government in 1984 and 1988 and the announcement by the Chief Secretary, Sir David Ford, of details of an expanded Legco in 1991 (see *Hong Kong 1991*, HK Government Printer) and the Basic Law of the HKSAR. The Decision to expand Legco came after the finalization of the text of the Basic Law in Guangzhou in February 1990 (Norman Miners, *The Government and Politics of Hong Kong*, 5th edition (Hong Kong: Oxford University Press, 1991)).

representative government in line with Hong Kong's economic and political progress, their policy, until the advent of the final text of the BL, was to expand functional constituency representation which, in effect, institutionalized the traditional practice of absorbing particular talents into the administrative system. In itself, that was no bad thing; it was, however, open to the challenge of remaining essentially undemocratic at a stage when a directly elected element in Legco was highly desirable. Moreover, as has been argued in the Patten proposals, the generation of functional constituency representatives could have come from an extended, rather than a narrowly based, franchise.

The expansion of the functional constituency representation and the confirmation of the role it is to play after 1997 is also a reflection of the reaction of the Hong Kong business elites to the changing situation. The business community, which for the past two decades has become increasingly dominated by Chinese capitalists, has consistently lobbied to restrict participation. Its lobbying was evident at the time of the issue of Green Papers in 1984 and 1987 and through representatives on the BLCC and BLDC between 1985 and 1990. The strength of this lobby was increasingly evident in the proceedings of Legco where its members always dominated the appointed cohort and where, in the 1991 chamber, it had eight representatives from functional constituencies.[26] Following the sweeping success of the liberal politicians in the 1991 direct elections (notably the United Democrats[27]) and the subsequent intensification of the trend away from an elite-dominated consensus towards a form of confrontational politics in Legco proceedings after the introduction of an elected element, the business community redoubled its efforts to safeguard its vested interests.

The remarkable change that was ushered in first by the results of the 1991 elections[28] and secondly by the policies of a new Governor in 1992 produced a more politicized legislature. The group that had hitherto supported the government, mainly the appointed members and their functional constituency allies, now found themselves in opposition to the Patten proposals and to many causes espoused by the liberal members. In the late 1980s the business community had seen no need for greater organization than that which had enabled them to lobby the British and Chinese authorities to safeguard their interests. It is noteworthy that Xu Jiatun not only courted the financial magnates of Hong Kong but, if his published memoirs are to be given credence, was congratulated either directly or indirectly by local and foreign members of the business elite for his stand against the proposals that appeared to herald direct elections in 1988. As already shown, this stand evidently led to the inauguration of

26. Commercial (2), industrial (2), financial (2), real estate and construction (1), tourism (1).

27. The United Democrats of Hong Kong, led by Martin Lee Chu-ming, Szeto Wah and Yeung Sam, became a party in 1990 on the basis of a 1989 coalition of democratic groups including the HKO, Meeting Point and the Hong Kong Affairs Society. See n. 17.

28. See n. 17. The only "conservative" party, the Liberal Democratic Federation, fielded five unsuccessful candidates who gained 5% of the vote.

the concept of convergence with the associated arrangement known as the "through train."

## Political Institutionalization

The reaction of the business elites led to the formation of the Liberal Party on 28 February 1993 prior to its official launching on 18 July 1993.[29] The preparatory committee for the party emerged from a group entitled the Co-operative Resources Centre (CRC) that was itself formed by 21 appointed and functional constituency members of Legco in November 1991, early in the term of the 1991–95 legislature when the United Democrats and their allies were flexing their political muscle. At the time, the CRC benefited from the privilege (if not the anomaly in a polity that was, according to the terms of the JD, ultimately to have an executive accountable to the legislature) of overlapping membership of the Exco and Legco. Four CRC members, including its leader Allen Lee Peng-fei, were Executive Councillors. Thus, on the one hand they advised the Governor on policy and, on the other, voted on it in the Legco in the fashion of the traditional system that was deemed to have served Hong Kong so well.

Shortly before the formation of the CRC, the overlapping membership of Councils was to generate a major problem for the Governor, Sir David Wilson. By declining to appoint any directly-elected member of the United Democrats (UD) to Exco despite the convincing electoral victory of that party, the Governor appeared to compound the illogicality of the situation and rub salt into the wound by elevating a less prominently partisan figure.[30] Sir David's successor, Christopher Patten, avoided this vexed question in 1992 by separating Council membership. This brought the CRC–UDHK dichotomy into sharp relief in the legislature. Together with the prospect of an all-elected legislature in 1995, when the business elites would no longer have support from appointed representatives, this was a strong incentive to minimize the gestation period of the Liberal Party.

The Liberal Party has links with the influential Business and Professionals Federation (BDF) and the "conservative" Liberal Democratic Federation (LDF). As an indicator of the non-confrontational bridging role it aimed to play, while still in its CRC embryonic phase it sent a delegation to Beijing. Its aims for the 1995 elections were evident in its efforts to reduce the prospects of the UD by promoting the adoption of

29. The section on the Liberal Party is based substantially on an interview with its leader Allen Lee Peng-fei on 14 July 1993 and documents made available at the time.

30. See n. 17. Although the explanation offered was based on the refusal of United Democrat Leaders to take the oath of confidentiality, it is widely believed that opposition by China to the elevation of the leaders was a major factor in British Hong Kong policy. Both Martin Lee Chu-ming and Szeto Wah (the former Hong Kong's most outspoken liberal campaigner for human rights, political reform and livelihood issues such as opposition to the Daya Bay nuclear power plant, the latter a "patriotic" liberal proponent of democratization in Hong Kong), had been accused of "counter revolutionary activities" in July 1989 and removed from the BLDC by the NPC on 31 October 1989.

a multi-seat, single vote constituency system in place of the existing dual seat, dual vote system. The latter, it was claimed, had enabled the UD to gain more seats than their support actually justified owing to the "coat-tails" effect it produced whereby a strongly preferred "best" candidate attracted support for a running mate.[31] A leading member of the CRC, Ronald Arculli, chaired a Legco committee whose recommendations included replacing the dual seat, dual vote constituency system.[32] In the 1991–92 session of the legislature, despite the strength of the UD, the CRC influence remained formidable. Its members headed over 50 per cent of the OMELCO panels, bill vetting *ad hoc* groups and sub-commit-tees compared to fewer than 10 per cent by members of the rival UD. Outside the legislature, the CRC, and now the Liberal Party (LP), enjoyed the support of the Hong Kong business elites and through them, in matters of common interest, that of Chinese business elites whose inter-ests in Hong Kong have increased dramatically in scope and substance in the 1990s.

The aim of the Hong Kong business elites is, above all, to safeguard their position after 1997. The business community in Hong Kong appears to take the view that the promotion of business and avoidance of confrontation are the keys to stability and prosperity in Hong Kong and China, and are a better guarantee for the future than the promotion of democracy. Accordingly, both Hong Kong and Chinese business elites have a shared interest in forging alliances. If the modernization and transformation of China accelerates without interruption, they may be vindicated and institutional development should follow. If, however, the process is interrupted, the absence of an established and adequate legal-institutional framework in Hong Kong, such as that required to meet new demands from civil society, could leave its business community more vulnerable to political interference than would otherwise have been the case.[33]

Having succeeded in establishing the parameters of political reform in the 1980s, the central government in Beijing focused in the 1990s on establishing the parameters of the high degree of autonomy promised for the HKSAR in the JD and on preparing the first generation of post-col-onial leaders. Together with the concept of an executive accountable to the legislature, a high degree of autonomy was one of the main features which enabled Britain to recommend the treaty to the people of Hong Kong.

The most conspicuous example of China curtailing the autonomy of Hong Kong was the controversy over the building of the new airport. In withholding support for an extended period from the announcement of the Port and Airport Development Strategy (PADS), in the terms of the

31. See Rowena Kwok, Joan Leung and Ian Scott (eds.), *Votes Without Power, The Hong Kong Legislative Council Elections 1991* (Hong Kong: Hong Kong University Press, 1992).

32. Legislative Council of Hong Kong, *Report of the Select Committee on the Legislative Council Elections* (Hong Kong: Government Printer, July 1992).

33. See John P. Burns, "The process of assimilation of Hong Kong (1997) and implications for Taiwan," *AEI Foreign Policy and Defense Review*, Vol. 6, No. 3 (1986), pp. 19–26.

Memorandum of Understanding (MOU), whose signing required the British Prime Minister's presence in Beijing in 1991, the Chinese government succeeded in establishing the parameters of Hong Kong's economic autonomy well before 1997. At the same time, the parameters of political autonomy have been further clarified by the central government's policy on maintaining the present relatively expansive, executive-led Hong Kong government. After the success of the UD in the 1991 elections, the call for a standing committee system for Legco, to supersede the specialist panels and the role of the *ad hoc* bills committees and create committees involved in policy-making – a step in the direction of a legislature-led government – was vigorously and successfully opposed by the central government and its state agencies in Hong Kong. Similarly, the proposals to corporatize Radio Television Hong Kong (RTHK) were criticized by China and subsequently dropped on the grounds that the department had increased its efficiency to the level at which corporatization was no longer deemed necessary.

### Enter Christopher Patten

While the Chinese government was successfully establishing the parameters of Hong Kong's political and economic autonomy, and preparing to groom the first generation of post-colonial leaders through the appointment of advisers and by supporting the launch of a new pro-Beijing political group, the Democratic Association for the Betterment of Hong Kong (DAB),[34] the British announced at the end of December 1991 that Sir David Wilson would retire in July 1992. The naming of his successor would await the results of the British general election in April 1992. The decision to replace the Governor was made shortly after the British Prime Minister's 1991 visit to Beijing to sign the MOU on the building of the new airport. It is therefore an inescapable conclusion that the wrangle over the airport project was one factor in the decision to retire Sir David. Following the election, it was announced that the new Governor would be the Rt. Hon. Christopher Patten P.C., a leading Conservative Party politician. Thus, while the Chinese government had replaced a politician with a career diplomat in Hong Kong, the British government now replaced a career diplomat with a politician. Within three months of taking office, Patten announced proposals indicating a major shift in policy on Hong Kong.

The so-called Patten Proposals were one part of a wide-ranging policy review by the British and Hong Kong governments.[35] Much of the review, while vitally important, was eclipsed by the attention subsequently devoted to the section in which the proposals were made, entitled "The

34. The first group of Hong Kong advisers (44 people) was inaugurated on 11 March 1992. See the *South China Morning Post*, 12 March 1992. The DAB was founded on 10 July 1992 by pro-China Hong Kong activists. Its programme, which includes dialogue with China, is aimed at grass-roots electoral politics.

35. *Our Next Five Years: The Agenda for Hong Kong* (Hong Kong; Government Printer, 1992).

Constitutional Package." The stated aims were to produce an executive-led government accountable to the legislature, to broaden the participation of the community in Hong Kong's affairs, and to devise arrangements for the 1994 and 1995 elections that would command the community's confidence and support. There were two main elements in the constitutional package which rankled Beijing: immediate changes to make representative institutions more effective and accountable; and the preparations for the 1994 District Board and 1995 Municipal Council and Legco elections.

The changes proposed addressed the question of the evolving relationship between Exco and Legco and, implicitly, between Legco and the government. The Governor proposed and implemented the separation of the two Councils to enable each to perform and develop different roles. For the foreseeable future, Exco would comprise distinguished independent members of the community and senior officials. Thus there would be no non-official members of Legco on Exco. Accordingly, the members of the legislature would enjoy greater autonomy, Legco would have its own secretariat, elect its own president and continue to determine its own rules of procedure. The gap thus created between the Councils, signalling the demise of OMELCO, was to have been bridged by the creation of a government–Legco committee to discuss legislative and financial programmes. That proved impossible to achieve in 1992–93 owing to disagreement over membership in Legco. Lastly, the Governor would attend Legco each month to answer questions on policies. The separation of Councils eliminated the embarrassing and illogical situation that had prevailed since 1991 when the most popular political party, the UD, had been excluded from Legco apparently because of Chinese opposition.

Regarding the 1994–95 elections, the stated aim was to develop democratic participation within the terms of the Joint Declaration and the Basic Law. The proposals advanced *for discussion* were: to lower the voting age to 18; to adopt a single-seat, single-vote first-past-the-post voting system; to expand the franchise for the functional constituencies by replacing corporate voting with individual voting and to add nine new functional constituencies (converging numerically on the BL), thus extending the franchise to 2.7 million people; to replace appointed membership of Municipal Councils with elected membership in 1995; to increase the role and funding of the District Boards which, with the exception of the New Territories ex-officio members, would be directly elected from 1994; and, unless the BL were changed, to generate ten seats in 1995 from an Election Committee composed entirely or mostly from the membership of directly elected District Boards. The Governor emphasized that he had two objectives in the proposals, namely to extend democracy while working within the BL.[36] The inference that may be drawn is that this shift in policy reflected British disappointment at the Chinese interpretation of the JD in the provisions of the BL, exasperation over the post-1989 wrangles and a wish to seek improvements, both

36. *Ibid.*

substantial and cosmetic, in the remainder of the transition, as a basis for a more honourable withdrawal.

The immediately negative Chinese response to the constitutional package was coupled with an ardent refusal to discuss it. The reasons given for the reaction were that the proposals breached the JD and the BL and violated an agreement reached between Britain and China in early 1990 on the method of constituting the Election Committee. The substantive reason was that, if implemented, they would make bureaucratic control of the three tiers of representative government less certain. When Patten subsequently visited Beijing he made no progress whatsoever. To judge by his public statements, the Chinese failed to demonstrate to him how the proposals actually breached the JD and the BL. To answer the claim that they broke an accord reached in early 1990, in late October 1992 the British side released the English text of secret exchanges, which disclosed that the agreement did not exist. A close reading suggested that it would have been possible had the Chinese side further increased the number of directly elected seats to the Legco, but that did not happen.[37] The Chinese side maintained its public position that it would not discuss the proposals until March 1993 when attempts through formal and informal channels brought the two principals close to agreement on opening talks. Meanwhile, the Governor, already designated a "triple violator," had been subjected to a colourful range of gratuitous insults. By gazetting two related items of legislation, the Boundaries and Electoral Commission Bill and the Electoral Provisions Miscellaneous Amendments Bill in February and March 1993, he appeared unilaterally bent upon introducing the constitutional package to the legislature. Had he done so, the intended outcome was finely balanced between liberal progressives and conservative pro-China members. Even if the package were rejected, the function of Legco would have been enhanced. In any event, the dispute in which Patten enjoyed majority but diminishing support further politicized the Hong Kong electorate.

### The Road to Resolution?

The principal obstacle to holding "talks about talks" was the issue of Hong Kong's participation. The Chinese side viewed this as a revival of the "three-legged stool" concept, unsuccessfully advanced by Britain in 1982 to enable Hong Kong to participate in the negotiations. It was surmounted by the principals agreeing that the two sides would be represented by the British Ambassador and a Chinese Vice-Minister for Foreign Affairs respectively, while the Hong Kong Secretary for Constitutional Affairs could attend as a non-negotiator.

Whether a compromise could be reached depended largely on the perception of the Chinese authorities, both central and local, of their

37. Exchanges between the British and Chinese Sides in January–February 1990 on constitutional development in Hong Kong, released by the Government Information Services, Hong Kong.

position and interests in Hong Kong. The central authorities represented by Lu Ping were stimulated to accelerate their plans for managing the transition and installing the first generation of post-colonial leaders. A second group of 49 advisers was named at the end of March; and the 57-member (30 from Hong Kong) Working Committee for the Preparatory Committee of the Special Administrative Region, under the Foreign Minister, Qian Qichen, was endorsed by the NPC on 2 July 1993. These moves showed that China had made significant progress towards establishing what had been threatened for Hong Kong soon after the promulgation of the Patten proposals, namely the setting up of a second "stove," or power centre, in Hong Kong. The profile of the advisers was revealing: among the 92 was a preponderance of NPC, CPPCC, Guangdong Provincial Congress members and pro-China business people. It was particularly noteworthy that the political group which had the greatest representation was the newly-founded Democratic Alliance for the Betterment of Hong Kong, followed by the Liberal Party, the New Hong Kong Alliance and the LDF, all in the pro-China camp. Significantly, no member of the UD, or any of the liberal political groups in Legco, was included among either the advisers or the members of the Preparatory Committee.[38]

While the central Chinese authorities orchestrated these constitutional and institutional measures for the resumption of sovereignty and the exercise of control, the policy of regional authorities, notably those in Guangdong and Shenzhen, was to continue to benefit from, and therefore to strive to preserve and develop, their lucrative economic links with Hong Kong. Over 60 per cent of the direct foreign investment in China, much of it located in the Pearl River Delta of Guangdong, comes from Hong Kong. Some three million people are employed there by almost 20,000 Hong Kong manufacturing enterprises engaged in outward processing.[39] Interest in the stability and prosperity of Hong Kong is therefore dominant. To a large extent this coincides with the interests of the central bureaucracies. Both seek capital investment from, economic integration with and an increasing return on investments in Hong Kong. It is evident that each of these quests is currently being met. Moreover, the capacity of the Hong Kong stock market both to list and to support the flotation of major Chinese enterprises, as geographically and functionally diverse as, for example, the Qingdao Brewery and the Guangzhou Shipyard, against the background of an acrimonious political dispute over the Patten proposals, is evidence of a sustained level of economic and political confidence in the Greater China economic region centred on Hong Kong.

Although central and regional economic interests may coincide, Guangdong and Shenzhen players have a much more hands-on relation

38. *Guangjiaojing (The Mirror)*, Hong Kong, 2 April 1993; *South China Morning Post*, Hong Kong, 23 June 1993.

39. See Edward K. Y. Chen, "Foreign direct investment in East Asia," *Asian Development Review*, Vol. 11, No. 1 (1993), pp. 24–59; and Robert F. Ash and Y. Y. Kueh's article in this volume.

ship with Hong Kong, based on export-orientated manufacturing and trading, than the central bureaucracies. They are therefore more sensitive to any political change that can disturb that relationship. Without Hong Kong in its present form, their economies and the growing aspirations of their populations would be the first to suffer. This implies that while a substantial degree of overlap exists between the Guangdong and Shenzhen perception of political change in Hong Kong and that of the Centre, at the regional level there are sensitivities enhanced by commercial interest. There is, therefore, an immediate awareness, because of local priorities, of the linkage between, for example, prosperity and the continuation of Most Favoured Nation trading status with the United States.

The phenomenal regional economic development that shapes provincial attitudes to Hong Kong is also a major consideration in determining mass reaction to political change in Hong Kong. It is regarded as essential to Hong Kong's continuation in its present form that the estimated 500,000 members of the key middle class should remain there, but for a large number of them the reversion of sovereignty, however patriotically satisfying and legitimate, is fraught with anxiety. For some, the solution is simply to leave, despite the uncertain economic future abroad. For others, the answer is to try to bring about political change in Hong Kong. Yet others, notably many in business for whom the buoyancy of the economy is of paramount importance, bend with the wind and try to work within the evolving system. For several years before 1989, emigration figures were rising. It took time, however, for the authorities to acknowledge their seriousness. 1989 confirmed the worst fears of many, and the number emigrating in 1990 rose to the present annual total of 60,000. Between a quarter and a third of them are key professionals. The government response was to increase the provision for tertiary education; in turn, the British government inaugurated the British Nationality Selection Scheme (BNSS) providing up to 50,000 heads of household with British nationality and the right of abode, as an insurance to discourage them from emigrating. It is arguable that had it not been for the economic recession of the 1990s which hit the favoured destinations of Canada, Australia and the United States, while the economy of the Greater China region boomed, the exodus would be even greater.

The economic growth and prospects of Greater China have not only stemmed a rising tide of emigration, but brought a slight ebbing as some people, with the right of foreign abode earned, returned to Hong Kong. Among those who remain in Hong Kong, the reaction to the controversy over political change ranges from the resigned powerlessness of some, notably the working and lower middle classes, who feel unable either to leave or to influence the situation, to the activism of those involved in local politics. Among the latter, are the mature political groups who fought the 1991 elections, seasoned campaigners in electoral politics, and the newcomers, the Liberals and the DAB. The Liberals, as noted above, are supported by most of the business community, for whom political change tends to be subordinated to a materialistic interpretation of stability and prosperity. They will, therefore, contest the next elections supported by the BPF and the Chinese Enterprises Association, a "chamber of commerce" for Chinese state corporations and provincial business interests launched in 1990 under the aegis of the NCNA, seeking to ensure their economic power is carried over to the all-elected 1995 Legco. The DAB, apparently enjoying the support of the PRC apparatus in Hong Kong and staffed by experienced activists, represents an important reaction to the debate over political change. Its performance, judged by the organization of the headquarters in Wanchai and the calibre of the staff, could have a significant political impact on the outcome of the 1994–95 elections. If the DAB does enjoy some success in the elections, it will be one example of the impact of political change to emerge from the interaction of the indigenous and exogenous factors described. The others include: a significant reduction in the autonomy of the Hong Kong administration, as shown by the elevation of the PADS and other issues to the JLG for bilateral agreement between Britain and China; and the functioning of the post-1991 Legco, which has brought a much greater transparency and accountability to the governing of Hong Kong.

## Prospects for the Future

Clearly, the impetus for political change and the reaction to it, both from the elites and various sections of the general population, have had a big impact on Hong Kong. This has intensified as the date of retrocession approaches. By 1990, with the publication of the Basic Law, the long-awaited scriptural authority for constraining the pace of development of representative government and for the perpetuation of the executive-led system, was put in place. Within a few months, China had also succeeded in wresting more control over major aspects of economic development from the Hong Kong government when Britain signed the Memorandum of Understanding on the new airport. In 1991, the elections, held against the background of the 1989 crisis, produced a "new-look Legco." This enhanced the accountability and transparency of the government of Hong Kong. Moreover, the government could no longer approach Legco with any certainty as to the outcome. The trend has been even more pronounced since the implementation of the Patten proposal to separate the two Councils, thereby encouraging the exercise of greater autonomy by Legco. Consequently, Legco has become an arena in which those with an electoral mandate seek, in practice, to substitute legislature-led for executive-led government. The internal and external impact of this contest, which dominates the 1991–95 term, is self-evident. In some areas, the government has been affected by immobilism, as in the case of matters connected with the airport and the abandoned attempt to corporatize RTHK; pressure on the civil service has mounted and unprecedented challenges become both enervating and potentially demoralizing. Through Chinese eyes, the continued politicization of Hong Kong, aided and abetted by the new Governor, is evidence that the political control of Legco is imperative.

The reaction to the Patten proposals has to be viewed in this general context. If, for example, a finely balanced Legco could thwart, however temporarily, the attempts by Britain and China to implement a proposal agreed by the JLG in 1991 to establish the Court of Final Appeal in Hong Kong, and in April 1992 force budgetary changes, what havoc could be wreaked after 1995 by an "uncontrolled" elected Legco? It could be composed of liberal democratic members generated not only in direct elections but also, in considerable proportion, from the old and new functional constituencies by virtue of the designation of new constituencies and a much wider franchise, and also from the electoral college, by virtue of being based on the directly elected members of the District Boards. It could, through re-distributive social policies, increase taxes and adversely affect business sentiment. It could emulate Taiwan's legislature and also encourage pluralism in China. Accordingly, the new Governor must either be forced to compromise or be faced with certain defeat in Legco. The independent non-aligned members of the Council will, therefore, be the focus of concerted "united front" pressure. What was perceived to be at stake accounted for the hostile reaction of China and its supporters in Hong Kong.

During the controversy, it is noteworthy that opinion polls (themselves testifying to the degree of politicization that had occurred in Hong Kong over the past decade) continued to show support for the political groups advocating greater democratization. This suggested that while popular opinion was against matters that generated confrontational politics, the Chinese counter-offensive had not yet achieved the results it sought. For example, see the results of three half-yearly polls by the Hong Kong Polling and Business Research Company of popular views of eight political groups and their leaders concerning their upholding of the interests of the people of Hong Kong, as shown in Table 2.

The Public Opinion Programme of the Social Science Research Centre of the University of Hong Kong, which tracked the popularity of the Governor and the public's satisfaction level over his policy speech, showed his popularity to have varied from a high of 65.5 in a poll taken on 7–8 October 1992, to 53.3 on 15–16 December, 54.35 on 27–28 April 1993 and 57.65 on 9–10 June 1993.[40] The level of satisfaction over the policy speech, on the basis of collapsed data (with dissatisfaction in brackets) has ranged from 33.5 (3.9) on 7–8 October 1992, 41.7 (9.7) on 3–4 November, 26.4 (13.9) on 11–12 January 1993, 26.1 (13.8) on 24–25 March to 30.1 (10.9) on 9–10 June. As a percentage of those expressing an opinion (omitting the 52.2 per cent "don't know"), the June poll showed 63.1 (22.9).

These polls indicate not only the level of politicization in Hong Kong

40. I am grateful to the Social Science Research Centre at the University of Hong Kong for giving me access to the data. I am responsible for the interpretation. The preceding (April–August 1992) and intervening trackings have been omitted; the aim here is to show the range and relative stability of the ratings. The shifts can be correlated with events such as the gazetting of the proposals and related legislation in February and March, and the progress of the talks.

**Table 2: Polls of Popular Approval of Political Groups and Leaders, 1992–93**

| Group | 16–18 July 1992 | 12–13 January 1993 | 1–5 July 1993 |
|---|---|---|---|
| *Those giving support for increasing the pace of democratization* | | | |
| UDHK (Xianggang Minzhu Tongmeng) | 67.70 | 61.79 | 61.74 |
| Association for Democracy and People's Livelihood (Minzhu Minsheng Xiejinhui) | 62.19 | 60.39 | 61.50 |
| Meeting Point (Huidian) | 57.71 | 56.35 | 58.14 |
| Hong Kong Democratic Foundation (Minzhu Cujinhui) | 55.90 | 53.11 | 56.39 |
| *Those giving little or no support for increasing the pace of democratization* | | | |
| The Liberal Party (formerly the Co-operative Resources Centre) (Ziyoudang, formerly the Qilian Zeyuan Zhongxin) | 55.28 | 55.56 | 58.55 |
| The Democratic Alliance for the Betterment of Hong Kong (Minzhu Jiangang Lianmeng) | 52.06 | 49.16 | 52.59 |
| The New Hong Kong Alliance (Xin Xianggang Lianmeng) | 53.58 | 52.05 | 52.57 |
| The Liberal Democratic Foundation (Ziyou Minzhu Lianmeng) | 53.03 | 52.11 | 51.91 |

*Note:*
Figures are mean ratings on a scale of approval of 1–100, with 50 as "pass."

*Source:*
Data from polls conducted in Cantonese provided by the Managing Director of the Hong Kong Polling and Business Research Company, Citi Hung Ching-tin. I am responsible for the interpretation and the categorization of the political attitudes of the groups towards democratization.

but also a popular perception of the need for some further advance in democratization. If the Patten proposals are implemented without any weakening adjustment – which, given China's hostility and the disposition of the forces in the legislature, is unlikely – the indigenous impetus for further political change, notably to the post-1997 political structure, would undoubtedly increase.[41] Under the present arrangements, unless there is a change of policy in China permitting improvements to the political structure, the conduct of government and the process of politics in Hong Kong could remain convoluted. This is illustrated by the procedure followed to determine the franchise for the Western (Third) Harbour Crossing, an airport core project.[42]

This deal, struck in July 1993, is instructive as a case study in that it reveals both the systemic problems characterizing the existing stage of political change in Hong Kong and an emerging degree of realism and pragmatism in the practice of government and the process of local politics. The details of this remarkable tripartite Legco, business interests and government deal are as follows. The government tabled the legislation following an agreement to award the HK$7.5 billion franchise to the sole bidder, a consortium. This is 48 per cent owned by the China-controlled CITIC Hong Kong, CITIC Pacific and China Merchants Holdings; the other members are the Hong Kong Cross Harbour Tunnel Company and Kerry Holdings. The deal had been submitted to and approved by the JLG before its presentation to Legco. Apparently, in view of Legco's disputatious record since 1991, a deputy director of the State Council's Hong Kong and Macau Affairs Office was moved to warn Legco against meddling with the agreed franchise. The Hong Kong government took a similar, if less minatory, position, fearing that any amendment to the bill, which affected a key part of the infrastructure for the new airport, would involve a bilateral re-negotiation in the JLG. Legco was offended about being asked, effectively, to "rubber stamp" a deal in which it had played no part, incorporating pre-determined fee levels that appeared to promise an unreasonably high return on investment. In the event, the threat of an all-party rebellion was averted, avoiding a direct confrontation between China and Legco, when the Liberal Party abandoned what was seen as its original vote-catching proposal. This had been to reduce the opening toll from HK$30 to HK$25. Instead, it proposed a ceiling of 16.5 per cent return on investments (in place of 15–18 per cent) with any surplus paid into a fee equalization fund which could be used to subsidize profit levels, thereby obviating the need for substantial fee increases, should traffic be less than predicted. This proposal, which was accepted and which allowed the bill to proceed, was thought to have been cleared outside Legco with the Chinese business interests concerned. Many of the more liberal members of Legco (such as the UD and their allies) remained

41. The potential for this is shown by the forming of a Full Democracy in 1995 Movement, by a number of legislators and other political activists. See *South China Morning Post*, 15 July 1993.

42. See *South China Morning Post*, 14 July 1993.

critical variously of the cost of the deal and of the implications of surrendering Legco autonomy over the determination of future fee levels, but they were not able to prevent it going ahead.

The significance of this case study is that it epitomizes the complexity of the present stage of political development in Hong Kong. The main players, the government, Legco with its two dominant parties, the Hong Kong business elites, the Chinese business elites and the two principals, Britain and China, are all represented and involved. As a core airport project, and in keeping with what is becoming a relatively common practice in important policy matters, the government submitted the franchise details to the JLG for approval prior to submitting them to Legco. The legislature was divided and the decision, by a majority vote in favour of a slightly amended version of the legislation, was a reflection of realism and pragmatism in face of heavy pressure. The outcome, judged by the approach of the government in the chamber, was not absolutely certain until the amendment was approved. Clearly, despite external pressures to adopt a realistic and pragmatic approach, Legco may not always be so amenable. In future it may indeed meddle substantially in agreements that have been reached elsewhere.

This suggests that political change has brought Hong Kong to the stage where unless China effectively gains control of the post-1995 Legco (which, as far as direct elections are concerned, the current opinion polls indicate may not be easy) a destabilizing confrontation in the legislature could indeed be difficult to avoid. In these circumstances, the control of Legco is likely to be determined by the new electoral arrangements for 1994–95. Accordingly, China may be expected to seek to maximize the etlectoralopportunities of its supporters in the new functional constituencies and to ensure that it can influence the indirect elections from the Election Committee. Meanwhile, the debate over the Western Harbour Crossing will characterize the political process in Hong Kong in the 1991–95 legislature.

# Social Change in Hong Kong: Hong Kong Man in Search of Majority

## Hugh D. R. Baker

In 1983 when *The China Quarterly* published a special issue on Hong Kong, I attempted to synthesize the history of its urban social life, coining the term "Hong Kong Man"[1] to describe what I considered to be the emergence of an identifiable unique social animal. Hong Kong Man, I suggested, was neither Chinese nor British. I characterized him as quick-thinking, flexible, tough for survival, excitement-craving, sophisticated in material tastes, and self-made in a strenuously competitive world. He operated in the context of a most uncertain future, control over which was in the hands of others, and for this as well as for historical reasons he lived "life in the short term."

In the past ten years much has happened to deal hard blows to this new being. Political events in China have shaken not only Hong Kong but the rest of the world, attempts at political reforms in the territory itself have led to soul-searching, and the conviction that others (notably China and Britain) were to shape its future more or less regardless of local opinion has strengthened after some heady glimpses of a greater degree of self-determination. This article asks whether the decade has brought about any substantial change in social life.[2]

*Population*

The population of Hong Kong in 1982 was estimated at 5,287,800. By the 1991 census it had risen to 5,822,500[3] and was rising at a rate of just 1 per cent per annum, giving an estimated total of 5,902,100 for the end of 1992. Of this figure 60 per cent were born in Hong Kong (57 per cent in 1981) and 34 per cent in China. Assuming that the proportion of non-Chinese in the population has remained more or less constant at around 3 per cent there is 3 per cent which is probably largely accounted for by ethnic Chinese born outside China and Hong Kong, some of whom will be the children of returned emigrants now holding foreign passports. The trend in natural increase of population is steadily downwards, from 12 per 1,000 in 1981 to seven per 1,000 in 1991, reflecting a decline in the birth rate from 17 per 1,000 to 12 per 1,000 in the same period. This trend has been shown clearly in census returns on the change in age distribution of the population: in 1981 24.6 per cent of the population

---

1. Hong Kong Man of course includes Hong Kong Woman, the attitudes I describe being common to both.

2. I am especially grateful to Professor Wong Siu-lun for his perceptive and constructive comments on my original draft and I have incorporated many of his suggestions in this final version.

3. Unless otherwise indicated statistics are taken from the Hong Kong Government's Annual Report *Hong Kong 1993* or from earlier reports in the same series.

were under 15 and 6.6 per cent were over 65, while in 1991 the equivalent figures were 20.9 per cent and 8.7 per cent. Mortality has remained constant at around 4.9 per 1,000, but suicide and self-inflicted injuries have risen from 520 in 1981 to 814 in 1991, a proportional increase of nearly half as much again. Life expectancy at birth is now 74.9 years for males and 80.5 years for females.

In 1983 it was still meaningful to divide discussion of social life between urban and rural, that is between Hong Kong and Kowloon on the one hand and the New Territories on the other. At that time the population of the New Territories had already risen steeply owing to resettlement to new towns (in 1971 17.2 per cent of the population lived in the New Territories, and this had risen to 26.1 per cent in 1981), but by 1992 43.6 per cent of the total population lived in the New Territories, the great majority in large new urban estates. This increase has had the effect of swamping (indeed well-nigh obliterating) what might have otherwise been called the "rural" people, though a 1983 article showed that even ten years ago they led a life of only doubtful rurality.[4]

There is little point today in drawing a distinction between urban and rural as virtually all Hong Kong now pursues an urban life-style, though it might be worth rehearsing here the vanished differences. When Hong Kong island was ceded by the Treaty of Nanking in 1842 and when Kowloon was ceded by the Convention of Peking in 1860, they were barely inhabited. Almost all the people of whatever origin who came to live in them were or had intended to be short-stayers only. Historical process turned many of these sojourners into permanent residents, and their children and grandchildren became the stuff of which Hong Kong Man was made. However, the 99-year lease of the New Territories which came into force in 1898 brought with it a large settled population of perhaps 84,000[5] who lived in villages and practised an almost entirely agricultural economy. Their forebears had in some cases inhabited the same settlements for up to 1,000 years, and they were permitted a considerable degree of freedom from interference by British administrators who honoured conscientiously enough the 1899 undertaking of Governor Sir Henry Blake "that your commercial and landed interests will be safeguarded, and that your usages and good customs will not in any way be interfered with."[6] These were not short-stayers but people who belonged. During the Japanese occupation of Hong Kong from 1941 to 1945, the population shrank by out-migration from about one-and-a-half million to a mere 600,000, but the decrease largely affected the urban populations of Hong Kong and Kowloon, not the rural New Territories people who had less need and almost no desire to leave the area. Similarly the great leap in Hong Kong's population from 600,000 in 1945

4. James L. Watson, "Rural society: Hong Kong's New Territories," *The China Quarterly*, No. 95 (September 1983), pp. 480–490.

5. H. D. R. Baker, *A Chinese Lineage Village: Sheung Shui* (London: Cass, 1968), p. 4.

6. In *Hong Kong Sessional Papers*, No. 93 (1900).

to nearly six million in 1993 has been as a result of in-migration to the cities and subsequent natural increase in this new population.

Generally speaking, then, it is useful to consider the indigenous rural population as a comparatively stable one, the dramatic volatility in numbers occurring in the urban areas. It was not until the late 1950s that there was any great change in the New Territories. The reasons for it were a push and a complementary pull: the push was the post-war boom in exports of cheap rice from South-east Asia and elsewhere which made it uneconomical to grow rice in Hong Kong as a means of livelihood. The rice-farmers abandoned their fields but could not easily find alternative employment with so many new immigrants flooding into the territory from China during and after the civil war which culminated in the Communist victory of 1949. The pull was the unexpected interest in exotic cuisine which swept Britain once the post-war austerity years had passed. Chinese food (or what passed for Chinese food) was different, it was cheap, and it could be provided with apparent authenticity only by Chinese cooks. Entry to Britain was denied the hungry but paperless refugees who had been pouring into Hong Kong, but the people of the New Territories had been born in British territory into settled communities and could provide plenty of witnesses to that effect. They were thus able to obtain British passports, which gave unrestricted access to Britain until the Commonwealth Immigrants Act of 1962 took effect. In 1951 there were only 36 Chinese restaurants in all of Britain,[7] but by 1984 the number had swelled to some 7,000 restaurants and take-aways.[8] The owners, managers, waiters, kitchen-hands and cooks, the vast majority of them men, came almost entirely from the New Territories. After the Commonwealth Immigrants Act it became much harder for new applicants to gain admission to Britain, but the dependents of those already granted admission could and did join them. An impetus to do so was provided by fears for the future engendered by the riots and uncertainties of the Cultural Revolution in China, and by 1971 over 2,000 were being admitted each year. The British Nationality Act of 1981 was implemented in 1983: it made it still harder for new immigrants to get into the country, but by that time a near-saturated restaurant market in Britain and Western Europe was no longer exercising the same magnetic influence, and probably most of those who had wanted to leave the New Territories had by then done so.

The old rural life based on a double-cropping season, traditional forms of periodic market activity, discrete tight-knit villages (in some cases walled and moated), large-scale patrilineal groups of kin with well-established affinal ties, and conservative immobile religions (especially ancestor worship) was heavily disrupted by the changes. And once the New Territories had become targeted for development and population overspill from Hong Kong and Kowloon, that rural life rapidly became a

7. Ng Kwee Choo, *The Chinese in London* (London: Institute of Race Relations, 1968), p. 10.

8. Anthony Shang, *The Chinese in Britain* (London: Batsford, 1984), p. 27.

thing of the past, neither familiar to nor wanted by the young people growing up there. In the past two or three decades the area has become urbanized not only in terms of settlement, but by the factories, power-stations, educational establishments, communication facilities and other trappings of urbanization which have moved there too. The indigeni still enjoy a certain privilege but they are few and can no longer be deemed a significant group, save perhaps that some of them have become more than averagely wealthy from land sales. It is now feasible to consider all three constituent parts of the territory as a whole.

## Housing

In 1983 more than 40 per cent of the population were housed in government-built accommodation, mostly in large new estates of high-rise blocks, serviced by schools, shops, light-industrial areas, and planned communications and transport networks. Historically the Hong Kong government involvement in public housing dates back to the early 1950s when large numbers of people were made homeless overnight in a series of disastrous squatter area fires. The earliest blocks had only the most primitive and basic facilities,[9] but as the programme developed so better and more spacious accommodation was planned, and the modern blocks, while not lavish, have been built to standards which compare with private-sector buildings. In 1992 some three million people (approximately half Hong Kong's population) were living in the 645,000 flats and 144,000 self-owned premises provided by the Hong Kong Housing Authority, and these were being built at the rate of 40,000 units a year, many of them (for obvious reasons of availability of space) in the New Territories. The trend to house-ownership noted in 1983 had become well-established, and the government had embarked on a scheme of selling off public housing to sitting tenants at preferential rates. Despite this extraordinary record of public housing provision which is matched by a vibrant private sector building programme, a government estimate of the squatter population at the end of 1992 is of nearly 274,000 people, and even if the playing-field remains level squatting will not be eliminated until the turn of the century.

Pressures of space of course impose limitations on the size of household groups, and it would be idle to seek for substantial evidence of large-scale co-residential kinship groupings in contemporary urban Hong Kong. The lineage and possibly the extended family group survive in the older-settled parts of the New Territories, though even there ties are weakening and it was never common for large numbers to live in one household. In 1983 I felt able to affirm that "the home and the family are at the centre of most people's lives," and it appears that as a general statement that still holds true, but it disguises some slippage in quality of adherence to traditional familial values. To measure that slippage qualita-

9. H. D. R. Baker, "Life in the cities: the emergence of Hong Kong Man," *The China Quarterly*, No. 95 (September 1983), pp. 469–479 at p. 472.

tively is not easy, but some indication is given by the steadily growing incidence of divorce. In 1983 3,734 divorce cases were heard in the District Court, while in 1992 the figure had risen to 8,067. I said in 1983 that "old people are nearly all looked after by their families and even the most hard-bitten town-dweller professes horror at the idea of putting the aged into nursing homes," yet the number of residential hostel and other care-and-attention places in the territory has increased from 5,845 in 1982 to 12,841 in 1992. This is despite the stated government policy of encouraging care of the aged inside the community, and while it may partly be a result of changing age ratios caused by greater longevity, there is also a growing reluctance or inability of families to take responsibility for their old people. Nelson Chow may have exaggerated the extent of the change when he stated that:

the family system here is rapidly losing most of its traditional functions, the family shedding most of its responsibilities on to society[10]

but there is some substance in the trend which he identified.

## Social Services

In 1983 social security was rudimentary and normally assisted only those who were in the direst need, seriously disabled or over the age of 70. At the end of 1982 218,069 people were drawing disability and old age allowance. This had risen to 501,200 by the end of 1992, the increase partly accounted for by a lowering of the minimum qualifying age to 65. Other social welfare benefits now include payments to single parent families, victims injured in crimes of violence, traffic accident victims and victims of disasters. The government also funds family services centres, child care centres, and youth services such as youth centres, social work teams targeted on areas of high juvenile crime rates, the Duke of Edinburgh's Award Scheme and services for young offenders. All social security benefits are non-contributory. Despite these provisions, the official philosophy has assumed that the family remains the proper seat of social care, and this philosophy is reflected in *Hong Kong 1993*:

The Social Welfare Department and a number of non-governmental welfare agencies provide a variety of family and child care services with the overall objective of preserving and strengthening the family as a unit through helping individuals and families to solve their problems or to avoid them altogether.[11]

Full-time education is compulsory between the ages of six and 15, and is provided free or at highly subsidized rates in government-run or government-aided schools, but private schools heavily outnumber public sector institutions and reflect the high value which parents continue to put on education. Eighteen per cent of the post-secondary school cohort go on

---

10. Nelson Chow, "The past and future development of social welfare in Hong Kong," in Joseph Y. S. Cheng (ed.), *Hong Kong in Transition* (Hong Kong: Oxford University Press, 1986), pp. 403–419 at p. 409.

11. Hong Kong Government, *Hong Kong 1993* (Hong Kong, 1993), p. 160.

to tertiary education in the territory. There are three universities, two polytechnics and two other degree-awarding colleges, as well as various other post-secondary institutions, and all these bar two offer adult education courses at various levels. Some 18,000 students leave Hong Kong to study abroad each year, with Australia, Britain, Canada and the United States being the main recipients.

Health care is partly government-run and partly subsidized or private. The total number of hospital beds of all kinds has increased from 22,500 in 1983 to 26,412 in 1992, though this represents only a slight improvement in the ratio of beds to population size. Cancer, heart disease and stroke are the principal causes of death but the general standard of health is high, and life expectancy continues to rise. AIDS appeared in the territory in the mid-1980s, with three deaths in 1985; of the total number of cases (73) 14 were reported in 1992. Drug abuse (mostly heroin: 94 per cent of reported cases) remains a serious problem. There are no accurate figures for the number of addicts, the Hong Kong government operating on the basis of an estimated 0.8 per cent of the population aged 11 and above (it was estimated at 0.75 per cent in 1982). Even this figure, which may be an underestimate, means that in 1992 there were some 38,000 active addicts, of whom 90 per cent were male. The 10 per cent who were female shows an increase on the 1982 figure of 6.5 per cent. A 1990 survey indicated that abuse of other drugs by students in secondary schools and technical institutes was on the increase.


*Employment*

Hong Kong has virtually no natural resources other than its people, and the majority of the work-force of 2.8 million employed are in the service trades (restaurants, hotels and shops) and the manufacturing sector (principally textiles and clothing, electronics, and fabricated metal products). In 1982 manufacturing was the largest employer (over 40 per cent of the territory's work-force) and the most important sector of the economy, but by 1992 it had lost that dominant position, employing only 23.5 per cent and slipping to third place in the GDP contribution table. Unemployment is estimated at just over 2 per cent, though in some sectors, notably the construction industry and domestic service, there is a labour shortage, and some foreign workers are recruited. The economy has remained buoyant, but recent high inflation has made life more difficult for many wage earners. The 1991 rate of 12 per cent, for example, reduced their purchasing power by more than 1 per cent, and in 1992 inflation was still running at 9.4 per cent. Direct taxes are light, not even the wealthiest paying more than 15 per cent of their total income, while goods attracting duty are limited to oils, alcohol and other beverages, tobacco, and cosmetics. The pace of work for everyone does not seem to have decreased over the past decade: many continue to work a seven-day week, "moon-lighting" helps to top-up family finances, and problems of commuting to work extend the working day to 12 or more hours for large numbers of people. Men comprise 64 per cent of the workforce, with 36 per cent women, a ratio unchanged over the past ten years.

## Leisure

The chief leisure activity for Hong Kong people remains eating. The proliferation of restaurants of all kinds and at all levels of cost and sophistication testifies to a concern with satisfaction of this basic and socially cohesive desire. From noodle and offal stalls, fast-food shops, and *dim-sam* restaurants at the cheaper end of the market, the choice rises through steak-houses, the standard Cantonese restaurants, other Chinese and exotic cuisines, gourmet sea-food restaurants, and up to exclusive dining clubs patronized by only the very wealthy or those with expense accounts. Even the old Bank of China building, in 1967 a bristling arsenal in support of the downfall of Hong Kong culture, now houses the gourmet China Club on its top floors. Families still compete for table space in restaurants on Sundays. Hong Kong people are among the world's highest consumers of protein, the territory's daily consumption being 8,060 pigs, 410 head of cattle, 280 tonnes of poultry and 550 tonnes of fish; these in addition to 920 tonnes of rice, 1,020 tonnes of vegetables and 1,460 tonnes of fruit.

Hong Kong remains a highly literate society. Nearly 40,000 people were employed in the printing and publishing industry in 1992, and while much of their product was exported (principally to Australia, Britain, China, Taiwan and the United States) there is a healthy local consumption of reading matter, with a growing number of bookshops and 54 public libraries stocking more than 4 million books. In 1983 55 Chinese and six English language newspapers were published daily. By 1992 these had reduced to 37 in Chinese and two in English, but there were also another 28 non-daily newspapers and over 600 periodicals. Censorship of the press is almost non-existent:

Two of the freedoms which Hong Kong presently enjoys are freedom of expression and freedom of the press. Compared to other Asian countries, Hong Kong probably has one of the most free news media, second only to Japan. Chang Kuo-sin, former head of the Communication Department at the Hong Kong Baptist College, has said that, except for the few occasions when the government has taken action against newspapers to protect public security, the press is allowed an extent of freedom that is equal to that in any democratic country. More significantly, Hong Kong is the only place ... where the Chinese language press enjoys press freedom. Publications which are banned in China and Taiwan are freely published and circulated here.[12]

The Hong Kong film industry produced 376 films in 1992 (the figure for 1983 was 118). There were 175 cinemas (90 in 1983) showing both local and imported films. Cinema audiences were down to 47 million in 1992 compared with 61 million in 1983, and this represents a drop in annual visits to the cinema from over 11 per head of population to just

12. Emily Lau, "The news media," in Cheng, *Hong Kong in Transition*, pp. 420–446 at p. 420.

under eight. Even so, the attraction of the cinema may be considered to have held up well when seen in the context of the competition from four local wireless television programmes (two broadcasting in Chinese and two in English), six satellite television programmes and burgeoning sales of video cassettes. In 1983 93 per cent of households owned a television set; in 1991 this figure had risen to over 98 per cent, and 68 per cent also owned a video recorder. From ten radio channels in 1983 there were 15 (some Chinese, some English and some bi-lingual) in operation in 1992, five of them broadcasting 24 hours a day.

It has been commonly said by expatriates over many years that Hong Kong is a cultural desert. There is little justice in that view whether levelled at Chinese or Western culture. World-class and world-famous orchestras, soloists, dancers, actors, artistes and artists pass through the territory in a constant stream, and many of them give performances while there. Nor is local talent unexploited. The Hong Kong Chinese Orchestra, the Hong Kong Philharmonic Orchestra, the Hong Kong Dance Company, the Chung Ying Theatre Company, the Hong Kong Ballet, the Exploration Theatre and the Hong Kong Repertory Theatre are the professional tip of a large iceberg of amateur drama and music groups; and training is provided by the well-appointed Hong Kong Academy for the Performing Arts which was awarded degree-granting status during 1992. The government and both corporate and private sponsorship support many artistic activities, and in 1990 the Foundation of Businesses in Support of the Arts was set up to channel funding for all kinds of artistic endeavour. The Hong Kong Arts Centre was visited by 1.1 million people in 1992, and the Hong Kong Cultural Centre by more than 3.5 million. The annual Hong Kong Arts Festival attracts artists from many countries and in 1992 was attended by more than 90,000 people. In the same year the Urban Council ran a programme of 325 cultural events attended by more than 230,000 people. With these and other activities, as well as ten museums, there is obviously a substantial and growing interest in the arts in Hong Kong. It is perhaps true, however, that something of an imbalance is developing between the Western and the Chinese side. Both traditional and modern Western art forms are well represented, but traditional Chinese arts are less in evidence (and sometimes then only in dubiously authentic or debased forms such as dragonboat racing or lion dancing), while the intrusive internationalization of contemporary music and drama may sap the development of modern Chinese forms.

Sport is highly popular, with soccer, swimming, basket-ball, badminton, table-tennis and athletics predominating. A large percentage of the population swim at either the 42 approved beaches or the 27 public swimming complexes (the official estimate is that some 20 million visitors used these facilities in 1992). About 40 per cent of the land area of the territory is occupied by 21 country parks, and their use for walking, picnicking and camping has increased steadily over the decade (there were more than 10 million visitors in 1992). Many parks and gardens of various sizes, a botanical garden and zoos provide some relief from the otherwise unrelieved concrete of the urban areas.

Horse-racing (or to be more accurate, gambling) is, as in 1983, the first love of many Hong Kong people. On race days, twice weekly from September to May, the two tracks are filled to capacity, and radio and television programmes give non-stop coverage. The government takes large sums in betting taxes and in a tax on admission charges, but the Royal Hong Kong Jockey Club is still able to make enormous sums available for charity work in the territory. The two race-tracks and associated off-course betting shops are the only places where gambling can legally take place in Hong Kong, and those gamblers who wish to indulge at other times but remain within the law take ship (or more usually hydrofoil or jetfoil) to Macao, 40 miles away across the Pearl River estuary. There they can gamble 24 hours a day at blackjack, roulette, *fantan*, big-and-small, baccarat and other games, or bet on dog-racing and *jai-alai*. Despite the law, many people in Hong Kong regularly play *mahjong*, snooker, cards and domino-games for large sums of money.

Many of the 3 per cent of the population who are non-Chinese are expatriate workers in white-collar and management positions. They are for the most part temporary residents only, working on contracts or perhaps on a career basis, and at the end of their time will move on or back to their country of origin. Most of them are employed on favourable terms with high salaries, subsidized or free housing, school fees paid for their children, and generous leave allowances with overseas passages paid. They live in the higher grades of accommodation in the quieter areas of the cities, entertain in their homes (few Chinese have the space to do so), patronize expensive restaurants, hotel bars and clubs, and enjoy the more costly sports such as sailing, riding, tennis and golf. Few of them learn to speak or understand Chinese: they tend to be confined to areas of activity which are normally conducted in English, and they consider themselves to be sojourners for whom it would be a waste of effort. For all that, they generally subscribe to the same "work hard – play hard" ethic as the Chinese. Of the many nationalities and ethnic groups who make up this non-Chinese community, those from the Philippines and the Indian subcontinent are the least typical. The vast majority of the former are employed on short-term contracts as domestic servants, and the latter tend to be permanent residents with a long family history of settlement in the territory, forming closed groups distinguished from others by their religion, their skin colour and their distribution among all socio-economic levels. They too conform to the strong work-ethic of Hong Kong.

## Recent Trends

In the past ten years Hong Kong has continued down the same path of social development: trends have become better established, and the people of the territory have shown a greater awareness of their own identity and a greater appreciation of the unique advantages of their situation. The most noticeable change has been in their becoming sensitive to political issues. Some of the issues are universal: the enactment of a justiciable Bill of Rights in June 1991 reflected considerable public concern with questions of human rights. Sexual equality, too, has become a focus of public and media attention. While the proportion of women in the labour force has remained unchanged over ten years, their spending power and voice in the community has been greatly heightened. The government implemented separate tax assessment for husband and wife in April 1990, and even the hallowed tradition of the male-biased inheritance system of the New Territories has recently been called seriously into question. Much of the politicization has been triggered by the imminence of the end of British rule.

When Hong Kong was founded in 1842 it is unlikely that many saw it as a place of permanent settlement. British, Chinese and other arrivals at the infant colony could only have considered it as a place in which to do business and from which to retire. For the expatriates that view has remained. There have been few (other than the South Asian community) who have decided positively to end their days in the territory, and many have stayed only a few years. For all these Hong Kong has been and is a place to live life in the short term.

For the Chinese it has been different. On the one hand there were the indigenous peoples of the New Territories, those who belonged but who were not fully drawn into the economic, political and social embrace of Hong Kong until the 1950s. Before that they could think in the long term, expecting no upheavals to change their established agricultural way of life, growing their crops, and trading their produce over the easily-crossed border with China and the small market town of Shenzhen. The suddenness and the totality of the change which was imposed upon them may paradoxically have saved them from much misery. In the space of a mere 30 years the "great wen" of urban Hong Kong had fastened upon their land, their way of life had been completely annihilated, their old landmarks had been built over, their villages abandoned or razed to be built higher for profit or for perceived comfort, and they themselves had in many cases deserted not just the countryside but the territory too. It may seem callous to do so, but it is objectively reasonable to assume that those who remain are hardly to be reckoned with.

On the other hand there were the newcomers, the people who had come to Hong Kong to seek their fortune in the early years, followed later by the hundreds of thousands who fled to Hong Kong in advance or in the aftermath of the Chinese Civil War. They and even their children may have thought of Hong Kong as a temporary haven, but history has taught them otherwise, and for their descendants Hong Kong is all they have ever known. The border with China is not physically hard to cross, but since 1949 there have been ample political, economic and social reasons why it was not desirable to leave Hong Kong for China. Stuck in Hong Kong without option of either advance or retreat from it, they have thrown themselves into building a good life there. It has been their hard work and energy which have fuelled the economic wonders of the past four decades, and they have with reason grown to be proud of what they have created. More than the indigenous New Territories people it is these people who really "belong" in Hong Kong and it is to them that Hong Kong may be said rightly to belong.

But belonging implies permanence, and permanence is what Hong Kong has never had. It was torn by boycotts and strikes between the world wars, taken by the Japanese in 1941 and held until 1945, threatened by the United States with return to China when the Japanese left, a poor relation of Shanghai until after the Pacific War, swamped to bursting with refugees in the late 1940s and early 1950s, economically crippled by the United Nations embargo on China trade during the Korean War of 1950–53, flooded with refugees again at the end of the three bad years following the Great Leap Forward in China, in danger of paralysis if not collapse during the Great Proletarian Cultural Revolution in 1967–68, hurt by the oil crisis of the early 1970s, barred by unfriendly tariffs from the free trade with others which it believed in practising, terrified and angered by the tragic events of 4 June 1989 in Tiananmen Square ... and always, whether the government in China was Imperial or Nationalist or Communist, there was the knowledge that Hong Kong was not recognized there as being a permanent separate entity. It was really only the fat years of the 1970s and early 1980s which could lull the territory into wishful belief in permanence, and the start of the Sino-British talks on Hong Kong's future soon dispelled that. In short, for those who might be said to belong, as much as for anyone else, the temptation has always been to live Hong Kong life in the short term.

The satisfactions which Hong Kong Man seems most to enjoy are those which come with speed and give a jolt to the senses. His dedication to eating is a realization of an ideal – food gives immediate satisfaction, once eaten it cannot be taken away from him, and hunger can return for satisfaction again and again. Drug-addiction works the same way. "Getting rich quick" and the seeking for material rewards by the shortest route are similarly satisfying. Gambling gives the kind of kick to the senses that he appreciates, and sometimes it brings rewards too. The old slow religion of ancestor worship taught patience and to think in terms of benefit to the family over many years, so that what you worked for perhaps your grandson might eventually obtain, but such a philosophy no longer fits: Hong Kong Man left his ancestors behind in China, and he now worships gods which move with the times, which promise him (not his son or his grandson) wealth and success, and which he can abandon for others if he finds them to be failing him. He goes to the powerful Wong Tai Sin Temple or to famous temples in the New Territories to worship and to consult the fortune tellers as to the best way forward. He consults and pays good money to geomancers, practitioners of a growth-industry quasi-science, specialists who claim to be able to find him the optimum siting for his office or his furniture so that he will prosper and his rivals flag. Corruption and bribery, evils which his government have tried valiantly to fight, do not necessarily seem so bad to him – they are ways of getting instant results which circumvent the (to him) wastefully slow procedures of legitimate operation. Forgery, possession of arms and ammunition and crimes against property have been at a high level for ten years and show no signs of decreasing, and recent armed robberies have involved more dangerous and indiscriminate weapons such as hand-grenades: crime (if successful) is another way to get satisfaction quickly. Suicide, which might be termed "death in the short term," the corollary of life in the short term, has increased in the past decade from 448 in 1982 to 705 in 1992.

A recent spate of student suicides has highlighted the importance attached to education by Hong Kong Man. This seems to contradict the prevalence of the temporary expediency attitude, since clearly education is a long-term process which looks even further into the future. Yet, as Wong Siu-lun has pointed out, Hong Kong people see it as something from which to expect quick returns, a form of transferable investment and mobile capital; hence an emphasis on quick-fix "practical" degrees such as Business Administration or Finance, and an apparent decline in the popularity of the lengthy medical degrees. Education can thus be interpreted as an adjunct and an aid to the Hong Kong ethos of flexibility and transience.

The continuing boom in the private housing market seems to be another noticeable exception to the strategies of adaptability and mobility. For those who do not wish to contemplate emigration or who are unable to do so because of lack of connections or marketable skills, house purchase makes good long-term sense. House prices have continued to rise steadily over the past ten years, and a relatively modest flat of 1,000 square feet can now easily cost as much as 5 million Hong Kong dollars (US$641,000). But while the market keeps rising, house ownership is probably the most effective way of building up a capital sum with which to finance emigration or diversification, and it appears that investment in this most permanent form of property is in many minds again a short-term expedient, another form of gambling. In this light house purchase is a good bet because the loser can at least retain his stake, but that will depend on whether he has paid off or can afford to pay off the huge mortgages which keep the market afloat at present. For those who bought ten or even five years ago the rewards for selling now would be high, but everything is predicated on the holding up of the market, and if (pessimists would say "when") the bubble bursts house prices could tumble rapidly. It could take no more than a rumour to bring about a collapse, and Hong Kong has in the past been no stranger to widely-believed rumours.[13]

13. The 1921 Census returns, for example, were thrown out by under-reporting of children, a rumour having spread that the information was required to locate babies who would be buried under the piers of a planned cross-harbour bridge to strengthen the foundations (J. D. Lloyd, "Census report," in *Hong Kong Sessional Papers* (Hong Kong, 1921)). Similar rumours spread at the time of a labour dispute over the Plover Cove Reservoir dam in the 1960s, and more recently there have been panic rumours over "ghosts" seen on a television advertisement for the Kowloon Canton Railway.

*Conclusions*

In 1983 it seemed to me that "life in the short term" aptly described Hong Kong society. In many ways the description has become more apt as the pace of life has quickened with economic progress and with the desire to find a solution to life in Hong Kong by the time sovereignty is handed back to China at the end of June 1997. One solution sought by many has been to leave before that date. *Hong Kong 1992* admits:

The brain drain problem resulting from emigration in recent years continued to cause concern. To ensure that the lost stock of professionals and experienced personnel could be replenished, the government ... established a joint venture company in July to attract qualified manpower from overseas countries, including former Hong Kong residents, to come to Hong Kong to work.[14]

It gives figures for emigration of an average of 20,000 a year in the early 1980s, 30,000 in 1987 and 60,000 in 1991 (more than 23,000 of whom were in professional, technical, administrative and managerial occupations). The estimate for 1992 was over 60,000. Clearly many people had no faith in Hong Kong's prosperity continuing after 1997, preferring to take their money and their families to start afresh elsewhere. It was helpful that their desire to leave coincided with a relaxation of immigration restrictions in a number of developed countries, notably Australia, Canada and the United States. Some, having fulfilled residence requirements in their adoptive country, have returned to Hong Kong to work and live, safe in the possession of a foreign passport. Some 50,000 British passports (which carry with them right of entry to Britain for dependents as well) are being issued under the British Nationality Scheme, the stated aim of which is to keep people from leaving Hong Kong by reassuring them that they can get out in future should they wish to do so. Entry visas to the United States are being issued under the Deferred Immigrant Visas Scheme with similar aims. Wong Siu-lun has argued persuasively that the desire for emigration may be naturally part and parcel of the kind of economic dynamism which has characterized the "four little dragons" of East Asia, and that the brain drain should be seen in this perspective.[15]

What has emerged from the tense period since the conclusion of the Sino-British Agreement on the future of Hong Kong is the loss of certainty of purpose of Hong Kong Man. If it is not too gross a paradox, one could say that he had grown accustomed to operating permanently in the short term, seeing his brash confident life-style as continuing into the future with constantly increasing rewards. The Agreement set a limit to the familiar pattern of that future and forced him to consider the long term. Despite the efforts of Britain and China to find a formula which would reassure him, he did not like what he saw, fearing that China's record of political control over its people was not such as to give him hope that he would be left to live his life as he had in the past. (That fear

14. Hong Kong Government, *Hong Kong 1992* (Hong Kong, 1992), p. 105.
15. Wong Siu-lun, *Emigration and Stability in Hong Kong* (Hong Kong: University of Hong Kong Social Sciences Research Centre and Department of Sociology, 1992).

was greatly heightened by the Chinese government's actions on 4 June 1989.) Emigration was one answer; another response was to press for political reforms. The introduction of democracy, he was told by eloquent intellectuals, would provide the bulwark against erosion of those features of his society – freedom of speech, freedom of the press, the rule of law – which he now realized he valued and needed. These were matters he had not concerned himself with before; they were the responsibility of government and government was something which he tolerated but if possible evaded. He was brought face-to-face with a long-term social responsibility he had previously not had to shoulder. Large numbers of people in Hong Kong decided that they should indeed take on that responsibility, and the pressure for democratic forms of government became strong. When in October 1992 the new Governor of Hong Kong, Christopher Patten, announced very modest proposals for a greater degree of democracy, the response of the Chinese government was loud and antagonistic, reawakening and confirming the fears which had been Hong Kong's first reaction to the prospect of rule from Beijing but which had been rather lost sight of in the pursuit of democracy.

Hong Kong Man has always been forced to make uncomfortable decisions to solve short-term problems. When tariff barriers were raised to block the trade in textiles on which he depended, he switched production to plastics and watches; when wigs were in demand to meet fashionable requirements for long hair, he retooled to make wigs; when fashion changed, the wig factories retooled again. When left-wing agitators tried to wreck his life-style in the late 1960s, he took the decision to ignore them. When progress demanded the latest in portable phones, faxes and computers, he equipped with them. His record for getting things right is an enviable one. The new dilemmas – to go or to stay, to democratize or to try to work the system in other ways – are tough but must be resolved. Those who have decided to stay or who have no choice but to stay have the hardest decisions to make, not least because along with the politicization of the past ten years has come a growing awareness of political impotence, and some are already advocating passive acceptance of China's will.

For those accustomed to thinking in the short term the four years that remain before Britain bows out still constitute a breathing-space and the gamblers still have good odds to calculate. Who knows better than Hong Kong Man that much can happen in four years.

# Macau and Greater China*

## Richard Louis Edmonds

Macau was the first port on the China coast to come under the influence of a foreign power and will be the last to return to Chinese sovereignty. Its historical importance in the early transmission of culture between East and West is well known.[1] After reaching its height as the centre of such contact in the second half of the 16th century Macau, like Portugal, languished in international affairs albeit with subsequent brief periods of relative importance.

Macau is by far the smallest entity in Greater China: neighbouring Hong Kong is more than 62 times larger and has roughly 11 times its population.[2] Although small, Macau has had a unique role to play in its relationship with the People's Republic (PRC), Hong Kong, Taiwan and overseas Chinese. The purpose of this article is to describe the internal workings and special functions of the territory and to assess Macau's position in Greater China in the coming century.

### Politics and Administration: Slow Localization

From the beginning the Portuguese in Macau were subject to constraints from the Chinese empire which did not recognize Portugal's claims to sovereignty until 1862. With the signing of a protocol in 1887, Macau's administration began to be amalgamated with Portugal. However, since the anti-government riots in Macau during 1966 and 1967, Portuguese control over the territory has been slipping although its presence in the administration is still evident. After the 25 April 1974 coup d'état in Portugal, the Portuguese government informed the PRC of its intention to leave Macau. China refused to discuss the issue as there were economic and political expediencies in maintaining Portuguese

*I should like to express my thanks to Bruce Taylor of the University of Macau for providing considerable literature as well as helpful comments on this paper. I would also like to thank Maria Gabriela dos Remédios César, former Director of the Direcção dos Serviços de Economia de Macau for supplying Macau trade statistics.

1. Books on the history of Macau in English include the works of Charles Ralph Boxer, *Seventeenth Century Macau in Contemporary Documents and Illustrations* (Hong Kong: Heinemann, 1984), *The Great Ship from Amacon: Annals of Macao and the Old Japan Trade, 1555–1640* (Macau: Instituto Cultural, Centro de Estudos Marítimos, 1988), and *Fidalgos in the Far East 1550–1770: Fact and Fancy in the History of Macao* (The Hague: Marinus Nijhoff, 1948) as well as the book by Carlos Augusto Monalto de Jesus, *Historic Macao* (Hong Kong: Oxford University Press, 1984), and there are numerous works by Portuguese authors including Benjamim Videira Pires and Manuel Teixeira as well as a smaller number in Chinese and other languages. For more on the historical literature see: Richard Louis Edmonds, *Macau* (Oxford: Clio Press, 1989) and Richard Louis Edmonds, "Resources for research: a bibliography," in R.D. Cremer (ed.), *Macau: City of Commerce and Culture, 2nd Edition: Continuity and Change* (Hong Kong: API Press, 1991), pp. 353–58.

2. Although its importance has increased due to rapid economic growth since the 1970s most discussions of Greater China to date have ignored the territory. As an example see Pamela Baldinger, "The birth of Greater China," *The China Business Review* (May–June 1992), pp. 13–17.

colonial rule.[3] However, from then on Chinese influence in Macau rivalled that of the Portuguese and Macau's administrative status began to change.

The promulgation of the *Estatuto Orgânico de Macau* (Macau Organic Statute) in 1976 can be taken as a turning point in Macau's administration as it gave the territory greater political autonomy. The sinification of Macau's political system began in 1979 when China and Portugal concluded a secret agreement defining Macau as Chinese territory under Portuguese administration.[4] Article 31 of the 1982 Chinese Constitution created the framework for the return of Macau's sovereignty by allowing the government to establish "special administrative regions" whenever necessary.[5] In May 1985, President António Ramalho Eanes and Prime Minister Zhao Ziyang issued a joint communiqué in Beijing agreeing to negotiate the question of Macau. Its fate was decided in March 1987 by the joint Sino-Portuguese declaration which went into effect on 15 January 1988.[6] Macau's current status will be maintained until 20 December 1999.[7] From that date, like Hong Kong in 1997, it will become a special administrative region of the People's Republic of China.

Since the mid-1980s the Portuguese government has resisted the Chinese government's complete domination by threatening to withdraw unilaterally from Macau. Such a move would not only destabilize Macau, but also affect Hong Kong. In this manner the Portuguese gained room to

3. Francisco Gonçalves Pereira, "The political status of Macau," in Cremer, *Macau*, pp. 270–72 points out the Chinese government's attitude that the Macau issue should be mutually settled at an appropriate time was contradictory to its calls for revolution in places such as Portuguese Africa. Chiu Hungdah, "Introduction," in Chiu Hungdah, Y.C. Jao and Wu Yuan-li (eds.), *The Future of Hong Kong* (New York: Quorum Books, 1987), p. 8 notes that according to the *Baltimore Sun* (2 February 1977), p. A4, Portugal offered to turn Macau over to China on three occasions between 1974 and 1977. Reasons why China wished to delay reversion included a desire not to upset Hong Kong which would upset the United Kingdom which could upset the United States, the fact that Macau was a good place for Chinese gold transactions as Portugal had not signed the Bretton Woods agreement of 1946, and the fact that the existence of Macau as a colony could be beneficial as a scapegoat if the government needed to take attention away from domestic problems.

4. The contents of this February 1979 Paris agreement were kept secret until the signing of the Sino-Portuguese joint agreement over Macau in 1987.

5. Pereira, "The political status of Macau," p. 275. At the same time as the special administrative region idea was promulgated, Deng Xiaoping put forward the now famous idea of one country, two systems.

6. After the signing of the Sino-British Joint Declaration over Hong Kong in 1984 Chinese officials repeatedly stated that the Hong Kong situation was not relevant to the future of Macau. These words, plus Macau's small size and the Portuguese government's admission that it was Chinese territory raised hopes amongst those wishing that Macau's status would remain unchanged. However, the Chinese had merely put aside the issue until Hong Kong's reversion was resolved. In contrast to the two years of negotiations over the future of Hong Kong, the Macau talks were finished in nine months. The Portuguese negotiating team included no China experts. It is said that the Portuguese approached the U.K. Foreign Office for advice on how to negotiate with the Chinese. Consultations between Portuguese and British officials continue although there has been no attempt at concerted efforts in negotiating the Macau and Hong Kong issues with China.

7. Although the Portuguese wanted to remain in Macau until 2007 in order to make their stay in the territory an even 450 years, China insisted that the country should "reunified" prior to 2000. In any case, it is not clear in which year the Portuguese first arrived in Macau.

manoeuvre which means that while their authority in Macau has weakened, they have been able to maintain more control over decisions affecting the territory than has sometimes been perceptible from the outside.

In many respects the Sino-Portuguese Joint Declaration over Macau copies the Sino-British declaration over Hong Kong. Macau's present economic order is supposed to be preserved for 50 years after 1999. During the intervening transitional period the Portuguese government is responsible for administration while a Joint Liaison Group is to aid in exchange of information between Beijing and Lisbon. However, one significant difference is that Portuguese passport holders in Macau as of 1999 will be able to pass on their full Portuguese citizenship to their children and grandchildren thus making Portugal a sanctuary for those who desire to leave Macau after 1999.[8] In addition the Portuguese government insisted that Portuguese remain an official language in Macau during the 50-year period. There is also no stipulation that the majority of legislators in Macau's *Assembleia Legislativa* (Legislative Assembly) be elected by the date of retrogression as in the case of Hong Kong.

Macau's current administrative process is rather complex, with both Portuguese and Macau bodies possessing legislative power. In 1990 the *Estatuto Orgânico de Macau* was modified granting more local autonomy in legislative, judicial and financial matters. These modifications were meant to bring the statute in line with plans for the post-1999 government and to resolve conflicts between the Portuguese parliament and President on one hand and the Macau *Assembleia Legislativa* and the Governor on the other.[9] Macau's foreign relations are still largely handled by Portugal but many matters, particularly in relation to economic affairs, are now being delegated to the Macau government.

The Macau *Assembleia Legislativa* is composed of 23 deputies (*deputados*) with four-year tenures of office. Only eight are elected by direct universal suffrage which was implemented in 1984, with seven appointed by the Governor and eight nominated by local civic associations.[10] As together they appoint the majority of deputies, the Portuguese government and the Chinese business and civic organizations dominate local politics, often by reaching an initial consensus behind closed doors.[11] Poor election turnouts with strong support to pro-Beijing candidates

8. According to *Macau*, Ser. 2, No. 5 (Setembro 1992), pp. 93–94 the 101,223 Portuguese citizens in Macau were being issued identity cards identical to those issued in Portugal.

9. Afonso and Pereira, "The constitution and legal system," pp. 284–85. The *Estatuto Orgânico* functions as the territory's constitution.

10. There are also municipal councils for the Macau peninsula (*Leal Senado*) and for the islands of Taipa and Coloane (*Camera Municipal das Ilhas*), each with a proportion of their representatives elected. Herbert S. Yee and Sonny S.H. Lo [Shiu-hing], "Macau in transition: the politics of decolonization," *Asian Survey*, Vol. 31, No. 10 (October 1991), pp. 909–910 note that domination of the municipal councils by Macaense (persons of mixed ancestry) came to an end with the 1988 elections. Now all the elected members are Chinese with the majority pro-PRC.

11. According to Yee and Lo, "Macau in transition: the politics of decolonization," p. 906 the Macaense members as well as a small number of independent liberal Chinese deputies have been known to play key roles by breaking deadlocks. The *Assembleia Legislativa* does have some

Table 1: **Voter Participation in Elections for the Macau** *Assembleia Legislativa* **(Legislative Assembly)**

| Year | Registered voters | Ballots cast | Percentage voting |
|------|------|------|------|
| 1976 | 3,647 | 2,846 | 78.04 |
| 1980 | 4,195 | 2,600 | 61.98 |
| 1984 | 51,454 | 28,970 | 56.30 |
| 1988 | 67,604 | 20,049 | 29.66 |
| 1991 | 97,648 | 18,202 | 18.64 |
| 1992 | 48,137 | 28,520 | 59.25 |

*Source:*
Paulo Godinho, "Macau nas urnas," *Macau* Sér. 2, No. 6 (Outubro 1992), p. 105.

suggest that the Macau electorate is resigned to indirect rule up to 1999 and to Beijing's firm control over the territory after 1999 (Table 1).[12]

The highest ranking executive in Macau is the Governor who is appointed by the President of Portugal and assisted by a support structure of adjunct secretaries.[13] The responsibilities and numbers of the latter are subject to frequent changes.[14] There is no fixed term but in practice the governorship changes at the end of the five-year term of office of the President of Portugal and the adjunct secretaries change with the Gover-

---

*footnote continued*

powers which its Hong Kong counterpart does not such as amending budgets and introducing spending measures.

12. In 1990 the pro-Beijing *União Promotora do Progresso* (Union for the Promotion of Progress) got slightly under 50% of the votes cast after losing with only 34% of total votes in 1988. "Corrente 'tradicional' conquista eleitorado," *Macau*, No. 33 (Março 1991), pp. 4–5 states that the two candidates for the *União Promotora do Progresso* won the intercalate elections in March 1991 obtaining 50% of the vote. In 1992, however, an increased number of voters turned out from a substantially reduced number of registered voters to elect four conservative Chinese from two parties (two of these deputies representing the *União Promotora do Progresso* and the other two the *União para o Desenvolvimento* (Union for Development)), two liberal Chinese from two parties, one Macaense and one pro-Macau government Chinese candidate while the traditionalist Macaense *União Eleitoral* did not elect a single candidate for the first time. The next elections will be in 1996.

13. In general, the appointment of the Governor and the adjunct secretaries are subject to changes in partisan politics in Portugal. The adjunct secretaries (*secretários-adjuntos*) have no statutory powers. Although the Governor suggests who will be the adjunct secretaries with the President of Portugal approving the Governor's suggestions, in reality these posts, along with the governorship, have often been given out by the Portuguese President as gifts for political support. In Macau it appears that some lower level division chiefs are also Portuguese political appointments.

14. The current seven adjunct secretaries are responsible for: judicial affairs; economic and financial affairs; public works and transport; education, administration and youth; health and social affairs; security; and communication, tourism and culture. Legally all the adjunct secretaries have equal power but in reality the strongest one emerges as number two in the Macau government. In contrast to Hong Kong, Macau only has *Forças de Segurança* or a local Security Force, since by agreement with China no Portuguese troops have been stationed in the territory since 1975. The Governor is also advised by a *Conselho Consultivo* or Consultative Council, half of whom are indirectly elected. The *Conselho Consultivo* must be consulted on bills to be introduced to the *Assembleia Legislativa* and on significant policy matters such as development plans.

nor. Apart from two recent civil appointments, Macau's Governors have generally been military officers.[15]

At the working level are government departments (*Direcção de Serviços*), autonomous bodies and monopolies for services granted to private companies. In general the government departments are responsible to the various adjunct secretaries.[16] They are usually further subdivided into bureaus, divisions (*divisões*) and sections (*secções*) all of which have shown a strong tendency to proliferate.

Pressure groups are important in Macau's political system. The most obvious are the Chinese business and civic organizations which can appoint members to the *Assembleia Legislativa*. The number and types of Chinese pressure groups has increased since the mid-1980s.[17] These include the Chinese General Chamber of Commerce, the Federation of Trade Unions, professional associations, groups supporting various causes, *kai fong* (local neighbourhood associations) and regional benevolent associations for groups of Chinese immigrants. Many of these groups indirectly represent Beijing's interests in Macau politics.

Since September 1987 China's political arm in Macau has been led by the New China (*Xinhua*) News Agency which is guided by the Hong Kong and Macau Affairs Office under the State Council. Its role in Macau's affairs has been growing continuously.[18] In 1988 the Chinese set up a Macau Basic Law Drafting Committee which was composed of 48 members, only 19 of whom are from Macau.[19] The 145-article Basic Law's provisional draft was made open for public consultation during four months in 1991 but little debate ensued. The blueprint was adopted in Guangzhou in the spring of 1992 and it was quietly promulgated in March 1993 with much of the wording similar to Hong Kong's basic law. China also makes its opinions known through its control of some Chinese

15. Governors Joaquim Pinto Machado (1986–87) and Carlos Melancia (1987–90) were the first two civil governors in 46 years. Pinto Machado quit after one year due to political isolation and dissatisfaction with the local administration. Melancia was attacked for involvement in a scandal surrounding the transformation of state-owned Teledifusão de Macau into a limited public company in 1988 and in a bribe scandal related to the West German company Weidleplan's construction contract for the Macau airport in 1990. T.C. Lam, "Administration and public service system in Macau," in Cremer, *Macau*, pp. 325–26 assumes that Governor Melancia was accused of these crimes to get control of the appointment of Macau's Governor out of the hands of President Mario Soares and the Socialist Party. In 1991 the post of Governor was returned to a military man, General Vasco Joaquim Rocha Vieira, in an attempt to reach a consensus over the appointment in Portugal and to achieve some stability in the run up to 1999.

16. According to Lam, "Administration and public service system in Macau," p. 330 in recent years the Macau government has attempted to privatize many functions of government performed by departments as has occurred in Hong Kong.

17. Rui António Craveiro Afonso and Francisco Gonçalves Pereira, "The constitution and legal system," in Cremer, *Macau*, p. 292.

18. Yee and Lo, "Macau in transition," p. 910 refer to a *South China Morning Post* of 9 September 1990 report that the Hong Kong and Macau Affairs Office was given more powers to supervise matters relating to Macau and Hong Kong in order to ensure that the territories received consistent messages about Beijing's politics rather than cross signals from several organizations.

19. Lo Shiu-hing, "Aspects of political development in Macao," *The China Quarterly*, No. 120 (December 1989), p. 839 says the members of this committee were less liberal than those in the Hong Kong committee which explains why there has been less controversy over the establishment of Macau's post-1999 legal system.

language newspapers, most notably the *Ou Mun Yat Pou (Macau Daily News)*.

Localization of the upper echelons of the civil service is considered by Beijing to be one of the three major political issues to be resolved in Macau prior to 1999, the other two being raising the status of the Chinese language and the reform of the legal system.[20] While localization has been stated policy since the signing of the Joint Declaration in 1987 it was not until December 1989 that the government put forward its plan to increase local "leadership staff" from 50 per cent locals in 1993 to 70 per cent in 1995, 80 per cent in 1997 and finally 100 per cent by 1999.[21] However, in contrast to official policy there was actually a slight rise in the number of Macau's civil servants who are from Portugal between 1988 and 1990.[22] Of the locals who have been promoted, the majority are Macaense with most of the upper echelons of the service still recruited from Portugal for fixed tenures (usually three years).[23]

The Macau government has been keen to establish a Portuguese imprint on the Macau civil service. As of 1991 the Macau government had sent about 100 local residents to Portugal for further study and integrated them into the Macau administration upon return.[24] However, in the late 1980s, the Portuguese also decided to integrate Macau's civil servants into the Portuguese civil service after 1999. In 1992 talks began

20. While the legal system is still Portuguese dominated, laws are now being translated into Chinese, and from the end of 1993, Macau's courts will offer simultaneous translation. *Asia Yearbook 1988*, p. 175 noted that all 11 judges and prosecutors in Macau were Portuguese and *Asia Yearbook 1989*, p. 164 that not one of the 30 lawyers in Macau is Chinese. Cantonese became an official language for legal translation in May 1988. Yee and Lo, "Macau in transition," p. 916–17 note some of the difficulties the government faces in translating Portuguese laws into Chinese. Portuguese higher courts used to hear appeals against decisions made by high ranking members of the Macau government. However, an independent local High Court (*Tribunal Superior de Justiça*) composed of seven judges to judge prosecution appeals, a Court of Audit (*Tribunal de Contas*) with three judges to deal with financial control of government departments and an Administrative Court (*Tribunal Administrativo*) were established in Macau in April 1993.

21. Yee and Lo, "Macau in transition," p. 913 cite the beginning of the localization policy to Governor Melancia's visit to Beijing in May 1990.

22. *Ibid.* p. 906 points out that the Portuguese expatriate percentage went up from 11.3 to 12.4% but note that the numbers of Portuguese passport holders went down from 73.6 to 71.4% over the same period. Although Macau government officials indicate there are about 8,500 civil servants, Yee and Lo give a figure of 14,664 for 1988, the *Asia Yearbook 1992* (Hong Kong: Far Eastern Economic Review, 1992), p. 147 gives a figure of 12,000, Afonso and Pereira, "The constitution and legal system," p. 289 indicate 11,500 based on 1988 data, and Lam, "Administration and public service system in Macau," pp. 338–39 gives a 1988 figure of 9,765. These discrepancies may be due to the large number of non-established short-term workers in the civil service. Some say the recent upsurge in the recruitment of Portuguese civil servants is due to a lack of skilled locals to handle the increasingly complex administration whereas others say it is a last ditch attempt to imprint the Portuguese presence on Macau in the post-1999 era.

23. Afonso and Pereira, "The constitution and legal system," pp. 289–290 state that 45% of the highest positions in Macau's administrative hierarchy are held by administrators from Portugal. A considerable number of short-term non-established posts are filled by Portuguese from Portugal. Only about one-third of the Portuguese professionals in the Macau government remain in the territory for longer than five years. Lam, "Administration and public service system in Macau," p. 340 notes that an article in the *Si Man Yat Pou (Shimm ribao)* from 14 May 1989 stated that only one-sixth of the directors of departments were local-born Macau residents.

24. "91 As linhas de acção governativa," *Macau*, No. 31 (Janeiro 1991), p. 45. This is known as the *Programa de Estudos em Portugal* or PEP programme. A small number of Macaense and Portuguese have also been sent to Beijing Normal University for Chinese language training. Lawyers are also being trained in Beijing and school teachers at Huanan University in Guangzhou.

on integration of the security forces into the Portuguese services, with a delegation from Macau visiting Portugal to express concern about the integration of civil servants in autumn 1993. This should lead to a substantial reduction in the Portuguese–Macaense presence in the territory as well as a possible drain of well-trained ethnic Chinese personnel. It appears that about 20 per cent of Macau's civil servants would be eligible to transfer.

It seems clear that Macau will maintain its own separate status in some international organizations after 1999. Its continued membership in various tourist associations has been assured.[25] In 1991 the territory joined the General Agreement on Tariffs and Trade (GATT) as its 101st member and was admitted to the Economic and Social Commission for Asia and the Pacific (ESCAP). It also recently joined the International Maritime Organization. If Chinese control over Macau and Hong Kong affairs continues to grow, this in effect will give the PRC three votes in many international organizations.

### Land Use, Infrastructure and Environment

Lack of resources and rugged terrain, in addition to the territory's small size, have limited Macau's economic and demographic growth perhaps to a greater degree than in Hong Kong, Taiwan or south-eastern coastal China. Apart from some rocks for quarrying there are no mineral resources to speak of.[26] The Macau peninsula already has a population density of about 70,000 persons per sq.km. and 96.4 per cent of the territory's population. The two islands to the south, Taipa and Coloane, remained largely undeveloped until the 1970s. As in most traditional Chinese cities the Macau peninsula has a complex mixture of residential and industrial land uses – often within the same building. Development of the islands has been rapid in recent years and it is likely that much of Taipa will be urbanized by 1999.[27] A number of major touristic and heavy industry projects have also been completed on Coloane. It is already impossible to describe any part of Macau as rural (Figure 1). By 1999 unused land will be restricted to steep hill slopes and the need for zoning of land use will be even more critical than now.

25. *Macau Travel Talk*, Series 2, No. 187 (March 1992), p. 8.

26. Wong Hon Keong [Huang Hanqiang], "Aomen guoduqi fazhan jingji miandui de maodun ji chulu de xuanze" ("Economic development of Macau during the transitional period – its difficulties and choices"), *Aomen Yanjiu/Journal of Macau Studies*, Vol. 1 (1988), p. 6 points out a Chinese phrase for describing Macau as a place of "Three nos" (*san wu*): no resources, no capital, and no domestic market.

27. Cheong Cheok Fu [Zhang Zhuofu], "Lun Hengqin de kaifa yu Aomen nongye, zhonggongye de zhuanyi" ("On the opening of Hengqin and its effect on trends in Macau's agriculture and industry"), *Hou Keng [Haojing]*, No. 9–10 (1992), pp. 93, 96–97 notes from paper clippings that between November 1989 and the end of May 1991 infrastructural and construction investments in Taipa and Coloane totaled 8,300 million patacas with another 13,800 million patacas committed to or being raised for planned investment. This represents a tremendous growth over past investment. Yang Daokuang [Yeong To-Kwong], "Luelun Aomen de jingji fazhan yu chengshi jianshe wenti" ("A design for the municipal construction and economic development of Macau"), *Aomen Yanjiu/Journal of Macau Studies*, Vol. 1 (1988), p. 17 notes housing for 120,000 people will shortly be completed on Taipa.

Figure 1: **Map of Macau and Surrounding Area**

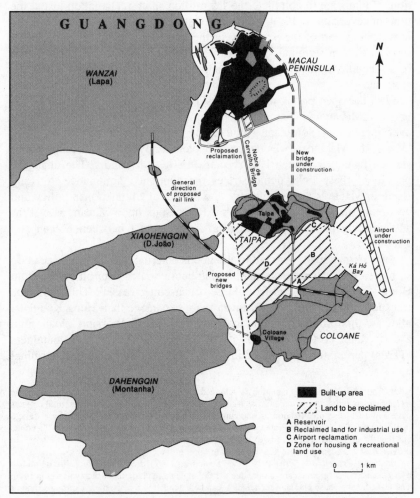

Lack of space and poor accessibility were recognized as obstacles to economic growth by the Macau government and in recent years a considerable number of infrastructural plans have begun. Ambitious reclamation plans for housing and industry were announced for areas north-east of the Macau peninsula (220,000 sq.m.) in 1988, along the Porto Exterior (1,900,000 sq.m.) on the east in 1991 and between Taipa and Coloane (4,400,000 sq.m.) in 1992.[28] However, it is unlikely that all this reclamation will be completed much before 1999. A further project to enclose and reclaim part of the territory's historic Praia Grande Bay at a cost of 15,000 million patacas began in July 1992 after delays caused

28. "Quatrocentos hectares de aterro vão ligar as duas ilhas," *Comércio de Macau* (29 de Fevereiro 1992), p. 7. According to *Macau*, Sér. 2, No. 14 (Junho 1993), p. 86 Macau and Chinese investors signed an agreement in May 1993 to develop newly reclaimed lands between Coloane and Taipa near the future airport. About one-fifth of the land is to be devoted to housing and almost two-fifths to industry.

by trouble between investors and the government over land-lease condi-tions.[29] Plans are to complete the 1.5 million sq.m. reclamation just at the time of reversion in 1999.[30] Other infrastructural projects recently begun in Macau as part of the planning for the transitional period include a new ferry passenger terminal, the port of Ka-Ho on Coloane, the construction of a second Macau–Taipa Bridge, and an airport to the east of Taipa and Coloane.

With the open policy of the 1980s, passenger vessels began travelling between Macau and Guangzhou, Jiangmen and Kao-hsiung as well as the ever increasing, dominant Hong Kong run.[31] The ferry link to Kao-hsiung, the Macmosa, was begun in September 1988 but was taken out of service from September 1992 because of low demand.[32] The changing pattern of these links demonstrates the continued dominance of Hong Kong in Macau's tourist industry, the impact of China's open policy and economic growth of the Pearl (Zhu) River delta upon Macau, as well as a continuing problem of furthering direct contact between Macau and Taiwan.[33]

Approximately 90 per cent of the goods entering and leaving Macau do so by sea with the majority of shipping being floated over on barges from Hong Kong after transfer from large ocean-going vessels. This has made transport costs in and out of Macau more expensive than Hong Kong. To alleviate this problem, a contract to expand Ká-Hó Bay on Coloane into a deep water port with a capacity to handle 80,000 standard containers (TEUs) per annum was signed in 1988.[34] Although the container terminal

29. The Praia Grande reclamation is financed jointly by Chinese, Macau and Portuguese interests as are most current major projects. Since the mid-1980s, all major infrastructural projects have had a Chinese organization as one consortium partner. Luís Santos, "Ambiente e tráfego justificam o fecho da Baía de Praia Grande," *Tribuna de Macau* (25 de Maio 1991), p. 11 points out that the enclosure will have two positive benefits: creation of a clean fresh water lake and provision of a six-lane by-pass alleviating congestion in the city centre.

30. *Macau Travel Talk*, Series 2, No. 193 (September 1992), p. 9. Twelve high-rise buildings, a hotel and an underground car park are due to be completed in phase one which will end in 1996. The lease for the phase one land reclamation can be extended to a convenient expiration date of 20 December 2049.

31. Edmonds, *Macau*, p. xlvii. Now about six million people arrive by sea annually with jetfoils carrying over two-thirds of the passengers. The increase of service has led to the construction of a new ferry terminal with a heliport on the roof to be opened in October 1993 at an estimated cost of 800 million patacas which should be able to handle a peak of 7,200 Hong Kong passengers an hour or about 13 million passengers per annum. With the link to former Portuguese Timor severed, all the current passenger sea links are with Hong Kong and China. The Hong Kong–Macau link has been useful for overseas Chinese many of whose ancestors came from the western side of the Pearl River delta and who have increasingly gone to visit this area via the territory since the early 1980s.

32. *Macau Travel Talk*, Series 2, No. 187 (March 1992), p. 9 gave 1991 loading figures for the Macmosa of 27% capacity.

33. According to Godfrey J. Harrison, "English in Macau," in Cremer, *Macau*, p. 150, Hong Kong's dominance led one Macau tourist poster to refer to the British colony as "Macau's airport." Paul Marriage and Kennis Chu, "Wu plans to transform Pearl delta," *South China Morning Post*, 29 June 1992 notes one of the most spectacular plans put forward for linking Hong Kong and Macau – a scheme proposed as early as 1988 by Hong Kong developer Gordon Wu Ying-sheung's Hopewell Holdings to build a 38-kilometre bridge and tunnel toll link between the two territories via Shekou and Zhuhai that would cut travel time to half an hour.

34. Roughly 5 to 7 tonnes of sand are deposited annually in the Lingdingyang waters near Macau adding a layer of about 1 to 2.5 centimetres of silt on the bed each year. The Ká-Hó port

at Ká-Hó was officially inaugurated in December 1991, local shippers have been reluctant to move their operations from the Porto Interior on the Macau peninsula to the new port. This problem began to be resolved in spring 1992 by the merger of some of the Porto Interior companies into the Ká-Hó operations.[35] In late 1992 work began on construction of an oil terminal near the container port site primarily to serve the new airport.[36] Future plans are to expand the total port area to 29 hectares and include construction of an industrial park.

The biggest change to the transport geography of Macau in the 20th century occurred in 1974 when Taipa was first linked to the Macau peninsula by the 2.56 kilometre Nobre de Carvalho Bridge. This began the rapid urbanization of Taipa which along with the airport project has necessitated the construction of a second bridge. The new 4.7 kilometre long, 18 metre wide four-lane bridge and viaduct was begun in 1991 and should be completed in December 1993. It will have three exits on the peninsula side, one of which goes directly to China via the Portas do Cerco and will allow passengers to go through Chinese customs at the planned airport without officially entering Macau.[37] Passing through the new Guia Tunnel, road transport will be able to get from the airport to the industrial areas in the north-western part of the Macau peninsula quickly and pressure will be taken off the Nobre de Carvalho Bridge.

Although the idea of building an airport in Macau dates back to the 1960s, it was not until September 1989 that reclamation of land and construction of an airport to the east of Taipa and Coloane began (Figure 1). However, the Macau International Airport with its 3,320 metre long runway which will be able to handle jumbo-jets should be completed by July 1995 at a cost of at least 7,500 million patacas (twice the original 1988 projected cost) and serve 4.5 million passengers plus 121,000 tonnes of cargo by the year 2000.[38] Its importance in Macau's links with

_footnote continued_

cost roughly MOP$120 million. It is being linked to Zhuhai and Hong Kong by a 200 TEU vessel feeder service.

35. Paulo Coutinho, "Um Porto-mar no Delta," _Macau_, Sér. 2, No. 13 (Maio 1993), p. 7. In 1992 Macau handled 72,000 TEUs. Approximately 20,000 TEUs were handled by Ká-Hó port.

36. This 350 million pataca terminal is being built by China's Nan Guang (Nam Kwong) Petroleum and Chemicals (95%) and the Ká-Hó port franchise holder, Macauport (5%) of which Nan Guang is a partner holding 12% of the shares. It should be completed in July 1994.

37. Clara Gomes, "Nova ponte emerge do Rio das Pérolas," _Macau_, No. 41 (Novembro 1991), pp. 46–53, "Administração e consórcio chegam a acordo," _Tribuna de Macau_ (30 de Abril 1992) and Paulo Coutinho, "A ponte do entendimento," _Macau_, Sér. 2, No. 13 (Maio 1993), pp. 10–12. The bridge is being built by a Portuguese–Chinese consortium and is estimated to cost 640 million patacas. There have been problems as the silt bed in the river cannot support the bridge without the insertion of deep concrete piles and also problems with granite boulders which required special drilling equipment, and damage caused by a typhoon during September 1993.

38. Jorge Silva, "Aeroporto: ordem para descolar," _Macau_, Sér. 2, No. 13 (Maio 1993), pp. 5–7. The Macau government's decision to start on the airport dates from a 1983 study. There have been problems which have slowed construction of the 136 hectare artificial island by about two years. This was apparently due to the slow supply and overcharging for sand and building materials from China. According to "Aeroporto em boa rota," _Macau_, No. 42 (Dezembro 1991/Janeiro 1992), p. 72 the airport reclamation requires 22.5 million cu.m. of sand. At first it was

Greater China are immense with the main route destinations expected to be mainland China and Taiwan.[39] However, it will not rival Hong Kong's new airport at Chek Lap Kok which should have capacity to handle ten times as many passengers.

A problem over the airport had developed between Macau and the neighbouring Zhuhai Special Economic Zone (SEZ). Zhuhai protested in 1990 that the development of an airport in Macau would create excessive noise levels over its area. What Zhuhai really wanted was approval by Beijing of its plan to expand a 1938 Japanese wartime airstrip on Sanzao Island into the SEZ's own airport. The consortium building the Macau airport, *Companhia do Aeroporto de Macau* (CAM), almost discontinued the project in 1990 because of the problems with Zhuhai.[40] Then Zhuhai's opposition disappeared, presumably upon Beijing's insistence, and the Macau airport plans went ahead. However, in April 1993, much to Macau's chagrin and against all odds, the Mayor of Zhuhai again proclaimed that an international airport would be built at Sanzao with

---

*footnote continued*

decided to build part of the airport on reclaimed land and part on piles as a compromise since the sand and soil will be bought from China and the piling work would probably be done by a consortium including Portuguese interests. In 1992 a decision was taken to build the whole project on reclaimed land. While there are several different consulting firms and companies involved in the project the reclamation work for the runway is being undertaken by a Chinese and Macau consortium, China Harbour Engineering. Management of the runway project has been given to a Hong Kong–Portuguese consortium known as SPP (Scott Wilson Kirkpatrick, Pengest Internacional, and Partex CPS). The terminal construction and aviation equipment was contracted to Siemans and Soares da Costa. However, over two-thirds of the construction tenders have gone to mainland Chinese interests. In December 1992 the Macau government announced its intention to become the majority shareholder in the airport by buying out other company shares. This was probably from Beijing's desire to have the airport largely under government control prior to 1999.

39. According to "Aomen guoji jichang 1995 nian wangong hou" ("After completion of the Macau International Airport in 1995"), *Zhongyang ribao* (International Edition), No. 23388 (24 October 1992), p. 7 a delegation from Macau in Taiwan during October 1992 stated that once there is direct air travel between the two territories, Nationalist Chinese citizens will be able to obtain on-the-spot visas upon arrival in Macau which will make travel between Taiwan and Guangdong faster than going through Hong Kong. Stanley Ho is supposedly interested in establishing the rights for flights between Macau and Taiwan through an airline company that he plans. According to *Macau*, Sér. 2, No. 14 (Junho 1993), p. 86 both the Chinese (CAAC) and Portuguese (TAP) national airline companies have expressed an interest in investing in a new airline called Air Macau which will initially make flights to selected Chinese destinations. Silva, "Aeroporto," p. 5 notes that airlines putting in applications to land in Macau include Lufthansa, Singapore Airlines, CAAC, TAP and KLM. Barry Grindrod, "Marketing of Macau," *South China Morning Post* (16 March 1991), stated that several East European airlines are also putting in such applications.

40. According to *Asia Yearbook 1991*, p. 156, CAM is made up of investors from Macau including Stanley Ho and the STDM (630 million patacas), the Macau government (500 million patacas), banker Edmundo Ho and real estate developer Ng Fok (120 million patacas each) as well as the Chinese consortium Chung Luen (*Zhong Lian*, 130 million patacas) and according to *Macau Travel Talk*, Ser. 2, No. 189 (May 1992), p. 1, the Portuguese investment corporation, Interfina. The *Zhongyang ribao (International Edition)*, 24 October 1992, p. 7 says the Portuguese government holds 30% of the stocks in the airport and that the group building it has a 30-year management concession. Chung Luen originally had a 500 million pataca share but was forced to reduce its investment due to foreign exchange shortages in 1990 with the STDM, E. Ho, and Ng picking up the slack.

planes being able to land on the strip by 1994.[41] Macau's small size dictates that it must follow the whims of Beijing on the airport issue in the future as the territory effectively has no air space of its own.[42] Such incidents do not bode well for future co-operation.[43]

A railway linking Guangzhou to Zhuhai is now scheduled to begin construction in 1993. The proposed line links Guangzhou to Foshan, Jiangmen and Zhongshan to Zhuhai's Gaolan Harbour and planned power station with a subsequent extension planned from Jiangmen via Kaiping to Xinxing where it will link up with the Guangzhou–Zhanjiang line.[44] During a visit by the Guangdong Governor, Zhu Senlin, to Macau in late September 1992, it was announced that the Guangzhou–Zhuhai Railway will be linked to Macau along with the planned 110 kilometre Guangzhou–Zhuhai motorway, which is due to be completed in 1996. This is a key step forward for Macau as it will give the territory a chance to compete with Hong Kong–Shenzhen for domination of the West (Xi) River delta hinterland. As well as bringing increased trade with Zhuhai, Zhongshan, Jiangmen and Foshan, where China has already made significant road improvements in recent years, these links should make Macau a favourable outport for goods from the neighbouring West River counties of Doumen, Xinhui, Heshan, Shunde and Kaiping as well as some rural areas further to the west. Plans to improve navigation on the West River will also be of great benefit to Macau's Ká-Hó port.

Current plans will enlarge the size of Macau from just under 17 sq. km. to over 28 sq. km. shortly after 1999 (Table 2). However, this geographical growth will not be enough to allow the territory to undergo the rapid economic expansion that many desire to help alleviate the estimated 250 million pataca budget deficit in 1992. One member of the Guangdong Provincial Academy of Social Sciences has advocated incorporation of Xiaohengqin and Dahengqin Islands into Macau in 1999 which would give the Special Economic Region a total area of over 50 sq. km. (Figure

41. Luís Cunha, "Guang Da: o jogador de póquer," *Comércio de Macau* (17 de Abril 1993), p. 4.

42. Silva, "Aeroporto," p. 7 says that Macau now has a guarantee of autonomy from China with regard to its own air space. "Aeroporto em boa rota," p. 73 notes that the Macau airport will have a very important role to fulfil by 1996 as its ability to handle 2.2 million passengers and 79,000 metric tonnes of cargo will take some of the strain off Hong Kong's Kai Tak Airport. Situ Huifen, "Zhuhai tun Aomen?" ("Will Zhuhai swallow Macau?"), *Guangjiaojing*, No. 238 (July 1992), pp. 42–43 gives 75,000 to 1,000,000 passengers and 11,354 tonnes of freight while *Asia Yearbook 1992*, p. 149 gives 2,000,000 passengers and 150,000 tonnes of cargo and mentions the possibility of a 6 million passenger–600,000 tonne freight capacity by 1999. Apart from these obvious functions the airport will serve as a wave blocking jetty for the Ká-Hó port. In view of this and the problems of flight traffic congestion, there will be no need for another airport at Sanzao. However, as of mid-1993, it appears that a domestic airport will be built at Sanzao.

43. According to Bruce Taylor (personal correspondence) Zhuhai has announced plans to have Formula One Grand Prix racing by 1996 which would become competition for the Macau Formula Three Grand Prix. Macau is now in the process of upgrading its own Grand Prix facilities. Zhuhai has also proposed a causeway link to Tuen Men in Hong Kong's New Territories thereby circumventing Macau's new airport and port.

44. Situ Huifen, "Zhuhai tun Aomen?" p. 43. Cheang Tin Cheong, "A coordenação das infraestruturas entre Macau e Zhuhai," *Tribuna de Macau* (27 de Abril 1991), p. 21. Gaolan Harbour should be able to handle 30 million tonnes of cargo by 1998.

Table 2: **Change in Areal Extent of Macau from Land Reclamation and Airport Construction** (in square kilometres)

|  | 1900 | 1927 | 1986 | With current projects |
|---|---|---|---|---|
| Macau peninsula | 3.38 | 5.42 | 6.05 | 11.42 |
| Taipa | 1.98 | 3.47 | 3.78 | |
| | | | | 16.63 |
| Coloane | 6.61 | 6.63 | 7.09 | |

*Note:*
    Future projects will link Taipa and Coloane.
*Sources:*
    Miguel Correia, "Em busca do centímetro perdido," *Comércio de Macau* (27 de Julho 1991), p. 9. Yang Daokuang, "Luelun Aomen de jingji fazhan yu chengshi jianshe wenti," p. 17. "Aeroporto em boa rota," *Macau*, No. 42 (Dezembro 1991/Janeiro 1992), p. 72. *Macau Travel Talk*, Series 2, No. 193 (September 1992), p. 9.

1).[45] There is historical precedent for this move as Portugal had put forward claims to these islands in the past.[46] Plans for development of Xiaohengqin and Dahengqin already exist and include bridges linking them to Taipa and Coloane. However, any decision to incorporate these islands into Macau is not likely to be made public before 1999 and will be dependent upon future socio-political developments as much as upon economic advantages.

Lack of telecommunications no longer hampers Macau's ability to compete with Hong Kong as it did in the 1970s. There has been major development which commenced in the 1980s, including the construction of a satellite communications dish on Coloane which became operational in 1984.

Recent economic growth has increased pollution at the same time as it generated the income necessary to allow Macau's populace to focus attention on environmental concerns. The hills on the Macau peninsula are still largely covered with vegetation except for Ilha Verde in the far north-west. On the islands some of the hilly areas are barren although the Macau government has been trying to revegetate them. The rapid development of Taipa and Coloane has put the remaining flora and fauna under severe threat. The lack of any wastewater treatment facilities has led to

45. Yang Daokuāng, "Luelun Aomen de jingji fazhan yu chengshi jianshe wenti," p. 21. This opinion was seconded by another member of the Academy: Chao Wai Peng, "O papel de Macau nas relações de cooperação económica entre Guangdong, Hong Kong e Macau," *Tribuna de Macau* (12 de Outubro 1991), p. A-6 who felt that these islands along with Wanzai should at the least be interlinked with Macau by bridges. According to Cheong Cheok Fu, "Lun Hengqin de kaifa yu Aomen nongye, zhonggongye de zhuanyi," p. 92 the rush to develop Xiaohengqin and Dahengqin (together known as Hengqin) began in 1990 with plans put forward to develop an export industrial processing zone. The islands' total area is 2.73 times that of Macau. Cheong feels that the economic climate is not right for developing Hengqin since Macau and foreign capital is lacking, there is little infrastructure on the islands, the population is only about 5,000 and the zone would compete with Macau for markets. Instead Cheong argues for development of agriculture as this activity has virtually disappeared in Macau.

46. Govêrno da Província de Macau & José Luis Marques, *Breve Memória Documentada acêrca da Soberania e Jurisdição de Portugal na Ilha de D. João, Macarira ou Sio-Vong-Cam* (Macau: Imprensa Nacional, 1923).

water pollution.[47] A water treatment plant and sewer are now being constructed, and a Solid Waste Incineration Centre on Taipa was completed in December 1992.[48] One waste dump in the north of the peninsula has already been filled and converted into a park but there are worries of toxic wastes polluting the surrounding waters.[49]

Since 1982 the government has been involved in sponsoring various activities during "green week."[50] The desire to continue to attract tourists has led to a growing concern for the preservation of historic buildings. Since the creation of the *Comissão de Defesa do Património Arquitectónico, Paisajístico e Cultural* (Committee for the Preservation of Macau's Heritage) in 1976, certain areas and buildings have been awarded protected status.[51] The government then gives tax reductions to proprietors as long as they maintain the building's historic character. Conservation and restoration programmes for paintings and monuments are being planned. A citizen's action group, a government standing committee on environmental problems and an environmental planning group have also been formed and a draft environmental law has recently been passed. However, the prospect of a "mundane city" with its remaining fragile areas under threat as described by Duncan and Figueira along with the rapid decay of the islands as noted by Batalha are ever more likely realities as the charm of old Macau gives way to prefabricated modernity.[52]

## The Economy: Has the Growth Bubble Burst?

It is difficult to talk about Macau's industrialization separately from foreign trade as apart from tourism the territory is totally dependent on its

47. For example according to *Tribuna de Macau*, 2 de Junho de 1990, p. 19 the government had to impose fines on anyone fishing for any species or collecting shellfish or seaweed in most of the waters adjacent to the territory.

48. According to Severo Portela, "A Central dos fumos brancos," *Macau*, Sér. 2, No. 13 (Maio 1993), pp. 14–15, the need to build a 550 million pataca waste incineration centre dates from Zhuhai's refusal to give the go ahead for a sanitary landfill of Macau rubbish in 1982. It is thought the Solid Waste Incineration Centre will provide enough capacity for Macau up to 2010.

49. "Aomen shengtai zaoshou pohuai jidai fa 'zhi' heshan," ("The destruction of Macau's environment"), *Zhongguo huanjing bao*, No. 888 (25 December 1990), p. 4.

50. Carlos Batalha, "Semana Verde de Macau," *Macau*, No. 34 (Abril 1991), pp. 56–63. In 1991 this event attracted over 22,300 participants.

51. Luís Santos, "25 edifícios e dois templos vão receber obras de restauro," *Tribuna de Macau* (19 de Outubro 1991), p. 9 notes that 18.3% of the total area of the Macau peninsula now has protected status. The functions of the *Comissão de Defesa* passed to the *Instituto Cultural de Macau* (Macau Cultural Institute) when it was formed in 1982.

52. Craig Duncan, "Development of Macau's city landscape," in Cremer, *Macau*, p. 182. For the stronger opinions of Francisco Figueira, a Portuguese architect who has been involved in preservation in Macau since the mid-1970s, see Clara Gomes, "Património indefeso," *Comércio de Macau* (12 de Dezembro 1992). For comments by Carlos Batalha see Luís Santos, "Ambiente e cimento," *Tribuna de Macau* (21 de Março 1992), p. 15. As the head of the Department of Traffic points out, Macau has already reached capacity for automobiles with ten new vehicles still entering the territory each day – Gilberto Lopes, "Carlos Nunes: 'Sem fiscalização, código da estrada não resolve nada'," *Tribuna de Macau* (19 de Dezembro 1992), pp. 16–17. Ho Wa Chun, "Melhorar o planeamento urbano," *Tribuna de Macau* (8 de Junho 1991), p. A-3 notes how serious noise pollution problems are, especially in low income areas, and suggests that the government must begin to think more about long-term environmental control.

Table 3: **Macau's Foreign Trade** (in million Macau patacas)

|         | 1987 | 1988 | 1989 | 1990 | 1991 | 1992 |
|---------|------|------|------|------|------|------|
| Exports | 11,233.5 | 12,003.2 | 13,193.8 | 13,638.1 | 13,326.0 | 14,080.1 |
| Imports | 9,017.1 | 10,375.5 | 11,879.1 | 12,343.1 | 14,832.4 | 15,684.7 |
| Balance | + 2,216.3 | + 1,627.7 | + 1,314.7 | + 1,295.0 | − 1,506.3 | − 1,604.5 |

*Source:*
Direcção dos Serviços de Economia de Macau.

ability to export. Starting from a weak base, Macau has experienced rapid growth since the early 1970s, led by textiles. The reasons for this growth include plentiful cheap labour coupled with laissez-faire government.[53] Between 1970 and 1979 textiles experienced a 29-fold increase in total exports, the GDP annual growth from 1971 to 1981 was a phenomenal 16.7 per cent and by 1990 the per capita GDP in Macau had reached 65,200 patacas or nearly double that of Portugal and roughly 20 times that of the PRC.

From 1983, diversification away from textiles and casinos began. Growth slowed and began to shift to the manufacture of artificial flowers, toys, electronic goods, ceramics and leather goods.[54] However, knitwear exports still accounted for 65 per cent of the value of all exports in 1990. Much of the industrial growth in the late 1980s was due to investors from Hong Kong taking advantage of the cheap unskilled labour, lower land prices, and their ability to export goods under a Macau rather than a Hong Kong quota to countries with protectionist tendencies. The growth in the 1980s was accompanied by an expansion of the banking sector and its services and thus complemented growth in Guangdong and Hong Kong.

Macau's source of imports can be difficult to measure as much passes through Hong Kong. Hong Kong and the PRC together accounted for more than 53.3 per cent of Macau's imports in 1992 while Japan, the USA, the EEC and increasingly Taiwan constitute other major sources. As Table 3 shows there has been a steady decline in Macau's balance of trade since the late 1980s with 1991 showing a negative balance for the first time in recent years. While this was due in part to increases in imports for the new infrastructural projects, the drop in the value of exports in 1991 is a worrying sign which was likely to have been caused by the world recession.

The problem of relative export slow-down since 1991 may also reflect

53. Renato Feitor and Rolf Dieter Cremer, "Macau's modern economy," in Cremer, *Macau*, p. 189 add geographical location, access to foreign markets and the existence of a nucleus of dynamic entrepreneurs as favourable economic growth factors.
54. Wong Hon Keong, "Aomen guoduqi fazhan jingji miandui de maodun ji chulu de xuanze," p. 5 gives a 8.6% annual growth rate for Macau from 1980 to 1985 compared with 6.9% for Hong Kong, 6.8% for Singapore, and 6.3% for Taiwan. According the the adjunct-secretary for Economics and Finance, Vítor Pessoa (Comércio de Macau (5 de Dezember 1992), p. 5), textiles in Macau still have labour costs on the order of 50% of those in Hong Kong but the levels of productivity are said to be lower than 50% of Hong Kong.

the lack of investment in manufacturing facilities. It has been hypothe-sized that lack of investment in equipment may be because of the abundance of cheap Chinese immigrant labour as well as undercapitaliza-tion of the many small family firms.[55] In addition Macau's industries have been criticized for their corruption, dependence on Hong Kong for trade promotion and lack of local training.[56] Such criticisms suggest, amongst other things, that Macau's industry would be wise to improve its average scale of operation to a preponderance of medium-sized firms producing more upgraded products.

There is another interesting trend. As Table 4 points out, Macau's negative balance of trade with other portions of Greater China has been generally growing in recent years. Taken individually we see a decline in trade balance with each polity over the six years from 1986 to 1991 with a slight rebound in the PRC and Hong Kong trade in 1992. In sum, Greater China still remains far more important as a source for imports to Macau than as a destination for exports.

As Table 4 shows, trade with the PRC has been running at a deficit. Exports are dominated by textile fabrics and thread. Imports from the People's Republic remain mainly primary materials and semi-assembled goods together with a strong growth in land fill material during 1992, presumably for the airport. To help promote Macau's trade with the PRC an Association of Chinese Enterprises of Macau was formed in mid-1992 with 148 companies represented. However, trade figures with China become increasingly less meaningful as many of Macau's enterprises are Chinese owned and a growing number of Macau entrepreneurs invest in factories in Guangdong. Kamm suggests that Chinese central control over Macau's economy has been increasing since 1985 despite claims that Guangdong's economy has become less and less controlled from the Centre.[57]

Table 5 focuses on Macau and Hong Kong's trade with the two mainland provinces most talked about in discussions of Greater China: Fujian and Guangdong. While questions can be raised about the validity of the Chinese data, the trends they show should be reliable.[58] Macau's

55. Feitor and Cremer, "Macau's modern economy," p. 190. Rolf Dieter Cremer, "Chinese entrepreneurs and enterprises," in Cremer, *Macau*, pp. 207–208.

56. Victor F.S. Sit, Rolf Dieter Cremer and Siu Lun Wong, *Entrepreneurs and Enterprises* in *Macau: A Study in Industrial Development* (Hong Kong: Hong Kong University Press, API Press, 1991), pp. 204–207. Rolf Dieter Cremer, "Economic development under conditions of inter-national dependency of the manufacturing industry," in R.D. Cremer (ed.), *Industrial Economy of Macau in the 1990s* (Hong Kong: API Press, 1990), pp. 23–24. Bao Yuhuang, "Guanyu Zhu Ao liangdi jingji guanxi de sikao" ("Economic relations between Macau and Zhuhai"), *Aomen Yanjiu/Journal of Macau Studies*, Vol. 1 (1988), p. 45. Lin Shiming, "Guoduqi Aomen jingji fazhan xuyao zhuyi de wenti de tantao" ("Economic development of Macau during the transitional period"), *Aomen Yanjiu/Journal of Macau Studies*, Vol. 1 (1988), p. 12 points out that as of the mid-1980s only one-quarter to one-third of Macau's workforce was literate or semi-literate in Chinese. Virtually the whole workforce is illiterate in Portuguese. One exception to the lack of training facilities is the government Hotel and Tourism Training Centre which saw its enrolment climb by 40% in 1990. In addition the University of Macau and the new Macau Polytechnic Institute are increasing their abilities to train people in various skills.

57. Kamm, "Macau's economic role in the West River Delta," p. 239.

58. For a start the data for Guangdong will include Hainan for 1986 and 1987.

Table 4: **Macau's Balance of Trade with the People's Republic of China, Hong Kong and Taiwan** (in million Macau patacas)

| | 1987 | 1988 | 1989 | 1990 | 1991 | 1992 |
|---|---|---|---|---|---|---|
| PRC[a] | − 1,490.5 | − 1,652.1 | − 1,877.5 | − 1,578.3 | − 2,069.4 | − 1,801.2 |
| Exports | 428.5 | 449.8 | 445.8 | 615.7 | 1,122.7 | 1,402.3 |
| Percentage of Macau exports | 3.8 | 3.7 | 3.3 | 4.5 | 8.4 | 9.9 |
| Imports | 1,919.1 | 2,102.0 | 2,323.3 | 2,194.0 | 3,192.2 | 3,203.6 |
| Percentage of Macau imports | 21.2 | 20.2 | 19.5 | 17.7 | 21.5 | 20.4 |
| Hong Kong | − 2,169.6 | − 2,819.7 | − 3,071.6 | − 3,439.8 | − 3,422.4 | − 3,396.7 |
| Exports | 1,738.4 | 1,682.9 | 1,934.8 | 1,770.1 | 1,743.1 | 1,763.3 |
| Percentage of Macau exports | 15.4 | 14.0 | 14.6 | 12.9 | 13.0 | 12.5 |
| Imports | 3,908.1 | 4,502.7 | 5,006.5 | 5,209.9 | 5,165.5 | 5,160.1 |
| Percentage of Macau imports | 43.3 | 43.3 | 42.1 | 42.2 | 34.8 | 32.8 |
| Taiwan | − 488.2 | − 541.2 | − 777.3 | − 847.0 | − 852.7 | − 918.9 |
| Exports | 2.2 | 6.0 | 16.6 | 30.9 | 44.6 | 92.2 |
| Percentage of Macau exports | 0 | 0 | 0.1 | 0.2 | 0.3 | 0.6 |
| Imports | 490.5 | 547.3 | 794.0 | 877.9 | 897.4 | 1,011.1 |
| Percentage of Macau imports | 5.4 | 5.2 | 6.6 | 7.1 | 6.0 | 6.4 |
| Overall trade with the PRC, Hong Kong and Taiwan | | | | | | |
| Balance | − 4,148.3 | − 5,013.0 | − 5,726.4 | − 5,865.1 | − 6,344.5 | − 6,117.8 |
| Percentage of Macau's total exports | 19.2 | 17.7 | 18.0 | 17.7 | 21.8 | 23.1 |
| Percentage of Macau's total imports | 69.9 | 68.7 | 68.2 | 67 | 62.4 | 59.8 |

*Note:*
[a] John T. Kamm, "Macau's economic role in the West River delta," in Cremer, *Macau*, pp. 229–230 points out that PRC and Macau government statistics on trade between the two territories often differ. Here I have relied on Macau government statistics.
*Source:*
Direcção dos Serviços de Economia de Macau.

trade with Fujian, while growing slightly in absolute value, is insignificant compared with the territory's trade with Guangdong. The level of Macau's trade with Fujian is also insignificant when compared with Hong Kong's Fujian trade. The overall picture of Macau's trade with Fujian is stagnant and there is no reason to suspect that it will ever be able to compete with Taiwan or Hong Kong.

The trends in the more important trade with Guangdong are much more worrying for Macau. The total value and proportions of Guangdong's imports from Macau have been stagnant or slipping since 1986 and while Guangdong exports to the territory have shown a modest growth in total value, their proportion in terms of both total Chinese exports to Macau and Guangdong's total exports has been stagnant. In contrast Guangdong exports are becoming more concentrated in Hong Kong and while the proportions of Guangdong imports from Hong Kong are stagnant, that performance is better than in the case of imports from Macau. To counteract this, it was jointly announced by the Governors of Macau and Guangdong in October 1992 that a semi-official organization has been founded for promotion of economic co-operation. However, it appears that Macau's small capacity is increasingly less capable of handling larger shares of the Guangdong trade.

Trade between Macau and Hong Kong is still best viewed as merely a part of Macau's general foreign trade as much merely passes through the British colony. However, the percentage of Macau's total exports going to Hong Kong slipped from 18.1 per cent in 1985 to 12.5 per cent in 1992. The leading trade items going to Hong Kong remain Macau's key export products – textile threads, fabrics and clothing along with leather products. Over 80 per cent of imports via Hong Kong remain primary materials and semi-assembled goods. Imports from Hong Kong consistently made up around 42 to 43 per cent of Macau's total imports until 1991 when they began to drop below 35 per cent (Table 4). Presumably this is a result of the direct import of products and material for the new infrastructural projects.

Trade with Taiwan, especially Macau's export trade, was negligible prior to 1989. The trade to Taiwan is dominated by Macau's key exports including knitwear, leather goods, textiles and furniture. Imports from Taiwan have exceeded exports by a substantial margin and almost quadrupled between 1985 and 1992. Almost 90 per cent of imports from Taiwan in recent years have been primary materials and semi-assembled goods. The growth in imports has been so strong that the Nationalist Chinese opened a commercial office in the territory in 1990 which sparked political squabbles between Portugal and the Communist Chinese.

Even though the trade deficit with Greater China has generally grown, recent trends suggest a reduction in Macau's dependence on mainland China, Hong Kong and Taiwan for imports while the proportion of exports to these areas remains relatively steady. The PRC's role in Macau's trade seems to be gradually increasing whereas Hong Kong's is slowly weakening and trade with Taiwan is just beginning.

Despite the poor overall trade performance with Greater China,

Table 5: **Trade Between Guangdong–Fujian and Hong Kong–Macau 1986–91** (in million United States dollars)

| | 1986 | 1987 | 1988 | 1989 | 1990 | 1991 |
|---|---|---|---|---|---|---|
| *PRC exports to Macau* | 299 | 427 | 442 | 469 | 506 | 526 |
|   Guangdong exports to Macau | 133 | 143 | 142 | 148 | 166 | 224 |
|   Guangdong share of PRC exports to Macau | 44.5% | 33.5% | 32.1% | 31.6% | 32.8% | 42.6% |
|   Per cent of Guangdong exports going to Macau | 3.1% | 2.6% | 1.9% | 1.8% | 1.6% | 1.6% |
|   Fujian exports to Macau | 5 | 6 | 4 | 9 | 8 | 8 |
|   Fujian share of PRC exports to Macau | 1.7% | 1.4% | 0.9% | 1.9% | 1.6% | 1.6% |
|   Per cent of Fujian exports going to Macau | 0.8% | 0.6% | 0.3% | 0.6% | 0.4% | 0.3% |
| *PRC exports to HK* | 9,941 | 13,778 | 18,269 | 21,916 | 26,650 | 32,137 |
|   Guangdong exports to HK | 2,955 | 3,751 | 5,725 | 6,366 | 8,543 | 11,369 |
|   Guangdong share of PRC exports to HK | 29.7% | 27.2% | 31.34% | 29.04% | 32.1% | 35.4% |
|   Per cent of Guangdong exports going to HK | 68.9% | 68.9% | 76.5% | 77.9% | 80.9% | 83.1% |
|   Fujian exports to HK | 261? | 374 | 637 | 752 | 1,057 | 1,067 |
|   Fujian share of PRC exports to HK | 2.6% | 2.7% | 3.5% | 3.4% | 4.0% | 3.3% |
|   Per cent of Fujian exports going to HK | 45.1% | 44% | 45.3% | 45.3% | 47.2% | 36.5% |
| *PRC imports from Macau* | 76 | 109 | 147 | 146 | 161 | 172 |
|   Guangdong imports from Macau | 41 | 66 | 64 | 57 | 36 | 64 |
|   Guangdong share of PRC imports coming from Macau | 53.9% | 60.6% | 43.5% | 39% | 22.4% | 37.2% |
|   Per cent of Guangdong imports coming from Macau | 1.7% | 1.8% | 1.2% | 1.2% | 0.6% | 0.7% |
|   Fujian imports from Macau | 1.0 | 1.4 | n.a. | 0.3 | 2.6 | 5.9 |
|   Fujian share of PRC imports from Macau | 1.7% | 1.3% | n.a. | 0.2% | 1.6% | 3.5% |
|   Per cent of Fujian imports coming from Macau | 0.3% | 0.3% | n.a. | 0.04% | 0.3% | 0.4% |
| *PRC imports from HK* | 5,696 | 8,437 | 11,973 | 12,541 | 14,254 | 17,463 |
|   Guangdong imports from HK | 1,874 | 2,895 | 4,089 | 3,497 | 4,116 | 6,230 |
|   Guangdong share of PRC imports coming from HK | 32.9% | 34.3% | 34.2% | 27.9% | 28.9% | 35.7% |
|   Per cent of Guangdong imports coming from HK | 77.2% | 79.8% | 80.0% | 72.4% | 71.6% | 73.2% |
|   Fujian imports from HK | 145 | 232 | n.a. | 373 | 457 | 741 |
|   Fujian share of PRC imports from HK | 2.5% | 2.7% | n.a. | 3.0% | 3.2% | 4.2% |
|   Per cent of Fujian imports coming from HK | 46.1% | 51.2% | n.a. | 50.7% | 49% | 52.6% |

*Sources:*
John T. Kamm, "Macau's economic role in the West River delta," p. 246. *Guangdong Sheng Tongji Nianjian* (*Guangdong Provincial Statistical Yearbook*). *Fujian Sheng Tongji Nianjian* (*Fujian Provincial Statistical Yearbook*).

Macau's tourism and gambling go some way to balance the deficit with Hong Kong and increasingly with Taiwan as well. The number of tourists expanded by 10 per cent per annum throughout the 1980s, although there has been a slippage in the rate of growth since about mid-1989. Hong Kong residents continue to make up over four-fifths of the tourist arrivals while tourists from Taiwan and mainland China have also been increasing in recent years (Table 6). Growth in the Taiwan market prompted the Macau government to appoint its first tourism public relations representative to the island in mid-1992. The Guangdong provincial government announced simplification of procedures for Chinese citizens to obtain visas for Macau in spring 1993. In general the tourism trends show an increase of East and South-east Asian tourists relative to European and North American guests. Gambling remains Macau's most popular diversion and accounts for roughly 20 per cent of Macau's gross domestic product.[59] Stanley Ho's Sociedade de Turismo e Diversões de Macau (STDM) has control of the gambling concession as well as the majority of the sea transport into the enclave. Currently Ho is trying to weave his company's fortunes deeper into the Macau economy so that the Chinese will find him impossible to oust in 1999.[60] Although Macau is likely to remain the gambling centre of East Asia for some time after 1999, competition is increasing as the Chinese have been thinking of allowing gambling in the Hainan Special Economic Zone and a race-track was opened in Guangzhou in 1992.

Hong Kong's ability to dominate the territory's economy can be seen in another sector – the property market. Land ownership falls into two categories: private land which can be purchased by individuals and public land which can be leased from the government on a long-term basis.[61] Either is open to non-resident investment and growth in property prices has been strong in recent years. Property booms on Taipa have been tied to Hong Kong and more recently also to Taiwan speculators. First there was an aborted mini-boom in the mid-1980s from the speculation that a loop-hole existed for Hong Kong people to get a Portuguese passport by owning property in Macau. Then with the beginning of the airport project to the east of Taipa, land prices on the island began to boom again in the early 1990s as Hong Kong and Taiwan speculators saw the potential for profit. Taiwan capital was sunk into the race-track on Taipa.[62] Macau

59. António Duarte de Almeida Pinho, "Gambling in Macau," in Cremer, *Macau*, pp. 255–56 states that the State of Nevada in the USA is the only place with a comparable amount of public expenditure financed from gambling. According to *O Jogo em Macau* (Macau: Inspecção dos Contratos de Jogos, 1985), p. 69 public revenue in Macau was 58% derived from gambling in 1984. The dominance of Hong Kong gamblers is implied by the fact that the average length of stay for a visitor to Macau is 1.35 days.

60. Jonathan Friedland, "A winning streak," *Far Eastern Economic Review*, 6 September 1990, pp. 56–59.

61. *Business Profile Series: Macau* (Hong Kong: The Hongkong and Shanghai Banking Corporation, 1989), p. 22.

62. During 1990 the races were televised in Taiwan, but telebets were blocked by the Nationalist government and, according to some, the Hong Kong Jockey Club. The track fell into deep financial trouble and had to be rescued by a consortium led by Stanley Ho's STDM in January 1991. Off-track uncrontrolled betting is increasing and it is said that the remaining Taiwan interests are dissatisfied with their investment

Table 6: **Tourist Arrivals by Sea in Macau by Nationality** (thousands of people)

|  | 1985 | 1986 | 1991 | 1992 | Change 1985–92 |
|---|---|---|---|---|---|
| Hong Kong | 3,443 | 3,466 | 4,951 | 6,163 | + 79% |
| Japan | 163 | 175 | 421 | 453 | + 178% |
| Taiwan, ROC | — | — | 109 | 236 | — |
| United Kingdom | 156 | 154 | 87 | 106 | − 31.1% |
| United States | 103 | 107 | 69 | 90 | − 12.7% |
| Thailand | 37 | 40 | 69 | 72 | + 94.6% |
| Rep. of Korea | — | — | 58 | 67 | — |
| Malaysia | 37 | 37 | 29 | 41 | + 10.8% |
| Australia | 55 | 52 | 32 | 40 | − 27.3% |
| Philippines | — | — | 21 | 38 | — |
| Germany[a] | 11 | 13 | 23 | 37 | + 236% |
| Canada | 23 | 26 | 22 | 29 | + 26% |
| PRC | 6 | 7 | 12 | 27 | + 350% |
| Portugal | — | — | 23 | 24 | — |
| Total | 4,182 | 4,238 | 6,080 | 7,699 | + 84.1% |

*Note:*
[a]Figures for Germany in 1985 and 1986 are for West Germany only.
*Sources:*
*Anuário Estatístico 1986/Yearbook of Statistics 1986/Tongji Nianjian 1986* (Macau: Governo de Macau, 1987), pp. 103–104. *Macau Travel Talk* 1992 and 1993.

residents, who on average only earn about half as much as their Hong Kong neighbours, see themselves being priced out of their own property market.[63]

The concentration of Macau's economy in textiles, tourism-gambling and to a lesser extent toys and artificial flowers has left it vulnerable to upturns and down-swings in these industries. By the late 1980s Macau's textile industry was facing serious protectionism problems as export quotas approached 100 per cent to the United States and in certain categories to the European Community, and further growth seems limited.[64] Competition in textiles as well as toys, artificial flowers and other low order goods from neighbouring countries with low wages, such as China, Vietnam and Thailand, is also increasing. Feitor and Cremer note that Macau manufacturers have already begun to upgrade their products.[65] However, diversification and improvement of labour skills during the 1980s has been slow.[66] Since 1989 the government has embarked on an

63. Richard Wigan, "A 'bit on the side' helps boost Macau," *South China Morning Post*, 14 August 1991 notes that it is even speculated that Hong Kong businessmen have fuelled the property boom by purchasing weekend hideaway flats for their mistresses.
64. Feitor and Cremer, "Macau's modern economy," p. 192. Wong Hon Keong, "Aomen guoduqi fazhan jingji miandui de maodun ji chulu de xuanze," p. 9 advocated further concentration of Macau's industry in certain specializations such as high quality textile products. However, he also noted that such a policy is dangerous in an era of growing protectionism.
65. Feitor and Cremer, "Macau's modern economy," p. 194.
66. Cremer, "Chinese entrepreneurs and enterprises," p. 218. Eric Yeung, "Uma questão de sovrevivência," *Comércio de Macau* (31 de Outubro 1992), pp. 9–10 feels that for Macau's industry to survive after 1999 it will be necessary that the current multi-fibre quotas continue, that

industrial diversification campaign first initiated by Governor Carlos Melancia. The hope is that low tech industries can be transferred out of Macau to Zhuhai and elsewhere while Macau goes for high tech manufacturing and services. However, by so doing Macau will enter into competition with Hong Kong, Taiwan and other NICs.

As has been shown, the small size of Macau limits its ability to function independently in several ways. For example, rapid growth of manufacturing and tourism has meant that agriculture has virtually disappeared during the last 30 years with what remains limited to market gardening.[67] Today 90 per cent of agricultural products, including freshwater fish, are supplied by China. Macau is also dependent on Guangdong for 70 per cent of its drinking water and about 10 per cent of its electricity.[68] This makes electricity costs in Macau higher than in Hong Kong and Taiwan.[69] Macau's small size also limits the amount of local capital available for investment. As of 1987 only an estimated 24 per cent of Macau's investment was from local sources with Hong Kong supplying 60 per cent and China 12 per cent.[70] Increasingly Macau investors will turn to China.

Despite these difficulties, Macau's economy has not ceased to grow although the world recession may slow it down in coming years. Infrastructural works may be costly but lack of investment in the airport and reclamation projects would leave Macau so far behind Hong Kong that the territory would lose its function as a local economic node for the western Pearl River delta.

## Society: Ethno-linguistic and Educational Problems

The people of Macau belong to three major groups: the Macaense, the Chinese and the Portuguese. Most people consider anyone of mixed ancestry who speaks Portuguese as a Macaense. Various figures are given for the Macaense population but most agree that there are now less than 10,000 in Macau. Their language was a Portuguese creole which along

---

*footnote continued*

Macau is viewed as a useful entry point to China, and that the government and industry introduce structural alterations to create a more flexible business environment.

67. Richard Louis Edmonds, "Land use in Macau: changes between 1972 and 1983," *Land Use Policy* (January 1986), pp. 58–60.

68. In 1988 Macau negotiated with Zhuhai to supply water up to 1999 to make up for shortages in the local supply. According to *Macau*, Sér. 2, No. 1 (Maio 1992), p. 97 the Companhia de Electricidade de Macau has invested enough funds in new electric generators on Coloane to ensure adequate electric supplies until 1995. Recent discoveries of natural gas on Hainan are more likely to be directed via pipeline towards Hong Kong than Macau.

69. Cheang Tin Cheong, "A coordenação das infraestruturas," p. 21 states that in 1987 the price of electricity in Macau was 71.6% higher than in Hong Kong and 112.5% higher than in Taiwan. There has been talk of laying a cable to channel Hong Kong electric power to Macau.

70. Wong Hon Keong, "Aomen guoduqi fazhan jingji miandui de maodun ji chulu de xuanze," p. 5.

with their cuisine and customs is rapidly disappearing.[71] Even though the Macau Basic Law does not limit the number of foreign passport holders allowed to sit in the *Assembleia Legislativa* and article 42 specifically protects the rights and customs of residents of Portuguese ancestry,[72] it is likely that many Macaense will emigrate prior to or shortly after 1999.

Cantonese speakers make up 86.3 per cent of the territory's population with the largest numbers coming from neighbouring counties. The Cantonese view themselves as part of Macau's larger Chinese ethnic group amongst which Fujianese and Shanghainese are the largest minorities. Today it is the Guangzhou (and Hong Kong) version of Cantonese that is the lingua franca of Macau. Recent attempts to make Chinese an official language in the territory have focused on Guangzhou Cantonese rather than on the official standard Chinese language (Mandarin), the later being spoken by only 1.1 per cent of the population.[73] No doubt the importance of Mandarin will increase after 1999.

The influx of Shanghainese, Fujianese, Hong Kong people and a number of entrepreneurs from Guangdong since 1949 has been cited as one of the main causes for the subsequent development of an entrepreneurial spirit in Macau.[74] However, many of these Chinese are planning to leave the territory prior to 1999 and those now coming in are not necessarily motivated by the same entrepreneurial tendencies.

Since 1988 the Macau government has allowed local industrialists to import labour from China. By April 1989, approximately 6,000 mainland workers had been brought in on contract.[75] However, there are even more illegal immigrants working in Macau. There has been a labour shortage since 1984, and immigration has caused resentment amongst the local resident population (despite the fact that over half of them were born in

71. For more on the Macaense dialect see José Miguel Riveiro Lume, "Centre of Portuguese language and culture," in Cremer, *Macau*, pp. 133–34 and Graciete Agostinho Noguiera Batalha, *Língua de Macau: O que foi e o que é* (Macau: Imprensa Nacional, 1974). According to Raymond A. Zepp, "Interface of Chinese and Portuguese cultures," in Cremer, *Macau*, p. 155 there are less than 20 people alive in Macau who can speak the Macaense dialect. For information on Macaense cuisine see Maria Margarida Gomes, *A Cozinha Macaense* (Macau: Imprensa Nacional, 1984) and Maria Celestina de Mello e Senna, *Bons Petiscos* (Macau: Direcção dos Serviços de Turismo, 1983).

72. Conselho Consultivo da Lei Básica da Região Administrativa Especial de Macau da República Popular da China (ed.), *Lei Básica da Região Administrativa Especial de Macau da República Popular da China* (Macau: Tipografia San Ngai, 1993), p. 19. On page 1, the preamble refers to the Portuguese gradual occupation of Macau since the mid-16th century. Bruce Taylor (personal communication) points out that this has caused considerable concern amongst the Macaense and Portuguese communities.

73. In 1991 9.2% of the population spoke Chinese languages other than Cantonese and Standard Chinese (Mandarin). For more discussion of issues related to the status of ethnic Chinese women, mainland Chinese migrant workers, and ethnic Chinese secondary school students in Macau see Chen Xinxin, *Aomen shehui chūtan* (*A Preliminary Discussion of Macau's Society*) (Hong Kong: Wanshiwei, 1992).

74. Wong Siu Lun, "Chinese entrepreneurship in Macau," in Cremer, *Industrial Economy of Macau in the 1990s*, pp. 27–36. Sit, Cremer and Siu Lun Wong, *Entrepreneurs and Enterprises in Macau*, p. 55.

75. *Business Profile Series: Macau*, p. 22.

mainland China), as it has led to reduced wages and social difficulties.[76] Perhaps the most serious social problem with illegal immigrants occurred in March 1990 when thousands of them took to the streets demonstrating for the right to register their children to reside legally in Macau. This led to a breakdown in law and order and to the creation of an Adjunct Secretary for Security (*Secretaria-Adjunta para a Segurança*) to ensure that such an event would not reoccur.[77] In 1991 an average of 100 illegal immigrants were repatriated to China each week.[78] While they represent a headache for the government, they are also a source of inexpensive labour and potential entrepreneurial talent and are therefore a key link between Macau and the rest of "Greater China."

Although as of 1991, 27.9 per cent of Macau's population had Portuguese nationality, only 1.8 per cent of the population spoke Portuguese. It is included as an official language during the period from 1999 to 2049, but it is doubtful whether Portuguese culture will survive in Macau. The short period of residence for most Portuguese expatriates in the territory and their relative isolation from the business sector means that few have made an effort to learn Cantonese or to attempt to integrate into the Chinese or Macaense communities. With 1999 approaching even fewer Portuguese will see their destiny as tied with that of Macau.[79]

76. The 1991 census gave Macau an official preliminary population figure of 354,537 although most agree that something closer to 450,000 or 500,000 is probably more accurate. Lin Shiming, "Guoduqi Aomen jingji fazhan xuyao zhuyi de wenti de tantao," p. 15 and Wong Hon Keong, "Aomen guoduqi fazhan jingji miandui de maodun ji chulu de xuanze," pp. 6–9 have even advocated allowing Macau's population to rise to one million by 2010, through immigration of selected Chinese labour and to a lesser extent natural increase in order to solve labour shortages and increase the size of the territory's domestic market. A Macau government planning report of 1987 estimates a population of 710,000 in 2010.

77. Lam, "Administration and public service system in Macau," pp. 326–27, notes that the Governor at that time, Carlos Melancia and the Chief of the Security Forces, Col. Proença de Almeida, who was responsible for military authorities in Portugal, used this incident as a political football. Putting the security forces under an adjunct secretary directly responsible to the Governor increases the power of the Governor and reduces the chance that this sort of incident could occur again.

78. *Asia Yearbook 1992*, p. 149.

79. Underlying tension between the small Macaense and Portuguese communities and the Chinese majority surfaced over the future of the statue to João Maria Ferreira do Amaral, a Governor of Macau assassinated by a group of Chinese on 22 August 1849. The statue had been standing in Macau since 24 June 1940. In 1990 the director of the Chinese State Council's Hong Kong and Macau Affairs Office, Lu Ping, stated that the statue should be removed prior to 1999 as it was a symbol of colonialism – a view echoed in the Beijing-controlled Macau newspapers and also held by many of Macau's ethnic Chinese. On Overseas Portuguese Day (10 June 1990) Governor Melancia deleted a passage referring to Ferreira do Amaral from a speech to be given by Portuguese Minister for Parliamentary Affairs, Dias Loureiro, in order not to offend the Chinese. Loureiro was delayed and the speech was read with this section and another passage deleted. This angered Portuguese politicians who saw the gesture as giving in to the Chinese. Melancia was called to Lisbon to answer questions about the affair. In August a project to build a car park was taken as the pretext to announce plans to remove Ferreira do Amaral's statue. In September 1990 it was said that the project would begin in December and be completed in ten months. However, Melancia fell from power. At roughly the same time the Bank of China building was completed to become the biggest symbol of growing Chinese influence while the statue stayed where it was as opinions about what to do with it multiplied. In September 1991 Governor Vasco Joaquim Rocha Vieira announced that the statue would be transferred to a proper place in Lisbon. However, it still aroused sensitivities prior to its removal in 1992. Some Macau Chinese stated that it should not have been removed as it was property of Macau not Portugal, many Macaense

In addition to various widely-practised Chinese beliefs (16.9 per cent of the total population are Buddhist), there are approximately 30,000 Roman Catholics in Macau. However, expansion of the Catholic congregation has been small, representing 6.8 per cent of the total population. Their position and relation to the Vatican after 1999 remains an unanswered question since Beijing continues to oppose links between Chinese Catholics and the Papal See. This religious group, which includes virtually the whole of the Macaense population, will resist severing its ties with Rome and it is likely that Beijing will make an exception on this point, at least in the short term.

The territory's small size and the Portuguese colonial connection has given Macau a very different education system from that found in other parts of Greater China.[80] The small scale has put what Brock calls a "ceiling of educational provision"[81] on Macau which is far lower than in Hong Kong or Taiwan. The territory also remains one of the few places in the world without free compulsory education. Instead of a unified system, there is a series of unco-ordinated educational institutions following models based on Portugal, Hong Kong, the PRC and Taiwan.[82] As in Hong Kong, government schools form about 12 per cent of the total.[83] Outside the government system more schools teach in Cantonese or in English than in Portuguese.[84] In sum, the education system is virtually unregulated with Hong Kong exerting the greatest amount of influence.

In 1990 the Macau government issued a document calling for government assistance to private schools, to be accompanied by controls. A Macau-wide examination system was also proposed along with new plans

---

*footnote continued*

worried that removal was a sign of their further disenfranchisement, while the Portuguese rejoiced that movement of the five tonne statue was completed with no major incident. For a recent Portuguese reflection on the matter see also João Fernandes, "Ferreira do Amaral tornou a ser polémico," *Macau*, Sér. 2, No. 14 (Junho 1993), pp. 92–93. According to Carlos Morais José, "Polémica à porta," *Ponto Final* (29 de Janeiro 1993), pp. 4–5 and Rachel Clarke, "Row over financing of public projects in Macau," *South China Morning Post* (12 April 1993), a plan to erect seven monuments to Sino-Portuguese friendship has been criticized locally as a waste of money. Presumably the purpose of these monuments is in part to replace the Ferreira do Amaral statue.

80. Mark Bray, "Colonialism, scale and politics: divergence and convergence of educational development in Hong Kong and Macau," *Comparative Education Review*, Vol. 36, No. 3 (1992), p. 322, has noted the differences in Macau's and Hong Kong's education systems. However, colonial heritage and proximity have led these two territories to share more educational features than either does with Taiwan or the People's Republic.

81. Colin Brock, "The educational context," in Kazim Bacchus and Colin Brock (eds.), *The Challenge of Scale: Educational Development in the Small States of the Commonwealth* (London: Commonwealth Secretariat, 1987), p. 8.

82. M. Conceição Alves Pinto, *Ensino em Macau: Uma Abordagem Sistémica da Realidade Educativa* (Macau: Gabinete do Secretário-Adjunto para a Educação e Cultura, 1987), pp. 20–21. Alexandre Rosa, "Educação em mudança," *Macau*, Sér. 2, No. 2 (Junho 1992), p. 63. For more detail on Macau's education system see Wong Hon Keong [Huang Hanqiang] (ed.), *Aomen jiaoyu gaige/Reforma da Educação de Macau/Education Reform in Macau* (Macau: Centro de Estudos de Macau, University of East Asia, 1991).

83. Bray, "Colonialism, scale, and politics," p. 329.

84. As of the 1991–92 academic year over 83% of the students in Macau were in Chinese schools and 9% were in Anglo-Chinese schools. Only 0.6% of the territory's population are native speakers of English.

to provide six years of compulsory education. In 1991, 12 per cent of Macau's budget was devoted to education, a 40 per cent increase in funds over 1990.[85] On 1 January 1993 a new Organic Education Law (*Lei Orgânica para a Educação*) came into effect which restructured the territory's Department of Education and Youth Services. Such moves suggest that it is likely that the government will get involved in curricula formulation prior to 1999. These developments will include last ditch efforts to entrench the Portuguese language as well as to teach the Macau Chinese people to speak standard Chinese (Mandarin).[86] In 1988, the government bought the main campus and majority of facilities of Macau's private University of East Asia which has now been renamed the University of Macau.[87] There has already been some effort to increase the amount of teaching in Portuguese and Cantonese and reduce that in English at the university as well as to increase total enrolment and to conduct a unified entrance examination. At the same time the government began to recognize qualifications from academic institutions outside Portugal.[88] Recent proposals have turned the university's education structure away from its English–Welsh foundations to a more Portuguese-style course and degree pattern. In September 1991 the *Instituto Politécnico de Macau* was founded to increase training opportunities and there are plans to establish an open university.

The use of Portuguese language in government has been seen by local Chinese and Anglophones as a blocking force limiting contact and creating suspicion to a greater degree than between the British administration and Chinese society in Hong Kong.[89] This reflects the greater willingness of Hong Kong Chinese to learn English than for Macau Chinese to learn Portuguese.

Although weakened Portuguese influence has meant less government interference in education, Macau's education system will have to adjust after 1999 to face the political reality of its new master. However, the Macau government seems determined to make its mark in these last years. The Sino-Portuguese joint accord's statement that Portuguese will remain an official language in Macau after 1999 suggests that some cosmetic level of Portuguese education may be maintained in the territory up to 2049. However, exchanges and contact with scholars in the PRC has been increasing in recent years. After 1999 there will no doubt be

85. "91 As linhas de acção governativa," p. 42.
86. According to Bray, "Colonialism, scale, and politics," p. 336, financial inducements for the study of Portuguese were introduced in 1987. In 1988 the government even tried to make Portuguese a compulsory subject in all private schools, but was forced by local opposition to retract this policy.
87. According to "91 As linhas de acção governativa," p. 43 nearly 700 Macau students were already studying with government scholarships at what is now the University of Macau in 1991. Between 1987 and 1992 close to 300 local pupils were trained at the University to take on responsibilities in the Macau government.
88. Yee and Lo, "Macau in transition," p. 916.
89. Lam, "Administration and public service system in Macau," p. 323. Harrison, "English in Macau," p. 150.

more integration of the education system with that of mainland China and gradual convergence of the Macau system with that of Hong Kong.

After the crushing of the pro-democracy movement in the People's Republic and the Tiananmen massacre on 4 June 1989, an estimated 100,000 people took to the streets of Macau to demonstrate. While crowds may have been bigger in Hong Kong, the Macau figure represents one-fifth of the territory's population. Demonstrations have continued on the anniversary of the massacre and these protests demonstrate that Macau society is not politically apathetic despite low turnouts in local elections.

In recent years corruption and crime have become more widely discussed issues. After many years of debate the *Assembleia Legislativa* endorsed a bill to establish a High Commissioner's Office Against Corruption and Maladministration in 1990. In recent years there has been a rise in the rate of violent crimes, particularly those involving rival triad groups.[90] Police protection rackets for Macau's 5,000 prostitutes and changing of police reports in the favour of certain criminals were also recently revealed. With the crackdown of Hong Kong authorities on smuggling to and from Shenzhen in the early 1990s there has been a rise in that between Macau and Zhuhai.

While the position of the Portuguese language, the Macaense and the Catholics could become precarious, it is not likely that there will be any serious conflicts amongst Macau's three major ethnic groups prior to 1999. However, problems related to education and crime within Macau and tension with mainland China will remain.

## Specialization and/or Expansion: The Alternatives for the Future

More than any other polity in Greater China, Macau is limited in its room to manoeuvre because of its small size. As much of the recent economic growth has been based upon Macau's legal status as a Portuguese-administered territory, the change in 1999 could provide a shock. One way to maintain economic prosperity would be specialization. The Portuguese element in Macau's past is one such area. Current efforts to secure a special place for Portuguese language and culture will ensure that Portuguese influence after 1999 will not disappear overnight. Whether Macau can again play a major role in East–West relations hinges in part on the ability of Latin countries to utilize the territory as a base for economic and cultural exchange.[91] The dominance of Hong Kong and

90. *Asia Yearbook 1992*, p. 149. Mariana Wan, "Macau in for bumpy landing," *South China Morning Post–Spectrum* (4 August 1991), p. 3.

91. While the Portuguese have often stressed the role that Macau can play in increasing contacts between China and the Latin world, it is interesting to see a Cuban, Enrique Bryon Rivero, "Macao," *Páginas* (Havana) No. 6 (1991), p. 47 reiterate this point. For a Macau Chinese voicing the economic potential of the Luso connection see Wong Hon Keong, "Aomen guoduqi fazhan jingji miandui de maodun ji chulu de xuanze," p. 8. For mainland Chinese see Lei Qiang and Zheng Tianxiang, "Aomen yu Zhu Jiang sanjiaozhou jingji guanxi fazhan de xinshiqi" ("A new era in the relation between Macau and the Pearl River delta"), *Aomen Yanjiu/Journal of*

the relative weakness of the Iberian peninsula and Latin America in the China trade do not bode well for this prospect. In particular, the Portuguese business presence in Macau is not as strong as that of the United Kingdom in Hong Kong. However, Macau's Portuguese past can be maintained as an attraction for tourists from the increasingly prosperous countries of East and South-east Asia. Therefore, the Macau Special Economic Region and China would be wise to control local developers and preserve as much of the remaining traditional Portuguese colonial flavour as national pride permits – particularly as Macau's other major current tourist revenue generator, the virtual monopoly of regional gambling, is likely to be broken after 1999.

In industry, Macau must upgrade and specialize if it is to end its dependency upon Hong Kong and to develop a more competitive relationship with Guangdong. To expand its economic role as an entrepôt for the western Pearl River delta in the same way as Hong Kong is for all of South China, Macau must grow both in geographic and demographic terms. In this context the infrastructural plans of the Macau government are indispensable. It will also be necessary for Macau to develop skills in value-added high technology industry as the territory will find it increasingly difficult in the coming decades to compete in labour intensive low cost production with south China. However, it is a real worry that rapid expansion of the territory's land area and population by 2010 could destroy the ecology and the remaining architectural legacy of old Macau. If so Macau would be better off if it gave up trying to compete with Hong Kong, Guangzhou and Zhuhai. It seems that specialization in tourism which preserves the territory's Portuguese heritage, high value-added low polluting industry, and financial services and information (particularly with the Latin world) provide the most reasonable package for the future.

Although they come under criticism, it seems that the overall policies of the Macau government and its backers are essentially correct if it is assumed that growth is desired. However, there are serious problems. Education has been neglected, local industry has yet to receive the kind of support it needs to compete with Hong Kong and Taiwan, planning for the new infrastructural projects and for the preservation of traditional architecture has only been piecemeal, and corruption, although not rampant, is still a problem. For Macau's growth-oriented policies to succeed, it will be necessary to rectify the above shortcomings, divorce Macau's politics from Portuguese politics and restrain Beijing's

---

*footnote continued*

*Macau Studies*, Vol. 1 (1988), p. 38 and Zhang Shouqian, "Aomen jingji de fazhan jiqi zai Ya Tai diqu de diwei he zuoyong" ("Economic development of Macau and its position in the Asia-Pacific region"), *Aomen Yanjiu/Journal of Macau Studies*, Vol. 1 (1988), p. 50.

influence in the territory in order to provide stability. It will also be important that Macau, Zhuhai, Zhongshan, Jiangmen and Foshan come to realize that their destinies are intertwined so that co-ordination between them will evolve to a higher degree.[92] Along with land reclamation, co-operation and integration with Zhuhai is the only way Macau can grow and compete for a significant economic role in a Greater China. However, growth and integration with Greater China so far has caused Macau to lose the characteristic which allows it to make a special contribution to this new economic force – its unique historical and cultural character.

92. Economic links between Zhuhai and Macau are already substantial. According to Paulo Nogueira, "Zhuhai e Cantão: o delta do futuro," *Macau*, Sér. 2, No. 7 (Novembro 1992), p. 9, Macau investments made up 38% of the total external investments in Zhuhai during 1991. Only the volume from Hong Kong was larger. Macau received 61.7% of Zhuhai's exports in 1990. This amounted to about 44% of Macau's imports from China. Over 76% of Macau's exports to China in U.S. dollar terms went to China via Zhuhai. Leonel Miranda, "Aproveitar as complementari-dades," *Comércio de Macau* (31 de Outubro 1992), p. 8 notes that as of 1991, 580 firms in Zhuhai were financed with Macau capital. Feitor and Cremer, "Macau's modern economy," p. 197 make the point that Macau and Zhuhai's products do not compete for local markets but for international markets which they suggest implies that Macau manufacturers are not likely to close their Macau operations if they open another plant in Zhuhai but rather may only shift labour intensive parts of their operation or some of their product lines out of the territory. Differing export quotas and tax preferences also encourage Macau investors in Zhuhai to continue to maintain their Macau operations.

# Go With Your Feelings: Hong Kong and Taiwan Popular Culture in Greater China*

## Thomas B. Gold

The people go with the Communist Party; the Communist Party goes with the Central Committee; the Central Committee goes with the Politburo; the Politburo goes with the Standing Committee; the Standing Committee goes with Deng Xiaoping; Deng Xiaoping goes with his feelings (*Deng Xiaoping genzhe ganjue zou*).

Trying to puzzle out the Communist leadership's reaction to the massive demonstrations then under way during the spring of 1989, some Chinese wits turned to "Go With Your Feelings," a well-known song recorded by the Taiwan pop singer Su Rui.[1] This not only indicated the critical role of one often unpredictable octogenarian, it also revealed the pervasiveness of popular culture from "peripheral China" on the mainland core: an allusion to a pop song from Taiwan could be used (and understood) to sum up an extremely volatile situation. As the economies of the mainland, Hong Kong and Taiwan move toward increased integration, with Hong Kong and Taiwan supplying the dynamism and the mainland the market, a comparable trend is emerging in the cultural realm: popular culture from Hong Kong and Taiwan is claiming a substantial share of the market and loyalties of mainland consumers. Furthermore, it is redefining the essence of what it means to be a "modern" Chinese at the end of the 20th century, and popularizing a new language for expressing individual sentiments.

This article will explore some aspects of the largely one-way influence of Hong Kong and Taiwan popular culture on the China mainland. It will address two central issues: why it has spread so quickly, and the implications for Greater China.

### Hong Kong and Taiwan Popular Culture

This article looks at various types of popular culture from Hong Kong and Taiwan, hereafter referred to as "Gangtai" (a contraction of the Chinese words Xiang*gang* and *Tai*wan), which have spread on the

*I would like to thank Ambrose King, Joseph Bosco, Andrew Jones, Rey Chow, Todd Gitlin, Lydia Liu and Orville Schell for comments on an earlier draft. Support came from the Center for Chinese Studies, University of California, Berkeley. Kang-ling Chang provided research assistance.

1. "Genzhe ganjue zou" ("Go with your feelings"), on the cassette *Taibei, Dongjing (Taipei, Tokyo)*, WEA Records, Ltd., 1988. According to a 1992 survey of 1,500 people in Beijing, 81.9% of those surveyed had heard this song (although only 49% claimed to like it). Liu Xiaobo, "Toushi dalu renmin di wenhua shenghuo" ("Perspective on the cultural life of mainland people"), *Zhongguo shibao zhoukan (China Times Weekly)* (hereafter, *ZGSBZK*), No. 61, 28 February–6 March 1993, pp. 70–77 at p. 76. In a speech at the University of California, Berkeley (12 April 1993), Liu Xiaobo noted that another Taiwan song, "Wo shi yizhi beifang laidi lang" ("I am a wolf from the north"), expressing sentiments of poverty, loneliness and authoritarianism, was also popular at the Square.

mainland of China.[2] These include music, film, television shows, literature, advertisements, decor, attire and leisure. Hong Kong and Taiwan are
market economies where culture, like virtually everything else, is a
commodity. In Hong Kong, the government imposes some controls, in
particular in the area of pornography. At times, bowing to pressure from
Beijing, it has banned the showing of anti-Communist films from Taiwan,
but in general, anything goes in the Crown Colony.

In Taiwan, the ruling Kuomintang (KMT or Nationalist Party) has a
Cultural Affairs Department which sets and oversees cultural policy. The
state has the Government Information Office[3] which engages in production, regulation and censorship, and the Council for Cultural Planning
and Development, founded in 1981 and due for upgrading to ministerial
status. The KMT additionally owns artistic enterprises, including a film
company and a radio and television station.[4] The party and government
have produced and disseminated a great number of ideological works,
both in the form of straight propaganda and entertainment. They have
also worked to preserve traditional Chinese culture, especially in the face
of the Communists' efforts to eradicate it, most noticeably during the
Cultural Revolution (1966–76). Over the years, the party-state on Taiwan
has exercised cultural control selectively, mostly in the political realm –
strictly controlling production or dissemination of works which challenge
its hegemony, raise questions about its past or legitimacy, spread Communist propaganda or even introduce life in Communist countries. It has
cut sexually suggestive scenes out of films and marked up periodicals to
blot out offensive text or illustrations.

In both Taiwan and Hong Kong, American popular culture has claimed
a major share of the market. Although Taiwan was a Japanese colony for
50 years and Japanese culture retains influence over many older Taiwanese, the mainland émigré regime's close ties with the United States
and enmity towards Japan (especially after Tokyo established diplomatic
relations with Beijing in 1972) brought about a strict control over the
import of Japanese culture into the island. The presence of American
soldiers, both as advisers since the Korean War and then for rest and
recreation during the Vietnam War, spawned a major industry designed to
entertain them. In addition to bars and brothels, Taiwanese entrepreneurs
vigorously pirated American records and books which made their way
into the mainstream. American Armed Forces Radio broadcast American
pop music, while subtitled (and censored) American movies dominated

2. I use "popular culture" to refer to cultural products produced for the mass market, which
reflect market-determined popular taste and are for enjoyment. This is in contrast to more elite or
high culture which has a much narrower appeal and poses more of an intellectual challenge to the
consumer. It is also in contrast to politically contrived directed culture. Taiwan and Hong Kong
do have high culture, but its spread on the mainland, by definition, has not been as great as popular
culture. The few cultural products which have gone from the mainland to Hong Kong and Taiwan
are generally of the less commercial variety.

3. *The Republic of China Yearbook 1993* (Taipei: Government Information Office, 1993),
p. 103.

4. Jeremy Mark and Julia Leung, "KMT's blend of business and politics draws fire," *The Asian
Wall Street Journal*, 2 December 1992, p. 1.

the film industry. Taiwan cultural figures began to imitate American popular culture.[5]

Being more open and virtually non-ideological, Hong Kong became the major centre for the production of Chinese popular culture. Many of the pioneers of the Hong Kong entertainment industry were refugees from Shanghai.[6] As the standard of living rose among Overseas Chinese communities in South-east Asia, Taiwan and Hong Kong films in Mandarin with indigenous-language subtitles, and songs, found a ready market. The Chinese mainland remained completely off-limits except for KMT propaganda radio, loudspeakers and balloons. The revolutionary decision of the Chinese Communists to reform their economy and open it to the outside world, taken at the Third Plenum of the 11th Central Committee in December 1978, provided an unprecedented opportunity for culture entrepreneurs to cultivate and then penetrate this potentially boundless market.

## A Reconnaissance of Gangtai Popular Culture on the Mainland[7]

Over the past decade, popular culture from Taiwan and Hong Kong has swept the mainland of China. From a base of close to zero at the time of the Third Plenum, the extent and multifariousness of this imported culture is striking. If anything, it has increased since the violent crackdown on dissent and bourgeois liberalization in June 1989 for reasons discussed below. This section provides an impressionistic reconnaissance of the presence of Taiwan and Hong Kong popular culture on the mainland as evidence of the phenomenon.

In early 1979, while an exchange student at Shanghai's Fudan University, I overheard Chinese students listening to smuggled or copied tapes by the Taiwanese crooner, Deng Lijun (Teresa Teng). In 1992, numerous singers from Taiwan and Hong Kong toured the mainland with lavish stage shows jointly produced by Hong Kong, Taiwan and local state enterprises which sold out quickly to a primarily youthful audience.[8]

---

5. American popular culture such as music, romance fiction and film was also disseminated and imitated during the KMT's rule on the mainland, at least in areas such as the Yangzi Delta.

6. Shanghai had been the centre and standard for everything "modern" in pre-Communist China. One could argue that the spread of Gangtai popular culture on the mainland now represents a return of Shanghai culture, since its émigrés have played such a major role in the culture industry in both places. I am grateful to Vice-Chancellor Wang Gungwu for these insights. Parenthetically, the Shanghainese who dominated the KMT émigré regime tried to recreate the Shanghai life-style in Taipei. For instance, the liveliest intersection was Nanjing Lu and Zhongshan Lu, and many nightclubs, restaurants and stores took their names from famous Shanghai establishments. As part of a nostalgia wave, beginning in 1992 EMI Hong Kong brought out compilations of old Shanghai popular songs.

7. Much of the following section is based on trips to Xiamen, Shanghai and Hangzhou in 1992. For an overview of the cultural scene in 1991, and references to post-1978 cultural developments, see Geremie Barme, "The greying of Chinese culture," in Kuan Hsin-chi and Maurice Brosseau (eds.), *China Review 1992* (Hong Kong: The Chinese University Press, 1992), ch. 13.

8. Although her tapes were banned, during the late 1970s it was said that "Old Deng [Xiao-ping] rules by day, little Teng [Lijun] rules by night." Significantly, Teresa Teng has not made a tour of the mainland. She has been outspoken in her anti-Communism and support of the Republic of China, making frequent trips to Quemoy to rally the troops. Nevertheless, her recordings are

Cassette tapes and compact discs by these singers, both legally imported (commonly through joint ventures between state enterprises and Hong Kong/Taiwan distributors) and pirated, are sold in once hidebound state enterprises such as the Xinhua Bookstore as well as by private enterprises.[9] The shops which sell them display large posters of the singers (mostly young males), in particular those of Hong Kong's "Four Great Kings" (*sida tianwang*) – Guo Fucheng (Aaron Kwok), Li Ming (Leon Lai),[10] Liu Dehua (Andy Lau) and Zhang Xueyou (Jacky Cheung) – as well as Tan Yonglin, Tong Ange, Lin Yilian (Sandy Lam), Xiaohudui (Taiwan's New Kids on the Block) and so on. Comparable posters of mainland artists are not seen. Fan magazines of Hong Kong and Taiwan singers and actors, referred to as giant stars (*juxing*) and idols (*ouxiang*), are published and sold on the mainland.[11] Staid publications such as Shanghai's *Jiefang Ribao* and *Wenhui Bao* run puff pieces about visiting Taiwan and Hong Kong celebrities with concert photos of them.[12] Official publications aimed at young readers are full of similar articles. China's own concerts frequently shown on television increasingly resemble those seen in Hong Kong and Taiwan: elaborately outfitted singers backed up by dancers, "mood" created by strobe lights and dry ice.

Television advertisements have the same rough jerky quality and off-time voice dubbing as Taiwan's. The stylishly dressed actors inhabit a world of consumption and interior decoration clearly reflecting the middle-class tastes of Taiwan and Hong Kong.[13]

Cities are densely packed with karaoke bars, featuring both public spaces and small rooms for private parties (KTV). These establishments feature expensive state-of-the art Japanese technology. Men entering them without female companions are likely to be approached by "hostesses" who sit with them and provide conversation, food, drink and petting. Karaoke demonstration tapes (with singers in addition to back-up music and on-screen lyrics) are played – loudly – in stores and restaurants to entertain customers and attract passers-by.

---

*footnote continued*

played and sold everywhere. Physician-turned songwriter/singer Luo Dayou has also not performed on the mainland. His song "Tongnian" ("Childhood"), expressing the frustrations of pubescence, a subject not publicly acknowledged on the mainland, was especially popular.

9. In November 1992, I tried to buy a tape by the mainland singer Mao Aming at a state store, but was told they only carried Hong Kong and Taiwan music.

10. Li Ming's 1992 concert tour was billed as "Li Ming's Return Home '92" (" '92 Li Ming huiguxiang") (*Renmin Ribao* (*People's Daily*), 11 November 1992, p. 3). The use of "*huiguxiang*" shows the effort to use a commercial tour to prove that Li Ming, like others in Hong Kong, sees his real "home" as being on the mainland and thus supports reunification.

11. I bought something called *Gangtai mingxing* (*Hong Kong and Taiwan Stars*), a series of six glossy fan magazines full of colour photographs and gossipy stories, published in Shenyang. Serious journals such as *Renmin yinyue* and *Yinyue yanjiu* have published articles discussing popular music, including that from Hong Kong and Taiwan.

12. Articles try to stress the mainland connection. For instance, "You Yiban Shanghai Xuetong di Yu Chengqing" ("Half-a-Shanghainese, Yu Chengqing") makes a big deal of the fact that this Taiwan singer has a Shanghainese mother and Yunnanese father (*Xinmin wanbao*, 8 November 1992, p. 4).

13. See Barme, "The greying of Chinese culture," pp. 13.22–23 for more on advertisements.

Films from Taiwan and Hong Kong play in theatres and on television, where one can also see soap operas from those areas.[14] Pirated video cassettes of Taiwan and Hong Kong films are sold quite openly on the streets.[15] Hong Kong television and Asian MTV can be accessed in much of the mainland.

As part of urban renewal and the need to compete, retail establishments owned by the state, collectives and private investors are investing great sums in redecorating. With their gleaming chrome columns, aquariums full of live and struggling (*shengmeng*) seafood (advertised by large signs in the windows), well-stocked bars, brightly lit interiors, polished linoleum or marble floors and costumed service personnel, restaurants resemble the same establishments one sees in Hong Kong and Taiwan. Cantonese food has become the rage in the Yangzi Delta region (and Taiwan as well). In addition to the main dining room, the private rooms upstairs often have "themes," such as the Western room, American West room, Japan room or bamboo room. Shanghai's once nondescript Zhapu Road now houses several glitzy multi-storey private restaurants which are popular after-hours haunts for small businessmen (*getihu*). With its neon and night-time bustle, Zhapu Road resembles Taipei's restaurant ghetto on Linsen North Road just off Nanking East Road. Restaurants throughout the cities string a canopy of small lights over the pavement, a style popularized by the beer halls (*pijiuwu*) of Shilin and other Taipei districts. Shenzhen's architecture and cityscape are a mirror image of Kowloon, and Xiamen is filling up with town-houses and apartment buildings with names such as "Taiwan Village" which duplicate the style of the burgeoning suburbs of Taipei. Taiwan film star Lin Qingxia appeared in late 1992 at the opening of the shiny multi-storey "Taiwan City" (*Taiwancheng*) entertainment centre located on Siping Road in Shanghai's Hongkou district. It has karaoke, KTV, bars, restaurants and shops. The investor is a 40-ish Shanghainese financier now based in the United States.[16]

Works of contemporary fiction by Taiwan and Hong Kong writers such as Qiong Yao, Ji Xiaotai, Xuan Xiaofo, San Mao, Yi Shu and Liang Fengyi (Leung Fung-yee), and knight errant novels by Gu Long and Jin Yong are widely published by mainland presses.[17] Business cards, store

14. For a list of Taiwan films which played on the mainland in 1986–91, see Gu Biling, Luo Rulan and Zhou Pinger, "Gangtai qunxing shanyao shenzhou" ("Hong Kong and Taiwan stars shine over the mainland"), *ZGSBZK*, 16–22 February 1992, pp. 66–69 at p. 69.

15. Privately-owned video cassette recorders are still not widespread. I went to a private restaurant in Shanghai where the owner provided a VCR on which diners could play their tapes. That particular evening, three young people eating hot pot watched a poor quality pirated Mandarin-language Hong Kong film. As far inland as Dali, Yunnan in 1985, I saw entrepreneurs selling tickets for Gangtai martial arts film videos.

16. *ZGSBZK*, No. 61, 28 February–6 March 1993, pp. 68–69.

17. On San Mao, particularly the effect of her suicide, see Barme, "The greying of Chinese culture," pp. 13.10–11. For a PRC perspective on Taiwan romance novels, see Huang Zhongtian, "Cun you suo chang, chi you suo duan: guanyu Taiwan yanqing xiaoshuo" ("An inch has its strengths, a foot has its shortcomings: concerning Taiwan's romance fiction"), *Taiwan yanjiu jikan* (*Taiwan Research Quarterly*), No. 4, 1991, pp. 84–89. For an overview of the state of the field, see Jeffrey C. Kinkley, "Mainland Chinese scholars' views of contemporary Taiwan literature,"

signs, advertisements and other published material increasingly use non-simplified characters (*fantizi*), ostensibly to assist readers from outside the mainland, including Japan, but also, one can speculate, because they signify differently from simplified characters. Instead of "comrade" or even "*shifu*" (master), young female service personnel are addressed, even by mainland Chinese, as "*xiaojie*," that is, "miss."

A Shanghai fad is to speak with a mock Hong Kong accent when introducing singers at karaoke bars. Many Hong Kong English-derived words have replaced Mandarin in common speech, such as *leishe* for laser (*jiguang* in Mandarin); *feilin* for film (*jiaojuan*); *dishi* for taxi (*chuzuche*); *bashi* for bus (*gonggong qiche*).[18] Advertisements in Shanghai newspapers solicit students to learn Cantonese. Hong Kong currency is widely used in Guangdong, and the New Taiwan dollar is tendered in some locations as well. Clothing styles, especially among young women, make it extremely difficult to distinguish Chinese from the mainland from those from Taiwan, Hong Kong or South-east Asia.

The cultural flow has not been one way, nor have all regions or art forms been equally affected. Mainland cultural works have always been available in Hong Kong, but have only appeared in Taiwan in the past few years. Printed works include those of leftist writers such as Lu Xun and others who stayed on the mainland after the KMT withdrew to Taiwan.[19] Their works have appeared in book form and on the literary page of the major news dailies. Video cassettes of mainland feature films, documentaries, travelogues, even *River Elegy* (*Heshang*) are also available, primarily in pirated versions sold in street stalls. Taiwan's underground cable Channel 4 (a generic term covering many small companies) regularly broadcasts mainland costume soap operas such as *Dream of the Red Chamber*, *The Three Song Sisters* and *The Last Emperor*.[20] Some performing art troupes from the mainland, from the Central Ballet Troupe to local opera companies, have begun to tour Taiwan.[21] After decades of banning contact with the mainland, the Kuomintang government belatedly uses this as a way of trying to emphasize Taiwan's Chinese roots in a rearguard effort to fend off

---

*footnote continued*

paper presented at the Annual Meeting of the Association for Asian Studies, Los Angeles, 25–28 March 1993. Cited with permission.

18. I am grateful to Ambrose King for this list.

19. Ma Hanmao (Helmut Martin), "Haixia liangan di wenxue jiaoliu" ("Literature flow across the Straits"), in Ma Hanmao (H. Martin) (ed.), *Zhengbuduan di Hongsixian* (*The Unbreakable Red Thread*) (Gaoxiong: Dunli Pub. Co., 1987), pp. 281–88.

20. Luo Rulan, "Dalu yingdai Taiwan remai" ("Taiwan enthusiastically sells mainland film tapes"), *ZGSBZK*, 16–22 February 1992, p. 67. Strictly speaking, broadcasting these tapes is illegal, and no royalties are paid. I am grateful to Joseph Bosco for clarification. Channel 4 achieved legal status in 1993.

21. "Liangan wenhua jiaoliu mairu xinlicheng – dalu yanyi tuanti jiang luxu futai" ("Cultural exchange across the Straits strides on a new course – mainland performing arts troupes will visit Taiwan one after another"), *ZGSBZK*, 19–25 July 1992, pp. 80–82. On 9 June 1992, the Republic of China government passed regulations permitting mainland performers to come to Taiwan for commercial performances.

increasingly strident demands for independence. But clearly, the direction of the cultural flow is overwhelmingly into the mainland and not out to Hong Kong and Taiwan.

## The Appeal of Gangtai Popular Culture

Why has the popular culture of Hong Kong and Taiwan spread so rapidly and widely on the mainland?

First, it has for some time demonstrated its enormous appeal in other Chinese communities, so why should mainland China be any different? In fact, many of its elements can also be found in non-Chinese societies in the region. The pop songs, musical extravaganzas, martial arts films, soap operas, romance fiction and so on seen in Japan and South Korea, for instance, are often identical (save the language) to the same things in Taiwan and Hong Kong.[22]

A second reason is its novelty. For decades, the Communist Party employed heavy-handed efforts to control cultural production, strictly define taste, and restrict and denigrate leisure-time activities and the service sector. This reached an extreme during the Cultural Revolution decade when only a very limited number of products passed official muster, and knowledge of foreign popular culture was virtually nil. For music, cultural workers created "light music" by adding Western pro-fessional techniques – which were seen as advanced – to traditional melodies (Han and minority), or by composing new pieces based on similar melodies.[23] By contrast, the pop culture from Hong Kong and Taiwan is clearly commercial and not produced to party dictates. When one contrasts the extraordinary intensity and dogmatism of mainland cultural goods throughout the 1970s, the sense of fun and relaxation conveyed by Gangtai imports is quite striking.[24]

The tracks on a concert recording released in the 1970s by the singer Guo Lanying – the original White-Haired Girl, popular with the Yan'an set – are unrelentingly ideological and shrill. They use traditional north China folk melodies and instruments. Teresa Teng, on the other hand, has

22. In the music area, Charles Hamm discusses a generic "Pacific Pop" with the following stylistic features: "moderate tempi, texts concerned with romantic love, string-dominated backings (now often generated by synthesizer), a singing style reminiscent of Olivia Newton-John and Barry Manilow, and the frequent use of rhythmic patterns derived from disco music of the 1970s." Charles Hamm, "Music and radio in the People's Republic of China," *Asian Music*, Vol. XXII, No. 2 (Spring/Summer 1991), pp. 1–42 at p. 17.

23. Hamm, "Music and radio," p. 7.

24. The characteristics of Gangtai popular music include: "smooth, flowing melodies, which usually have no direct or obvious relationship with traditional Chinese melodic construction; a type of vocal production which was described to me as the 'middle way' (a term carrying a positive connotation) between Western full, ringing vocal style and Chinese folksong style; lyrics emphasizing feelings of love between young men and young women; a relatively high level of technical sophistication, from the standpoint of studio production; and an easy dance beat back-ground (provided by the instruments most commonly used in Western popular music), which Americans might commonly associate with 'light' disco-inspired dance music, or with the popular music style commonly known as 'easy-listening'." Tim Brace, "Popular music in contemporary Beijing: modernism and cultural identity," *Asian Music*, Vol. XXII, No. 2 (Spring/Summer 1991), pp. 43–66 at p. 47.

a soft, slightly tremulous (actually, quite Japanese-sounding, reflecting her training there) and seductive voice. Andrew Jones quotes songwriter Jia Ding as being virtually transfixed upon first hearing Teng's songs in 1978, and we can assume a similar reaction throughout society.[25] This is not to argue that all Chinese prefer the Teng sound, just to emphasize the glaring novelty.

A third reason for its appeal is its content. Where Communist culture is heavily ideological and addresses large themes of modernization, nationalism, socialism and so on, Hong Kong/Taiwan culture is intensely personal. As a young man in Hangzhou explained, the strong point of Hong Kong and Taiwan song lyrics is their ability to concentrate on small incidents and feelings that people can identify with, and not the great issues of the motherland or reform.[26] These songs, and by extension other art forms, express individual emotions (*yanqing*). A Shanghainese referred to these songs as "*shenghuoxing*," more related to actual life as opposed to abstract concepts.[27] Song lyrics and written words provide a language for mainland Chinese to express individual emotions – the word "I" occurs frequently – which had previously been denigrated.

A popular song of 1979, which in its musical arrangement (heavy use of a synthesizer) and lyrics already reflected the influence of Teresa Teng, still illustrated the mainland lyricists' attention to large issues even while attempting to express an individual emotion:

> The flowers of prosperity blossom in our hearts,
> Songs of love are blowing in the wind.
> Our hearts fly to faraway places,
> Looking for that beautiful revolutionary ideal.
> Ah! Beloved, let's hold hands and march forward,
> Our life is full of sunshine.[28]

Contrast this with the lyrics to "Go With Your Feelings":

> Go with your feelings,
> Tightly grasp the dream hand.
> Footsteps grow lighter and lighter,
> Livelier and livelier.
> With all your emotion, spread around your smile
> Love can grasp me at any place.[29]

The romance novels of Taiwan's Qiong Yao offer a similar sort of emotional expression and release.[30] Some consumers like the fact that

25. Andrew F. Jones, *Like a Knife: Ideology and Genre in Contemporary Chinese Popular Music* (Ithaca: Cornell University East Asia Program, 1992), p. 16.

26. Interview, Hangzhou, 19 November 1992.

27. Interview, Berkeley, 5 March 1993.

28. "Women di shenghuo chunman yangguang" ("Our life is full of sunshine"), on the cassette *1979nian Zhongguo Jinqu Shiwushou* (*15 Chinese Golden Hits 1979*), Baili Record Co., 1980.

29. "Genzhe ganjue zou" ("Go with your feelings"), lyrics by Chen Jiali.

30. In the poll referred to in n. 1, Qiong Yao ranked first among eight authors for name recognition: 85.8%. The runner up, interestingly enough, was Cultural Revolution writer Hao Ran (79.8%). Third was the nihilistic Beijing writer Wang Shuo (70.3%) and fourth was martial arts writer Jin Yong (64.3%). When asked which of eight authors they had actually read, the rankings

they can more readily identify with the lives of people in Gangtai fiction. For instance, the prolific Hong Kong writer Leung Fung-yee, herself a businesswomen, specializes in novels about business people. Mainland Chinese private entrepreneurs and stock traders, still with somewhat low status politically and socially, find her works especially appealing as she legitimates their activities in their own eyes, making them feel they are engaged in a moral enterprise.[31]

A fourth appeal of the culture is its accessibility; it is in Chinese. It is a hybrid of modern Western culture and East Asian traditions, but being in Chinese makes it easier to comprehend than unmediated Western or Japanese works.[32] Fifth and related, it is at the same time decidedly foreign and modern – it comes from outside the PRC.[33] The music itself, apart from the Chinese lyrics, bears little in the way of Chinese character-istics. Consuming it gives one a sense of participating in a sophisticated global activity. Because mainland Chinese now know that Hong Kong and Taiwan have achieved miraculous economic development and their people have a high standard of living, they provide a model of a modern Chinese life-style for mainland Chinese to emulate. There is a prestige attached to demonstrating familiarity with Hong Kong and Taiwan fashion, colloquialisms, behaviour and taste.

A final appeal lies in the escapist aspect of Hong Kong/Taiwan culture. Martial arts adventures are from a different time of course, but the contemporary romantic songs and novels lift consumers out of the generally harsh reality of life on the mainland. Qiong Yao's stories, soap operas and ubiquitous advertisements bespeak a middle-class world of passion and indulgence far removed from that of most Chinese. It provides an escape. Going to a glitzy Hong Kong-style restaurant with courteous and attentive service provides another sort of escape not only from cramped living quarters, but also from the insulting service and decrepit ambience of most state-owned eating establishments.

## Explaining the Spread of Gangtai Popular Culture

No single factor explains the rapid and extensive spread of Hong Kong and Taiwan popular culture throughout mainland China, but four variables – technology, social structure, economics and politics – should be explored.

---

*footnote continued*

were: Qiong 71.8%; Hao 69.8%; Wang 57.4%; and Jin 55.2%. Respondents were asked to rank the eight by preference (1,2,3). Hao Ran received the highest number of first ranks (29.9%), while Qiong Yao came in second with 27.6%. Jin Yong scored 19.4% and Wang Shuo 13.2%. Liu Xiaobo, "Toushi dalu renmin di wenhua shenghuo," part 2, *ZGSBZK*, No. 62, 7–13 March 1993, pp. 74–79 at p. 75.

31. Interview, Shanghai, 12 November 1992.

32. Western (especially American) and Japanese popular culture are also wildly popular, although being in a foreign language makes them harder to identify with.

33. This point is also made by Brace, "Popular music," p. 48. Although official propaganda treats Gangtai people as blood compatriots, many Chinese on the street with whom I spoke included them in the category of "foreigners."

*Technology.* The post-1978 reforms have introduced and popularized the technological means to facilitate the spread of culture. This includes domestic as well as foreign culture, high and low, ideological and popular. Prior to the reforms, privately-owned televisions and short-wave radios were virtually non-existent except for the elite. People watched television in the office of the neighbourhood committee, production brigade or other collective setting. The masses could not own short-wave radios, and foreign stations were jammed in any case. Although personal radios, including transistors, were not uncommon, what went out over the airwaves was tightly controlled by the party-state. The same was true for gramophone records, publishing, cinema and stage performances.

The introduction of cassette recorders at the end of the 1970s must be considered a revolution. They were much less expensive than televisions or record players, were mobile, and were capable of making instant copies of other tapes or records. One could listen to and copy tapes in the privacy of one's home. The advent of the walkman facilitated this even more – listening through personal earphones put one beyond the reach of snooping neighbours.

Video cassette recorders and karaoke equipment, which add a visual dimension, are not as common or inexpensive as televisions and cassettes, but serve the same functions of spreading cultural products widely and permitting private enjoyment. During the 1980s, privately-owned short-wave radios began to appear, receiving the foreign broadcasts which the regime stopped jamming at the same time. Private telephones – including cellular phones – have become widespread in the cities, making it possible to speak directly with people abroad. Fax machines, now quite common in offices, make possible the spread of printed materials; during the 1989 demonstrations they were crucial in disseminating information from abroad and around China. In a further escalation, satellite dishes have begun to appear throughout China.[34] This has opened the airwaves to a wide variety of non-officially approved programmes, in particular Hong Kong's Television Broadcasts Ltd. (TVB) and its rival, Star Television which broadcasts MTV Asia, entertainment, news and sports shows.[35]

34. Nicholas D. Kristof, "Via satellite, information revolution stirs China," *The New York Times*, 11 April 1993, p. 1.

35. *Ibid.* Kristof writes that "at last count, 1,800 cable television systems were operating in China, with 429 set up in just the first three months of this year. . . . A State Statistical Bureau survey several months ago found that 4.8 million households in China can receive Star Television – presumably a significant underestimation, since the bureau counted only Government-authorized satellite dishes" (p. 6). With more than 11 million viewers in Asia, Star TV is contributing disproportionately to the unification of Asian (including Chinese) popular culture. It can be accessed virtually everywhere in China, and it brings PRC programming directly into Taiwan, bypassing government restrictions there. It was established in 1991 by Richard Li, son of Hong Kong tycoon Li Ka-Shing. Liam Fitzpatrick, "Does Asia want my MTV? An interview with Richard Li," *Hemispheres*, July 1993, p. 21; Rachel F.F. Lee, "TV viewers star-struck by satellite broadcasts," *Free China Journal*, 25 May 1993, p. 5. Media mogul Rupert Murdoch bought 64% of Star TV in July 1993. Andrew Tanzer, "Four heavenly kings," *Forbes*, 30 August 1993, p. 51.

*Social structure.* Although the technology became available to enable popular culture to spread from Taiwan, Hong Kong and elsewhere, social structural changes have been crucial in making this actually happen. Of primary importance has been the improved standard of living which has made it possible for increasing numbers of Chinese to purchase cassette recorders, televisions and now satellite dishes.[36] Once out-of-reach status symbols, cassettes and colour televisions, at least, have become household necessities in cities and quite widespread in rural areas as well.

The single child family policy has induced many Chinese adults, who now have the financial wherewithal, to indulge their children and grandchildren, buying them electronic equipment and cultural goods. Young workers commonly still live with their parents until they are married; even if they contribute to family expenses, they retain much of their wages. Married couples who delay childbirth combine two incomes and low rents, leaving a surplus. The millions of small-scale entrepreneurs (*getihu*) who have appeared as a consequence of the reforms have set a new standard for conspicuous consumption and indulgence. They frequent expensive Gangtai-style restaurants and clubs.

Knowledge of the outside world, improved education and disposable income have changed tastes, making many citizens dissatisfied with the sterile output of Party culture workers and receptive to the appeals discussed above. Opening to the outside world has brought in millions of tourists who bring electronics as well as objects of popular culture for their own enjoyment and to give to friends and relatives. Overseas Chinese, who bring in Chinese-language material, have the greatest impact. By now, millions of mainland Chinese have gone abroad for short or long stays, and are virtually obliged to return home laden with electronics ("The Eight Great Treasures") as well as other items. The ones who stay abroad for a long time are likelier to have cultivated a taste for foreign things, which they carry back and introduce to their fellows.

A survey in Beijing of some 14,000 students, teachers, parents and principals revealed that television watching was the major extracurricular activity among students, and

that there is a bias in favor of foreign-made films and television productions, and those made in Hong Kong or Taiwan. Of the students surveyed, 47.4 per cent indicated that they especially liked foreign-made and dubbed (translated) films, and 44.9 per cent indicated that they liked films made in Hong Kong or Taiwan, whereas only 6.6 per cent indicated that they liked films produced in Mainland China.[37]

The survey revealed similar preference in music:

Our survey of 234 students in the third year of lower middle school in six schools in the Chongwen District in Beijing Municipality indicates that 84.5 percent of these

36. In his "Report on the Work of the Government," Premier Li Peng claimed that, "In 1992 the average amount of per-capita income that city dwellers used for living expenses was 1,826 *yuan*, an increase of 910 *yuan* over the 1987 figure. The average per-capita net income of farmers was 784 *yuan*, an increase of 321 *yuan*." In *Beijing Review*, 12–18 April 1993, p. III.

37. "Report on the survey on 'Social and Cultural Life and Ethics Education in the Middle Schools'," *Chinese Education and Society*, Vol. 26, No. 2 (March–April 1993), pp. 6–39 at p. 15. I want to thank Stanley Rosen for bringing this survey to my attention.

students like Hong Kong and Taiwan popular singers, and when students were asked to write down titles of their favorite songs, twenty of the thirty most popular songs, or 66.7 percent, were songs from Hong Kong and Taiwan.[38]

The survey revealed a general "confusion" about the cultural market-place, values and taste which make young people more susceptible to these newly available things, and their elders (parents and teachers) unsure of how best to deal with it. This should not be surprising, given the inconsistent cultural policies of the Communists. Most traditional Chinese culture as well as most of what was produced under Party stewardship up until the Cultural Revolution was criticized and banned for more than a decade. The paucity and sterility of much of what was promoted to replace it created a vacuum which Gangtai culture has filled. There are hundreds of millions of Chinese who do not know how to appreciate traditional high culture but who find Gangtai culture appealing.

*Economics.* "Opening to the outside world and enlivening the domestic economy," the watchword of the reforms, has dramatically altered China's economic institutions, paving the way for the introduction and dissemination of Gangtai popular culture. In particular, with the marke-tization and privatization of much of economic life, culture included, producers by necessity have become keenly sensitive to what sells. The introduction of enterprise responsibility for profits and losses has created very real pressure to make money. State enterprises, including military companies turning to the civilian market, are flooding stores with elec-tronics and other items. Both local and Gangtai entrepreneurs have moved aggressively to get a piece of the action. With the increase in disposable income and leisure time, the opportunities to develop and penetrate the expanding market are irresistible. As an indication of its size, Taiwan's Chen Shuhua sold 800,000 cassette tapes; after performing on the mainland, Tong Ange sold more than 10 million audio and karaoke tapes; and Taiwan singers with a mainland following, such as Zhao Chuan and Pan Meichen, now produce at least one million copies of each tape.[39]

Much of Gangtai cultural production is spread through pirating. The wide availability of equipment facilitates this, and copies of audio and video cassette tapes are easily available and quite inexpensive. Following complaints by Hong Kong and Taiwan businessmen (ironic because many of them practised the same trade), mainland distributors have begun to negotiate contracts for distribution of Gangtai works. Hong Kong middle-men dominate this market.[40] Taiwan and Hong Kong promoters

38. *Ibid.* p. 16.
39. Gu Biling, Luo Rulan and Zhou Pinger, "Hong Kong and Taiwan stars," pp. 66–67.
40. Hong Kong's underworld is known to be heavily involved in the entertainment industry, so we can conclude gangsters are also involved in distributing Gangtai works on the mainland ("Heishili changjue yingquan han jiuwang" ("The film industry cries for help from underworld violence"), *Jiushi Niandai* (*Nineties*), June 1992, pp. 23–27). Because of the rationing of distribu-tion rights by the PRC government to domestic enterprises, we can speculate that there is a certain

have become crucial to the careers of many mainland artists. For instance, Taiwan's *Gunshi* (Rolling Stone) Company and Hong Kong's *Dadi* (Great Earth) have stepped in to promote mainland rock-and-roll and popular music. Dadi has its own promotional show on Central Television. Mainland rock groups (as opposed to the much softer popular or light music) have more trouble finding investors. Groups such as Tang Dynasty and Black Panther have received Taiwan and Hong Kong support,[41] which is useful not only at home, but for penetrating the international market.[42] Actors, directors and writers are signing up with outside promoters with lots of money. Xie Jin, a leading mainland film director, met Taiwan's prominent director Li Xing and Hong Kong producer Qiu Fusheng just after Taiwan's Golden Horse Film Awards.[43] The internationally acclaimed director Zhang Yimou has received Japanese funding for some of his recent films, and Taiwan director Hou Hsiao-hsien was involved in Zhang's 1992 work, *The Story of Qiuju*.[44]

As well as the pirating of Gangtai works, economic necessity compelled mainland performers to include them in their repertoire and writers and composers to imitate them.[45] In popular music, this is apparent in

---

*footnote continued*

amount of corruption in this part of the business. I am grateful to John Burns and Andrew Jones for raising these issues.

41. "Shangpinhua weixie Beijing yaogunyue" ("Commoditization threatens Beijing's rock-and-roll"); *ZGSBZK*, No. 60, 21–27 February 1993, pp. 66–67.

42. Gu Biling, "Changchu zheyidai Zhongguoren di xinsheng" ("Sing out the aspirations of this generation of Chinese"), *ZGSBZK*, No. 53, 3–9 January 1993, p. 76–77; Matei P. Mihalca, "Chinese rock stars," *Far Eastern Economic Review*, 19 November 1992, pp. 34–36; Song Chunsen, "Dalu mingxing haiwai zhanshenshou" ("Mainland stars reach out abroad"), *ZGSBZK*, No. 50, 13–19 December 1992, pp. 78–79.

43. "Liangan dianyingjie sanlongtou wei Zhongguo dianying bamai" ("Three dragons of the film world from two sides of the Straits stimulate Chinese cinema"), *ZGSBZK*, No. 54, 10–16 January 1993, pp. 94–95.

44. For additional information, see Jiao Xiongping, "Cong bingfeng gejue dao jiedong huiliu – huaren dianying di guoqu yu weilai" ("From frozen isolation to thawed confluence – past and future of Chinese cinema"), *ZGSBZK*, 2–15 February 1992, pp. 45–51.

45. There was also an effort at competition. This took the form of emphasizing and reincorporating some of the traditions of inland peasant China which had been neglected in the focus on the coastal regions and opening to the outside world. The "root-seeking" fiction and peasant films of such "fifth generation" directors as Chen Kaige and Zhang Yimou (and their mentor Wu Tianming) generated interest among intellectuals in particular and the films attracted much international attention and acclaim. They presented very unglamorous portraits of the North China peasantry. Some hardliners criticized the directors for emphasizing China's backwardness and pandering to foreign audiences who seemed to enjoy seeing such degradation. The controversial 1988 television documentary *Heshang* (*River Elegy*) argued that these same traditions were responsible for China's continued failure to modernize. The film scores utilized traditional instruments, singing styles and themes, resulting in a "north-west wind" (*xibeifeng*) style which was popular for a time in 1987–89. While reincorporating elements of traditional music, they also incorporated some of the new qualities of instrumental accompaniment and production imported from Hong Kong/Taiwan. On these matters, see Brace, "Popular music," pp. 49–53; and Jones, *Like a Knife*, pp. 52–63. To compete head-on, in 1991 the Ministry of Propaganda produced an extensive series of karaoke audio and video tapes of officially-produced mainland music, including highly politicized songs and selections from the Cultural Revolution's model operas. Nevertheless, Chinese statistics indicated that "over 80% of the most popular 600 songs used in the bars originated outside the mainland (mostly Taiwan and Hong Kong)." Barme, "The greying of Chinese culture," p. 13.18.

melody, orchestration, lyrics and performance style. Literature and drama reveal increased attention to matters of love, personal appearance, leisure and consumption, all of which characterize Gangtai works. Much more of this can be expected following the official call to intellectuals to *xiahai* (literally, go down into the sea), meaning enter the market economy part or full-time.

*Politics.* One might ask why the Communist Party, which has exerted so much effort over its entire life span to directing and monopolizing the entire superstructural realm, has failed to stem this pandemic. On several occasions during the reform era, conservative elements, with the acquiescence of moderates, did try to launch attacks on vague targets variously condemned as bourgeois liberalization, spiritual pollution, wholesale Westernization, negative social effects, pornography, the six pests, and so on. Gangtai popular culture was criticized as part of these movements.[46]

These efforts failed ignominiously. Their most outspoken advocates were perceived as relics of the Yan'an or Cultural Revolution mind-set, hopelessly out of touch with the reality of the reformist, open China of the 1980s. As gossip about corruption and sybaritism among the elite and especially its children spread, their tiresome trumpeting of asceticism, sacrifice, struggle, Chinese tradition (odd, for revolutionaries) and the Lei Feng way appeared increasingly hypocritical and ludicrous. The gap between official ideology and the reality that Chinese, especially young urbanites, experienced, turned them decisively away from the lofty collectivist ideals which the authorities defined as central to a good life towards the individualist values expressed in Gangtai and other foreign culture.[47] Heavily ideological works, as well as traditional art forms such as Peking opera, are facing tough times.[48]

The confused signals emanating from the authorities at the Centre greatly harmed the work of teachers and others charged with transmitting official values. As the post-4 June survey cited above revealed, teachers, who were raised in a different social and cultural environment, have trouble understanding the students' world.[49] Parents are likewise out of touch, and the increasingly busy lives of parents and teachers have caused a breakdown in the former close co-operation between the two in the cause of socialization of youth. The authors of the survey put forward no proposals more imaginative or fresh than strengthening Party leadership,

---

46. See Thomas B. Gold, " 'Just in time!' China battles spiritual pollution on the eve of 1984," *Asian Survey*, Vol. XXIV, No. 9 (September 1984), pp. 947–974; and Orville Schell, *Discos and Democracy: China in the Throes of Reform* (New York: Pantheon, 1988).

47. Stanley Rosen has published several essays providing empirical evidence for popular attitudes – especially youth attitudes – toward the party-state and ideology. For an example, see "Students and the state in China: the crisis in ideology and organization," in Arthur Lewis Rosenbaum (ed.), *State and Society in China: The Consequences of Reform* (Boulder: Westview Press, 1992), pp. 167–191.

48. The state continues to subsidize many of these traditional units and their leaders are trying to think of ways to "modernize" them enough to appeal to youth. Meanwhile, faced with the need to make money, many troupes are opening restaurants and clubs.

49. "Report on the survey," p. 13.

formulating a unified plan, "providing good intellectual and spiritual food for the middle school students and creating a better social environment," and so on.[50]

Although the combined traditional–Communist urge impelling "directed culture" in China remains strong,[51] the bankruptcy of what it has to offer, combined with the technological, social and economic changes analysed above, certainly seems to doom it to failure. The authorities have failed to promulgate a coherent or appealing set of guidelines for popular culture in the current era.[52] The Communist Party is in an impossible situation of its own making: it is encouraging and compelling cultural units and individuals to assume responsibility for their own economic health, even to the point of urging artists to leave their units and go on their own, while simultaneously drastically reducing political demands on them, relying instead on a "velvet prison," where most willingly censor themselves, make money and avoid trouble.[53] Material imperatives dictate that they produce what the market wants, and what the most free-spending segment of the market wants is either Gangtai culture or close approximations to it. The Party has in effect yielded a "zone of indifference" in the cultural realm to producers and consumers, where it will not intrude excessively as the costs outweigh the benefits.[54]

Permitting Gangtai culture to circulate on the mainland does however perform something of a positive function for the Party. In the early 1980s, a handful of Gangtai artists came to the mainland with the Party's blessing to promote manifestly pro-reunification works. This extremely selective promotion was a way for the regime to show to its own people the veracity of its propaganda about the people of Hong Kong and Taiwan yearning for reunification. The premier example is Taiwan's popular singer/songwriter Hou Dejian, who slipped from Hong Kong to Beijing in 1983.[55] Hou's signature work was his own composition, "Descendants of the Dragon" (*Long di Chuanren*), something between a dirge and a chant, which expresses the frustrations of a Chinese who has

50. *Ibid.* pp. 33–39.

51. Timothy Cheek, "A literature of protest, a literature of change: on the role of directed culture in Chinese literature," in Bih-Jaw Lin and James T. Myers (eds.), *Forces for Change in Contemporary China* (Taipei: Institute of International Relations, 1992), pp. 239–250.

52. See the discussion in Geremie Barme, "The Chinese velvet prison: culture in the 'new age,' 1976–89," *Issues and Studies*, Vol. 25, No. 8 (August 1989), pp. 54–79 at pp. 70–75.

53. Geremie Barme applies the Hungarian writer Miklos Haraszti's concept to China in "The Chinese velvet prison." See also, Richard Curt Kraus, "Four trends in the politics of Chinese culture," in Lin and Myers, *Forces for Change in Contemporary China*, pp. 213–24.

54. One area where it has intruded more is rock-and-roll (*yaogun yinyue*) as contrasted with the popular music (*tongsu yinyue*) discussed above. This appeals to a more fringe audience. See Jones, *Like a Knife*, and "Beijing bastards," *Spin*, October 1992, pp. 80–90, 122–23; and Orville Schell, "China's rock and roll underground," *San Francisco Chronicle This World*, 29 November 1992, pp. 7, 12–13.

55. Ironically, given the fact that he was one of a group of four intellectuals left at Tiananmen Square in the early hours of 4 June 1989, Hou's defection to Beijing occurred on 4 June 1983. Much of the following information on Hou comes from Yang Zujun, " 'Long di chuanren' shi zenma dao Beijing di?" ("How did the 'descendant of the dragon' get to Beijing?"), *Qianjin* (*Progress*), No. 12, 18 June 1983, pp. 4–8; "Hou Dejian di jueze" ("Hou Dejian's choice"), *ibid.* pp. 6–7.

never been to the mainland. After his defection, the song received aggressive promotion on the mainland and Hou became an instant celebrity.[56] Another of Hou's Taiwan compositions, "Do You Have Old Bottles to Sell?" (*Jiugan tang maiwu*) – the theme from the film, *Papa Can You Hear Me Sing?* (*Dacuoche*) – was also broadcast frequently in the mid-1980s.[57]

During the summer of 1984, Hong Kong singer Zhang Mingmin's uplifting "My Chinese Heart" (*Wodi Zhongguo Xin*) was broadcast endlessly and he performed on the mainland. Against the backdrop of the Sino-British talks on Hong Kong then under way, Zhang's actions ostensibly underscored the yearning of Hong Kong residents for re-unification.

Unfortunately for the cultural commissars, the import of Gangtai popular culture expanded well beyond such patriots. Tolerating this uncontrolled influx can have a positive political payoff for the regime, in that it demonstrates to Hong Kong and Taiwan residents living on or visiting the mainland that life under the Chinese Communist Party is not as terribly restrictive as they feared, and that leisure time can be constructed pretty much as at home.

If anything, performers from Taiwan and Hong Kong have become more ubiquitous since 4 June, including over the party-state-controlled airwaves. This is a way of profiting from as well as attempting to co-opt their popularity. It is evidence of the CCP's implicit acknowledgement of its problematic relationship with society and its reduction in political demands on the people at large.

Pulling together the four variables discussed in this section, it can be seen that the Party undertook economic reforms to regain the legitimacy damaged by the Cultural Revolution. It redefined its primary task as modernization, which involved marketizing and privatizing the domestic economy and opening to foreign investment, trade, tourism, experts, students, and so on. The Party greatly relaxed its control over the superstructure, both in terms of ideology and directed culture. Rapid, although unequally distributed, economic development ensued, with shops well stocked with consumer goods, and citizens with money to spend. The state stressed the importance of the tertiary sector, legitimiz-

---

56. Prior to his defection, the KMT also approved of the song and invited Hou to compose "Uniting China with the three principles of the people." See Yang Zujun, " 'Long di Chuanren'," p. 5.

57. The very popular (in Taiwan) soundtrack for this forgettable film was sung by Su Rui, who also recorded "Go With Your Feelings." In 1985 I saw the Changsha Opera Troupe's performance of its stage version of the film entitled *Jiugan Tang Maiwu* in Changsha. Hou does not appear to have been very productive while on the mainland. He issued one recording, *Hou Dejian zuopinji* (*Collected Works of Hou Dejian*) through the China Audio and Video Recording Company, undated. He does not sing all of the tracks, and many songs predate his defection. Interestingly, in retrospect, there is one song in English which he does sing, "Well, I Need to Be Alone." Hou hid in the Australian Embassy for a time after the Tiananmen killings. After emerging with assurances of no reprisals, he granted several outspoken interviews to foreign journalists, and was unceremoniously put on a fishing boat in Fujian and shipped off to Taiwan in mid-1990, where he remains very quiet. See Geremie Barme and Linda Jaivin (eds.), *New Ghosts, Old Dreams: Chinese Rebel Voices* (New York: Times Books, 1992), pp. xix–xx, 48, 72, 82n.

ing personal enjoyment and leisure time, and leaving it to individuals to decide how to structure it. Gangtai popular culture demonstrated its appeal to mainland Chinese, and aggressive domestic and external entrepreneurs moved to cultivate and satisfy this market.

*Implications for Greater China*

Together with increased economic and personal linkages, the spread of a common popular culture among Taiwan, Hong Kong and the mainland is an additional force for the formation and integration of a Greater China. As in the economy, the mainland is supplying the market, while Hong Kong and Taiwan are supplying the commodities, expertise, networks and capital. What might the ultimate political consequences be?

It needs to be stressed again that the flow is overwhelmingly unidirectional, from Hong Kong and Taiwan into the mainland. It is also not evenly distributed: the kindred regions of Guangdong and Fujian have been exposed longer and more deeply than the interior, and cities more than countryside. For Hong Kong and Taiwan, the main impact is economic – an increasingly larger dependence on the mainland market. There may also be revived interest in Chinese traditional arts and curiosity about the mainland pop scene. This forces us to reconsider the idea of "core and periphery" in terms of the creativity and dynamism of contemporary Chinese culture, and ability of the old, increasingly moribund core, to exert control over the regions far away. The geographically peripheral Chinese societies of Hong Kong and Taiwan (one might also include Overseas Chinese communities in South-east Asia) have risen into the semi-periphery of the global economy. Through their investments they are pulling selected regions of the mainland out of poverty and isolation. The cultural challenge from the geographical periphery toward the core is something altogether new and quite different.

As Tu Wei-ming argues in an important paper:

Although the phenomenon of Chinese culture disintegrating at the center and later being revived from the periphery is a recurring theme in Chinese history, it is unprecedented for the geopolitical center to remain entrenched while the periphery presents such powerful and persistent economic and cultural challenges. Either the center will bifurcate or, as is more likely, the periphery will come to set the economic and cultural agenda for the center, thereby undermining its political effectiveness.[58]

This clearly seems to sum up the situation at present. While they derive from a common root, elements of which undeniably survive, the decades of colonialism and autonomy have clearly caused Hong Kong and Taiwan to develop economic, social, political and cultural systems quite different from the mainland's. These differences are far greater than those among regions of the mainland itself. The phenomenal economic success has emboldened the people of Hong Kong and Taiwan, who are fanning out

58. Tu Wei-ming, "Cultural China: the periphery as the center," *Daedalus*, Vol. 120, No. 2 (Spring 1991), pp. 1–32 at p. 12.

across the world to engage in multifarious activities. This success needs to be contrasted with the recurrent failure of the mainland to achieve sustained economic development until it began to implement, on a piecemeal basis, central elements of the East Asian capitalist model.[59] In yet another failed reprise of the *ti/yong* dichotomy of trying to adopt foreign technology while maintaining a "Chinese" essence, the Communists have found that culture (including values) cannot be entirely separated from technology, certainly not by fiat from a regime struggling with fundamental problems of delegitimation and moral bankruptcy.

Gangtai popular culture has short and long-term consequences for the mainland. In the short run, it might actually have a stabilizing effect on the regime. To understand this, it is necessary to look at how it is "read" by mainland audiences, youth in particular. Andrew Jones discusses three forms of reception of popular culture which are useful here.[60] First is hegemonic, where the ideology reflects and reinforces the domination of the ruling class, and the masses consent to it. As argued above, popular culture produced by the regime now has little market. In effect, there is no longer a clearly hegemonic popular culture as the regime's control over society and the superstructure continues to erode.

The second form is negotiated reception, where some ground is left for expressing emotions such as anger, "without confronting the social mechanics of domination per se." Gangtai popular culture fits in here. Reading the message of individuality and feelings does not directly challenge the regime's remaining political hegemony, but neither does it reflect consent. One may argue that it helps to carve out a private sphere apart from the collective. It institutionalizes the zone of indifference. It does not provide the release of frustrations which a safety valve might, but does offer an outlet for simply ignoring the authorities and opting out of the world they continue to try to dominate. This is returned to below.

The third mode of reception is emancipatory, which is explicitly subversive of the hegemonic codes. This includes what Haraszti calls "Maverick Artists," those "willing to sacrifice the privileges of the assimilated in order to retain their independence" although "by so doing they are doomed to eek [*sic*] out a meager existence as fringe-dwellers in a state-owned cultural desert crowded with mirages."[61] Explicit producers and consumers of this type of culture are still few, with rock-and-roll their main form of expression.[62] Gangtai music does have the potential for

---

59. I noted above the "search for roots" cultural movement on the mainland. In Taiwan, and to a lesser extent in Hong Kong, many intellectuals and artists have initiated a conscious movement to define the elements of what they argue is their unique identity. I discuss this in "Civil society and Taiwan's quest for identity," in Steven Harrell and Huang Chun-chieh (eds.), *Culture Change in Postwar Taiwan* (forthcoming).

60. Jones, *Like A Knife*, p. 46.

61. Barmé, "The Chinese velvet prison," p. 69.

62. Jones, *Like A Knife* and "Beijing bastards"; Mihalca, "Chinese rock stars"; Schell, "China's rock and roll underground." I attended a concert by China's premier rocker, Cui Jian, in Hangzhou in November 1992. The concert had a very definite cathartic effect on the youthful audience, but they did not turn their emotions outward into a rampage on the streets. They left the concert venue in a very orderly and quiet fashion. The heavy police presence may have had something to do with this.

emancipatory readings, however, as the use of "Go With Your Feelings" illustrates – it expresses not only Gangtai values but was also used to satirize the leadership.

Because the most common form of reception is the second, negotiated one, it represents something of a pact between the regime, which has given up both trying to eradicate Gangtai culture and to impose its own culture monopolistically, and the consumers, who do not translate dissatisfaction into unrest. This facilitates stability, at least in the short term. But in the long term, Gangtai popular culture is corrosive and potentially destabilizing, especially in league with the other changes under way in China which are gradually eroding the party-state's domination of the economy and superstructure. It is a central element of peaceful evolution. It provides a model of a modern Chinese life-style and a new language that breaks the hegemonic lock of Communist Newspeak.[63] The emergence of new social forces, continued integration into the outside world, spread of development from the coastal areas into the heartland, and increased local autonomy, increase the degree of complexity in China making it more difficult for the Party to enforce any sort of uniform domination.

Increasing societal autonomy is forcing the creation and expansion of a genuine public sphere, of which Gangtai culture is an important part. The funding of Chinese dissidents abroad, especially by Taiwan interests, brings a more explicit political element into it. The public sphere exists at many levels: national, local, and between local power and the Centre. It is already becoming contested terrain within and between these levels. This raises a central issue: what is the geographical scope of "Greater China"? Does the south, where Gangtai interests are strongest, wish to embark on a new Northern Expedition, or merely protect its autonomy?

As in 1989, this presents a very dangerous puzzle: how much will the Centre tolerate? And if it decides its limits of tolerance have been reached, how far, and in what fashion, is it prepared to go to reimpose control?

---

63. Jeffrey C. Goldfarb, *Beyond Glasnost: The Post-Totalitarian Mind* (Chicago: University of Chicago Press, 1989).

# Greater China and the Chinese Overseas

## Wang Gungwu

Some of the most important developments of the last quarter of the century have taken place in the Asia-Pacific region. Of these, the Chinese shift from Communist ideology and central planning to a commitment to build a market economy has had extensive ramifications. These have led to much speculation about the re-emergence of China as a powerful actor in world politics. The idea of Greater China is one of the products of that speculation. The lack of precision in the term "Greater China" – whether it should cover Hong Kong–Macao (hereafter Hong Kong), Taiwan and all of the People's Republic of China (PRC) or only parts of it – should not prevent it being used to explore some current and future developments. In this article, which examines the impact the concept of Greater China has on the Chinese overseas, the term would obviously not include those Chinese who live outside.[1] Nevertheless, depending on which aspect is emphasized, the actual area covered can be significant.

For example, if politics is the focus, then Greater China may be used to refer to a future unified China, the unitary state of Zhongguo, when the PRC, Taiwan (Republic of China) and Hong Kong (including Macao) are brought together. If the stress is on the dynamic process of economic integration, then Greater China may mean only the southern coastal provinces, Taiwan and Hong Kong, that is, the South China Economic Periphery, or perhaps more accurately "Lesser China." However, if the emphasis is on the broader picture of cultural China, the term may refer to the traditions of Chinese civilization and what has transformed them in modern times. In this context, it may be said that Great China has become Greater because its store of cultural values has been enhanced by modern borrowings, influences and adaptations. As a result, millions of ethnic Chinese now residing abroad might find it possible to identify with it.

A drawback of the term Greater China is that when used politically, there is an implication of expansionism towards the neighbouring regions, and when used culturally, it suggests a grandiosity which is at best misleading and at worst boastful. At this stage in history, only the apparent near-integration of the "Lesser China" of the South China Economic Periphery bears close scrutiny. All the same, since Greater China is becoming more used today, this article will try to bring out the effect the term has for the Chinese overseas.

"Chinese overseas" as a term is no more precise than Greater China. I have deliberately avoided the older term "Overseas Chinese" which translates the Chinese term *huaqiao*. That refers to Chinese sojourners, Chinese subjects or nationals temporarily residing abroad. Until recently, it was a term used for all people of Chinese descent, that is, all those descended from a Chinese father who were still recognizable as Chinese.

1. Harry Harding, "The concept of 'Greater China'," in this issue.

Today, *huaqiao* no longer includes those who have become foreign nationals. Since most Chinese living in foreign countries have adopted local nationalities, it is important to distinguish between the minority of "Overseas Chinese" who are Chinese nationals and the majority of foreign nationals who are ethnic Chinese.[2] For the purpose of this article, however, the distinction may not be necessary. Unfortunately, there is now no universally accepted term that includes all Chinese living abroad, both Chinese nationals and the ethnic Chinese. "Chinese Diaspora" is sometimes used but is unsatisfactory because its association with Jewish history is unacceptable in South-east Asia. I have therefore chosen to use "Chinese overseas" to refer to everyone of Chinese descent living outside Greater China.[3]

One further point should be noted. Some writings in the media have made estimates of the "Chinese Diaspora" that include the populations of Taiwan and Hong Kong.[4] Since Greater China in this volume includes the people of China, Taiwan and Hong Kong, clearly the term "Chinese overseas" does not include such populations. It refers here to all the people who live outside those three territories but acknowledge their Chinese origins, or are so regarded by demographers. There is no accurate figure of how many such Chinese there are. The most widely accepted numbers range between 25 and 30 million, four-fifths of whom live in South-east Asia.[5]

## Greater China in Economic, Political and Cultural Perspective

Other articles in this volume describe the developments within Greater China, and the emphasis is mainly on the Lesser (South) China of the southern provinces, Hong Kong and Taiwan. It is important to note that the majority of the Chinese overseas originated from the southern provinces. Even among those who did not, the majority emigrated after a period staying in either Hong Kong or Taiwan, especially those who left more recently after the end of the Second World War. The close relationship between these Chinese and the South China Economic Periphery, therefore, can be described as organic and deep-rooted and yet, at the same time, ongoing and dynamic. It has great potential, but is also full of historical memories and rich in emotional ties. Most of the current economic dimensions of the relationship cannot be separated from that thickly-knit background. This is not to deny that there has always been a link with political and cultural China of the Great Tradition, of the Empire and of the Confucian State, but for most Chinese overseas most

2. Wang Gungwu, "The origins of Hua-ch'iao," in Wang Gungwu, *Community and Nation: China, Southeast Asia and Australia (New Edition)* (Sydney: Allen and Unwin, 1992), pp. 1–10.

3. I have used this in the title of my book, *China and the Chinese Overseas* (Singapore: Times Academic Press, 1991).

4. *The Economist*, 21 November 1992.

5. Leo Suryadinata, "Ethnic Chinese in Southeast Asia: problems and prospects," *Journal of International Affairs*, Vol. 41, No. 1 (1987). Compare these figures with my estimates in "External China" in Brian Hook (ed.), *The Cambridge Encyclopaedia of China* (Cambridge: Cambridge University Press, 1982), pp. 104–110; and its new edition (1991), pp. 84–90.

of the time, it is South China which they know and care for. For them, the difference between the close-knit organic relationship with South China and the formal symbolic one with Greater China is an important part of their socialization at home and any Chinese education they may have.[6]

An important distinction can also be made about two other sets of relationships. One consists of the ancient relationships between coastal Chinese and the neighbouring countries like Korea, Japan, Vietnam and other countries in South-east Asia, with whom they have traded for millennia and to which many have emigrated continuously for centuries. The other are the relatively new relationships between the Chinese, again mostly coastal people from South China, and the Americas, Australasia, the rest of Asia, Europe and Africa, relationships which came after Western expansion into the Chinese area. That distinction will be indicated where it is relevant for this article. Otherwise, references to the Chinese overseas will include all those outside China who call themselves Chinese or are identified as Chinese, wherever they have chosen to settle down.

For recent decades, from 1949 to about 1980, when the Chinese mainland was largely outside the international trading system, there is yet another set of distinctions. This derives from the imbalance in the triangular relationships of Guangdong–Hong Kong–Taiwan and how the Chinese overseas were sensitive to that imbalance. Hong Kong was recognized by all as the pivot for the most effective economic links with China, especially for all non-official relationships through and with South China. Taiwan established in the 1950s, and for at least the next 20 years, many direct and profitable ties with the Chinese overseas in the non-Communist world, and was particularly successful in Japan, South Korea, the Philippines, Thailand, the United States and parts of Latin America and some countries in the rest of Asia, Europe and Africa. But for obvious reasons, it had no connections with the mainland of South China.[7]

The Chinese mainland had, for a while, its own special relationships with the Chinese in Indonesia, Burma, the Indo-Chinese states, the Soviet Union and other Communist or fraternal socialist states in Europe, Asia and Africa, but it was mostly a turbulent political relationship rather than a profitable commercial one.[8] This imbalance in the Guangdong–Hong Kong–Taiwan triangle clearly did not contribute directly to the growth of Greater China, or for that matter the South China Economic Periphery as defined here. It has, in any case, become much less significant since the

6. C.F. Yong, "Patterns and traditions of loyalty in the Chinese community of Singapore, 1900–1941," *The New Zealand Journal of History*, Vol. 4, No. 1 (1970) provides interesting examples of this experience.

7. The series of country by country volumes on the distribution of Overseas Chinese around the world, the *Hua-ch'iao chih* published in Taiwan from the mid-1950s, provides a useful, if not always accurate, record of these successes.

8. Stephen FitzGerald, *China and the Overseas Chinese* (Cambridge: Cambridge University Press, 1972), pp. 162–195.

mid-1980s, but it still needs to be kept in mind when considering how the present integrating forces are working on the economy and how the Chinese overseas as a whole might respond to them.

Within a brief article it is only possible to distinguish the main features of the remarkable developments of Greater China and survey briefly the impact they are having on the great variety of Chinese overseas. They are viewed from three perspectives. In economic affairs, the new investment opportunities and enhanced communications are clearly attractive. In terms of political changes, there has been unending drama in all parts of Greater China. Hopes have been aroused for major reforms, but there have also been events which produced depths of anguish and despair.[9] As for the cultural debates that have followed, they have led to both pride and incomprehension.

The most striking is clearly the economic perspective.[10] Chinese financiers, industrialists, hoteliers and property magnates from Hong Kong have been investing more and more in South China since the Joint Declaration was signed in 1984. Increasingly, similar investments are being made from Taiwan. And, of course, there have recently been public sector organizations from China making large investments in Hong Kong. Hence the prospect of integration that would make the whole area a single economic region. In the midst of all this, there are numerous reports that the Chinese overseas are joining the rush to invest in China. How significant is this?

Several prominent firms and businessmen in South-east Asia have recently attracted newspaper headlines, notably Liem Sioe Liong, Sinar Mas and Mochtar Riady from Indonesia,[11] Charoen Pokphand and the Sophonphanich family from Thailand,[12] and the Kuok brothers and the Hong Leong Group from Malaysia.[13] In every case, they had been doing business with Hong Kong and had established bases in the territory. Many have extended their business empires to America and Europe and can be described as multinationals. As such, they could still be identified as Indonesian, Thai or Malaysian in origin, but many local politicians as well as commentators in the media tend to stress the fact that their founders and successors are mainly Chinese.

These "Chinese multinationals" had, since the early 1980s, been

9. The example of responses among the Chinese overseas to the tragedy at Tiananmen in June 1989 is instructive. In North America, Western Europe and Australasia, media reports were filled with emotional outbursts, especially from the younger generation. In South-east Asia and elsewhere in Asia, the reports of their responses were very muted.

10. There are numerous reports, ranging from the sensational to the matter-of-fact. The account in *The Economist*, 21 November 1992 remains one of the most useful to date.

11. Leo Suryadinata, "Chinese economic elites in Indonesia: a preliminary study," in Jennifer Cushman and Wang Gungwu (eds.), *Changing Identities of the Southeast Asian Chinese since World War II* (Hong Kong: Hong Kong University Press, 1988), pp. 269–277; Richard Robison, *Indonesia: The Rise of Capital* (Sydney: Allen and Unwin, 1986), pp. 278–288.

12. Akira Suehiro, "Capitalist development in Postwar Thailand: commercial bankers, industrial elite, and agribusiness groups," in Ruth McVey (ed.), *Southeast Asian Capitalists*, (Ithaca, NY: Cornell University Southeast Asia Program, 1992), pp. 42–61.

13. Lim Mah Hui, *Ownership and Control of the One Hundred Largest Corporations in Malaysia* (Kuala Lumpur: Oxford University Press, 1981), pp. 82–112.

looking for opportunities to invest in China from their Hong Kong bases. Some are known to have made investments and contributions on a smaller scale to specific areas, especially to their ancestral villages and towns if they still had relatives there. There is little evidence that they were investing in China for any reason other than an opportunity to set up a profitable business. But they were clearly preparing themselves for large-scale investments when the chances were there. All they were waiting for was a firm commitment from China to expand and sustain economic growth and welcome and protect foreign ventures. There is also no doubt that, when that moment came, the knowledge of China that these firms and entrepreneurs had, and their considerable familiarity with the evolving system of "market socialism," would be seen by the Chinese authorities as a great advantage. In that context, these enterprises expected that they would be favoured.

These South-east Asian Chinese are somewhat different from the few prominent Chinese businesses in the Americas and elsewhere, who showed enthusiasm for investing in China very early in the 1980s and who dealt directly with Beijing and not through bases in Hong Kong. The best-known example of this approach is Wang An in the United States, but others like Cyrus Tang and Charles Wang were also active.[14] For all of them, important changes in policy occurred when Deng Xiaoping visited the United States.[15] Responses from the Chinese there, however, varied considerably, ranging from enthusiasm to extreme caution. The real difference between past and present practice began after 1990 when it became clear that China would make major commitments to a market economy. With that assurance, these outside companies began to make long-term investments of large sums of money.

There were, of course, many other smaller investors from South-east Asia, and also Japan, Europe, the Americas and Australasia, who had been exploring the Chinese market, learning from hard experience and looking for appropriate connections for future ventures. There is no reliable data of how many there were. Most material is anecdotal, but the impression of abiding interest and a readiness to plunge in is strong. All one can say at this stage is that the many investors, unnamed and unnoticed, who made modest remittances and contributions to businesses and to their respective families during the past decade or so, provided the large reservoir of capital and experience for the explosion of activity after 1990.[16]

Most of these smaller firms are difficult to pin down because they rarely sent sizeable amounts of money directly to China from their own countries. The standard operation required that branches or agencies be

14. Mai Liqian (Him Mark Lai), *Cong Huaqiao dao Huaren–Ershi shiji Meiguo Huaren shehui fazhan shi* (*From Huaqiao to Huaren: A History of the Development of Chinese Communities in America*) (Hong Kong: Joint Publishing, 1992), pp. 392–416, 437–463.

15. Deng Xiaoping's visit in January 1979 met with mixed receptions from the politicized sections of the Chinese American population, but was greeted with relief by most businessmen.

16. The only reports are to be found in the Hong Kong daily press. They are desultory and often unsourced, but the impression of steady and continuous activity is unmistakable.

set up in Hong Kong to prepare the ground and make the contacts. By the time China was ready for them, many firms could act in fact as Hong Kong firms. The line between them and firms that represent overseas interests is blurred, making it difficult to identify investments from the Chinese overseas except when public announcements are made by prominent companies. For these Chinese multinationals, especially from South-east Asia, it is clear that they are investing with the full knowledge of their governments, and often with direct support from their national leaders.[17] The significance of this will be discussed later.

It should also be noted that the Hong Kong-based companies began by following their Hong Kong allies and competitors and concentrating on Guangdong, especially the Pearl River delta beyond Shenzhen and Zhuhai. For them, security rested on the growing economic integration of the South China Economic Periphery, which increasingly included Fujian and Zhejiang.[18] This was strengthened further by the entry of more Taiwan firms during the late 1980s.[19] The relative profitability of all these investments encouraged some to move further afield gradually until early 1992. Then the gates began to open widely, to the Yangzi valley, to the provinces of Hubei and Sichuan in the interior, and beyond Beijing to the north-east.[20] The mounting excitement over ever larger areas of China being equally profitable was a great spur. There is no doubt that the effect was like taking the cork out of a champagne bottle.

The result is a picture of Greater China enveloped in a mad scramble, troubled by a degree of anarchy verging on chaos, with increasing examples of corruption and lawlessness and clear cases where the central government has little control. This state of affairs stems from structural problems within China and has little to do with what the Chinese overseas are doing as actual and potential investors. Nor is it one that such Chinese would welcome for the long-term investments which they have made or are ready to make. A few of them may be swayed from time to time to make sentimental gestures, but all the evidence points to hard-headed calculations of profit behind their every move.[21] If the investment conditions of China should deteriorate, if there is civil disorder, if a fierce struggle for power develops either at the Centre or between the Centre and the provinces, these Chinese will be quick to withdraw their money and put it elsewhere.

Political Greater China, however, belongs to a different dimension. The

17. Interviews with Indonesian and Malaysian consular officials in Hong Kong confirm this.

18. The material on investments in the Pearl River delta can be found almost daily, but the small but significant communities of Chaozhou, Minnan (Southern Fujian) and Ningbo businessmen ensured that Hong Kong enterprises would move further afield.

19. As government policy in Taiwan towards relations across the Straits began to change in the mid-1980s, its businessmen pushed ahead by using Hong Kong as a base. From 1988 onwards, a veritable flood of visitors from Taiwan to the mainland was a prelude to intensive funding of joint enterprises which the Taiwan government could do little to curb.

20. After the Deng Xiaoping visit to South China in January 1992, Hong Kong businesses, led by Peter Woo, began to look seriously at opening up the interior provinces and the north.

21. Regular interviews with South-east Asian businessmen from Singapore and Malaysia since the early 1980s have confirmed that sentiment will always be accompanied by assurances of profit.

idea of future unification points to the prospect of a strong and prosperous China being taken seriously again in world affairs. The Chinese overseas have always been particularly sensitive to the way China's international position gave them self-respect and pride, if not also added status in the countries they have made their homes. Are those overseas today very different from their predecessors? Probably not if they still identify themselves as ethnic Chinese and have resisted total assimilation to the majority community. The difference between generations may be sharper where the host community has been relatively tolerant and the descendants of Chinese immigrants have become comfortable and successful. In countries where discrimination is pervasive and ethnicity has constructed little walls between distinctive groups, ethnic Chinese today may well be as defensive and proud as their forefathers.[22] But all countries are different and the variables are too many to allow for generalizations. A generation gap is to be expected, but no less important are the nature of national policies, the legal system under which they live, educational and business opportunities and attitudes towards traditional cultural values, factors that would make the difference between, on the one hand, a quiet and private pride in being Chinese and, on the other, a willingness to contemplate a disloyal expression of Chineseness in their adopted countries.

At the same time, there is the spectre of an expansionist empire under the last powerful Communist Party in the world, the successor state to the Soviet Union.[23] The Chinese overseas react differently depending on where they live. In South-east Asia, in the area where the power of China can easily be felt, there is great ambivalence. Few respond to the blandishments of Communism today. Many are relieved that the new policies towards "market socialism" make China more acceptable to South-east Asian governments. Greater China not only makes it profitable to deal with it, but also holds out the promise that Communism will before long be dead. If that happens, the Chinese overseas, who have generally benefited greatly from the freer economies under which they live, will have fewer obstacles to trading with, and investing in, Greater China and even to their children learning Chinese as one of the major languages of economic development.

However, the Chinese overseas have no control over the future, whatever their hopes for a political Greater China. That is largely a matter for China itself and for their own respective governments in their diplomatic and security policies. Cultural China, however, is more accessible and the response to that is much more a matter for them to determine themselves. There are many levels at which this restoration of cultural Greater China can be received. There is the most basic level of

22. This is common all over Asia, notably in Japan and South Korea and still true, despite strong assimilationist policies, in South-east Asia. But the examples of Chinatowns in the migrant states of the Americas and Australasia suggest that ghetto-like lives are historically widespread and may persevere.

23. There is a growing number of commentaries in the Western media since 1991 which stress this, but South-east Asian reports have also played on this theme from time to time.

simply loving and being proud of everything Chinese, starting with language and dialect, customs, festivals, foods and news of China, then ranging from joining Chinese organizations and attending all their functions, to the urge to visit China, to give donations to all Chinese charities and parties for all visiting Chinese dignitaries, and to the determination that one's children and grandchildren should master the Chinese language and maintain and even improve the quality of their Chineseness. At that level, the contrasting bits of cultural China on the mainland, in Taiwan and Hong Kong pose no problems.[24] They may be bewilderingly different, sometimes contradictory, but what they stand for is still Chinese.

At another level, however, a rejuvenated and enhanced Chinese culture arouses in those already educated in Chinese the desire for sustained action and intellectual effort. This can take many forms, depending on what these Chinese perceive to be the direction of cultural change. They divide into those who think that the modern culture in Greater China has been distorted by foreign borrowings and those who think that too much of cultural China is still clinging on to the past, whether to the burdensome traditions of history, or to the discredited revolutionary values of Marx, Lenin and Mao, or several positions in between.[25] Such Chinese may want to return to Greater China to see for themselves and offer better models for the future, that is, models that are more democratic and have more respect for the law. At the same time, they may also be concerned that the younger generation should appreciate the Four Books, Han and Tang poetry, Sung paintings and prose, even Ming-Qing romances – just about anything that would save Chinese civilization from decay or contamination.[26]

There is yet another level at which cultural Greater China might deter young Chinese overseas from assimilation and loss of identity. In Southeast Asia, where Chinese ethnicity has to remain subdued, the culture, literature and arts of Greater China can be learned through non-Chinese languages. For example, during the 19th century Ming-Qing novels were translated into Malay, Thai and Vietnamese.[27] Today, selections from the classics can be read in an international language like English. Similarly, modern works, whether politically correct or not, are followed with interest as part of the globalization of modern culture of which cultural China is an important part.[28] Non-verbal arts and expressions can be even

24. The Chinese newspapers published among the Chinese overseas demonstrate this clearly, more so perhaps in North America, but also in much more carefully chosen words in Singapore and Malaysia.

25. The vigorous debates among new *huaqiao*, and especially the better-educated students and dissidents from the mainland, since 1989 have been found in newspapers and magazines not only in North America but also in Hong Kong and Taiwan.

26. The literature of this genre is now vast, mostly published in Hong Kong and Taiwan, but also in various forms in mainland magazines as well.

27. Claudine Salmon (ed.), *Literary Migrations: Traditional Chinese Fiction in Asia (17th–20th centuries)* (Beijing: International Culture, 1990).

28. This subject is yet to be studied. The campaign to introduce Confucian values through translated texts in Singapore in the early 1980s is a good example; Tu Wei-ming, "Iconoclasm, holistic vision, and patient watchfulness: a personal reflection on the modern intellectual quest," *Daedalus*, Vol. 116, No. 2. Perhaps from the sublime to the not so ridiculous, the cartoon versions

more powerful. Paintings and music might reach only a small discerning audience, but film, television, video and other information technologies have a much larger impact.[29] As long as cultural China is presented in all its variety, with both verve and skill, no Chinese overseas today can be far away from its attractions. Few would find it possible to reject its claim to their attention.

The positive view above assumes that the perspectives of most Chinese overseas today about China are shallow. They have little sense of the past and either follow their immediate interests, or follow their instincts about what they like or dislike about being ethnically Chinese. It also assumes that the countries in which the Chinese overseas have gained acceptance believe in non-interference in their ethnic Chinese communities and the ideas and sentiments these communities may have about China. But this is not true in many countries, notably those in various parts of Asia, particularly South-east Asia. Even in the migrant states of the Americas and Australasia, where civic tolerance and liberal laws have often left the ethnic Chinese more free to remain Chinese, the very dominance of the majority culture can exercise great pressures on the descendants of immigrants.[30]

Both these assumptions have to be juxtaposed with the fact that there have been several hundred years of history of the Chinese overseas and the fact that the polities in which most Chinese overseas have lived, or grown up, have undergone radical changes during the 20th century. No study of the response by these Chinese overseas to Greater China today can ignore the significance of that changing historical background. This article will look at two questions in recent history which may throw light on the impact that Greater China can have on the Chinese overseas today.

The first question the Chinese overseas want to know is whether the success of Greater China so far has been determined by the recent shifts in the PRC's foreign and economic policies. These Chinese expect that the prospects for Greater China depend on those policies being sustained by a stable regime and remaining unchallenged by the policies of other powers. The second question is whether this development of Greater China is the result of irrevocable changes to the global economic and political environment, in which all three governments (of the PRC, Taiwan and Hong Kong) have had no choice but to promote the development of the South China Economic Periphery in the different ways they

---

*footnote continued*

of the Chinese classics by Tsai Chih Chung now translated into English are read by the younger generation of the Chinese overseas. They are easily available in a Singapore edition published by Asiapac.

29. The impact of Hong Kong films, television and video tapes on the Chinese overseas is widely acknowledged.

30. The literature on this topic is growing. A good example of the genre is Joann Faung Jean Lee, *Asian Americans: Oral histories of First to Fourth Generation Americans from China, the Philippines, Japan, India, the Pacific Islands, Vietnam and Cambodia* (New York: The New Press, 1991), pp. 99–139.

have done. If the changes are fundamental and permanent, they will profoundly influence the attitudes of the Chinese overseas towards the future of Greater China.

In order to answer these questions, there are several historical points that are pertinent. How do the recent policies of the central government on the mainland compare with those of earlier governments and how much do the changes represent a fundamental move to a stable set of policies and a new equilibrium in the region? How vulnerable is the PRC to the future development towards a new world order, or at least towards new regional relationships? The perceptions of different groups of Chinese overseas towards Greater China may depend on the answers to these questions. The different groups may need to re-examine their various roles in their respective regions, countries or territories. What impact then would an economically dynamic Greater China have on what they decide to do in Greater China, on their loyalty to their respective adopted countries and on their feelings about their own ethnicity? The rest of this article will first focus on the experiences of the Chinese overseas with China's policies towards them and try to place the current situation in perspective; and secondly, deal with the way a successful Greater China may affect different groups of the Chinese overseas and the decisions they make about their national and cultural identity and their political and economic future.

## The Chinese State and the Chinese Overseas Cycle

It is not necessary to dwell on the centuries of Chinese imperial policies before the last decades of the Qing dynasty. Suffice it to say that from the Tang to the Song and then to the Yuan dynasties, private trade by Chinese with other Asians went on side by side with the officially permitted tributary trade. The volume was never great and the numbers of Chinese involved were never very large. But there was a major shift in policy at the end of the 14th century[31] when the Ming founder banned private trade with foreign countries in reaction to the disorder which he believed foreign traders had brought to the China coast. This was some time after a small number of Chinese overseas communities had appeared in South-east Asia. The Ming ban on private overseas trade in effect cut these communities off from China. All future trade had to be conducted through official tributary missions tightly controlled by the Ming court.

This policy was eventually modified, but the growing number of Chinese merchant communities outside China traded increasingly with European companies and eventually were subjected to European administrations. The sharp contrast between the lack of support for the Chinese merchants by the Qing mandarins and the official financial and military backing given to the European traders by their respective governments

31. Wang Gungwu, "Early Ming relations with Southeast Asia – a background essay," in Wang Gungwu, *Community and Nation: Essays on Southeast Asia and the Chinese* (Singapore and Sydney: Heinemann Educational Books and Allen and Unwin, 1981), pp. 43–57.

helped to shape the trading mentality and culture of the Chinese overseas. It led to resentment against the uncaring Chinese government mixed with envy towards the advantages held by the European traders. But it also led to a high degree of independence and self-reliance within the Chinese communities. This self-reliance was coupled with an adaptability towards foreign institutions of authority.[32]

Nevertheless, what most of the Chinese overseas increasingly wanted was a strong China to protect them against the state-supported Western-ers. Neither the Qing after the 1850s nor the Republic of China after 1911 could really do that. But, although weakened by divisions and impover-ished by Western competition, both those governments did care and try to offer diplomatic support. This was widely welcomed among the Chinese abroad and, by the 1920s and 1930s, their success in commerce, growing wealth and heartfelt gratitude led to the perception that it was the Chinese overseas who could now save a poor and war-torn China: through investment, through patriotism and a new nationalism and, if necessary, through revolution, they could make China wealthy and strong again. This provided many of them with inspiration, idealism and a willingness to die for their country.[33] The defeat of China by Japan in 1895, followed by many encroachments on Chinese sovereignty year after year until the 1930s, had enhanced that sense of devotion. The only reason why huaqiao (Overseas Chinese) investments in China were not more successful for most of those 40 years was because China suffered from civil wars and foreign invasion. Throughout that period, the huaqiao invested not primarily for profit but largely out of the duty to support the Chinese economy.[34] When they realized that investments in China were not necessarily the best way to be helpful under the circumstances, many concentrated on making money elsewhere so that they could remit funds to support the government in its efforts to defend China.

After 1949, a new image of a united and strong China replaced that of division and helplessness. But what did this bring to the Chinese over-seas? Hundreds of thousands returned to rebuild their country, but many more left China for Taiwan and Hong Kong and, from there, sought to emigrate to any place in the world that would accept them. And millions of those already outside stayed where they were and learnt to cope with newly independent nation-states, especially the large minorities who had

---

32. Three essays by L. Eve Armentrout Ma, Yen Ching-hwang and Mak Lau Fong, in Lee Lai To (ed.), *Early Chinese Immigrant Societies: Case Studies from North America and British Southeast Asia* (Singapore: Heinemann Asia, 1988), pp. 159–243, bring this out clearly.

33. Two examples from British Malaya and the Philippines are of interest: *Dazhan yu Nanqiao* [ *Ta-chan yu Nan-ch'iao*] (*The Great War and the Overseas Chinese in South-east Asia*) (Singa-pore: Southseas China Relief Fund Union, 1947) and Antonio S. Tan, *The Chinese in Manila During the Japanese Occupation, 1942–1945* (Quezon City: University of the Philippines, Asian Center, 1981).

34. The classic example is Chen Jiageng (Tan Kah Kee). C.F. Yong, *Tan Kah Kee: The Making of an Overseas Chinese Legend* (Singapore: Oxford University Press, 1987). Tan had many loyal supporters who followed his example, pp. 175–297.

chosen to settle in South-east Asia.[35] When the doors began to open in the migrant states of the Americas and Australasia, new generations of *huaqiao* went there to join the earlier immigrants and their small communities, including significant numbers of re-migrants from South-east Asia.[36]

This outline of the responses to the cycle of strong China, weak China, strong China, by the Chinese overseas needs to be taken into account when the present confidence and enthusiasm in Greater China is being examined. Most South-east Asian Chinese of the older generation are familiar with this history. Their children and grandchildren may have heard the often-told stories about China's policies towards the Chinese abroad, but they are unlikely to have constituted a systematic account. Elsewhere, especially in the migrant states of the Americas and Australasia, even less was known until recently.[37] It would, therefore, be possible for many of the Chinese overseas today to misread the emergence of Greater China and the formation of new policies to welcome them to help restore China to greatness as an unprecedented event.

The historical context helps us to appreciate what is happening. This is not the place for a full account, but the following provides a schematic summary of the relationship between China and the Chinese overseas since the beginning of the Qing dynasty in terms of the Chinese overseas cycle, or the CG/CO cycle.

1. Strong and prosperous Qing empire from 1680s to 1840s.[38]

   Chinese Government (CG) neglectful of, and indifferent to, the fates of the Chinese overseas;

   Chinese Overseas (CO) faced great obstacles, but learnt to be self-sufficient and independent, and increasingly successful in commerce.

2. The Hundred Years' weakness and poverty, 1840s to 1949 (the weak and poor Qing empire followed by a republic divided by civil wars and invaded by Japan).

   CG offered recognition of, and support to, the CO, but expected political loyalty from them, and also economic investments from the rich CO;

   CO numbers grew rapidly but the *huaqiao* were responsive to China's needs and

---

35. C.P. FitzGerald, *The Third China: The Chinese Communities in South-East Asia* (Melbourne: F.W. Cheshire, 1965); Mary Somers-Heidhues, *Southeast Asia's Chinese Minorities* (Melbourne: Longman, 1976).

36. Mai Liqian, *Huaqiao to Huaren*, chs. 10–12; and Edgar Wickberg (ed.) *From China to Canada; A History of the Chinese Communities in Canada* (Toronto: McClelland and Stewart, 1982), pp. 204–267, for North America.

37. Progress in North American research on Chinese communities has been remarkable; Him Mark Lai, "Chinese American studies: a historical survey," *Chinese America: History and Perspectives 1988* (San Francisco: Chinese Historical Society of America, 1988), pp. 11–29. Also Wing Chung Ng, "Scholarship on post-World War II Chinese societies in North America: a thematic discussion," *Chinese America: History and Perspectives 1992* (San Francisco), pp. 177–210.

38. The Qing government was not always prosperous, nor consistent in its policies towards the Chinese overseas; see Jennifer Wayne Cushman, *Fields from the Sea: Chinese Junk Trade with Siam During the Late Eighteenth and Early Nineteenth Centuries* (Ithaca, NY: Cornell University Southeast Asia Program, 1993), chs. 4 and 5.

were, on the whole, caring; they continued to be economically prosperous but were also angry and ashamed at the failure of successive Chinese governments.[39]

3. The Mao era of strength and promise unfulfilled, 1949–76: strong country, poor people, living under the shadow of the Cold War and the U.S.–Soviet "central balance."

CG imperious but constrained, forced by diplomatic isolation and ideology to ineffectual policies amounting to a return to neglect of, if not indifference to, the CO;

CO faced new obstacles and relearnt how to be self-sufficient and economically autonomous; became politically localized and naturalized, if not still divided by the forces of China politics.[40]

4. The reforming PRC since 1978 has become potentially strong and prosperous relative to China's neighbours and its place in the world, but is still on the margins of Third World poverty.

CG returns to recognition and modest support of the CO, but defensively, welcoming investments but not expecting loyalty;

CO once again grows fast but they remain sympathetic, even caring; being better educated, they adapt to conditions abroad more easily and are divided in the ways they are attracted to the promise of Greater China but dismayed by the PRC's political system.[41]

The CG/CO cycle briefly summarized above is a rather simple depiction of the way the Chinese governments and the Chinese overseas interacted during alternating periods of strength and weakness in the Chinese polity. It suggests a pattern of behaviour discernible in the Chinese overseas which seems to have been sensitized to the ebb and flow of Chinese political struggles and their effect on foreign and economic policies. After the range of experiences they have had, most of the long-settled and naturalized are unlikely to be easily swayed by current developments towards Greater China and would tend to await much clearer signs of stability in the PRC and in the Beijing government's capacity to adjust to new global and regional relationships. Some of the wealthiest Chinese overseas with bases in Hong Kong have been interested in the economy of South China for several years and have shown that they are willing to take a limited range of risks. The evidence so far is that they have preferred, or at least limited themselves to, short-term investments made through their Hong Kong bases.[42] Given their increasing sophistication about political, economic and financial matters, even these entrepreneurial Chinese have balked at being exposed

39. Yen Ching-hwang, *Coolies and Mandarins: China's Protection of Overseas Chinese During the Late Ch'ing Period (1851–1911)* (Singapore: Singapore University Press, 1985).

40. Several essays in Cushman and Wang, *Changing Identities*, provide examples of what happened in South-east Asia during this period: notably essays by J.A.C. Mackie, Chinben See and Tan Chee-Beng (pp. 217–260, 319–334 and 139–164).

41. This is analysed in the last part of this paper, "Changing groups and different responses"; see also my essay, "Among non-Chinese," in *Daedalus*, Vol. 120, No. 2 (Spring 1991), pp. 135–157.

42. There have been some exceptions. Sino-Land, an offshoot of a Singapore company, and Kerry Trading, a Hong Kong arm of a Malaysian company, had begun to make large investments by the mid-1980s.

to the uncertainties that still hover around the future growth of Greater China.

As for the ordinary Chinese overseas, they are divided among themselves and are still straining to adapt to their very complex local societies. Whatever appeal the idea of Greater China may have for them, it has always had to be screened through the many layers of their own new national loyalties and their decades of separation from their ancestral homes. In addition, their local commitments to their own families and their minority communities have become deeper. The nationalist education of their young and the steady acculturation and modernization of their value-systems have greatly increased their distance from China and things Chinese. Many have, in fact, kept up their skills with the Chinese language, and others have begun to relearn the language in response to recent developments in Greater China, but the majority of the Chinese overseas are likely to admit that they have lost their capacity to understand, and do not have the determination to study, what is happening in China today.[43]

It is not suggested here that the CG/CO cycle is uppermost in the consciousness of the Chinese overseas. Nor would such an understanding of historical relationships be decisive in the Chinese overseas response to Greater China developments. But it forms a background to the widespread caution and wariness that accompanies the calculations that the Chinese overseas are likely to make when they contemplate committing themselves in any way to Greater China.

## Changing Groups and Different Responses

Anyone who studies the Chinese overseas knows that, despite the efforts this century by successive governments in China and by patriotic and nationalistic Chinese to bring the *huaqiao* together, there has never been one single Chinese community abroad. There has been no uniform view of China nor one about how the Chinese overseas should respond to their respective places of settlement or residence. It is widely understood that different groups of Chinese have had very different perceptions of their roles outside China.

About 20 years ago, in two articles about the Chinese in South-east Asia published in *The China Quarterly*[44] and *Southeast Asia in the*

43. The literature on the Chinese overseas written by scholars in Hong Kong, Taiwan and the PRC and by Western sinologists tend to focus on those Chinese who can still speak, read and write Chinese. This is less true of the anthropologists, notably the studies of Thailand by G. William Skinner, of Cambodia by William Willmott, of Indonesia by Donald E. Willmott and Mely Tan Giok Lan, and of Malaysia by Judith Strauch and Tan Chee-Beng. The latter studies show that most Chinese in the second or third generation were losing their ability to communicate in Chinese. Hence Maurice Freedman's reference to the need for re-sinification, see John R. Clammer, "Overseas Chinese assimilation and resinification: a Malaysian case study," *Southeast Asian Journal of Social Science*, Vol. 3, No. 2, pp. 9–23; also Tan Chee Beng, *The Baba of Melaka: Culture and Identity of a Chinese Peranakan Community in Malaysia* (Petaling Jaya: Pelanduk Publications, 1988).

44. Wang Gungwu, "Chinese politics in Malaya," *The China Quarterly*, No. 43 (1970), pp. 1–30, also in *Community and Nation* (1981), pp. 173–200.

*Modern World*,[45] I suggested that the Chinese, in terms of their political activities, could be divided into three groups. Their economic activities were touched on, but not emphasized because it was assumed that these activities would be determined by the various pressures to demonstrate political loyalty to the new nation-states of which the Chinese were citizens. The major issue was one of political loyalty and that was the focus of the studies. This article provides the opportunity to re-examine the question beyond South-east Asia, especially the growing communities in North America and Australasia. There is a new situation involving all Chinese overseas widely distributed around the world at a time when political and economic loyalties may no longer coincide and may diverge widely in a more open and international business environment.

A full description of the three groups of political Chinese can be found in the two articles referred to above.[46] Here, only a summary definition is offered:

Group A Chinese, a relatively small group that had become smaller; they maintained links with the politics of China, either directly or indirectly, and were concerned always to identify with the destiny of China.

Group B Chinese formed the majority group everywhere; they were hard-headed and realistic and concentrated on making a living in occupations which allowed them to behave openly as ethnic Chinese. In the political sphere, they tended to limit their activities to the low posture and indirect politics of trade, professional and community associations.

Group C Chinese were generally committed to the new nation-building politics, even though they remained uncertain of their future as ethnic Chinese and were never sure whether they would ever be fully accepted as loyal nationals.

The conclusions were that, in South-east Asia, Group A Chinese would grow even smaller and that Group B would also grow smaller if the new national policies were enlightened and, by removing discriminatory policies against Chinese minorities, encouraged Group C Chinese to confirm their loyalty. These groups were examined by other scholars and refinements were suggested.[47] In some South-east Asian countries, it was pointed out that there should also be a fourth group which had accepted assimilation and no longer insisted on being known as Chinese.[48]

It would be interesting to see if the three-group division (not including here the fourth group of those who did not identify themselves as ethnic Chinese) can help approach the question of the response of the Chinese overseas in general to the development of Greater China, and their present and future roles in Greater China and within their own countries. It is recognized that Chinese overseas communities are different from one

45. Wang Gungwu, "Political Chinese: their contribution to modern Southeast Asian history," in Bernhard Grossman (ed.) *Southeast Asia in the Modern World* (Wiesbaden: Otto Harrassowitz, 1972), also in Wang Gungwu, *Chinese Overseas*, pp. 130–146.

46. Wang Gungwu, "Chinese politics," pp. 4–6, 21–30; "Political Chinese," pp. 132, 139–146.

47. Loh Kok Wah, *The Politics of Chinese Unity in Malaysia* (Singapore: Maruzen Asia, 1982) is the best example.

48. Charles A. Coppel, "Patterns of Chinese political activity in Indonesia," in J.A.C. Mackie (ed.), *The Chinese in Indonesia: Five Essays* (Melbourne: Nelson, 1976), pp. 19–76.

another, but the questions will focus on two regions or types of host countries where the communities are large: the new nation-states of South-east Asia and the migrant states of the Americas and Australasia.

*Group A Chinese.* In the new nation-states, there has not been much immigration from Hong Kong, Taiwan or the PRC, and this group which identifies with the destiny of China is indeed smaller than it was 20 years ago and consists mainly of aged and aging people. In the migrant states, however, there has been a considerable influx of fresh immigrants from Taiwan, Hong Kong and the Chinese mainland as well as from Chinese communities in South-east Asia. Thus, many more Chinese in the migrant states meet the criteria of Group A Chinese.[49] It is possible to generalize that Group A Chinese will be found in larger proportions, relative to Groups B and C, in areas which have seen a strong recent influx of new *huaqiao* from Taiwan, Hong Kong and the mainland.

Where the development of Greater China is concerned, Group A Chinese are expected to be enthusiastic and excited by its potential to make China strong and prosperous again. They include critics of both the PRC and Taiwan and those who want to bring democracy and human rights to Greater China. In the new nation-states, they have not themselves made any significant contribution to that development. This is because the older and more successful of the group in South-east Asia have by and large retired and have been succeeded by their local-born and educated, and also less sentimental, progeny who may well be recognized as Group B Chinese, with some even identifying fully with the new nation-states as Group C Chinese.

In the migrant states of the Americas and Australasia, however, where new immigrants have swelled the ranks of Group A Chinese, they have close direct links with one or other of the three parts of economic Greater China, and strong emotional ties with cultural China and the PRC or Taiwan and even Hong Kong. Although few of them have had the economic resources to support the recent growth of Greater China directly, there have been notable entrepreneurial successes among those who have specialized in trading and investing in China.[50]

When the two types of host countries are compared, Group A Chinese in the migrant states are more likely to play a political role in Greater China than those from the new nation-states. Most of those in the migrant states are recent arrivals and they originate from the most dynamic part

49. Detailed studies of this phenomenon have begun to be published, for example two new books about New York City: Hsiang-shui Chen, *Chinatown No More: Taiwan Immigrants in Contemporary New York* (Ithaca, NY: Cornell University Press, 1992) and Min Zhou, *Chinatown: The Socioeconomic Potential of an Urban Enclave* (Philadelphia: Temple University Press, 1992). They should be read together with an earlier study of New York's Chinese community by Bernard Wong, *Chinatown: Economic Adaption and Ethnic Identity of the Chinese* (New York: Holt, Rinehart and Winston, 1982).

50. A good measure of one of the consequences of the growth in numbers of Group A Chinese can be seen in H.M. Lai, "The Chinese press in the United States and Canada since World War II: a diversity of voices," *Chinese America: History and Perspectives 1990* (San Francisco: Chinese Historical Society of America, 1990), pp. 107–155.

of Greater China. Many have become successful professionals in the fields of science and technology.[51] The expertise that these newcomers possess has enabled them to contribute directly to Greater China. Their sub-groups of Hong Kongers, Taiwanese and mainlanders include people who are also seen as having the ability to build economic bridges between each territory and anyone in their adopted homes overseas who wish to participate in the Greater China adventure. Given the circumstances, there is no need for these recent immigrants to demonstrate openly any kind of Group A political allegiance to China. But if they are perceived to have a special understanding of the workings of the governments of the PRC, or better still have connections with useful levels of the economic centres of Greater China, that will enable some of them to play a role out of proportion to their relatively small numbers.

The interesting question is, if Greater China moves inexorably towards a strong and rich "Unified China" during the 21st century, will such a group in the migrant states grow much larger? Will it be swelled by more and more sojourning businessmen and professionals from Greater China? Will some of those born and educated in the Americas and Australasia, who might have been grouped as either Group B or Group C Chinese, be won over from their present comfortably established positions and identify with Group A Chinese? Much depends, of course, on whether they can combine their Greater China interests with a semblance of loyalty towards their adopted countries, and on whether, and for how long, these migrant states will tolerate the potentially divisive features of ethnicity and allow their citizens to play such bridging and ambiguous roles. And that in turn depends on whether the relatively open international economy that has dominated the world for the past four decades is here to stay and whether the direction of recent developments in Greater China is now firmly locked in. Otherwise, Group A Chinese in the migrant states are likely to undergo what their counterparts in South-east Asia experienced and be forced to diminish in number and influence as their children seek integration and new local identities.[52]

*Group B Chinese.* There are historical reasons why this group has always been the majority in the new nation-states and is likely to remain so. This has much to do with the size of early Chinese trading communities in South-east Asia and their deep roots in South China, now the key territories of rapid economic development. With their preference for "the low-posture and indirect politics of trade and community associations"[53] and their commitment to cultural maintenance for both sentimental and

---

51. Given the increasingly complex relationship between China and the United States and the large number of American sinologists who know Taiwan, Hong Kong and the PRC reasonably well, such Chinese may not find themselves all that useful. But elsewhere in the Americas and Australasia, many of them could render their governments considerable help.

52. Unless large numbers of fresh immigrants continue to come from Greater China, this may be unavoidable. On the other hand, it is difficult to predict what new factors might appear to change the course of development.

53. Wang Gungwu, "Chinese politics," p. 4.

practical commercial reasons, they are, almost by definition, the best placed in South-east Asia to respond both to the opportunities of Greater China as well as to the new environment of multinationals and cross-border economic actors now active in the Asia-Pacific region.

In the migrant states, Group B Chinese can be identified through the plethora of traditional organizations in dozens of Chinatowns which emphasize Chinese ethnicity, but it is unlikely that they form the majority in their respective communities. In any case, the distinction between them and Group A and Group C Chinese respectively is likely to be a little blurred. In countries where the opposition to involvement in China politics is not strong and the pressures to integrate or identify politically with local nationalist symbols are more subtle and less direct, the three groups cannot be as sharply delineated as in the new nation-states in South-east Asia. On the contrary, wherever ethnicity and multicultural rights are protected by legislation, Group B Chinese who are openly proud of their Chineseness tend to think and act with Group A Chinese, the group that has been augmented by recent immigrants from Chinese-speaking Taiwan, Hong Kong and the mainland.[54] At the same time, where political participation and social mixing with the majority host communities are relatively free and open, second and third generation Chinese have moved comfortably into the category of loyal ethnic minorities, something akin to the Group C Chinese that survive more precariously in South-east Asia.[55] In short, Group B Chinese in the migrant states form what would appear to be a diminishing middle group between growing numbers of Group A Chinese openly active in Greater China affairs and the large numbers of Group C Chinese who are proud to be loyal nationals.

The contrast here between Group B Chinese in the migrant states and in the new nation-states is of particular interest. Those in the former are rarely as wealthy as their counterparts in South-east Asia. Few could make the sustained impact on the future development of Greater China in ways that those in South-east Asia can hope to do if present conditions continue. In fact, in the migrant states, wealthy Group A Chinese entrepreneurs, rather than Group B Chinese, are more likely to be the successful ones who invest in Greater China.[56] Thus, wealthy and powerful Group B Chinese are largely a South-east Asian phenomenon. Many Group B Chinese there recognized the opportunities offered by the economic reforms in the PRC during the 1980s and have made modest contributions to the emergence of Greater China by investing, mainly through Hong Kong, in at least two of its territories (that is, Hong Kong and the Pearl River delta; or Hong Kong and Taiwan) and making linkages between the South China Economic Periphery and the economies of their own respective countries. With the further develop-

54. Using the New York example, see Min Zhou, *Chinatown*, pp. 219–233.
55. For a Canadian perspective, Wickberg, *China to Canada*, pp. 244–267. Somewhat different is that in Australia, see Marig Loh, *Sojourners and Settlers: Chinese in Victoria, 1848–1985* (Melbourne: Barradene Press, 1985).
56. Mai Liqian, *From Huaqiao to Huaren*, pp. 437–467.

ment of all the coastal regions of Greater China and the prospect of opening up most of the interior, many more are asking themselves how they should respond. The need for new capital investments is vast. Although Group B Chinese entrepreneurs in South-east Asia have more capital and are better equipped to invest in Greater China than their counterparts elsewhere, there are limits to what even they can do. At this stage, they would be wise to ensure that their investments do not exceed what they invest within their own countries and that at least some of their ventures are done together with local nationals, and others are what their respective governments have approved.[57]

They do still have advantages because most of them have access, either directly or indirectly, to family connections and other Chinese trading networks. Some Chinese have, in addition, links with foreign multinationals in their own countries or their respective government's agencies or companies.[58] Some of these non-Chinese companies readily use their help and advice. They themselves could, through these companies, then participate in the larger ventures which they might not have been allowed to undertake on their own or with other Chinese. Excellent examples are the entourage that accompanied the Prime Minister of Malaysia to China.[59] There had been similar Indonesian Chinese, largely Group B Chinese, who guided the Chamber of Commerce delegations to the PRC during the 1980s.[60]

On the whole, however, the constraints on their activities in Greater China are likely to remain great. Apart from the need to show loyalty to their adopted countries, there are also the growing opportunities for profitable investment at home. Several of the countries in South-east Asia, notably Malaysia, Indonesia and Thailand, have been keenly determined to join the club of "Little Dragons" and want the help of their compatriots of Chinese descent, notably the Group B Chinese who have both affirmed their political loyalty and successfully retained their own trading networks. With few exceptions, these Chinese would not be distracted from the opportunities, some greater and mostly safer than those offered in Greater China, which they now have within the region and within their own countries.[61]

57. I am not aware of any case where a South-east Asian Chinese entrepreneur has invested more money in either Taiwan or the PRC than he has invested in his own country. It is harder, of course, to determine if funds are transferred over time to Hong Kong and later re-invested in the PRC as Hong Kong investment.

58. Suehiro, "Postwar Thailand," pp. 54–57, gives examples of joint ventures with several multinationals from Japan, Germany, Britain and Hong Kong. Heng Pek Koon, "The Chinese business elite of Malaysia," in McVey, *Southeast Asian Capitalists*, pp. 127–144, has many examples of close associations with public companies. Similarly, Richard Robison, "Industrialisation and the economic and political development of capital: the case of Indonesia," in the same volume of essays, provides examples from Indonesia.

59. *Asiaweek*, 23 June 1993.

60. Interview with two delegations from Indonesia in 1987 and 1988.

61. The essays in n. 58 also show what enormous opportunities the entrepreneurs have within their own countries. The reports of what the Chinese overseas are doing in Greater China should be compared with what they are doing back home. For example, the report "SE Asian Chinese head for home," in *Asian Business*, April 1993 would be alarming if it is thought that firms like

But will the enhanced future of Greater China change the nature of Group B Chinese whether or not they contribute to its success? Will their political loyalty to their adopted countries be sorely tested? The answer to both these questions is probably not much. They have been probing the limits of what is and is not acceptable within their own countries for at least four decades. As long as the modern nation-states survive and the regional structure is working, the parameters of minority ethnic identities are clear.[62] Group B Chinese have never been geared to challenge authority, only to defend against its abuse. After observing the volatile political and economic changes in China this century, they are not about to let another prospect of China's revived greatness move them from their hard-won position as loyal citizens of new nations.

All the same, it is likely that they will be subject to suspicion and closer scrutiny by their national governments which have always feared the rise of a rich, united and powerful China. These Chinese will have to make greater efforts to assure their governments of their ultimate political loyalties by showing that they can resist Greater China's blandishments and by ploughing their savings and profits into investments in their home countries. On the other hand, an economically successful China will almost certainly give most of them greater confidence in themselves as ethnic Chinese, though not to the extent of fortifying their organizations against what their respective countries want from them. Nevertheless, their greater confidence can help support the policy of cultural mainte-nance among their descendants, and even consolidate the sense of ethnicity of a permanent Chinese minority.

*Group C Chinese.* This group was difficult to define for South-east Asia 20 years ago, and is no less difficult to pin down in the new nation-states today. In South-east Asia Group C Chinese referred to those Chinese, largely local-born, whose education in a national system had led them to eschew the symbols and rituals of a culturally defensive Chinese community and had prepared them to be fully integrated into the larger national identity. In the new nation-states, where the national identity was still somewhat fluid and yet to be fully developed, it was expected that these Chinese themselves would help in the shaping of that national identity. To the extent that such Chinese did believe this to be possible, they would give greater attention to nation-building efforts and would by and large opt out of matters aimed at strengthening the Chinese com-munity itself. By definition, such Chinese would not be involved in the

---

*footnote continued*

Lippo, Kuok Group, Charoen Pokphand, Bangkok Land were taking most of their capital out to "bring home" to the PRC. If true, then Ian Stewart's story in the *South China Morning Post*, 22 May 1993, "Wrath of Asia as Chinese venture forth" would be justified.

62. Ruth McVey, "The materialisation of the Southeast Asian entrepreneur," in McVey, *South-east Asian Capitalists*, pp. 7–33, analyses how the ethnic Chinese entrepreneurs perform successfully in the South-east Asian context.

emergence of Greater China and would not be interested in furthering its cause.[63]

If national policies encouraged more and more Chinese to participate fully in the social and political life of the new nations, it is likely that this group of Chinese would grow in number. For the greater part, this has happened. In practice, many tensions remain, mainly because some of the assimilationist ideas earlier this century which were widely accepted by South-east Asian governments during the 1950s have left a legacy of deep distrust of those Chinese who did not pledge total denial of their Chinese culture, such as it was, when affirming their political loyalty to the new nations. There is, therefore, much variety in the region where this phenomenon is concerned, ranging from the exceptional Singapore Chinese majority to the delicate equilibrium of Malaysia across to the relatively successful integration of Group C Chinese in Thailand.[64] More than with the other two groups, Group C Chinese are highly sensitive to local conditions and vulnerable to their government's changing policies and moods about China.

Nevertheless, it is clear that Group C Chinese have greater room for manoeuvre than originally envisaged. This is partly because the world has become more sophisticated about the nature of ethnicity and partly because the global trading system has made ideas about national interest broader and more flexible.[65] Those Chinese who could prove that they were politically and economically integrated into the national community have attained the trust of their respective national governments. Thereafter, whether as professionals, skilled technicians or businessmen, whether in private or in public service, they were in a position to represent larger national interests and engage in the affairs of Greater China. Political loyalty to their new nations certainly did not preclude them from active involvement in the development of South China through Hong Kong, nor in the bilateral contracts which their governments signed with either the PRC or Taiwan. Indeed, many such Chinese are particularly well equipped to serve their countries in this way. At the same time, they can also function as a bridge between Chinese ethnic organizations and the national governments and thus allay any fears their governments may have about future loyalties.

The rise of Greater China may have some longer-term impact on these Group C Chinese. If the developments in China and the region are orderly and non-threatening, such Chinese could also play a major role in blurring the differences between themselves and the defensive Group B Chinese and truly establish a loyal and domesticated ethnic Chinese

63. The case studies by Tan Chee-Beng (Malaysia) and Antonio S. Tan (The Philippines) in Cushman and Wang, *Changing Identities*, pp. 139–164 and 177–203, show how this is happening.
64. The case of Thailand has always been special, as illustrated in the Chearavanont family, *Asiaweek*, 23 June 1993, "The growth machine."
65. Group C Chinese in Indonesia and Malaysia can be said to be still discovering themselves in a very fluid world of Muslim politics. With leaders like Suharto and Mahathir in power, however, they have been given a reasonable chance to prove themselves valuable as well as loyal. The relationships are personalized, so they may still be very unreliable.

identity in each of the countries. If, on the other hand, a rich and strong Greater China turns out to be destabilizing, they may have to choose either total assimilation to the majority culture to retain the trust of the national governments or return to the attenuated loyalties and ethnic defensiveness of their Group B compatriots.

The situation of Group C Chinese is different in the migrant states of the Americas and Australasia where similar kinds of Chinese have settled down to become loyal nationals with little difficulty and have made strong political commitments to their adopted countries. In each case, local conditions vary considerably and the Group C Chinese will always have to be alert and sensitive to changes in national policies and attitudes towards what happens in Greater China. Unlike in South-east Asia, the number of such Chinese had been growing fast and would have been the largest group had it not been for the steady influx of new immigrants (and illegal immigrants) from Taiwan and Hong Kong for the past four decades and from the mainland more recently.[66] But, with the current trends, Group C Chinese may remain a minority, albeit a large and growing minority added to by the descendants of Group B Chinese, for some time. Eventually, however, when new immigration slows down, this will be the group to which most Chinese gravitate. It will be a more stable Group C than in South-east Asia. While more will disappear into the ranks of the assimilated than elsewhere, the presence of Group C Chinese in the migrant states will be guaranteed by the commitment to plural societies, multi-culturalism and the multi-ethnic nation by their respective governments.[67]

The idea of Greater China and the economic successes of the South China Economic Periphery must both seem barely relevant to the normal lives of Group C Chinese. All the same, they too can serve their countries by being actively concerned in developments in Greater China. Whether or not that involvement affects their political loyalties will vary from individual to individual. Where the national identity is well-developed and where their pluralistic societies continue to be just and harmonious, it is doubtful if any changes in Greater China will ever affect the lives of such Chinese. What matters is the larger issue which they will be quick to appreciate: that the integration of Greater China will increasingly be seen as part of the globalization of the market economy, and as the result of irresistible forces that have come to dominate all future political and economic developments.

From the outline above, it is clear that the three-group approach to the Chinese overseas continues to be useful for the study of the communities in South-east Asia. It can explain how, through the continued and growing economic strength of Group B Chinese, so many new entrepreneurs from Malaysia, Indonesia, Thailand and the Philippines have

66. Census figures showed a majority of local-born Chinese in both the migrant states and the new nation-states during the 1950s. Since then, however, the figures for Canada and the United States have changed significantly in favour of those born in Greater China.

67. I refer specially to the multi-cultural policies laid down by countries like Canada, Australia and the United States.

been ready to contribute to, and benefit from, the development of Greater China. It is less certain how useful the grouping is for understanding the migrant states of the Americas and Australasia. For the better-documented countries, like Canada, the United States and Australia, the approach certainly brings out the contrast with South-east Asia. Instead of the dominance of Group B Chinese in the affairs of Greater China, it is Group A Chinese who now have the ascendancy, and also Group C Chinese, who appear far more stable and secure, and who are freer to participate in the future development of Greater China than their counterparts in South-east Asia.

China's historical record has left most Chinese overseas cautious about close direct involvement with its internal affairs. But it is important to distinguish the many groups of Chinese and the many ways that each group can participate in the growth of Greater China. There are those who are narrowly concerned with China's resurgence and those who are narrowly concerned with the survival of ethnic Chinese communities wherever they are. But all Chinese overseas want future developments to proceed without serious conflict. They have nothing to gain and everything to lose if the integration of Greater China fails and the constituent Chinese territories attract major confrontations into the region. Even if they are in no position directly to contribute to, or to profit from, the rise of Greater China, they cannot but be aware that it is a development of global significance which could change the lives of everyone involved.

# Index

*Note*: Names of individuals mentioned only once in footnotes have been omitted